FLAGRANT, SELF-DESTRUCTIVE GESTURES

FLAGRANT, SELF-DESTRUCTIVE GESTURES

A BIOGRAPHY OF DENIS JOHNSON

TED GELTNER

University of Iowa Press Iowa City

University of Iowa Press, Iowa City 52242

uipress.uiowa.edu
Printed in the United States of America

Design by Nola Burger

Printed on acid-free paper

Library of Congress Cataloging-in-Publication Data

Names: Geltner, Ted author
Title: Flagrant, Self-Destructive Gestures: A Biography of Denis Johnson / by Ted Geltner.
Description: Iowa City: University of Iowa Press, 2025. | Includes bibliographical references.
Identifiers: LCCN 2025006787 (print) | LCCN 2025006788 (ebook) | ISBN 9781685970376 paperback | ISBN 9781685970383 ebook
Subjects: LCSH: Johnson, Denis, 1949–2017 | Authors, American—20th century—Biography | LCGFT: Biographies
Classification: LCC PS3560.O3745 Z64 2025 (print) | LCC PS3560.O3745 (ebook) | DDC 813/.54 [B]—dc23/eng/20250505
LC record available at https://lccn.loc.gov/2025006787
LC ebook record available at https://lccn.loc.gov/2025006788

Vivas to those who have fail'd!
And to those whose war-vessels sank in the sea!
And to those themselves who sank in the sea!
And to all generals that lost engagements, and
  all overcome heroes!
And the numberless unknown heroes equal to the
  greatest heroes known!

—Walt Whitman

For Dale Plumb, a newspaper man through and through

CONTENTS

FLAGRANT, SELF-DESTRUCTIVE GESTURES

PROLOGUE

Big Creek Bridge lies at the bottom of a gently sloping valley about five miles south of Bethany, Missouri. The Milledgeville Church, a simple white A-frame building with a stone driveway, sits amid fields of knee-high grass and the occasional plowed field. The tips of a few silos in the distance are the only other man-made structures visible from the bridge. The two lanes of Highway 69 cut through the valley, bending slightly on the north side of the bridge, with a more pronounced curve on the south side. Today, you can stand near the bridge for an hour and count the number of vehicles that pass on two hands. It's quiet enough in the valley that when the road is empty, the sounds of water lapping onto the shore of Big Creek is audible. When a vehicle does appear on the horizon, it can be heard for several seconds before it comes into view, and when it crosses over the bridge, the roar of the engine in the silent valley sounds like a 747 landing in your backyard.

I went to Bethany, Missouri, in the summer of 2022, looking for the spot where Denis Johnson spent the most harrowing moments of a life filled with them. Bethany is a small town of a little under three thousand citizens surrounded by farmland, a few miles from the interstate. To get to the bridge, you drive through Bethany, past a dusty, decrepit downtown and a few streets of hundred-year-old houses that have seen better days. Soon you reach an intersection that features a historical marker that tells the history of Harrison County, Missouri, home of Edgar (Ed) W. Howe, famed author of another century, best known for the 1863 novel *The Story of a County Town*. There, you take a left and head south, toward the bridge. I was in the only car on Highway 69 that morning, driving past empty fields under a clear blue sky.

The scene on Big Creek Bridge was quite different on the night of April 20, 1972. That was the night that Denis Johnson spent a few short minutes there. The rain was coming down hard that night. The highway was slick. Traffic was much heavier, because in those days, Highway 69 was the only way to get from Kansas City to Iowa. If you were driving between Kansas City and Des Moines in 1972, you could drive seventy miles per hour on a four-lane interstate highway the entire way, save the twenty-two-mile stretch from near Pattonsburg, Missouri, to the Iowa border—the stretch that includes the Big Creek Bridge. Those twenty-two miles on Highway 69 were two lanes the whole way, with hills and sharp curves, and the result, as traffic through the area grew, was a long string of fatalities. The Bethany Chamber of Commerce erected signs, created rest stops, and began a safety campaign to alert drivers to the oncoming danger, but the accidents and the deaths continued. As they did, the area's reputation as a death trap spread. Local residents and truckers who drove the stretch frequently referred to it as the Ho Chi Minh Trail, after the supply route from North to South Vietnam where many thousands of soldiers had been killed.

Denis Johnson had hitched a ride earlier that evening with the Eckhart family of Wichita, Kansas, Craig and Janice, and their little daughters, Lori and Cindy, four and one. The family was headed to Northwood, Iowa, to visit relatives, and so Craig could look for a job. Denis approached them at a gas station, dripping wet from standing in the rain on the side of the highway. He'd been on the road for days. Craig considered himself a Good Samaritan and had a habit of picking up hitchhikers, but never when Janice and the kids were in the car. But this young man seemed friendly and unthreatening, so Craig asked his wife if they could help him. She reluctantly agreed.

Janice brought Lori up to the front seat as Denis threw his bag in the trunk and climbed into the back seat. Craig chatted with their new passenger while they drove through the rain. Denis was quiet but friendly. He said he was hitching from Arizona, where his parents lived, back to the University of Iowa. Craig told him about his job opportunity in Marshalltown, near Northwood. He told Denis he could take him as far as the interstate near Iowa City, but because of the weather, he'd be taking it slow.

Toward midnight, the car turned onto Highway 69. Nobody inside had any idea of the danger associated with that stretch of road. The rain was still coming down hard as they reached the outskirts of Bethany a little after midnight. Around the same time, William Webb, a thirty-nine-year-old mechanic at the Cadillac dealership in town who was on his way home, passed the historical marker about Harrison County and turned onto Highway 69 heading south.

In the Buick, Denis rested his head on the window and dozed off. The baby, wrapped in a blanket, slept on the seat beside him. The radio was tuned to a Top 40 station. Cher's pop/folk hit "Gypsys, Tramps & Thieves" came on. In the front seat, Janice and Lori perked up as the wipers ineffectively pushed water back and forth across the windshield. "She just loved Cher," Janice told me later. "So we were just singing along."

As the song played on, the Buick rounded a sharp curve and headed toward Big Creek Bridge, an arch bridge that crosses over a small tributary. On the other side of the bridge, Webb's Ford headed south, traveling at a high rate of speed on the slick, wet asphalt. Webb drifted to the right. The Ford collided with the north end of the bridge, then spun around into the northbound lane, where it was struck, at full speed, by the Eckharts' Buick.

The front end of the Buick was mangled. Janice, Lori, and Craig were thrown forward into the windshield and the dashboard on impact. Red liquid sprayed through the car and across the back seat. Nobody in the car was moving. The hiss of the radiator was the only sound in the valley.

On the other side of the bridge, Webb's Ford had been smashed beyond recognition. Webb hung out the passenger-side door, soaked with blood and convulsing. He would be dead within the hour. Craig regained consciousness a minute later and began calling out to his wife and shaking her. His face was covered in blood. Janice showed no signs of life.

In the back seat, Denis gathered himself and realized that, inexplicably, he was unharmed. He asked Craig if his wife was okay and tried to reassure him that she was still alive. Then he picked up the baby, opened the car door, and started walking off Big Creek Bridge, toward oncoming traffic. The slam of the door barely registered with Craig. "I heard the back door open up," he told me. "I didn't even pay it much attention. I was taking care of them. I got out and he was gone."

Twenty years would pass before Denis would take the events of April 20, 1972, and turn them into a story that would be read by millions and would become the opening to a classic work of American literature. On that night, he was a twenty-two-year-old graduate student returning to school for one last shot at earning a degree from the famed Iowa Writers' Workshop. A few years earlier, he had been the undisputed star of the program. He had published his first book of poetry in 1969 when he was just nineteen. An anthology released by a major publisher featuring the work of the nation's most promising poets used one of his poems as its title. He had begun writing fiction as well, with stories accepted by national publications. He was even featured in the pages of *Rolling Stone* magazine.

In 1972, however, he seemed on the way to squandering all of it. He had a taste for illicit substances, the more dangerous, the better. The habit had gotten him involved with a dubious crowd. He'd been in Iowa City since 1967, during which time he'd gotten married and had a son. His drinking and drug use had landed him in a psych ward, then ended his marriage the previous fall. The night of the crash, he was hitchhiking his way back to the University of Iowa after a short, failed effort to right the ship at his parents' home in Arizona.

There were to be many more years in the wilderness before Denis would put pen to paper and tell the story of the night of April 20, 1972. When he finally did, he was on the other side of his addictions, an experienced and respected young writer. By that time, he could look back on that night with distance while at the same time placing himself back on the side of the road and into the mind of that twenty-two-year-old, thrill-seeking junkie poet. "My jaw ached," he wrote. "I knew every raindrop by its name. I sensed everything before it happened. I knew a certain Oldsmobile would stop for me before it slowed, and by the sweet voices of the family inside it I knew we'd have an accident in the storm."

That story, "Car Crash While Hitchhiking," became part of the collection he entitled *Jesus' Son,* the book that made Denis famous. Later, after *Jesus' Son* had become a cultural marker and a totem for a new generation of writers and readers, the night on Big Creek Bridge would be recreated on-screen as part of the Hollywood version of the book. In the opening scene of the 1999 film, the actor Billy Crudup stands by the road wrapped in a sleeping bag and dripping wet, just as Denis had. Crudup's voice repeats the words Denis had written: "My jaw ached. I knew every raindrop by its name."

By then, Denis had made good on the promise he had shown in his early days at Iowa. He had written a string of acclaimed novels and would go on to write many more. He had established himself as a master of the language in both poetry and fiction, reported from the most dangerous war zones in the world, and written for stage and screen. The phrase "like a Denis Johnson story" had begun to take on cultural meaning. Those words told you to expect a certain level of weirdness. It told you that you were entering a world where behind a door, you might find a pathway to redemption and bliss, or you might find a stairway down into the heart of darkness. Readers knew that a Denis Johnson story would be populated by characters on the fringes of society—dangerous characters, but characters with humanity, searching for life's ecstasy and terror, and characters who may be afforded an unlikely moment of grace. You never knew where you were headed in a Denis Johnson story, but you knew it was worth the ride.

I left my car in the driveway in front of Milledgeville Church and walked a half mile down Highway 69 to the bridge. The sky was nearly cloudless. The valley was serene. It was hard to imagine that this was the same place that Denis had his closest brush with death, an experience so frightening, yet somehow so exhilarating, that he searched for the feeling it generated for the rest of his life. I walked across the eighty-nine-foot length of the bridge, then down the embankment to Big Creek, where the hood of William Webb's Ford had come to rest that night after the collision. Afterward, I walked a bit farther down the road on Highway 69, trying to picture the same surroundings as they were fifty years before.

It was only then that I saw it, on a telephone pole by the side of the highway. It was really the only sign I found that day that I was walking through a Denis Johnson story. Someone had nailed a jagged board to the pole. On it, written in bright red letters, was a question: "ARE U RIGHT WITH GOD?"

INTERNATIONAL MATTERS

1

I believe that it must be the policy of the United States to support free peoples who are resisting attempted subjugation by armed minorities or by outside pressures. I believe that we must assist free peoples to work out their own destinies in their own way. I believe that our help should be primarily through economic and financial aid, which is essential to economic stability and orderly political processes.

—President Harry S. Truman, March 12, 1947

One of the memories Denis Johnson liked to share when describing his childhood abroad recalled an incident that took place outside the American embassy in Tokyo. In his telling, it was the early 1950s and the Cold War was raging. Japanese demonstrations against America's continued military presence in the country were a regular occurrence. On this day, an enormous crowd of demonstrators had commandeered the streets in front of the embassy and were moving in a tightly choreographed formation, chanting anti-American slogans to all who would listen. Young Denis was noticeably frightened. His father, Alfred, took his hand, and the two descended the steps of the embassy and caught the attention of the demonstrators. Immediately the chanting ceased, the street went silent, and the crowd parted to offer father and son a clear path through the throng. One by one, the demonstrators bowed their heads in deference to the symbol of American global power as Alfred Johnson, U.S. diplomat and World War II hero, led his boy down the street.

Though he was not born on American soil and would spend the majority of his formative years living in foreign lands, Denis Johnson was raised in a world where the idea of American preeminence was an unquestioned truth, the one bedrock concept on which all knowledge would rest. Just a few years before Denis was born, his father had been in Germany in May 1945, part of the great Allied advance, a cog in the war machine that was Patton's army as it swept through Western Europe and conquered the Nazis, once and for all.

Denis would grow up in a home where the American ideal was sacrosanct. The greatest cause one could aspire to was to extend the influence of America, to bring democracy and capitalism to the unenlightened, and to bestow on them the wisdom of the greatest country on earth, all in the name of the common good. "American prestige throughout the world," wrote that era's leading media baron and philosopher, Henry Luce of Time Inc., "is faith in the good intentions as well as the ultimate intelligence and ultimate strength of the whole American people." The men who served as young Denis's role models, starting with his father, Alfred, were the leading edge of that movement.

Alfred Nair Johnson was born in the fall of 1914, right in the middle of an America just stepping into its rightful place on the world stage. Just a few short months before his birth, Archduke Ferdinand of Austria had been assassinated in Sarajevo, the first shot fired in World War I and the first act in the unraveling of the great monarchist powers of Europe. Though the record of how he got there is murky, Alfred was destined to have a front-row seat to both the last gasp of Europe's hold on world domination and the ascension of his own country into the vacuum created by the devastations of the Great War.

Oshkosh, Wisconsin, is a small city roughly ninety miles north of Milwaukee on the banks of Lake Winnebago. It is best known as the home to OshKosh B'gosh, a manufacturer of overalls founded in 1895. Alfred listed Oshkosh as his birthplace when he filled out his draft card in 1940, and he listed his mother, Beatrice, as the person closest to him. According to newspaper articles, his parents parted ways and Beatrice married Alvin Niehoff, a mason who moved his new family to Clintonville, another small Wisconsin town about an hour north. Alvin and Beatrice had three children together, but by the time Alfred was in high school, Alvin was out of the picture and Beatrice was left to raise the family herself.

It was the early 1930s, the heart of the Great Depression. Alfred held down jobs and helped Beatrice support the family while he worked his way through high school. Doing his part to keep food on the table for the family kept Alfred from participating in extracurricular activities at Clintonville High. There's nary a mention of him in the Clintonville yearbook. (Years later, Alfred would tell his children that his family eventually went their separate ways during the Depression. He played pool for money and attended night school to earn his degree.)

By the time he filled out the U.S. Census form in 1940, Alfred (who went by Al as an adult), was living in Washington, D.C., and listed his highest year of education completed as the fourth year of high school. After the war, however, he would report obtaining degrees from the University of Wisconsin, George Washington University, and at the University of Glasgow in Scotland, where he "studied economic planning aspects of international food programs." By 1940, he was a working as classifier for the Federal Bureau of Investigation. While at the FBI, he also spent time as a fingerprint technician in an office in which each desk was adorned with evidence from the famous Charles Lindbergh baby-kidnapping case, a physical reminder of the one of the FBI's greatest achievements. J. Edgar Hoover was already decades into his reign as founder and director of the institution when Al came aboard. Al would later recall the complicated cleaning and organizational rituals the technicians would have to go through to make sure the appearance of the office was acceptable on the rare occasions that Hoover would unexpectedly drop in for a visit.

*

Al went before the draft board at Hilton Elementary School in Washington, D.C., in the fall of 1940, an act that would, across the country over the next five years, be undertaken by more than fifty million American men. Adolf Hitler, leader of the fascist Nazi Party, had become the führer and supreme commander of Germany in August 1934. Hitler had commanded a German invasion of Poland in 1939—the beginning of World War II, the deadliest war in human history, and one that would result in twenty-eight million deaths over the next six years. The war would consume Al's life and lay out the path for the rest of his professional career.

In the summer of 1940, the same week that Hitler's forces captured France and the Battle of Britain began, the U.S. Congress opened debate on the Selective Training and Service Act, which would install the first peacetime draft in American history. It came to a vote in September, the news sharing the fronts of American newspapers with stories about the Luftwaffe, Germany's air force, raining bombs onto the streets of London. The draft was just a few weeks old when Alfred Johnson—age 26, height 5 foot 7 ½ inches, 133 pounds—came before the board to make himself eligible for military service.

It was nearly three years before Al became a soldier. He was working for the War Food Administration when his number was called in early 1943. By the summer, he was on a train to the desert of Southern California, destined to spend the next two and a half years of his life as part of the 567th Anti-Aircraft Artillery Battalion, Charlie Battery. He trained in various camps across the United States before his unit finally made its way across the Atlantic in the fall of 1944. By then, the Allies had pushed the Germans back from the Atlantic across France. Now, Al and the 567th would march across the continent on the way to join General George Patton's famed Third Army in its thrust into Germany.

Al was, by this point in the war, a staff sergeant in charge of a squad of soldiers reporting to him. On March 31, 1945, Al and the 567th were at the Rhine River, providing support fire when the Allies crossed into Germany. The battalion had arrived in advance of infantry to set up headquarters. Al and his fellow soldiers were the first Americans seen by German civilians in the region. The Allied forces constructed a

632-foot floating pontoon bridge while under fire, then crossed into the Rhineland. The next month was spent on a race through Germany as the Nazi military unraveled and the country deteriorated into chaos. Members of Al's battalion visited "the gruesome concentration camp of Ohrdruf just at the time that former prison guards and local civilians were burying the many bodies of the slaughtered prisoners."

The German military unconditionally surrendered on May 7, 1945, and Al's days as an active soldier ended with the conclusion of the war in Europe. His next duty was under the auspices of the Office of Military Government, United States (OMGUS), the newly created organization tasked with the democratization of Germany. In addition to maintaining order and providing food distribution, the OMGUS undertook a massive propaganda effort to convince the population that Nazi Germany was dead and that the future was American democracy. Al would begin his postwar career working toward these goals.

Before leaving Europe, Al spent time in Glasgow, Scotland, studying agriculture at the university there. He eventually returned to the nation's capital and soon was once again working for the federal government. He was discharged from the army in February 1946 and began a job as a budget analyst at the Department of Agriculture, eventually to transfer to OMGUS. He started taking graduate classes at American University in Washington. He met a southern girl and former high school basketball player named Vera Louise Childress. Vera, the daughter of a farmer, had grown up in the quiet North Carolina burg of Mt. Airy, hometown of television actor Andy Griffith and, residents later claimed, the basis for Mayberry, the fictional home of Aunt Bee, Floyd the Barber, and the rest of the characters in *The Andy Griffith Show.* An earlier marriage had brought Vera from North Carolina to Washington, but the marriage was over by the time she met Al. Al had also been married for a short time before the war. Al and Vera became a couple, and they were married in Prince George's County, Maryland, on July 1, 1948.

Just a few months later, Al was appointed deputy chief of food process and distribution for the food and agriculture division of the Office of Military Government for Bavaria and sent to Munich, Germany. Al was headed back to Europe, with Vera soon to follow. The newlyweds settled in Munich in the fall of 1948, and less than a year later, the Johnsons welcomed their first child. At 12:45 in the morning on the first day of July in 1949, a baby boy weighing 7 pounds, 8 ½ ounces was delivered at 98th General Hospital, an American military hospital housed in the former Krankenhaus Schwabing, on the northern outskirts of Munich, Germany.

Al and Vera both wanted their children to have names that were distinct. They liked the name "Dennis," but they preferred the less common French spelling. The child had been delivered by Dr. Hale, which they thought sounded nice when it came after "Denis" and was also just as uncommon. Their first child, they decided, would be called Denis Hale Johnson.

*

The Cold War, the struggle for control of territory between the Soviet Union and the United States, quickly became the dominant power struggle around the globe. Alfred Johnson made a career of it, as did thousands of others in the postwar U.S. government. Al was successful enough at it to give his family a life of diplomatic privilege, complete with state dinners, international schooling for his children, and a professional existence in the shadows of true power.

The Johnsons were now a family, but their time in Munich was to be short. When Denis was just over three months old, Al was called back to the States. The family boarded the USNS *Henry Gibbins* for a two-week journey from Bremerhaven, Germany, to New York. A faded black-and-white photo, with the note "Welcome to the U.S.," shows the new parents posing with their baby in a park in Manhattan shortly after disembarking. Al, sporting a dark gray suit and black tie, squints into the camera, while Vera, in a black skirt and white blouse covered by a dark sweater, glances down toward the baby. The final destination the family listed was Mt. Airy, North Carolina, but Al was soon back to work for the federal government, initially with the Department of Agriculture. By the end of the year, he had been transferred to the Department of State, where he would spend the next two decades. The family settled in Alexandria, Virginia, just across the Potomac River from Washington, D.C. Shortly, Vera was pregnant again, and in September 1951, Denis and his parents welcomed his little brother, Randall.

Denis and his brother were born into the great generational anomaly that would come to be known as the baby boom, a phenomenon destined to cast its shadow over American culture and life as long as he would live. Today, the tremendous rise in the birthrate after World War II is viewed as an obvious result of millions of soldiers returning home to start families. At the time, however, the general consensus was that birthrates were about to decrease significantly. Americans were moving off the farm, the thinking went, where large families were needed to keep the operation going. The population was migrating to the suburbs, and the average middle-class suburban existence called for two parents and two kids. Women who had joined the workforce during the war effort would not all be prepared to return to a life of child-rearing. According to *Life* magazine, the United States was headed for "an eight percent cut in its youth base between 1940 and 1970."

The experts, of course, had it wrong. More babies were born between 1947 and 1953 than in the previous thirty years combined. Family size continued to decline, but a variety of other factors sent the birthrate skyrocketing. The postwar economic prosperity throughout the Western world led to a general optimism about the future, which encouraged procreation. In America, baby mania blossomed. Movies, television, and magazines all painted a picture of the ideal life for the American woman: get married, have babies, stay home, and take care of them. Marriage rates shot up, while the average age for marriage went down. Marriages without children, or just one child, became rare. The medium-sized family, between two and four kids, dominated. The ideal was reflected in popular television programs of the time, such as *Father Knows Best* and *Leave It to Beaver*, with dad at the office and mom in the kitchen, and it was an arrangement that held in the Johnson household throughout Denis's childhood.

Al did his part and continued to work his way up the ranks. His entry in the U.S. State Department's *Biographic Register* reflects an employee earning the respect of his supervisors and being rewarded for it. Promotions came regularly. According to the *Biographic Register,* Al first joined the State Department Foreign Service in 1953, doing a temporary stint at the U.S. embassy in Kabul, Afghanistan, as an executive officer. At one point, the plan was for the Johnson family to relocate to Kabul to join him. The family received vaccines, and Vera purchased two years' worth of American supplies that were unavailable in Afghanistan in preparation for the move, but then Al was told by superiors that the move was no longer necessary.

In August of that year, he transferred into the United States Information Agency, a new organization created to streamline the elements within the State Department that were primarily tasked with messaging, in all its forms. With the USIA, the State Department would use a variety of cultural and informational strategies—books, magazines, radio broadcasts, films, educational materials, cultural events—to win support for American political initiatives across the globe. Al survived the agency's vigorous security clearance procedure, in place to weed out radicals and communists.

At home, Vera and Al enrolled the boys in Trinity Methodist Church in Alexandria for preschool, then entered them into the public school system. Denis showed early aptitude for reading, less for math, and his early teachers mentioned his deficient listening skills. Vera noticed his early love for reading as well. "At home, Denis spends a great deal of time trying to read the books we have around our home," she wrote to one teacher. Vera encouraged her son's interest in books. Televisions were becoming ubiquitous in American households in the 1950s, and the Johnsons bought one in 1954. Vera, however, thought TV was for adults only. "When I went to school, everybody'd be talking about *The Life and Legend of Wyatt Earp, Gunsmoke,* some of these shows that I hadn't been allowed to see," Denis said. The shows did, however, help turn the five-year-olds of Alexandria into little gunfighters, and Denis was happy to take part. He and his friends would hide in the bushes, waiting for adults to come home from work. When one arrived, they would leap out of the bushes and demand, "Yankee or rebel?" Rebels would be granted a pass, but Yankees were shot on sight. "I didn't know what a yankee was and I didn't know what a rebel was, but I was living in the Virginia suburbs, in the early 1950s, and I knew we were rebels," he recalled years later.

*

Denis wouldn't remain in rebel territory for long. In May 1956, Alfred received word that he would be transferred to the American embassy in Tokyo. Immediately after Denis finished first grade, the family relocated to Japan, where they would spend the next five years. What had begun as a typical suburban American childhood was now to be something entirely different.

In Japan, the Johnsons settled into a life of diplomatic privilege and domestic comfort. Al, as an executive officer for the USIA, was involved in efforts to get the population behind America's political goals. The USIA preferred to call its activities "public diplomacy," a term that one analyst referred to as "a perfect piece of propaganda about propaganda." The agency worked to get the American point of view into the eyes and ears of the Japanese populace. USIA officials recorded and broadcast hundreds of pro-American radio programs, imported and distributed American books and periodicals, organized in-person events throughout the country, and even made sure newly created Japanese baseball fans could listen to the American World Series.

Denis and Randy attended Yoshi Elementary at the Tokyo American School. As early as age seven, Denis was commended for his storytelling abilities. "Perhaps his greatest achievement has been in the field of creative writing," his second-grade teacher gushed on his report card. "He does 'long stories' with ease and vivid imagination." The Johnsons' television didn't make the trip from Virginia to Tokyo, so Denis used books to entertain himself. He liked the children's mystery series the Hardy Boys and read many elementary-level science fiction books. At around age nine, he moved up to more advanced books, such as *Tom Sawyer* and *Huckleberry Finn.* He was particularly taken by *Penrod,* a 1914 adventure tale about an elementary-school-age boy and his dog in the Midwest. The hero of Booth Tarkington's classic children's tale battles a bully with a garden scythe, puts tar in a man's hat, and has other adolescent adventures. Denis, also an elementary-school-age boy at the time, decided someone needed to write a book about him, and Denis himself was the only one he could think of who would take on the task. He updated the story from the pre–World War I era to Tokyo of the 1950s and set off, like the hero of the book, to become a writer. "I hid out and wrote a novel, and it was very much like *Penrod,* only it was about me," Denis said later.

Life in Tokyo suited the Johnsons. At the embassy, Al monitored Japanese media—books, magazines, television, radio—for attitudes toward America. Vera enjoyed being the wife of a diplomat, the state dinners with visiting dignitaries, the perks of life overseas as a representative of the State Department. She became an officer in the Tokyo Women's Club and devoted time to one her passions: the game of bridge. In 1958, she competed in a worldwide bridge tournament sponsored by the State Department with more than a thousand other players, and took first place. For her effort, she was presented with a silver bowl by the ambassador, Douglas MacArthur II.

Vera had an outgoing personality and made friends easily. She was a southern girl who had no problem leaning into what was left of her accent. She also had a flair for fashion and soaked up attention, which came to her naturally. A photo of her in a family scrapbook shows her posing proudly with her two sons. Two Japanese men surround them, each with their hands on the shoulders of the boys. Denis, with his dark hair and complexion, shows a strong resemblance to his mother, while blond Randy appears to take after Al. The anti-American demonstrations that were common during those years posed no real threat, and Denis was allowed the freedom to explore the city by rail without adult supervision, a privilege he later looked back on fondly.

Four years in the same location is a fairly long assignment in the U.S. foreign service, and the Johnsons lasted just beyond that in Tokyo. In October 1960, Alfred was promoted to deputy public affairs officer at the American embassy in Manila. In the fall of Denis's sixth-grade year, the family packed up and moved to the Philippines. The Johnsons settled into a comfortable apartment in the Perry House on embassy property. Their arrangement included maids to run the household and free Vera up for social pursuits. The family adopted a dog and named him Oki. Al diligently trained the new pet, but the dog, a boxer by breed, was difficult to walk on a leash and got into scraps with other dogs, so Oki spent most of his time in the backyard. Because of the Filipino view of dog meat as a delicacy, the maids were constantly worried that Oki would be kidnapped and served for dinner.

The promotion to deputy public affairs officer gave Al more responsibility along with more authority. Now he was second in command in one of the agency's largest offices. USIA branches in other cities across the Philippines now reported directly to him. Al had climbed higher on the organizational chart of the State Department and spent more of his time hobnobbing with the rich and powerful element of Manila high society. The most compelling stories from these fancy dinners and interactions would be retold to Denis and Randy in the Johnson household. Al was invited to a dinner to celebrate John Kennedy's inauguration in January 1961. The party, held in one of Manila's largest and most ostentatious mansions, included some of the wealthiest Filipinos along with several State Department higher-ups. Dinner was served around a long, elegantly arranged dining-room table. Dozens of servants presented the elaborately prepared meal to the guests at the table. Suddenly, in the middle of dinner, one of the Filipino guests stood up, grabbed a chair, and hurled it toward the other end of the table. It came crashing down, shattering fancy china and sending guests scurrying to the floor. It seemed that another guest had brought this man's long-estranged ex-wife to the dinner as an insult—clearly one he considered worthy of a violent response. As an adult, Denis would recall this story as an example of the power of passion to break through the guardrails of polite society.

It was in Manila that Denis began to exhibit a rebellious streak. He wrote later that when he moved to a new school, he would use bad behavior to get attention, and as he grew older, he graduated from "Cutup to Hoodlum." He attended the private American School in Manila along with the children of other corporate executives and career diplomats. His grades were usually average, mostly Bs and Cs with the occasional A or D. Sometimes his misdeeds drew the attention of administrators, who passed along their concerns to his parents. In eighth grade, the principal of the American School in Manila suspended him for two days for disruptive behavior. "Any repetition will cause a harsher penalty and may even endanger his place in the school," the principal wrote to Vera. "Perhaps Denis had better consider his need for attention." Manila was also where Denis began to experiment with illicit activities. Drinking at a young age was prevalent in the Philippines. Denis tried rum for the first time at age fourteen and soon began drinking it regularly.

But it was reading and writing that consumed the larger part of his time as he moved deeper into his teenage years. "You could go to the library, you go to the shelf, some title catches your eye, you check it out, read it, and it makes you feel at home on the earth," he remembered. "I was already claiming that I wanted to be a writer because it was the only thing I could do at school that sort of mollified the authorities, or made me credible to them, anyway."

*

In April 1965, the USIA sent Al back to headquarters in Washington. The Johnsons' decade-long international experience had come to an end. The family settled back into a suburban existence at the modest Fort Ward Tower Apartments in Alexandria, close enough for Al to commute to his new office across the Potomac River in Washington, D.C., but a step down from the residence provided by the State Department overseas. Vera found the role of American housewife far less appealing than her previous position of foreign-service spouse. Occasionally she would "go on strike" to show her displeasure with domestic duties.

For Al, however, the move put him even closer to the halls of power. His position in the government had become elevated enough to even warrant the occasional trip to the Oval Office. Once, he and his direct supervisor were called in to meet with President Johnson. Whatever the subject of the meeting was, it proved to have sufficient gravity that Johnson felt the need to use one of his trademark Texas idioms on Al and his boss. It must be done, and it must be done right, the president told them. "If not, I'll have your pecker in my pocket!"

Denis enrolled at T. C. Williams High School. His performance in school continued to be lacking in most areas, save the humanities. One teacher, after gifting Denis a D, wrote, "This grade reflects lack of work, not ability. Thoroughly enjoyed having you as a student, Denis!"

A few of his classmates from T. C. Williams would become lifelong friends. One of his closest pals during this period was Joe Cohen. Cohen's older sister, Helen, would later be known as Cass Elliot of the Mamas & the Papas. Another good friend at the time was Bobby Zimmerman, a short, sickly kid with frizzy hair (who just happened to share his birth name with the folk-rock poet who was already an idol for Denis). The three of them, along with another T. C. Williams student, Carter Batchellor, had a life-altering experience that bonded them forever when they decided to try LSD.

In 1966, lysergic acid diethylamide, commonly known as acid, was still a legal drug. Thanks to its celebrity champion, Timothy Leary, it was by then widely known to be extremely potent in inducing visual and auditory hallucinations and increased emotional reaction to stimuli. The four buddies got their hands on five hundred micrograms of White Owsley. Owsley acid was the first mass-produced LSD, created by Grateful Dead soundman Owsley Stanley, who began shipping it across the United States in 1965. Stanley's acid was considered the purest version of the drug. Denis and his friends could vouch for its purity after their experience. They consumed the drug in Denis's Chevrolet and embarked on what Denis later called "an absurd odyssey for which none of us had been the slightest bit prepared." The boys sat in the car for six straight hours, listening to the radio and barely speaking.

When the drug's effects began to ease, Denis started the car and drove while still hallucinating. The streetlights looked like dandelions and the car a "giant teacup." He managed to get Cohen and Batchellor safely to their houses, then arrived back at the Fort Ward Towers at 5 a.m. with Zimmerman. Vera was awake and distraught. She asked where they had been. Denis turned to his friend and waited for Bobby to respond. In the past, when the two had gotten in trouble together,

Denis could count on his friend to talk them out of the situation. But with his brain still in the grip of the Owsley, Bobby could not generate a response. Instead, both boys asked each other "Where have we been?" several times, until Vera relented and sent them on their way.

By this time, writing, specifically poetry, had become Denis's identity. He and his friends called themselves beatniks. They were devotees of the Beat Generation writers—Jack Kerouac, Allen Ginsberg, Gregory Corso—and discussed T. S. Eliot at length. Denis got a job at a bookstore and began telling people he was going to be a poet. Those who discouraged him from his new career goal only hardened his position. Denis's English teacher at T. C. Williams told him that if he tried to make a career out of poetry, he'd starve, but Denis was unmoved.

The summer before his senior year, he spent time with the family of Vera's brother in North Carolina. His Uncle C.S. said that if Denis took engineering in college, he would make sure there would be a job waiting for his nephew when he graduated. "I told him that I wanted to be a writer," Denis wrote to his parents in July 1966. "He was shocked, and completely unable to understand why anyone would want to devote himself to such a worthless profession. I think that if I was his child, he would have beaten me. But it doesn't really bother me what Uncle C.S. thinks."

Fortunately for Denis, his decision to devote himself to a life of poetry had the backing of the two most important people at the time: his parents. Both Vera and Al appreciated the arts and saw writing as a serious pursuit. By the time the Johnson family watched Denis accept his diploma in the T. C. Williams gym on June 8, 1967, Denis knew where he'd be heading after high school, and that knowledge was partly due to assistance from his father. Al was an acquaintance of a young poet named Stanley Plumly. He told Plumly that his son wanted to be a poet and asked what Denis should do. Plumly responded, in dramatic enough fashion that the Johnsons needed no further convincing: "He should get himself to the Writers' Workshop in Iowa City, indubitably."

BLOOD ON THE STEPS 2

We are not about to send American boys 9 or 10 thousand miles away from home to do what Asian boys ought to be doing for themselves. **—President Lyndon Baines Johnson, October 21, 1964**

Denis was just two months past his eighteenth birthday when he arrived on the University of Iowa campus in September 1967, but he was already a nonconformist through and through. He wore his curly hair long, but not past his shoulders in the popular hippie fashion of the time. He preferred clothing picked up at secondhand stores. He dressed plainly and wore boxy, Boy Scout–style shoes and oversized khaki work pants. But he was also a worldly, urban kid from the nation's capital about to share a dorm and classrooms with thousands of teenagers from the farms of rural Iowa who viewed Iowa City, population below fifty thousand, as the big city.

Denis arrived at Hillcrest Residence Hall before the start of the semester, eager to start life on his own. He went on a shopping expedition and found a little store owned by an Armenian couple where he bargained the price of a World War I–era knapsack down to $2.50. He negotiated for a Victrola record player and a Civil War uniform but couldn't reach a deal with the couple. Then he headed to the Goodwill store and picked up a bunch of worn baby blankets he planned to use as towels.

In addition to poetry, Denis had developed an abiding interest in music. He played both guitar and harmonica and had studied the history of American blues music. Early in the semester, he came downstairs in Hillcrest carrying a stack of blues records—Lightning Hopkins, Lead Belly, Mississippi John Hurt—looking for a room with a record player. He ended up in the apartment belonging to Bob Stall and his roommates. Stall was a Des Moines native who had come to the University of Iowa to study English. He and Denis would soon become close friends. That night, and on many nights to follow, Denis, Stall, and a few others who came to comprise Denis's social circle in the dorm sat around, talking about guitar styles and playing whatever blues songs they could with the three chords they had mastered.

Another cadre of friends that Denis developed early in his first semester was a group of fledgling antiwar activists. The members of his new cohort had come to the debate over the war in Vietnam recently. Denis, though, had been intimately involved for years, thanks to the work of his father.

*

During Alfred Johnson's years in Manila, Vietnam was the focal point of American foreign policy in the struggle for Cold War supremacy with the Soviet Union. President Dwight Eisenhower's domino theory, which stated that the scourge of communism would infest countries one by one if the United States didn't stop it, placed a foreign-policy emphasis on Southeast Asia in the 1950s. Vietnam had become the top priority for Al's USIA office in the Philippines, as it had in all American embassies in Asia. Messaging about Vietnam became central to the USIA mission. Al and his colleagues spent their days creating and disseminating the American message, both directly into Vietnam to promote loyalty to the pro-American government in Saigon, and around the world to portray the U.S. effort as a noble cause. Indeed, the agency's efforts concerning Vietnam in the 1960s account for the largest funding in its history. USIA efforts were instrumental in coining the phrase "Viet Cong," to tie the North Vietnamese forces to the USSR.

Al's own feelings about the war in Vietnam were conflicted. Professionally, he was a committed soldier in the American war effort. In private, Al, whose core political beliefs had been formed while supporting the efforts of Franklin Delano Roosevelt and the New Deal Democrats in the 1930s, often voiced antiwar views and questioned the U.S. strategy toward Southeast Asia. But his understanding of international conflict had also been shaped by his experiences in World War II. Denis's brother, Randy, recalled a heated discussion with their father during the height of the Vietnam War. Al saw a headline in the *Arizona Republic* indicating that William Calley Jr. had been convicted of murder in connection with the infamous My Lai massacre, in which hundreds of Vietnamese civilians were killed by U.S. soldiers. The news enraged Al. War is war, he told his son. Soldiers are trained to be killers and are subjected to unimaginable situations, sent by men in offices thousands of miles away. They can't be held accountable when their most brutal instincts are unleashed by the conditions of battle. That sentiment couldn't help but seep into his feelings toward his professional activities, many of which undoubtedly ran counter to his own political beliefs.

The work that Al did for the USIA while the Johnsons were in the Philippines was shrouded in mystery for his family. Throughout his life, when describing his father, Denis would say that Al was the liaison between the USIA and the Central Intelligence Agency. Like the USIA, the CIA was another new agency created to streamline American operations in the aftermath of World War II. It was tasked with all information gathering for the United States internationally, including covert operations. Because both CIA and USIA personnel often operated out of embassies, it's likely that Al coordinated regularly with CIA officials working out of the embassy in Manila rather than acting as a liaison, as Denis believed. Because of the similarity of the agencies' missions and their proximity, it was a common implication that someone holding a USIA title was actually hiding the fact they were spying for the CIA. In fact, USIA leadership went out of its way to avoid being used as CIA cover because it was thought that it would undercut the USIA's credibility around the world.

Denis did not pick up on his father's internal conflict during his adolescence. His peers all were part of families similar to his own, with the head of the household's paycheck coming from the U.S. government. As a child growing up in a community that believed collectively in the righteousness of the American cause in Southeast Asia, Denis's beliefs followed the consensus. He bought into the anticommunist crusade, and as a young teenager, he was eager to jump into the fray. "I was very against communism," he said. "I didn't care what war we were in at that age, I wanted to get in it, and blow some things up."

His awakening to anti–Vietnam War sentiment came once Al was transferred back to Washington, D.C. The Johnsons returned from the Philippines while Denis was still in high school. They left their tight-knit community made up mostly of government officials and their families and moved back to United States just as the American population was hardening into pro- and antiwar factions. It wasn't long after he arrived back in America that Denis was confronted with the other side of the argument. In Alexandria, he spotted a car in the parking lot with a bumper sticker that read, "America: Get Out of Vietnam." "I couldn't believe it," he said. "I was drawn in, like Satan, to find out more and more and more about why somebody would think that."

*

Early in his first semester at Iowa, Denis began to meet informally with a group of students who shared his burgeoning antiwar views. It was at one of these meetings that Denis first encountered a young woman named Nancy Jo Lister. Nancy was a freshman art major from the tiny Iowa town of Dallas Center, 130 miles due west of Iowa City. Nancy's upbringing was the stuff of Norman Rockwellian Americana: five siblings, a father who was the town doctor and made house calls every night before dinner, and a mother who stayed home and taught her daughters how to master the sewing machine. There were sixty people in her high school graduating class, and they had been in the same school building since kindergarten.

The Listers voted Republican, but more out of tradition than ideology. They taught their children compassion, however, and it rubbed off on their daughter enough to turn her against the Vietnam War. When she arrived on campus, she had begun to dress in full hippie regalia—flowing dresses, the more colorful the better. She got to know Denis and was intrigued by his interest in writing, by his East Coast origins, and by his international experience. She found him an exotic, romantic figure, and the two became friends.

In October, Denis went to a meeting of the student senate. There was talk of antiwar rallies and demonstrations. The idea of burning down the Iowa state capitol was discussed and received considerable support. Vietnam had seeped into the classroom as well. Denis wrote to his parents about philosophy class: "My teacher devoted half a discussion period to explaining why God does not exist. The rest of the period, and of all periods, he devotes to explaining why America should get out of Vietnam."

*

Across the country, the United States was experiencing a similar phenomenon. The American cause in Vietnam, which Alfred Johnson had worked so diligently to promote, had been increasing exponentially in the public sphere as his son had grown to comprehend it. President Lyndon Johnson had campaigned and been reelected in 1964 as the peace candidate, but he had become the opposite once the election was over. In 1964, North Vietnamese boats fired on the USS *Maddox* in the Gulf of Tonkin, an incident President Johnson used to gain support for the United States to launch retaliatory attacks against North Vietnam. In 1965, the United States moved to full-scale bombing raids against North Vietnam. More than 125,000 American troops were deployed by the end of that year. The Selective Service draft call was doubled, then doubled again. By the summer of 1965, thirty-five thousand men were being drafted into the army each month. The first major ground offensive started that summer as well. American battle casualties began to accumulate right around the time Alfred moved his family moved back to the States. Images of flag-draped coffins seeped in the country's consciousness. U.S. battlefield deaths went from 116 in 1964 to 11,363 in 1967. By that year, half a million American troops were stationed in Vietnam.

The protest movement in America was on the same trajectory as the American war effort through the 1960s. College students were at the core of the movement from the beginning. The early '60s saw the growth of civil-rights protests. Freedom rides were launched; buses filled with protesters, many of them college students, drove into the Deep South to demonstrate against segregation. What started in the South spread up the East and West Coasts. Student protest organizations formed, first at elite colleges, then, as Vietnam crept into the conversation, at large public universities in America's heartland. Students for a Democratic Society (SDS) was formed at the University of Michigan in 1960 and became an umbrella organization that fueled the engine of protest on campuses across the country. SDS and the New Left, as it was termed, grew through the early part of the decade. In 1965, an SDS march on Washington attracted more than twenty-five thousand protesters. While Denis was finishing his last semester of high school, it was clear that the antiwar movement was spreading across American college campuses. Early in 1967, college newspaper editors and presidents of the student body at a hundred universities sent a letter to Lyndon Johnson in opposition to the war effort. The fuse of student activism had been lit, and now it was burning toward an inevitable explosion.

*

The moment when the Vietnam War truly arrived at the University of Iowa was just after 10 a.m. on November 1, 1967. That was when a Hawkeye defensive lineman rushed a line of peaceful protesters, knocked several of them down, and started stepping on their heads.

About an hour earlier, Denis had taken his place in the line with approximately 150 other student demonstrators in front of the Iowa Memorial Union, locked arms, and braced for battle. It was a damp, cool Wednesday, just another day in the middle of the semester on campus. Students casually walked by the protesters on the way to class, silently noting the appearance of something they were heretofore unfamiliar with, but would, in the coming months, come to expect.

Outside organizers had come to campus early in the fall semester of 1967 to foment antiwar activity. The strategy that had developed for that Wednesday was for student demonstrators to disrupt a scheduled recruiting drive for the United States Marine Corps. SDS had launched a campaign of similar demonstrations across the country. The University of Wisconsin in Madison had been the site of the infamous Dow riot just a week before, where police had violently dispersed a peaceful student sit-in against a Dow Chemical recruiting event, sending seventy people to the hospital and shutting down the university for several days. (Dow produced the chemical weapon known as napalm that was used extensively in the American war effort.) Now, the University of Iowa students were using some of the same tactics against the Marines.

Along with Denis, writers were well represented on the line of defense against the aspiring Marines. Phil Schultz, a future winner of the Pulitzer Prize in poetry, was, like Denis, newly arrived in Iowa City in the fall of '67. He and Denis did not know each other yet, but a few years later, they would become close friends and fellow students in the Writers' Workshop. Unlike most of his coconspirators, Schultz was an experienced veteran of the movement. He had gone to college as an undergraduate in California at San Francisco State, where antiwar demonstrations had started years earlier. "You couldn't walk from one class to another without being part of a protest and being locked up," he recalled. Schultz was in Iowa as a graduate student primarily because, like many young men of the time, he preferred a campus in the Midwest to the jungles of Vietnam. Over the summer, the New York draft board had tracked him down in Paris, where he was living with his girlfriend, and given him forty-eight hours to enroll in school or report for military duty. So now he was in Iowa City, trying—and failing—to keep a low profile. "I was a real troublemaker. I did not see fit for others to be arrested and not me," he said.

Schultz had become close with Robert Coover, then a young professor who taught a fiction workshop in which Schultz was a student. Coover would eventually become a leading figure in postmodern experimental fiction, defining the movement with contemporaries such as Donald Barthelme and William Gass. In the fall of 1967, Coover was as new to campus as Denis when he joined the demonstration that Wednesday morning. A month later, he would dive into what he termed "advocacy journalism," filming a documentary when Dow Chemical showed up on Iowa's campus to recruit. Coover's new boss was George Starbuck, the director of the Writers' Workshop at the time and a poet of some renown himself. George and his wife, Judy, took their place on the steps in front of the Memorial Union as well, bringing several other students from the workshop along with them.

The sky was gray, and a cold rain had started falling on the demonstrators when the first Marine recruits began to approach the Union. Campus police, who had been tipped off to the demonstration, set up outside the front doors to the building, barring entry to the protesters. As the rain intensified, Denis and his fellow combatants organized outside, took their positions in several rows, and waited.

At about 9:15, a few clean-cut, determined youths arrived, climbed the steps, and demanded entry to the building. The demonstrators refused, words were exchanged, and what would become a five-hour battle was officially underway. Many of the Marine wannabes, after failing to talk their way past the protesters, rushed the lines of defense and were repelled. Others went to the flanks and fought their way through. Shouting and scuffles broke out. A crowd began to gather.

The tide turned with the arrival of the Hawkeye defensive lineman John Evenden. He approached the line "with a determined gleam in his eye that made us all a little nervous," one of the protestors wrote afterward. Evenden casually took off his coat, then rushed the line as if he were attacking an opposing quarterback on a Saturday afternoon. He stiff-armed, elbowed, and kicked his way through the defenses, leaving several injured protesters in his wake.

The atmosphere turned to one of impending violence as the number of antiprotesters grew. Though the percentage of the student body opposed to the war was increasing, the majority still supported it, and many viewed those who had bought into the protest movement as commies or freaks. It wasn't uncommon for someone whose appearance marked them as a hippie to be pelted with rocks or frozen hard-boiled eggs by fraternity members who remained on the other side of the argument.

As the morning leaked away, the opposition quickly expanded beyond potential Marines to include anybody who either hated hippies or wanted to have a little fun at their expense. They began pulling protesters out of the line and beating them. One protester was knocked to the ground and kicked in the stomach and head. A young woman was punched in the face. "The screams of the hecklers became increasingly brutal, obscene and mindless," a reporter for the student newspaper wrote.

Schultz was attacked and punched, and the fight led to one of his attackers rolling down the stairs. That resulted in more combatants coming after him. "They knew the guy, or they took his cause on, and they came after me, and they were all big," he said. "And I remember someone on our side grabbing me by the arm, pulling me out of there and saying, 'you've done enough fighting.'"

Throughout the day, Denis and the students on the steps maintained the nonviolent approach, even as the opposition became increasingly menacing. Arms locked, they remained stoic as their situation grew more dire. The campus police, who had been lined up behind the protest on the steps for most of the morning as a bulwark against anarchy, now abandoned them and moved inside. By early afternoon, the gathering of hecklers and spectators numbered near a thousand. A dean with a megaphone implored the protesters to go home. A state senator arrived, only to egg the mob on, shouting, "Go get 'em!" The mob obliged, and the attacks intensified.

Finally, at around 2 p.m., nearly 120 police officers from Iowa City and surrounding counties, wearing full riot gear, shields and batons raised, pulled up and joined the fray. The hecklers immediately dispersed. The police set their sights on the protesters. The Iowa River flows past the front of the Memorial Union, and beyond the steps a steep hill runs down toward the water. Some of the protesters bolted the line and were chased across the grass by police waving billy clubs. In the commotion, one hefty officer, depleted from the chase, suffered a heart attack and rolled down the hill.

The police were more benevolent than usual that day. They turned their backs and gave the remaining protesters a minute to disappear.

Those who considered themselves too poor to suffer the financial consequences of being arrested scattered. Denis fit into that category but did not take the police up on the offer. Instead, like most of his fellow protesters, he stayed on the steps and waited to be arrested. The grim-faced officers began the process. Some protesters went limp and had to be dragged off the steps. Each of them, limp or not, was numbered with chalk on his or her back, and then, one by one, was loaded into school buses and driven away. Eventually, all who had been arrested made their way to the Johnson County Jail, where they were charged with disturbing the peace. Denis, like most of his comrades, pled not guilty and went back to his dorm room to await the consequences.

The protest had been planned as a series of events, and two days later, Denis joined another demonstration. Students met at the office of an English instructor named Paul Kleinberger. Under the supervision of a medical technician and a medical student, they used hollow needles to drain blood from their arms into cups. Other students pricked their fingers, dipped toothpicks in blood, and signed petitions excoriating both the war effort and the university's handling of the earlier protest. Then they went back to the Memorial Union and splashed blood on the steps, leaving what the student newspaper deemed a "gory mess." Afterward, they gathered in groups of two and three and marched across campus to the Iowa Old Capitol Building, a campus landmark that had served as the state capitol when Iowa had first become a state in the mid-nineteenth century. Six of the protesters carried a casket wrapped in black crepe. At the Old Capitol, they served university president Howard Bowen with the blood-drenched petitions. Police were prepared this time, so physical confrontation was avoided, but the opposition whipped coins at the protesters as they made speeches and performed antiwar skits. Later in the day, a Dow Chemical event that was on the upcoming schedule was quietly canceled.

The following week, Denis and the other 107 protesters who had been arrested on November 1 began appearing in court to plead innocent to charges of disturbing the peace. One by one, Iowa City police judge Marion Neely found them guilty. Denis told his friend Bob Stall that he planned to go to jail rather than pay a fine. Stall, who had been ambivalent about the war, was just beginning to wrestle with the issues involving Vietnam and to form his own political views. He was amazed by his new friend's steadfast devotion to principle. "Only a damn fool gets himself arrested, and nobody goes to jail on purpose," Stall thought at the time. "That's when I realized that this guy is really unusual. This guy's extraordinary." Stall also had an inkling, however, that part of the reason behind Denis's decision was for the experience—and for the material it would provide him to write about down the road.

A little over two weeks later, seventy-seven student and faculty protesters appeared before Judge Neely in Iowa City police court. The judge admonished them, telling them they'd been led astray and should seek the truth in the future. Then he found all of them guilty and fined them $54. If the convicts could not come up with the money to pay the fine, they could pay it off, at the rate of $5 a day, by serving time in the jail.

The $54 figure caused an audible gasp among the arrestees, who had been expecting a $25 fine. Still, nearly all of the students informed the court that they planned to pay the fine. One student marched to the podium to declare loudly that it was the U.S. government, not he, who was guilty of disturbing the peace. After the impassioned speech, the student paid his fine and went back to campus.

Most of the students had the money or could call their parents to cover it. None of them, however, had a father who championed the American war effort in Vietnam for a living, and who had devoted his life to promoting the nobility of American foreign policy. Denis chose not to make that call. Instead, whether for principle, lack of funds, or just to see what it was like, or for all those reasons, he decided he would do the time. Most of the other students were paying the fine or making arrangements to pay it before the December 1 deadline, so Denis approached the clerk of the court and said he'd like to be incarcerated immediately. After the necessary forms were completed, a guard placed him in handcuffs, took him by the arm, and led him past the murmuring throng of student convicts, through the doors, out of the courtroom, and into the custody of the state of Iowa.

*

From Friday afternoon until the following Thursday, Denis resided in the Johnson County Jail. On campus in Iowa City, the excitement of the protest had worn off. Life proceeded as usual. On Monday of the week Denis was in jail, another antiwar activist came to the University of Iowa campus. Muhammad Ali, the former heavyweight boxing champion of the world, had refused induction into the U.S. military in April, citing his Muslim beliefs. He'd been stripped of his title and indicted, but he remained the shadow heavyweight champion of the world, until, as one prominent columnist wrote, "somebody besides a fat lawyer with a cigar and a fountain pen" defeated him. Now, to earn some money, he was giving speeches on college campuses across the country, airing his antiwar views and reciting poetic contempt about his chief ring rival, Sonny Liston. Hundreds of chairs were added to the auditorium in the Memorial Union; the hallways overflowed with people who came to hear Ali speak and answer questions. He was asked why he wouldn't fight in Vietnam. "I don't take part in no wars," Ali said. "I don't care if we fought Russia tomorrow, jumped up and fought Africa, jumped up and fought Israel, jumped up and fought Mexico, I take part in no wars that take the lives of humans."

Denis remained incarcerated. A friend from Hillcrest, Peggy Lamar, led the effort among his dorm comrades to get him out. She went to the jail with enough money to free her friend but was told he'd have to stay another day. Before she went back to campus, she bought Denis a greeting card and wrote him a note. Denis opened the envelope while in his cell. On the front of the Hallmark card was pictured a group of cartoon figures, with sad expressions and a few tears, with the caption, "Please come back, we all miss you very much, and besides. . . ." Inside, the punch line read, "The coast is clear!" Lamar told Denis that she had paid his court costs and was trying to get him out of jail. "Take care of yourself," she wrote. "We're anxiously awaiting your return to the city of the politically dispossessed."

On November 22, Denis was finally free. If it was material for future writing that he was after, that goal was most definitely accomplished. One particular person whom he met during those six days would become both a partner in crime and, decades later, the basis for a character in Denis's masterpiece of fiction. Serving time alongside Denis was an eighteen-year-old Iowa City kid with a long juvenile rap sheet who had just been arrested for the first time as an adult. John Dundon hadn't been at the protest at the Memorial Union. In fact, he had no idea the protest had taken place. Denis's newest friend was in jail for a decidedly different crime: he had broken into the house of an elderly woman, robbed her, and used the money to buy drugs. Through Dundon, Denis would be introduced to a new cohort that had nothing to do with the art of poetry and everything to do with the Iowa City illicit drug trade.

Denis's days as an antiwar protester, and indeed as an activist of any type, had come to an end. For the rest of his life, he would express his political beliefs through writing but never again take part in political demonstrations. Nearly sixty years later, when he was in his last year of life, Denis would still be drawing on his experiences inside the walls of that jail as he was writing what would be his final short story. "I've seen those same men many times throughout my life, repeatedly in dreams and sometimes in actuality," he wrote, "and it makes me feel each person's universe is really very small, no bigger than a county jail, a collection of cells in which he encounters the same fellow prisoners over and over."

3

ADULT EDUCATION

You win a few, you lose a few. Some get rained out. But you gotta dress for all of them. —**Leroy (Satchel) Paige**

When his week in jail was over, Denis announced the official end to his career as a war protester. In a letter to his parents, he devoted all of two sentences to his break with the peace movement. The true goals of the organizers were destructive, not the peaceful motives they stated publicly, so his association with them was finished, he wrote to Al and Vera. No mention of the arrest or the week in jail made it into the letter. The rest of the page was devoted to the results of his midterm exams, and to telling his parents that he was too broke to afford to do his laundry.

The events of November 1 and the aftermath had a clarifying effect on Denis. He was at the University of Iowa to study poetry, and that was where his focus should be. His involvement with the anti-Vietnam movement on campus faded away, remembered Nancy Lister, his dorm mate and fellow protester. "He was actually a pretty serious student, and he knew why he was there in Iowa City, and he knew why he had chosen that school to attend, and he took it seriously," she said. He began to write what he called "a ditty a day." Monday through Sunday, without exception, he would write lines, phrases, and thoughts, in longhand into a little spiral notebook. Sometimes he would share his work with Nancy, but more often, he kept it to himself. There was a single-mindedness to it, Nancy believed. He was accumulating ideas and observations that he would soon be crafting into poetry.

Denis and Nancy began spending more time together. What had started as a dorm friendship blossomed into a romantic relationship. Nancy began joining Denis when he went to poetry class. She was captivated by his writing and enjoyed hearing it discussed by the rest of the students. The privilege made her feel special. Nobody else brought their girlfriend to class. Soon Denis was asking Nancy to type up his handwritten pages before he would submit them. By the end of the year, they were seeing each other exclusively.

Near the end of the spring semester in 1968, Denis walked into the cafeteria in Hillcrest carrying a pint of whiskey. Alcohol was strictly forbidden in the cafeteria. Denis had already consumed much of the bottle before he got there. He began sipping as he ate his supper, casually flouting the rules to the astonishment of his friends. A few bites in, the cafeteria monitor noticed the whiskey bottle and headed toward the table. Denis picked up the bottle, walked over to the window, and opened it. Then he calmly tossed the bottle out. The entire dining room heard the crash of glass against the pavement, two floors below. Denis was not an attention seeker; this behavior was out of character. It had been brought on by something he had learned earlier in the day: Nancy was pregnant.

Now Denis had two issues confronting him: a student conduct code charge and a pregnant girlfriend. The details of the first problem appeared in his campus mailbox five days later in the form of a letter from the associate dean. "On the basis of your witnessed and admitted behavior which involved your drinking hard liquor from a bottle during dinner in the Hillcrest cafeteria on May 24, 1968, I am recommending that you be suspended from the University of Iowa for semesters 1 and 2 of the 1968–69 academic year," the associate dean wrote. A hearing was set for later that summer. The College of Liberal Arts piled on, placing Denis on academic probation, thanks to D grades in philosophy and French and an F in literature. The A he received in poetry wasn't enough to save him.

The second problem, the pregnancy, would have to be dealt with first. The information was communicated to parents, and the families decided to make the best of the situation. Decisions were made in accordance with the mores of the older generation. A baby was on the way, so a marriage was in order. A little less than two months later, an item announcing the engagement of Nancy Jo Lister to Denis Hale Johnson appeared in a Washington, D.C., newspaper.

A late August wedding was planned, to be held in Nancy's hometown of Dallas Center. Invitations were prepared and mailed. In mid-August, Denis and Nancy took letters of consent from their parents and went down to the courthouse, where they applied for a marriage license. Vera and Nancy's mother, Norma Jean, spoke on the phone and exchanged letters in preparation for the wedding. "We're getting acquainted with Denis more each day," Norma Jean wrote to Vera. "Neither he nor Nancy Jo are what you could call 'talkative,' but we are quite pleased that they are willing to discuss with us any suggestions we may have."

The wedding was scheduled for August 31. The Johnsons arrived in Iowa a few days early. Nancy had already sewn dresses for herself and her wedding party. Denis asked his high school friend, Joe Cohen, to be his best man. When Cohen sent his regrets, Nancy drafted Bob Stall, their friend from Hillcrest, for the job. The two families got together for the first time the night before the wedding. Nancy's parents had chosen, for the rehearsal dinner, Alice's Spaghetti Land in Waukee, a local favorite, owned by the Nizzi family, patients of Nancy's father, Eugene. At the dinner, Eugene pulled Denis aside and asked him why Stall hadn't gotten his hair cut for the wedding. The subtext of the question, Stall thought, was, why hadn't Denis himself gotten his hair cut so it would be appropriately short when Denis walked down the aisle with Eugene's daughter?

The plan was for Denis to spend the night before the wedding at Stall's parents' house in suburban Des Moines. Stall was embarrassed to have his friend, a "diplomat's son" who he thought was above him in economic and social class, see how the Stall family lived. But if Denis noticed, he didn't mention it to Stall. He did, however, complain about the behavior of Stall's cat. In the middle of the night, Denis appeared in Stall's bedroom to tell him the cat had evicted him from the guest bedroom. He told Stall he was hitchhiking to Dallas Center, packed up his clothes, and left.

Bouquets of white gladiolas decorated the altar the following afternoon when the families and guests settled into their pews at the United Presbyterian Church in Dallas Center to watch Denis and Nancy take their vows. It was a traditional affair, with attention paid to every detail. Nancy had been busy at the sewing machine, creating for herself a floor-length gown of ivory French crepe, topped with a crown of Swedish lace. For her sisters, the bridesmaids, she had sewn floor-length green and blue gowns, and presented each with a single glamelia encircled with leather leaf, along with streamers of miniature pearls. Denis and his groomsmen eschewed tuxedos and wore their own suits. Along with Stall as best man, Denis's wedding party consisted of a high school friend who had made the trip from Virginia, and Tim Griffith, a friend from Iowa City with a thriving marijuana business who would, a quarter century later, become the model for a character in *Jesus' Son*.

After the ceremony, the guests came back to the Lister house for a reception. Many of the dignitaries of Dallas Center joined Al and Vera; Denis's grandmother, Maggie Childress; and the extended Lister family to enjoy coffee and punch and to watch Denis and Nancy slice into the three-tier cake. Nancy's mother, Norma Jean, recorded every detail, down to who presided over the guest book and who oversaw the gifts, and later reported those details to the local Dallas Center newspaper for publication in the next edition. The Johnson and Lister families cautiously mingled. Vera worked the room, embracing all she approached with southern warmth, while Al blended into the background. The refreshments were served, the guest book signed, and the cake distributed; then the guests went back to their respective homes and states, leaving Denis and Nancy, now officially married teenagers, to prepare for the impending birth of their firstborn.

*

The newlyweds made their first home at Hawkeye Drive, the University of Iowa's married housing complex. The Hawkeye Drive apartments were a series of plain brick structures that had been built eight years before to accommodate the growing number of married students attending the university. The were populated by student couples of varied disciplines. Because the apartments were more than a mile from campus, most residents took shuttle buses to their classes. Denis and Nancy moved into a small second-floor apartment with two bedrooms, a small living area and kitchen, and a single bathroom. Their friends from the dormitories were no longer living just a few steps away, but Nancy made the best of it, chatting up their new neighbors: a doctoral student in chemistry on one side, a business major on the other.

Denis had beaten the rap from the whiskey-in-the-cafeteria incident—or at least gotten the suspension reduced to probation—so he worked on raising his grade point average and getting himself back into the good graces of the student affairs office. Nancy dropped out of college in preparation for the baby, which was due in January 1969. As that date approached, Denis continued the lifestyle he'd become accustomed to: going to bars, drinking with friends, and selling nickel bags of marijuana in College Green Park. The upheaval of this way of life that would inevitably come with the addition of a child was not something they discussed much. "We seemed to just jump from one circumstance to the next without a lot of worry," Nancy said. "We didn't really talk about it. It just was something that was going to happen, and we just took it in stride."

Instead, the apprehension bubbled to the surface in other ways. Nancy's blood pressure went up. She worried about their financial situation and what costs they would incur as parents. Once, she decided the apartment was so dirty as to be unlivable for a baby. She demanded that Denis remove all the furniture and wax and scrub the floors until it was germ-free and baby-safe. Denis thought she'd lost her mind, but he waxed and scrubbed and scrubbed and waxed until his wife was satisfied.

The story of the birth of his child was not destined to be one that would bathe Denis in paternal glory. The due date was a few weeks behind them when Nancy finally felt serious labor pains in February 1969. Denis and his friend Oren Peterson bought a case of beer and brought it to the Hawkeye Drive apartment to drink while they waited for Nancy's condition to progress. By the time the contractions were coming often enough for Nancy to be taken to the hospital, the case of beer had been consumed. Peterson owned a small two-door Chevrolet Corvair that they planned to use to transport Nancy for the birth. The three teenagers descended the apartment stairs, then headed toward their car parked in the lot. Peterson climbed in the driver's seat, and Denis pulled up the passenger seat and motioned for Nancy, who was nine and a half months pregnant and the person they were supposedly assisting, to climb into the back seat.

Peterson successfully piloted the Corvair to the hospital, where he let the couple out and drove away. Denis was supposed to accompany Nancy into the room where the birth would take place. The notion of fathers in the birth room was a relatively new concept at the time, but Denis planned to witness the momentous occasion and help his wife through the ordeal. Denis and Nancy had planned to experience the birth together. However, when the nurse began to grasp Denis's obvious intoxication, plans changed. Denis was denied entry and relegated to the waiting room. Nancy was scared and distraught. Fortunately, the doctor on call happened to be the former boyfriend of one of the Lister sisters and a close family friend. He calmed Nancy, and the delivery proceeded uneventfully for both mother and child.

Denis sobered up once the baby was delivered and was on his best behavior when his in-laws arrived the following day. The next hurdle to be accomplished was the naming of the newborn. On this subject, Denis had strong opinions, which he had shared well in advance. If it was a girl, Denis had decided she should be called Tangerine. The child was a boy. Denis had decreed that a male child would be christened Changer D'avis, which, translated from French, means "change your mind." Nancy, however, would not sign off on Changer D'avis Johnson as the name for her firstborn.

Luckily, the new parents were able to find common ground thanks in part to a movie. They had both recently seen and enjoyed the British slapstick comedy *Morgan!* The film, starring David Warner and Vanessa Redgrave, tells the story of a madcap London artist who mimics a gorilla, concocts increasingly bizarre situations in an attempt to win back his girlfriend, fails, and winds up in a mental institution. Nancy's father had a close friend of the family whose last name was Morgan, so she saw some additional meaning in the choice and agreed to go along with the name.

For a middle name, Denis pushed for Paige, after the baseball player Satchel Paige, one of the first players to move from the Negro leagues to the major leagues after baseball was desegregated. He had also gained fame by playing professionally well into his fifties. Denis told Nancy that he liked the exceptionalism in the Satchel Paige narrative.

Thus it was that Denis Johnson's first and only biological child, Morgan Paige, named for a fictional eccentric artist with an ape obsession and an age-defying knuckleballer, made his entry into the world and joined his young parents in their little second-floor apartment on Hawkeye Drive. In less than a year, a series of circumstances and the advice and direction of their parents had turned Denis and Nancy from carefree college students into teenagers with heavy responsibilities and little capacity to meet them. Now they were left to live out the results.

FROM NOWHERE IN PARTICULAR

4

I teach genius. I teach genius, not necessarily to geniuses. It takes jiujitsu. It requires knowing how to create momentum and getting out of the way.

—Marvin Bell

Sometime during the spring of his freshman year, Denis took a walk over to the English-Philosophy Building, where the offices of the Iowa Writers' Workshop had recently moved. The workshop had resided in a group of nondescript Quonset huts along the Iowa River since the World War II era two decades before. Its year-old home was a four-story redbrick structure with a prisonlike facade that would, many years later, be voted the ugliest building in the state of Iowa by a national publication. Denis entered the building, ascended the stairs, and found his way to the workshop offices, which sported shiny new office furniture that gave it the feel of a corporate office more than a hall of academia.

Denis was there to find his very first college poetry teacher, John Morgan. He had a question to ask Morgan, one that had been weighing on him since long before he arrived in Iowa City. Morgan was only a few years older than Denis and in his third year of teaching poetry to undergrads at the University of Iowa. But he had studied with Robert Lowell at Harvard. More importantly, however, he had been granted the authority by the legendary Iowa Writers' Workshop to evaluate the writing of aspiring poets from across the country, so to Denis his opinion mattered. Morgan sat with Denis and went over some of the poems Denis had submitted in his class. He told Denis that his work was slightly heavy on adjectives. It was also, however, exceptional for a freshman and superior to the work of his classmates.

Denis was not satisfied.

"I know that," he responded. "What I need you to tell me is—do I really have it? Can I make it as a writer?"

Morgan took a deep breath and considered the importance his answer would mean to this young student, brimming with ambition. Though he was a teacher of the art of writing, he himself still wrestled with that question. He knew from experience that all the other fledgling poets and writers working their way through the program struggled with the question every single day. He gave Denis a reasoned answer about how each writer finds a way forward at a different pace, and about how each must achieve personal breakthroughs with language and self.

Denis was still not satisfied. Morgan thought he could sense the anxiety in his young student. Denis told Morgan that he'd come to Iowa for one reason: to find out the answer to this question. Did he have what it takes to make it as a writer?

Now the stakes had been raised. Morgan thought that his answer had the power to either launch Denis toward stardom or crater his writing career before it got off the ground. He took another look at the poems on the desk and decided in that moment that the poems, and his student, were worthy of encouragement.

"Since you really want to write, you should keep at it," he told Denis. "Because it's clear that you have talent."

When he released that word, *talent,* into the air, Morgan wrote later, he could feel the release of tension from Denis's body. Morgan pushed the point further. "If you stick to it, I don't see why you can't make it," he said.

Denis had the answer he needed. He stood up, reached across the desk, grinned, and told Morgan, "That's really great to hear."

Then, as Morgan remembered, Denis grabbed Morgan's hand and shook it vigorously, "partly from gratitude, it seemed, but also, to clinch the deal."

*

In the fall of 1968, Denis enrolled in a poetry workshop that was to be taught by a young instructor named Marvin Bell. Bell was a New Yorker who had discovered a love of poetry at the University of Chicago in the late '50s and then attended the Writers' Workshop for his MFA. After a two-year stint in the army, he'd come back to the workshop and settled in for what would be four-decade run as a poetry instructor and mentor to hundreds of writers and poets. When Denis met him, he was about ten or twelve years older than his students—far enough into life to radiate an aura of experience, but young enough to swim in the same generational pool. He was a "ball of energy who couldn't sit still for a minute," always moving around and talking, in the classroom and out. On the spectrum of teacher–student relationships, with one side being a relationship that ends at the door to the classroom and the other side representing true personal friendship along with occasional life coaching, Bell landed on the far end of the friendship side. His workshops would often begin with a communal lunch an hour before class time and conclude hours after the scheduled end time, at an alternative location of the members' choosing. Occasionally class would be moved to his house, where his wife, Dorothy, would prepare and serve her famous lasagna or some other home-cooked dish to the assembled poets.

Sometimes Bell's services went well beyond recommending classes or critiquing poems. Two of his students, Tess Gallagher and Michael Burkard, got married in his backyard. One evening less than a year later, Bell received a phone call from Gallagher. She told her professor that her husband had apparently reached an emotional breaking point and had snapped. Burkard had been shouting incomprehensibly and throwing his poems out the attic window. Gallagher began retrieving Burkard's rain-soaked pages, but when she brought them back into the house, Burkard was holding a knife and seemed unhinged. "I didn't know if the knife was me, or for himself. I assumed it was for him, but I wasn't going to find out." Bell arrived at the apartment in minutes and calmly went up to the attic. Burkard was still stewing, knife in hand, bottle of whiskey on the table. Bell spoke softly to his student, assuring him that his troubles, which seemed unbearable in the moment, would ease with time. After a while, Burkard put down the knife and calmly descended the stairs, Bell following closely behind. "Marvin took that knife away from him," Gallagher remembered. "The way he talked to Michael, and the way he brought that whole thing down, was so amazing to me."

Bell took as deep an interest in his students' poems as he did in their lives. He would perform deep, line-by-line readings of their work, gently providing directions for revision while managing not to come across as harshly critical. He emphasized the fact that he was a writer as well as a teacher, so he was fighting the same intellectual battle as his students. He created a list of rules about poetry and teaching, one of which was that he, as the teacher, would always do each of the exercises that he assigned to the class. He saw his role as being as much an instructor of writing as an example for how one ought to live the life of a writer. "Good writers who teach provide models for the writing life, which encompasses craft, knowledge, nerve, attitude, and even, sometimes, lifestyle," he wrote.

Bell's poetry workshop, which Denis walked into that September, would become a particularly close-knit group. Each student, following the process for undergraduate participation in the IWW at the time, had applied and been admitted to the class after samples of their work had been deemed worthy. Among those around the table on the first day of class were Denis's friend, Bob Stall; Alan Soldofsky, an Iowa City native who had started studying in the workshop as a sixteen-year-old high school student the previous summer; Carolyn Maisel, a single mother struggling to work her way through college; Sue Fletcher, a Catholic school graduate who had come from a small town in Minnesota after winning a national poetry prize; and Danny Schabilion, "a bearded psychedelic Jimmy Stewart–type" who liked to walk his pet rabbit on a leash. The group quickly bonded, and soon the members, along with their teacher, were meeting for lunch before class in the River Room of the Iowa Memorial Union to gossip and talk poetry, then heading back again after class to continue the discussion.

The standard design of an Iowa workshop had developed into its current form over many years. It had been passed down from instructor to instructor and was, by then, set in stone. A student would distribute copies of a work to classmates and teacher, all would read the work, and then, during class, they would go around the table delivering their reactions, critical and complimentary, giving, it was hoped, the writer both an evaluation of what had been created and a direction for improvement.

The first poem Denis turned in that semester was "A Poem about Baseballs." In it, the narrator, a frightened young boy in a baseball game, waits in fear as a fly ball descends toward him in the outfield, while at the same time his adult self contemplates his lived reality and where humanity fits into the universe. It was a work that merged nostalgic Americana with man's search for meaning in about a hundred words containing both humor and deep insight. Years later, when, as an accomplished professor of poetry at a major university, he could recognize it for what it was, Soldofsky would call it "an amazing, freely associative poem, containing an external narrative frame story and a contrapuntal interior voice." But in the moment, he and his fellow classmates were dumbstruck. Nobody was able to manage any suggestions for improvement, so they decided to adjourn and, as a group, go listen to some Bob Dylan records.

As the semester wore on, a pattern developed. When it was Denis's turn to submit work to the class, he would present them with a poem that everybody sitting around the table would recognize as a work of poetic genius. Each one contained "wild rhetorical and surreal figurative effects" that they all emulated but knew they could not equal. Denis, for his part, was reticent. He had little to add to the discussion about how it had been created or what it meant, and he was visibly embarrassed by the attention. After the students expressed their shock and stammered out compliments, Bell would take over to provide analysis and explain to the class what, exactly, Denis had just given them. During one class, Bell read a poem Denis had turned in, and after he was through, every student seated around the table looked down or stared into their hands, each one unable to respond. Nobody was able to muster as much as a sound. Finally, Schabilion broke the silence. "Well," he said. "It's another Denis Johnson poem."

"Nobody could really critique his stuff, because he was so unique already at that time," Fletcher remembered. "He just did what he did. It was very different. The rest of us were much more amateur. Denis could write a complete poem, whereas the rest of us, our poems were just half good, and half not up to par."

Bell recognized it as well. "It was immediately obvious that he was an extraordinary talent," Bell said years later. "His poems were already original in their narratives, personal without being beholden to ego, and charming too." He began to include Denis's poems on the class worksheets. Each week, a new Denis Johnson poem would be part of the paper Bell handed the students with their assignment—poems that would become iconic pieces of the Johnson opus—"Quickly Aging Here," "Checking the Traps," "The Dry, Dry Land," "The Man among the Seals"—all were first published at age nineteen as worksheets and distributed in Bell's afternoon poetry workshop through the fall of 1968.

Though the other members of Bell's class harbored some jealousy toward their class genius, they developed into a tight group that took their art deadly seriously and viewed themselves as poets of the future. They would gather at Carolyn Maisel's house on Iowa Avenue and conduct poetry salons to further discuss their work in an atmosphere where illicit substances could enhance the conversations. The gatherings were rife with literary pretension. Iowa City was the Paris of the American heartland, Maisel was a latter-day Alice B. Toklas, and they all were the voices of the latest Lost Generation. Word of the salons got around, and soon the doors had to be locked to keep out groupies and wannabes.

It wasn't all analysis of poetry at the Maisel poetry salons. Sometimes the brew of alcohol, marijuana, and iambic pentameter led to a communal desire to partake in a little lighthearted mischief. Once night, the group heard that Canadian pop singer Gordon Lightfoot was in Iowa City for a concert. Somehow they managed to get Lightfoot on the phone. One of the assembled poets graciously invited him to join them at Maisel's house for some poetry and refreshments. Lightfoot declined. This nearly successful attempt at celebrity wrangling led to a string of attempts to contact other big-name artists. Numbers were solicited and calls were made. In the crowning achievement of their celebrity artist telephone hunt, they got the phone number to the Factory, pop-artist extraordinaire Andy Warhol's famed studio on East Forty-Seventh Street in Manhattan. The number was dialed, and the call was placed. Warhol would not come to the phone, but they spoke with an unidentified woman, who, after the rejection had been completed, was thoroughly analyzed to determine which of Warhol's famous posse she may have been.

*

The reaction to the poems he wrote for Marvin Bell's workshop, as well as his association with Bell, launched Denis on the path to publication. There, too, he found almost immediate success. Since 1964, Bell had been the poetry editor for the *North American Review*. The *Review* had been one of the most important magazines in America through the nineteenth century and the first half of the twentieth century but had been shuttered in 1940, when its then-publisher was arrested for taking money from the Japanese consul in Manhattan to spread pro-Japan propaganda. Cornell College, a small liberal arts school just up the road from the University of Iowa in the town of Mount Vernon, employed an ambitious poet and professor named Robert Dana, who had come through the Writers' Workshop in the early 1950s. Under Dana's direction, Cornell assumed the rights to the *Review* and resumed publication in 1964. Bell became the new journal's poetry editor. The *Review* changed hands again when it was purchased by the University of Northern Iowa in 1968. Bell continued editing its poetry, and in the fall of 1968, he selected two of the poems Denis had submitted to his workshop: one entitled only "Poem," and another called "Boy Aged Six Remembering." The tagline noted that Denis had been born in Munich, Germany, that he was a sophomore at the University of Iowa, and that this was his very first publication.

Denis's excitement was palpable when he wrote his parents of his success. He told them that he'd written to the editor of the *Review* and managed to obtain eight copies of the issue, one of which was on the way to them in Virginia. He didn't receive any money for the poems, he said, so he was now planning to limit his future submissions to magazines that paid. They should be ready, he told Al and Vera, because he would be sending them copies of all magazines that published his work. Pretty soon they would be able to fill a whole bookcase with them, he wrote.

There was soon evidence that his prediction was correct. The next issue of the *North American Review,* spring 1969, included another of Denis's worksheet poems, "Checking the Traps," and the one after that, summer 1969, had another two, "The Man among the Seals" and "A Consequence of Gravity." For those two, he received his first payment, which, at 50 cents a line, added up to a much-needed forty bucks. He pocketed another $100 when he won the Hallmark Honor Prize, part of the Kansas City poetry contest, for a poem called "The Woman at the Slot Machine." The literary journal of Southern Illinois University, *Sou'Wester,* published yet another poem from Bell's class, "Quickly Aging Here." Denis got his hands on a list of seventy-five publications that were buying poetry, created by the Writers' Workshop for graduate students in the MFA program, and, buoyed by his success, pumped out more submissions.

Journal publications were exciting and envied by Denis's undergraduate pals, but the feat was also something that was regularly accomplished by many of the workshop graduate students. Getting a poem or story published in a book marked an even higher level of achievement. Around that time, a twenty-six-year-old professor of English at University of Hawai'i by the name of Geof Hewitt pitched an anthology of emerging poets to Doubleday in New York and received a contract. He had proposed to the editors at Doubleday to find the best American poets who had yet to publish a book or have their work published in a major anthology. Hewitt had studied at the University of Iowa and knew Bell, so it wasn't long into his hunt when he became acquainted with Denis's work. After reading more than four thousand poems for consideration and finally arriving at his list of thirty-five poets who made the cut, Hewitt let Denis know that he had been selected. It was to be another paid gig. Denis would receive a $10 check with "Doubleday" imprinted on it for his hard work. He wrote home to share the news with Al and Vera. Not only would five of his poems be included in the anthology, but he had also been asked to write a page about "poetics" to accompany the poems. It would be his first prose publication, he told his parents.

Quickly Aging Here: Some Poets of the 1970s was released in the fall of 1969. Hewitt used one of Denis's poems as his title, which he noted in the introduction, along with the fact that Denis, at age twenty, was the youngest contributor to the collection. Hewitt declared that his book was a representation of "some of the best poetry being written by unrecognized poets during the last half of the sixties." The short essays on poetics served as the contributors' notes at the back of the book. In his brief treatise, Denis did his best to explain some of his work, something he eschewed when he had originally presented them to Bell's workshop. "Checking the Traps," he wrote, "was the beginning of a minor obsession I had for syncopating two concerns of the poem within what I hoped was a coherent whole." "A Poem about Baseballs" "was the culmination of this experiment." His favorite of the group was "A Man among the Seals," which, he wrote, "came from nowhere in particular, which seems to be a good place for poems to come from."

*

The extended life of that particular poem would continue just a few months later. It would go on to be the verse most associated with early Denis Johnson poetry.

The poem had grown out of a small Associated Press article Denis had come across in the newspaper one day during the spring of his freshman year. The newspaper's headline writer had already crafted a line of poetry even before Denis got his hands on it: "Seals' Tipsy Pal Fined after Dip." Denis, of course, had to read further:

> NEW YORK (AP) Sometimes seals act almost like humans. And in the case of John Giordano, vice versa.
>
> A waiter, Giordano appeared before Criminal Court Judge Amos Basel Tuesday, accused of stripping to his underwear and joining the seals in their Central Park pool at 5 a.m. last July 25.
>
> "Were you stewed?" Basel inquired.
>
> "I wasn't drunk. But I was on my way," Giordano conceded.
>
> "How long were you there?"
>
> "Am I going to get charged by the minute?" the defendant asked. "Fifteen minutes."
>
> "Did you have rapport with the seals?"
>
> "I guess I did have rapport with the seals."
>
> Despite the rapport, Basel fined Giordano $50 for annoying the seals.

In Denis's interpretation of the scene in the article, the seals perform their expected clumsy ritual for the parents and children "jerking under balloons" through the day at the zoo in the city. But at night, the seals become masters of the water. The appearance of a drunken interloper in his underwear only acts to emphasize the seals' grace. Mr. Giordano most likely paid his fine and did not return to breach the walls of the seal tank, but the drunk in Denis's creation is destined to return daily, "wetness forever staining him through his pants, to watch his seals as they rise above the rocks" and perform acts of natural beauty lost on their captors. Like much of Denis's early poetry, it was a charming, lyrical bit of verse, a scene filled with humor but with a bit of darkness at its core.

The raft of publications, combined with Bell's advocacy throughout the English-Philosophy Building, made the phenomenon that was Denis Johnson widely known among students and faculty alike. It wasn't long before Denis's growing fame came to the attention of somebody with the power and facility to extend it even further. Kim Merker was a New Yorker who had come to the University of Iowa in 1956 to write poetry in the Writers' Workshop. The form of his contributions to the art of poetry changed when, shortly after his arrival in Iowa City, Merker met Harry Duncan, the University of Iowa's foremost expert in printing and typography, and the owner and operator of a boutique publisher called Cummington Press.

Merker soon became an expert in the art of fine-press printing, bookmaking as it was practiced before the advent of mass production. He founded Stone Wall Press in 1957. Using the same iron handpress that Duncan had first used in 1939 and had brought to Iowa with him in the 1950s, Merker began to publish books by worthy poets. He meticulously planned the design, chose paper and typefaces, and printed and bound each volume by hand. By 1967, he had published books by renowned poets such as William Carlos Williams and Ezra Pound, along with books by young poets whose talents would soon be widely recognized, including Mark Strand, W. S. Merwin, and another fledgling Iowa wordsmith, Marvin Bell.

In the spring of 1969, Merker told Denis that Stone Wall Press was considering publishing a book of his poems. Denis wrote home to share the news. First, he swore his parents to secrecy and told them the news he was about to deliver was nothing to get excited about yet. Then, he enthusiastically laid out all the reasons that this opportunity would be an unbelievable boon to his future career. He had seen some of the other books published by Stone Wall, and they were "very classy." Thanks to Stone Wall Press, important people would no doubt read his work. The rights to the poems would stay with Denis, so he could resell them later. Indeed, he and Bell had gotten deep into the planning of Denis's career strategy, and they surmised that a book from Stone Wall Press would put them several moves further along on the chessboard. A published book would relieve Denis of the pressure to win a big award to have his work widely read. Big awards inevitably led to career slumps—something Denis might avoid, Bell said. This opportunity, Denis thought, was almost too good to imagine. Don't even talk about it, don't even think about it, he wrote to Al and Vera, "lest a terrible jinx occur."

The jinx was avoided. Though Denis thought it would take more than a year for even a decision to be made, in fact Merker called him before the end of the spring semester to tell him that Stone Wall Press would indeed publish the first book of poetry by Denis Johnson. Merker allowed Denis to choose the title poem, and he selected *A Man among the Seals*. The poem, written for Bell's workshop, was dedicated to a friend from Hillcrest, Ed Schroeder, because Schroeder had generously given Denis a dose of LSD.

Publication was scheduled for September 1969. It was to be a limited-edition print run of 260 copies with hand-set Romanée type on fifty-six pages of rag paper from the Curtis Paper Mill, the oldest mill in America. Denis would get one copy for free and 10 percent royalties, which Merker told him might amount to another copy or two. Merker also told Denis to prepare a list of people who should receive an announcement about the book—the more, the better. Denis relayed the request to Al and Vera, who put together four pages of friends, relatives, and State Department colleagues from across the Washington, D.C., suburbs. Even Mrs. Pfeiffer, Denis's counselor at T. C. Williams High, got an announcement.

Among his friends and throughout the workshop community, Denis kept the news under guard. The embarrassment he felt as the star pupil in Bell's workshop was magnified now that he was on the cusp of achieving the goal that each and every Writers' Workshop student hoped for. He pulled Stall aside and dropped the bombshell on him quietly. He was very discreet about it, Stall remembered. "He kept it on the QT. He didn't want to be set aside from the rest of us."

Merker printed the last of the 260 copies and made *The Man among the Seals* available to the reading public in the fall of 1969. On the opening page, Bell revealed his discovery, whom he'd been championing across the University of Iowa for the past year, to the wider world: "Denis Johnson began writing seriously when he was sixteen. Now, at nineteen, an age when most poets have barely begun, he has put together a collection of thirty-two poems having a vision, a voice, and a music we have not known before."

The following year, Denis added another item to his long list of firsts: his first rave review. The sole published review for *A Man among the Seals* came from the *Virginia Quarterly.* There it was, among reviews of works by James Dickey, W. S. Merwin, even the ghost of Hemingway, whose posthumous novel *Islands in the Stream* made an appearance in the same section. The reviewer for the *Quarterly,* like almost everyone who had read Denis's poetry in the past two years, focused on the fact that it had come from a teenager. "This is an astonishing first book. The sophistication and controlled intensity are those from a mature writer in midcareer. Denis Johnson finds moments of psychological nakedness, moments when the devious corners of our mind are illuminated and presents them in an imaginative and gracefully colloquial manner."

Denis remained conflicted about the prestige and veneration that came with his newfound status. Soon he would start receiving offers to give public readings, and after accepting some of the offers, he would begin to understand how ill-equipped he was for the experience. Years later, when enough time had passed since the publication of *A Man among Seals* that it ceased to be the boon to his career that he had envisioned and instead became a symbol of past success and lost promise that hung around his neck like a weight, he would view the book in a different light. But in the glow of initial triumph, he could find pleasure in his status on campus and around the EPB. "He was the wunderkind of the workshop for a long time," Nancy recalled, "and when that mantle passed to somebody else, I could tell that he felt, I wouldn't call it jealousy, but it was kind of an emotional thing for him when he finally lost that title."

BERKELEY OF THE MIDWEST

5

Iowa City is a college town and nothing else. Every so often you will go nuts. All of the sudden the cornfields will get you. —**Kurt Vonnegut**

The Iowa City that Denis called home in those years was a small islet of the 1960s floating in the middle of a vast sea of the '50s. The counterculture movement that started on the coasts had moved into the interior of the country, and it found a perfect habitat in the small central Iowa town. The fashion, the music, the drugs, and the cultural revolution that was taking place in urban America had blossomed in and around the university. "If you were a hippie in Iowa, you found your way to Iowa City," remembered Susan Fletcher, Denis's classmate. "Iowa City was the San Francisco of Iowa."

For a small city surrounded by endless miles of farmland, it managed to stay culturally relevant despite its size. Interstate 80 runs straight across the middle of the state and cuts to within miles of the university. In an easy, flat three and a half hours, you can get from Maxwell Street on the west side of Chicago to the Iowa Memorial Union, and national musical acts, performers, and political figures or celebrities with something to say would regularly make the trek. Great Chicago blues artists like Hound Dog Taylor, Willie Dixon's All-Stars, Duke Tumatoe and the All-Star Frogs, and nationally blues known acts, like Buddy Guy, John Lee Hooker, and Muddy Waters, would drive across the prairie to play shows at the C.O.D. Steam Laundry, a combination deli, bar, and music venue on Iowa Avenue that could hold five hundred on a good night. The Chicago-to-Iowa-City corridor brought the biggest of the big concert tours as well, like Jefferson Airplane and Led Zeppelin, both of which came to town in 1969.

LSD advocate and counterculture hero Timothy Leary announced he was coming to Iowa City while Denis was a sophomore. Leary missed his plane in San Francisco, showed up the next day, and, after a four-hour rain delay, regaled the remaining crowd with his philosophies of life, which boiled down to "all of nature's creatures should essentially do what is in that being's innateness to do." Charles Bukowski, the "laureate of lowlife" who was just then achieving widespread recognition, came to town to read his underground poetry at the Boulevard Room on East Market Street. He reeked of whiskey and looked like a hobo who had been wearing the same clothes for three weeks, but he managed to get through the evening without fighting any members of the audience.

It was a town where the local karate dojo served alcoholic beverages to its students, on the theory that most fights took place in bars, so those who planned to defend themselves by using martial arts should, of course, be able to kick and chop with a few drinks in them. It was a town where you could go to Epstein's Books on Clinton Street and find poetry shelved, alphabetically, directly next to porn. Or you might decide to drop by Epstein's to witness the "actualist" poet Dave Morice attempt to write a thousand poems in twelve hours. Above all, it was a town where an intrinsic appreciation of works of art and their creation carried more weight than social status or economic class. It was an atmosphere that produced virtuoso art and attracted the eccentric personality types that go along with it.

The environment in Iowa City suited Denis. He cultivated friendships with the oddballs and intriguing characters who populated the bars, bookstores, and other gathering spots from one end of town to the other and beyond. "He would sit down and start conversations with people who he considered characters," Nancy said. "He was always trying to harvest words or emotions or outlooks that he could then file away in his head. It was part of who he was from when I first met him. Iowa City had its share of oddballs, and Denis knew them all."

*

The idea was to collect characters who would eventually end up on the page, and the collection grew not only from Iowa City's cast of odd birds but also from Denis's own circle of friends and coconspirators. One of the first to secure a spot in the collection was John Dundon, the pal he'd made during his stay in the Johnson County Jail. Denis had found him fascinating from the moment he encountered him on the cellblock. Dundon was very close in age to Denis, but that was where the similarities ended. John was the first child of Lewis Dundon, a World War II veteran from New Jersey who landed in San Antonio, Texas, after the war and married a local woman named Helen Perales. The couple had seven more children after John, moving to Cedar Rapids, Iowa, before they had the final two. Lewis Dundon was a diesel mechanic with an alcohol problem and a mean streak that often showed up in the disciplining of his children. John's fights with him grew worse as he got older. He inherited his father's addictive personality, which appeared when he discovered the local drug scene. The first time he tried heroin, he blurted out to anyone in earshot, "I'm in trouble!"

Indeed he was. He racked up a number of juvenile convictions. He began leaving hypodermic needles around the house—something that didn't sit well with his parents when his younger siblings began to discover them. Eventually he was thrown out of the family house. He began spending time at a farmhouse about four miles southwest of Iowa City with fellow members of the drug scene. At the farmhouse, Dundon was a friend of a University of Iowa student named Tim Griffith, who had migrated to Iowa City from Ames, Iowa, and Steve McCurdy, from Oskaloosa, a small town in between Iowa City and Des Moines. Griffith and McCurdy happened to have a successful marijuana and hashish business that operated out of the farmhouse. Denis, through his friendship with Dundon, began to spend time there. He got to know all of the regulars as well as those who wandered in and out to do business. As they appeared, he added them to his notebook of Iowa City oddballs.

Dundon and Griffith both liked guns, and it wasn't long before Denis began to share their interest. Shooting at cans and other targets was a popular way to pass the time around the farmhouse. Griffith eventually decided Denis should have a gun of his own and bought one for him. He brought it to the apartment on Hawkeye Drive, wrapped in a cloth. Denis accepted it gratefully and put it in the top of the bedroom closet. He promised Nancy he would keep it unloaded and separate from the bullets, but this new development worried her, especially with a child in the apartment. "I remember them having a fascination with guns. They were just guys who liked to dare or risk things, and that appealed to Denis. That was a period of time where that was his thrill, too," Nancy said. "It freaked me out that he had that gun in the house, and he knew that."

Nancy's fear was not unfounded. The mixture of weapons and illicit substances, not surprisingly, soon resulted in a gunshot wound, though it wasn't Denis's weapon that did the damage. The series of events that unfolded that afternoon would create the elements from which, twenty years later, Denis would compose "Dundun," his fictional tribute of sorts to his gun-and-heroin-loving friend. A .32 caliber bullet from the gun of Dundon ended up in the stomach of McCurdy that day. The circumstances were cloudy. The story that circulated afterward was so outlandish that it did little to clear things up. Apparently someone's child had been at the farmhouse and fell asleep on a bed. Dundon had left his gun and bullets in that same bed. The kid wet the bed, soaking the gun and bullets—and enraging Dundon. In the ensuing argument, Dundon fired at McCurdy, but, because the kid had urinated on the gun, it misfired, thereby saving McCurdy's life. The bullet did not pierce his stomach lining and resulted in only a superficial wound.

Dundon reluctantly brought McCurdy to the hospital, where he was confronted by a member of the Johnson County sheriff's department. At this point, Dundon chose to relate a more believable, less legally perilous version of events. He told the authorities that he and McCurdy had been shooting at targets when the gun misfired. The misfire caused them to examine the gun, which they believed incorrectly to be empty, whereupon it fired again, sending the slug in question into the gut of McCurdy. The sheriff's department officer apparently didn't see the need to look into the legality of the gun or the criminal history of the gun's owner. The entire incident found its way into the pages of the local newspaper—and, of course, into Denis's notebook. (His fictionalized version of that afternoon would eventually appear in the March 1989 issue of *Esquire* and later as the fourth story in *Jesus' Son*.)

The farmhouse gang made another appearance in the *Iowa City Press-Citizen* less than two months later—an appearance that Denis luckily avoided. The Johnson County sheriff's department, perhaps intrigued by the earlier "accidental" shooting, dispatched some deputies to the farmhouse early one morning when he was not present. The officers were greeted, not very hospitably, by McCurdy, Griffith, and another friend, Barbara Blair. The officers found their way to a shed behind the farmhouse, where they discovered seven large plastic bags and seven cardboard boxes of marijuana (later valued at $36,000), several knives, two machetes, a sawed-off shotgun, two .22 caliber pistols, eleven hypodermic needles, and a syringe. McCurdy and Griffith were arrested without incident, but Blair managed to take a bite out of the upper arm of the police captain, Richard Lee, causing Captain Lee to be treated for possible tetanus later that morning at the University hospital. The three arrestees spent a few days in jail and would make court appearances related to the raid for the next two years, eventually making a plea deal to receive suspended jail sentences and pay $200 fines.

Another friend of Denis and regular guest at the farmhouse was a local musician and fledgling criminal named Jeff Hottel, another member of the gang who would become a model for a character in the *Jesus' Son* stories. Hottel was a blond teenager who sometimes dressed like a cowboy in a ten-gallon hat and boots, and he occasionally played the drums for a local band called the Rocket 88s when he wasn't running from somebody he owed money to. He was the son of a local optometrist and came from a well-respected Iowa City family, but he gravitated toward the local drug scene. One night he teamed up with Dundon for the crime that resulted in the farmhouse gang's second appearance on the front page of the *Iowa City Press-Citizen*. According to the newspaper's report, the two of them, along with two other accomplices, approached a local man named Arthur Sierra and offered him a ride to a "free beer party." Sierra couldn't resist such an enticing offer, but he well should have. Instead of taking him to the party, the gang drove him to a cemetery, where they separated Sierra from the hundred dollars he was carrying, then pushed him out of the car.

Sierra told his story to the police. He related the "free beer party" version of events, which was evidently accepted, although the nature of the dispute between him and Dundon most likely involved substances other than beer. Officers found Dundon at his house later that night. Hottel and the other two accomplices jumped out the window and fled. Two of them, Hottel and David Thomas, were later apprehended while carrying marijuana and heroin, arrested, and brought to the jail, where Dundon waited. Police were unable to apprehend the other accomplice, who might or might not have been a "local poet" who owned a gun. Denis, whether he had intimate knowledge of the events of the evening or had heard about them secondhand, duly recorded the details and filed them away to be used, to great effect, in the distant future.

Because it was now clear that money from the sale of poetry wasn't going to keep the Johnson family clothed and fed, Denis and Nancy needed to find a way to produce income to support themselves and their baby. Al and Vera helped out occasionally in the financing of Denis's tuition with gifts and loans, but the couple largely had decided to try to make it on their own financially. Their rent was a reasonable $105 per week. Denis had a fifteen-hour-a-week work-study job arranging campus tours. They applied for and received welfare and food stamps, which were easy to come by in those days. They signed

Morgan up for a co-op day care group that operated out of a local church basement. Each of the parents in the co-op was responsible for watching the kids for four hours each week. Denis preferred to sign up for his hours in the morning, so he could read the paper and drink coffee before most of the babies and toddlers, all under three, arrived. When he couldn't, he would beg Nancy to take his hours, usually to no avail. "I suppose the experience is good for me," he wrote. "Already I've learned not to like children."

The need for money led to innovative thinking. Nancy began to apply to magazine and department-store contests, and even won a few, including a $200 sewing machine. Denis found a lab that would buy his plasma. They managed to stockpile 25-cent cartons of milk meant for elementary school lunches, which they used to keep Morgan fed. The development that would prove to be the greatest boost to the Johnsons' finances, however, occurred when Denis made the acquaintance of Paul Engle.

The illustrious institution known as the Iowa Writers' Workshop had achieved its status largely under the direction of Paul Engle, who led the program from its infancy in the early 1940s until the year Denis arrived in town. In the storied history of the workshop, Engle was, by far, the most important name.

The genesis of the Iowa Writers' Workshop, and of writers' workshops in general, can be traced to a class called "Versification," taught initially at the University of Iowa in 1896 by a poet-teacher named George Cram Cook. The method of teaching creative writing evolved over the decades at the university, passed from one professor to another through the early twentieth century. The form of a workshop class—students submitting work to be critiqued by their classmates under the tutelage of a veteran writer—developed slowly. The philosophical underpinning of the workshop came from Norman Foerster, who arrived in 1930 from the University of North Carolina and brought with him the belief that "a creative writer must by the nature of his art be additionally a literary critic." The term "writers' workshop" first appeared in the course catalog in 1939.

The English department at the University of Iowa awarded its first master of arts degree for creative works in 1931. Five more were handed out in 1932, one of them to Engle, a native Iowan from Cedar Rapids. After earning the degree, he established himself as a poet thanks to a book called *Worn Earth,* which became the first creative writing thesis to be published and also part of the Yale Series of Younger Poets. On July 29, 1934, the entire front page of the *New York Times Book Review* was devoted to Engle, under the headline "A New Voice in American Poetry." He spent a few years at Oxford; then he was back on campus in Iowa in 1937 to await his ascension to the directorship of the workshop in 1941.

Engle took the Iowa Writers' Workshop from a misunderstood wing of the English department to a nationally recognized entity. He knew how to raise money. He also had a knack for publicity and for ingratiating himself with the powerful. He was an inaugural member of the National Council of the Arts, a celebrity-filled board created during the Johnson administration to hand out awards and grants to artists. He networked his way into the halls of political power in Iowa and Washington and dined at the White House. When in 1956 he wrote and dedicated sonnets to Iowa's fallen war heroes, his photo appeared prominently in *Life* magazine, and the Writers' Workshop took another step toward national status.

The program soon achieved widespread recognition, to the point that a prospective student from India could send a letter without an address, just the words "Paul Engle, Iowa City, USA," and it would be safely delivered to his office in the workshop's Quonset huts by the Iowa River. Bell called him a "country slicker" because in public he affected the manner of a farm-raised son of the heartland but was actually always "in the know" and two steps ahead of everyone else. Engle could talk legislators and administrators into funding his programs, talk famous writers into relocating to out-of-the-way Iowa to teach, and once, in an oft-told tale in the Engle legend, talked a group of escaped convicts who had taken him and his family hostage in their home into letting him go into his study to finish writing a book review. (He eventually talked the prisoners into leaving as well.)

Engle was in his sixties when Denis first encountered him and was enough of a revered figure around campus that Denis referred to him as "Mr. Engle" in correspondence. By the time Denis met him, the reins of the workshop had recently passed to George Starbuck, Denis's fellow war protester. Engle and his wife, Hualing, started the International Writing Program in 1967, with the goal of bringing international writers to Iowa and providing them the physical and intellectual support to practice their craft. Bell introduced Denis to Engle, who took a liking to Bell's young protégé. Engle offered guidance to Denis as well as fatherly advice. When Engle was badly injured in a car accident, Denis went to visit his new mentor at the hospital. Soon Engle had made it his business to find Denis a job in his new international program.

In the fall of his sophomore year, one opportunity arose that would lead to years of further work and valuable experience. Engle got Denis an interview to be a translator for Zbigniew Bieńkowski, a Polish writer who was translating the work of a nineteenth-century poet from his country to English. One of the two English-speaking translators who was assisting Bieńkowski left the country, leaving a vacancy for Engle to fill. Denis wrote home and described the interview. The other translator took one look him and decided he didn't need any help, especially from Denis. That's what happens when people find out how young I am, Denis said. Engle pushed for him, however, and soon Denis was officially in the translating business.

Denis was provided a desk in the International Writing Program suite and began working with a variety of international writers. On top of the job, Engle tried to find Denis grants to boost his income. One grant Engle told Denis about was for $1,000. Denis wrote home about it, telling his parents that in his "ocean of indebtedness," $1,000 was like "an old man carrying water away in a thimble." On another occasion, Engle found out Denis was at the bottom of a list for a grant, so he wrote letters to the committee and got Denis moved up the list.

Denis enjoyed the work and recognized the advantages of being aligned with Engle. His main responsibility at the IWP was to work with writers who spoke English as a second language but did not have the vocabulary to coherently translate their work into English. Denis would welcome new writers and their families to campus, help them get set up in their apartments, and, with the help of the IWP, provide them with a television to further assist them in becoming acquainted with the American vernacular. Early on, he was assigned poets from Japan and Brazil. He and Nancy would often tag along on adventures in Americana that Engle arranged to introduce international writers to the glories of his beloved Iowa.

Being in the orbit of Paul Engle brought other rewards as well. Engle invited Denis to join him for a reading in celebration of National Poetry Day in the summer of 1970. The event was to be hosted by Iowa governor Robert Ray and would honor Engle himself. Engle told Denis that Governor Ray took poetry seriously and wanted contemporary poets, as opposed to "part-time sonneteers." Engle also recognized Denis's reticence and, because this was to be Denis's public reading debut, offered to coach him before the event. Denis agreed but remained apprehensive. He suffered from stage fright and worried that his voice would break, the lines would blur, or he would drop sentences.

When the day arrived, Denis survived and even enjoyed the experience to a degree, perhaps because his time under the microscope was short. The day was largely to celebrate the father of the Writers' Workshop. Engle, Denis, and Anselm Hollo, a professor in the workshop, took the stage in the Levitt Auditorium of the Des Moines Arts Center and looked out on an audience of two hundred people, mostly women. Denis was allotted ten minutes, and he filled them with exclusively poetry because he was afraid to offer any remarks or explanations of the poems. He read the poem "A Child Is Born in the Midwest," about the birth of Morgan, and several others.

After the poetry portion of the event concluded, the exaltation of Engle began. He was presented with letters of commendation from the governor, and members of the National Arts Council paid him tribute. Ray read telegrams from a number of other dignitaries around the country saluting Engle and his achievements. When it was his turn to speak, the honoree played to the crowd. "The state of Iowa is an example that great art can flourish a great distance from salt," he told them.

The hard part was over. The celebration moved to the governor's mansion. Denis mingled with the glitterati of Iowa politics and arts. He marveled at how everybody remained standing and chatting for hours amid all the comfortable-looking furniture. Later, he compared it to a scene from the movie *The Bridge on the River Kwai,* where a prisoner of war is forced to stand at attention all day until he finally pitches forward and falls on his face. Denis nibbled hors d'oeuvres and nodded in agreement, silently mocking the upper-class pretensions of his fellow attendees as they complained that Europe had become too Americanized and declared that he should spend only the briefest time possible on the continent. Sometime during the evening, he said yes to another reading in the fall in Waterloo, Iowa, an offer that had been sweetened by the promise of a $50 payment. "I actually enjoyed the whole affair a great deal," he wrote to his parents. "Next time I go to one of these things I'll bring a rope and lash myself to a floor lamp for support."

The event received widespread coverage across the state. Denis's name appeared in the newspaper, a distinction he now shared with his friends at the farmhouse. For him, though, it was poetry that was bringing him attention in public and in print. Unbeknownst to his new fans and his mentors, however, Denis's creative energy had shifted, his seemingly endless well of original verse had finally been depleted, and for the next few years, the focus of his writing would move in another direction.

INTRODUCING THE TOWN MORON

6

Summer's a discouraging time to work—You don't feel death coming on the way it does in the fall when the boys really put pen to paper. —Ernest Hemingway to F. Scott Fitzgerald, 1929

It was a review in *Newsweek* that first brought the novel *Fat City* to Denis's attention in 1969. Later, he remembered that it was something in the tone of the review, a sincere reverence that lacked the usual overheated praise, that caught his attention. He searched out a copy and read the book shortly after it was published. The story of a pair of working-class boxers struggling to get by on the seedy side of Stockton, California, would become something of a textbook for Denis as he began to explore the art of fiction. "I sensed some mystical connection between what I found in the style itself and its ability to draw my sympathy for a type of character whom I'd surely never meet," Denis wrote later in an appreciation of the book. "Its measured tone, its attitude of respect for all, its keen eye and appreciation for passing details. . . ." These would be characteristics of his own writing for the rest of his life. He thought, at first, that it was his own personal discovery, but soon learned that in Iowa City, "admirers were everywhere."

Leonard Gardner, the author of *Fat City,* grew up in Stockton and started boxing at age eight. His father, a former amateur fighter himself, hung a speed bag in the garage and infused Gardner with passion for the ring. Gardner went to the Lido Gym in Stockton when he was old enough, fought a few times as a welterweight, and, after getting his nose broken in a match, quickly transitioned from boxer to chronicler of the lives of boxers. He studied writing at San Francisco State in the 1960s, where he got the idea to write a novel about skid row boxers. He made trips back to Stockton for research so he could experience what he hoped to recreate on the page. He topped onions and weeded tomatoes with destitute day workers, slept in flophouses, and hung around the gym to observe the fighters, trainers, and assorted hangers-on of the Stockton boxing community. He translated his observations and experiences into vivid descriptions of life on the streets of Stockton.

Gardner worked on his book for four years, tinkering and cutting until he had a 400-page manuscript down to a sleek 180 pages. Its release brought him grants, awards, and eventually a career as a writer of television and movie scripts. In 1972, *Fat City* was made into a movie, directed by John Huston, and starring Jeff Bridges and Stacy Keach. The book would be Gardner's one and only novel.

Gardner's other fans in the Iowa writing community began to show themselves soon after Denis found the book. One of his neighbors in the married housing complex on Hawkeye Drive was Philip Schultz, who had been among the true believers from Denis's side of the anti-Vietnam demonstrations when Denis was a freshman. Schultz had left Iowa shortly after the demonstration and moved back to San Francisco for a few years before returning to Iowa City. While he was away, he met Gardner after recognizing him from his book jacket photo. "He loved that," Schultz remembered. "He wasn't used to being famous. He was in his midthirties. I was twenty-two or twenty-three, and we hit it off." Schultz and Gardner met regularly for lunches to discuss writing. Gardner told Schultz boxing stories and described battles he had with John Huston on the set during the filming of *Fat City*. One day, Schultz said the wrong thing at lunch, and the friendship was over. "He was very temperamental," Schultz said.

Denis asked his neighbor to tell him his Gardner stories regularly.

Later, Denis made the *Fat City* connection with another workshop student, Tracy Kidder. Kidder was a Vietnam vet who came to Iowa City to become a novelist but eventually left with battle scars from the workshop and the impulse to pursue a career in journalism. He could recite lines from *Fat City* verbatim, and did so liberally. Many years later, after Kidder had won the Pulitzer Prize for nonfiction, Denis would remember sitting in the graduate school office and listening to his friend quote Gardner's opening to chapter 4: "Days were like long twilights in the house under the black walnut trees; through untrimmed shrubs screening the windows the sun scarcely shone."

The phrasing and tone and structure of Gardner's masterpiece were clues Denis used in his early understanding of the architecture of fiction. Gardner crafted gritty, spare sentences imbued with precise, sensory details pulled from lived experience. He incorporated vivid descriptions of the stifling, arid Central California environs in which he placed his desperate, aimless characters. Denis intuited how Gardner's spare language and rich imagery created the bleak landscape in which his characters fought their battles. He read, over and over, a particular five-page exchange of dialogue between a boxer and his girlfriend to teach himself how to create believable and realistic speech. "Between the ages of nineteen and twenty-five I studied *Fat City* so closely that I began to fear I'd never be able write anything but imitations of it, so I swore it off," he wrote years later. Beyond the craft, though, Denis found something in the book that focused him on what he wanted to accomplish with his fiction, something that even molded his philosophy of life. Gardner taught him, he said, "that in the world's grays and sepias, in its shadows and lonely nights, a fine beauty is visible to the eye that stays open."

*

Even as Denis was astounding everyone with his poems, he was harboring visions of future success as a fiction writer. While he was enrolled in Bell's poetry workshop as a sophomore, he was also taking a fiction workshop taught by Gina Berriault, a novelist and short-story writer. She was one of the prominent names who had been wooed to the land of cornfields to teach that particular semester. Berriault had a reputation as a meticulous crafter of sentences and had, the year before, published a well-regarded novel called *The Son*, about an incestuous relationship. Though Berriault found Denis's performance worthy only of a C, it was in her classroom that he began work on what would become his first published short story.

One of those oddball Iowa City characters was the spark for the story. Bob Stall and a few other friends and acquaintances of Denis's were renting a house in town from a local landlord who happened to be extremely protective about the house. The landlord thought he had rented his house to a group of 1950s' choirboys and became infuriated when he began to see late '60s behavior, in the form of pot smoking and partying, under his roof. His response was to put his own house under twenty-four-hour surveillance. Stall and the other residents saw him outside in the early morning hours, sitting alone in his car across the street, staring at them menacingly. Inevitably, there was a confrontation between landlord and residents, which was discussed ad nauseum among Denis and his friends. Denis recognized in the landlord a character around which to build a story when it was time to write one for Berriault's class.

In his typewriter, the obsessive Iowa City landlord became Riggs Northrup, who, in the opening of the story, sits in his truck near midnight under a moon that resembles a "great round orange," watching a house with a loaded rifle in the back seat and a pistol on his lap. The story follows Northrup as he shoots through the window of the house, speeds home to argue with his Bible-thumping mother, laments his failed army career, and eventually robs a gas station, kills an acquaintance, and puts a bullet in his own head. It was an intimate portrait of a particular type of American loser: a beer-guzzling, low-IQ misfit, and it was told with the religious overtones found in Flannery O'Connor's stories that appealed to the tastes of writers and editors at the time.

Denis showed the story to Bell while he was enrolled in another of Bell's poetry workshops. Then, with Bell's blessing, he sent it to Robley Wilson Jr., fiction editor at the *North American Review,* who promptly accepted it and scheduled it for publication. "The Taking of Our Own Lives" was published in the winter 1970 issue of the *Review.* It contained an opening sentence that gave a proper introduction to Denis's first of many antihero protagonists: "Riggs Northrup, whose life so far had progressed like that of any other town moron, sat in his battered Chevrolet until nearly midnight and staved off any inkling as to what everything in him had led to." The publication further enhanced Denis's reputation around the English department. Like his first published poems, "The Taking of Our Own Lives" would live on beyond the pages of the *Review.* Wilson happened to be in the process of editing a fiction anthology with another writer, Stephen Minot, a professor at Trinity College in Connecticut. The collection, entitled *Three Stances of Modern Fiction,* was to include classics along with recently published stories and would be broken into various types of fiction. When it came time to select the stories that fit the definition of "mimetic," or realistic, fiction, Wilson remembered the story of Riggs Northrup and proposed it for the section. "The Taking of Our Own Lives" ran alongside stories by Anton Chekhov, John Updike, and Franz Kafka. For his contributions, Denis earned $50.

This initial success in fiction led Denis to pour more of his time and concentration in that area. Ideas were coming to him faster and more frequently than he could turn them into stories. His inability to take these ideas and produce quality writing was discouraging, however. He joked to his parents that he was learning to blame his typewriter, the weather, the president, or anything else he could think of his for his failures.

Soon he was planning to start a novel. He told Al and Vera that he had pages and pages of notes for the new project, but no plot or interesting action to use them in. It would probably be a "practice novel," he said, and it would take him eight or nine years to complete. He began hunting for topics. Vietnam, a popular subject of choice around the workshop and in the wider world, was a nonstarter, he said, because he wasn't willing to do the research.

The concept of "the debut novel of Denis Johnson" was most

definitely on his mind. He began to devote time to reading published first books by contemporary literary novelists. "He did a kind of study of first novels, because he knew he was going to write one himself," said Stall. "He was taking mental notes, no doubt." If he liked one of the books, he would recommend the author to Stall. Recommendations included books by Robert Stone, S. E. Hinton, and Joan Didion.

Progress on the "practice novel" moved slowly. Work slowed to a trickle in the summer, the pain from which, Denis told people, was somewhat eased because a summer slowdown was a phenomenon also experienced by Hemingway. By the fall of 1971, he was "working like mad" and had three completed chapters. Soon it would be time to send it off to potential agents and publishers for review, he said, but he still felt he did not know what he was truly writing about. The world of publishing would have to wait until he could knowledgeably answer questions about the partial manuscript he was planning to submit.

*

It was Denis's next successful fiction project that alerted the wider publishing world to his existence. He learned that he could submit stories to larger national consumer magazines like the *Atlantic* and *Esquire* without an agent, and, because his novel wasn't going anywhere, he thought that this was a good avenue to pursue. Having a story published in an academic journal like the *North American Review* was a tremendous accomplishment, but having your work in one of the few high-circulation magazines that published fiction was an even higher level of success. *Esquire,* the *Atlantic*, the *New Yorker*, and *New York Magazine* all sat on the coffee tables at the literary agencies and publishing houses of Manhattan and represented the clearest path to novelistic glory.

An incident on a bus would be the genesis of the story that would get Denis's name onto those coffee tables. That same serendipitous observation would also lead to the birth of a character that would, a decade and a half later, figure significantly in one of his signature works of fiction. Late one night, Denis was on a Greyhound bus when he heard a young mother loudly reprimanding her young daughter.

"Move your foot," she said. "I'm tired now. Move your foot or I'm going to have the bus driver stop the bus and we're going to put you off the bus in the dark and we're going to drive away."

Denis filed it away. The exchange resonated with him deeply. "I kept thinking about that woman," he said later. "I didn't really dislike her when I heard her talking. I could understand. It was late and, in fact, the kid was a nuisance to all of us. I wouldn't have minded a bit if she'd gone ahead and done it."

From that moment, the story grew. The woman on the bus became Jamie. The irritating kid was Miranda. The bus was headed east, driving through the night near Chicago. Jamie was on the bus because she'd just left her husband, who had cheated on her with a neighbor in a California trailer park, and now she was taking her kids (in the fictional version, there was also an infant, Baby Ellen) to "Choklit Town," Hershey, Pennsylvania, to escape. As the story developed in Denis's mind and onto the page, Jamie begins to tell her troubles to a man named Bill Houston, who calls himself "Leather Bill." (Houston would become the character Denis would write about more often than any other in his lifetime, and he would appear in several books.) In the bus story, Houston provides Jamie with beer after beer, until she's roaming the aisles of the bus, berating the passengers and the driver, and threatening to vomit on them.

Once he had revised it to his satisfaction, he put the story into an envelope, added a stamp, sent it off to New York City, and waited. The response he hoped for came from the *Atlantic.* In existence since a decade before the Civil War, the *Atlantic* had been the initial publisher of many writers who would appear in American textbooks, including luminaries like Ralph Waldo Emerson, Harriet Beecher Stowe, and Mark Twain. In the early '70s, it was a mix of politics, commentary, and reviews, with a generous portion of the magazine devoted to the arts, including short stories, poetry, and interviews with prominent people from cinema, literature, and music.

Denis entitled his story "There Comes After Here." It appeared in the April 1972 edition of the *Atlantic,* in an issue that contained an interview with Italian film director Federico Fellini; poetry by the winner of the previous year's Nobel Prize for literature, Pablo Neruda; and reports regarding the 1972 presidential campaign. The cover story was an interview, by Ralph Ellison, of another workshop writer, James Alan McPherson, who had received his MFA the year before. In the contributors' notes, Denis mentioned that he was at work on a novel, offering a quasi business card to potential publishers. That moment of reality that had been the spark for the story, the late-night exchange on the bus, had moved into the realm of fiction:

> "Move-yer-*fut,*" Jamie whispered fiercely and grabbed Miranda's ankle and moved it. "You behave. Or I'll tell the driver and he'll take you and put you off the bus right there in that cornfield. Right in the dark with the scarecrow. Do you hear me?" She jerked Miranda's foot away again. "Don't you play like you're asleep when I can see goddamn it you ain't!"

The business card drew business quickly. Denis had been planning to offer the "practice novel" that he'd started a few years earlier, which had evolved into a tale about some of the characters around Iowa City and the farmhouse. But when the inquiries came, editors asked Denis if the *Atlantic* story was part of a novel. In Denis's mind, it was not. He didn't have any idea how to build the story of Jamie on the bus into a complete novel. Nevertheless, he told interested publishers that he was indeed at work on a novel that contained the characters from "There Comes After Here."

A phone conversation was held with an editor from Houghton Mifflin, the Boston-based publisher that had come to prominence in the mid-nineteenth century with writers such as Emerson, Thoreau, and Nathaniel Hawthorne. It was a publishing house that specialized in publishing unproven writers. Denis agreed to give Houghton Mifflin an option on his unwritten, unimagined novel in exchange for an advance payment. He promised that three chapters would arrive in Boston shortly.

Denis signed the agreement without an agent, a decision he would almost immediately regret. Shortly after the agreement was signed,

Denis, finding himself in need of money, wrote to his editor in Boston asking for a larger advance, "making no threats." Perhaps he should have been more threatening, because the request was denied. For the next few years, he continued to work on the project, making progress when he could, but it would be many wrong turns and several iterations before, as an older man in a different phase of his life, he would find the key that would unlock the wider story that began late in the night in the back of that eastbound Greyhound bus.

MARRIAGE STORY 7

If two lie down together, they will keep warm.
But how can one keep warm alone? —Ecclesiastes 4:9–12

Money, or the lack of it, continued to put a strain on the young Johnson family of Hawkeye Drive. Denis had a knack for finding jobs and winning grants and fellowships, but still the family seemed to be always on the brink of bankruptcy and starvation. He wrote regularly to Al and Vera asking for a few bucks to tide them over, always promising quick repayment. His intention, he wrote, was to pay for his education and support his family on his own, and only to ask for help in desperation. Still, most of his letters home during this period include discussions of money—requests, promises, fiscal breakdowns of the situation. Marvin Bell, poetry mentor and career coach, was brought in to take on a new role and act as family economic counselor. "He was in desperate straits financially," Bell remembered. "I called him in, took out a piece of paper, drew a line down the middle, and said, 'What have you got and what do you owe?'" Bell went over the Johnson family financial statement, advised Denis take time off from school, and recommended a few job opportunities, including one with a local paper company. He also suggested Denis try his hand at plumbing.

They weathered the day-to-day repercussions of their financial situation and tried to laugh at the more glaring indications of their poverty. Denis said they were spending this period of their lives experiencing the clichés of working-class existence. One of those clichéd experiences occurred around the time when Morgan was first mobile. He made his way into the kitchen, opened the broiler, gasped, and ran to tell Nancy that the "berler" was going to bite him. Nancy assured him it was safe, so Morgan went to find somebody who would be more receptive to his tale. He found Denis, who followed him into the kitchen so that his son could present the evidence. Morgan delightedly pointed at the door to the broiler. Denis opened it, looked inside, and locked eyes with a healthy rat who was, despite his time in the broiler, quite alive. Denis quickly shut the door and got Nancy. When they opened the door again, ready to capture the creature, it was gone. The next several days were spent hunting for the rat and trying to locate a safe place to put rat poison where it wouldn't be consumed by their son.

Not all of Nancy and Denis's stories about child-rearing involved desperate straits. Denis enjoyed watching his son develop. He relished teaching new words and listening to his son's attempts at speech. He chronicled Morgan's developmental milestones for his parents. When Morgan first began to communicate verbally, Denis proudly related the first words he and Nancy could understand—"thank you," "mama," "dada," and "ball." When Morgan started walking, Denis reported that his son had a habit of looking around after he fell to see if anybody was watching. His parents would look away to save Morgan from embarrassment. Denis also reported on Morgan's mischievous habit of choosing to play with whatever items his parents had specifically barred him from touching. "He has no morals," Denis joked. "He worries only about the possibility of getting caught."

During the summer of Morgan's second year, the Johnsons took their first family vacation. They packed for the trip and drove to Dallas Center, where they traded their unreliable car for Nancy's father's Ford Thunderbird, and drove north to Ely, Minnesota. They checked into a cabin at the Northernair Lodge, a rustic resort on the shore of Lake Mitchell, just a few miles from the Canadian border. They enjoyed the tranquility of nature and the time away from campus life. Denis took a boat out on the lake every day and fished for bass and walleye. Parents and child went swimming in the crystal-clear waters of Mitchell Lake. In the evenings, they lounged in the sauna and dined on the fresh fish Denis had caught. When the vacation was over, Denis was entertaining visions of living in the wilds of the north, which he believed would improve both his health and his writing ability. It was a fantasy that would eventually become reality, but not until many years later. "He's all enthused about the North woods and wants to live here," Nancy wrote to Denis's parents. "He's never seen a Minnesota winter!"

Back in Iowa City, Denis and Nancy decided to tackle their food insecurity head on by seeding a patch of ground in a community garden. They proved to be inept farmers. They planted a variety of vegetables in May, then didn't return to the garden until three months had passed. Predictably, weeds now accounted for the majority of the vegetation. They salvaged some lettuce, and while Denis was pulling what he thought were giant weeds, they realized these were the radishes they'd planted three months before. The harvest netted the family a nice salad.

Denis followed Bell's advice and went out on the Iowa City job market. He landed a position as a public-relations man for a marketing and advertising firm. To fit in with the rest of the ad men, he grew a mustache, but he shaved it soon after because, he said, he was becoming unable to discern "who was me and who wasn't." He wrote advertising copy for a bank trying to attract the business of local farmers, for which he had to learn the intricacies of corn production. Another client was the director of an Iowa City nonprofit organization. Denis wrote a speech for the director that included a single joke. The joke worked so well that the director used it three times during the same speech, then tried it in a newspaper article as well. Denis resolved to spend more time writing jokes.

The same director soon turned out to be a problem client. He began to return all of the copy Denis wrote for him with notes asking for changes. Denis, apparently as emotionally committed to his advertising copy as he was to his poetry and fiction, usually ignored the suggestions and hoped for the best.

Denis's real skill lay in the creation of press releases, however. In this area, he also relied on his abilities as a fiction writer. His releases were mostly composed of phony quotes by made-up sources. Still, the releases were well received. Whenever his boss was in a sour mood, Denis would concoct another press release to cheer him up. The agency was relatively new, and Denis came into work every day unsure if the business would still be in operation. Despite these concerns, he began planning to ask for a raise only two weeks after he was hired. The plan was never put into action, though, because he was laid off after the third week. It was a rickety outfit, he said, and a small setback for the company led to what would be an early conclusion to Denis's fledgling public-relations career.

Living day after day without enough money weighed on them. "We were pretty poor," Nancy recalled. "We ate a lot of bologna. We pretty much lived on a shoestring. We just managed to get by. We just managed it somehow. We didn't ask for much help from our families, so we lived frugally."

There were other cracks in the foundation of the marriage that, over time, grew into fissures. Much of the problem had to do with Denis's continued alcohol and drug use. He was using hard drugs more often, staying out late drinking with friends, and inviting those same friends to the apartment and engaging in the same behaviors. Nancy, who had once been part of the action, was now left to handle the child-rearing and keep the household running. She worried more and more about how her husband's lifestyle was affecting Morgan. When she confronted Denis, he was "manipulative." This is who I am, this is who you married, he told her, so you better get used to it.

Often Denis would fall into dark moods, punctuated by fits of rage. During one marital blowout, the argument became so heated, and Denis's behavior so frightening, that Nancy ran to the bathroom and locked the door behind her. Denis went to the bedroom closet, retrieved the gun, and took it out of its cloth. He went back to the bathroom and, with Nancy screaming from within, put the gun on the floor and slid it partway under the door so that she could see he had it.

Nancy said that, given the circumstances, this situation may have been inevitable. "I can hardly blame him, because there he was, married at nineteen, and a father immediately, and trying to pursue a career that meant everything to him," she said. "I just think at the time it was kind of scary for us, but, thinking back, I just kind of understand how that all came to be."

The family moved from the apartment on Hawkeye Drive and relocated to a house in town, which they shared with a friend of Denis's and his son. Soon, though, the good times were receding, and the dark, dangerous times were becoming more and more common. Denis recognized the root of the problem lay in his growing dependence on alcohol and drugs. He began to feel that although he understood his addictions, he was unable to control them. When his desperation reached a breaking point, he decided to act. To resolve the situation, he thought, he would have to separate himself from it. In the fall of 1971, he checked himself into a psychiatric clinic and asked to be treated for his addictions.

Nancy took Morgan to visit his father regularly during his stay at the clinic. She thought she could see improvement in Denis over the course of his stay. But with him out of the house, she also felt a tremendous release of pressure. She began to spend more time with some of the friends she had made through the cooperative day-care organization. Life, in general, was calmer. She could see it reflected in the behavior and mood of her son as well.

After a three-week stay in the clinic, during which he was selected for and participated in a study on creativity conducted by one of the researchers, Denis was released. He was a self-referred patient, so although he consulted with his therapist at the clinic, it was up to him to decide when he was ready to return to society. Some of his friends were surprised by the entire episode. "I was out of town, and when I came back, he was in the hospital," remembered Stall. "Then, you know, he was back out, and he seemed completely fine."

It was soon apparent to Nancy, however, that everything was not fine. The changes she had seen during her visits to the clinic did not persist when he came back to the family. The same behaviors that had led him to enter the clinic returned almost immediately. The same people returned as well. The calm she felt during his stay in the clinic evaporated, and the realization that life was demonstrably worse when she and Denis were together caused more conflict. During one intense argument, Denis lashed out at Nancy and hit her in the ear. Afterward, she was unable to hear out of that ear. She went to the emergency room, where she learned that she had a ruptured eardrum. "They asked me about domestic violence, and I said 'no, no, no, it was an accident,' that I just walked into a gesture. And, of course, I knew they didn't believe me." Denis apologized profusely, and Nancy felt he was sincere, but still his conduct did not change.

Not long after that incident, Nancy decided it was time for drastic action. The inevitable split was not brought about by a final detonation but by the gradual accumulation of evidence that proved to her that the problems in their relationship had become unresolvable. At a certain point, she understood that she was going to have to leave if Denis was ever going to change his behavior—or Denis would have to be the one to leave, and she knew that Denis would never go on his own. Nancy's sister, Jane, was a student at the university and lived in a rented house a few blocks away. So Nancy packed up a few belongings, walked her son through the neighborhood to her sister's house, and moved in.

Denis's reaction was muted. "It was like he expected bad things to happen," she said. "I don't remember him saying 'Oh, please come back' ever." Instead, he told Nancy to call Vera and tell her about the breakup. Nancy dutifully telephoned her mother-in-law, expecting the worst. She delivered the news and anticipated a fiery reaction.

"Well, I wondered how long it would take," Vera said.

Nancy breathed a sigh of relief. She had been worried that Vera would blame her.

Denis eventually felt the need to inform his parents himself. He sat down at the typewriter and typed a short note a few weeks before

Christmas. Nancy and he were getting a divorce, he wrote, and there was virtually no hope of reconciliation. Nancy was not as happy in the marriage as he had thought. She had supported him when he was in the clinic, but she didn't want to wait around for round two. Denis assured his parents that he would not spiral into another breakdown. He planned to concentrate on his studies, stick to a routine, and adjust to his new reality. He signed the letter, and then added a handwritten addendum: Please don't call me. When the time is right, I will call. He told them he loved them and apologized for delivering bad news so close to Christmas.

The marriage had lasted two and a half years. During that period, Denis achieved a level of productivity and success as a writer of both poetry and fiction that he would not reach again until he was a much older man. Although he was a hard drinker and an enthusiastic drug user throughout his relationship with Nancy, the responsibilities of marriage and fatherhood had turned out to be a stabilizing force, to a degree. Now, without those guardrails, Denis was entering a new phase. Increasingly, he would find it difficult to pull off his balancing act when the freedom to leap into the abyss was all around him.

CRASH LANDING 8

There were doubts from the start. Could the writer keep his native frenzy in the academic air? Would not the place be overrun with aesthetes come not to work, but to dabble their delicate fingers in the Iowa River?

—Paul Engle, "The Writer and the Place"

The students in the Iowa Writers' Workshop's MFA program who would eventually make up the graduating class of 1974 included a grand total of two who had already published a book of poetry before they took a seat in their first classroom. One was Denis, the youngest member of the class, at the University of Iowa since he turned eighteen. The other, the oldest member of the class at thirty-five, had taken a much different route to Iowa City. Tom Meschery's prepoetry claim to fame was that he was the second highest scorer in one of the most famous basketball games of all time: Wilt Chamberlain's hundred-point game. (Meschery had sixteen that night.) He was traded to the Seattle SuperSonics, where he began dabbling in poetry. An editor at a publishing house thought the rhymes and stanzas of a six-foot, eight-inch jump-shooting poet might sell a few books, leading to Meschery's first published collection, *Above the Rim*. After the book came out, he was introduced to poet and former workshop instructor Mark Strand. The two became friends, and a few years later, when Meschery was an unhappy coach of the struggling Carolina Cougars in the American Basketball Association, Strand told his tall friend that there might just be an opening at the workshop for a power forward/ poetry student.

The quixotic journey that led a former NBA star to the English-Philosophy Building in Iowa City for a place among the nation's budding poets was one that illustrated the unconventional makeup of the Iowa Writers' Workshop's student body during that era. Like Meschery, many of Denis's fellow students who arrived in 1972 to start the program came in Iowa City via circuitous routes. Tess Gallagher, who grew up in Northwest logging camps, followed her first husband, an aspiring astronaut, to military bases across the South, until he ended up in Vietnam and she came back to Washington to study with Mark Strand, who sent her to Iowa. (Strand's name comes up in several of the students' backstories; he was instrumental in recruiting five poetry students into the Washington-state-to-Iowa pipeline that year.) Stuart Dybek had been teaching and spearfishing on the Caribbean island of St. Thomas when he decided he wanted to study with Robert Coover in Iowa. Tracy Kidder had earned an English degree at Harvard, then done three years as a first lieutenant in military intelligence in Vietnam. Allan Gurganus had also been in the war, serving three years aboard the USS *Yorktown* in the South China Sea on his way to Iowa. T. C. Boyle had spent four years teaching high school in New York, much of that time shooting heroin on the side. He had never been west of New Jersey when he sent his lone application to the Writers' Workshop. Jane Smiley had followed her husband to Iowa and wasn't even in the workshop yet. She was taking classes toward a doctorate in English when she began sneaking up to the floor that housed the Writers' Workshop and surreptitiously grabbing stories out of the bin where the writing students submitted their work. Soon she had joined her fellow writers on the fourth floor.

It was a time of transformation for the Writers' Workshop. While the number of creative writing programs at major universities in America could still be counted on one's fingers, the University of Iowa was the original, and as such, it had the most name recognition and a wide applicant pool filled with searchers and wild cards and free-thinkers from all walks of life. It was a program that was still larger in reputation than in actual operation. Engle and some of his original protégés, like Bell and Donald Justice, were living links to the genesis of the concept of the writing workshop. The program was less than a decade removed from the days in the World War II barracks building by the Iowa River. Bell could remember the times when Engle, in the middle of conducting class, would excuse himself to answer the phone in the next room, providing the students with a lesson of another sort as they listened through the thin walls to their professor convincing yet another donor that it was in their interest to part with a little more of their money so Engle could keep the program growing.

In just a few short years, creative writing programs would begin to proliferate and would quickly number in the hundreds. The Association of Writers & Writing Programs had been founded the year Denis arrived in Iowa, the beginnings of a network of writers, teachers, and administrators that would accelerate the corporatization of university creative writing programs and homogenize the experience of the college writing student. As the world of university creative writing widened, the variety of applicants narrowed, and the vagabonds, cowboys, and working-class denizens were gradually replaced by a steady stream of Ivy Leaguers and graduates of good schools looking to add another prestigious line to their résumé. In 1972, however, that evolution had not yet occurred, and the students arriving in Iowa City were seeking something much more elusive.

Denis had explored the idea of leaving Iowa and beginning studies for a graduate degree at another university. For a while he considered applying to Syracuse University and later was recruited by Columbia. Bell recommended he move on and continue his studies somewhere else, but he was pleased when Denis ignored his advice. By this time, Denis's reputation as a young star poet had spread well beyond Iowa. Some of the new students arrived not only aware of Denis but in awe of his work. "All of us who came to Iowa, all the poets, they all knew about Denis, and that he was the success story," remembered Michael Waters, who arrived in the fall of 1972 from Brockport, New York, to begin work on his MFA. "He had published a poem that we all knew and loved called 'Checking the Traps.' I remember that he had long hair, and he looked like Dennis Wilson of the Beach Boys. He was this golden god kind of guy."

His reputation would be further enhanced a year into his graduate studies, when he was given perhaps the most important stamp of approval of the era among his peer group. Right around the time Denis had enrolled at the University of Iowa, a twenty-one-year-old Cal-Berkeley dropout named Jann Wenner had the idea to create the country's first rock 'n' roll magazine. The inaugural issue of *Rolling Stone* magazine, featuring John Lennon on the cover, was published on November 9, 1967. Wenner's creation quickly found its footing. It evolved into his original vision, featured the most important rock celebrities of the era, and by the early '70s, was the hippie bible of what remained of the countercultural movement. Editors at *Rolling Stone* turned their attention to poetry and went looking for the rock 'n' roll poets of America, promising to offer readers "an abridged but representative list of who's writing poems these days, where and why." Denis made the list.

When the article appeared, the entry for "Dennis Johnson" (his first name misspelled) was accompanied by a silhouetted profile shot of Denis with his face obscured, apparently shirtless, with a flowing mane of hair falling to his shoulders. The photo was conspicuously distinct among a sea of standard headshots of smiling, tie-wearing poets. Denis's views on "poetics" had changed since he stated his case for the anthology that published his work four years earlier. For *Rolling Stone,* he explained his evolving views. "Before, the act of writing helped me to understand things. Now, it's just an act of writing.... In the end my work becomes an expression of my total inability to figure anything out. And that's perfectly all right with me. It's enough now to see something and say, there it is."

*

Denis arrived back on campus in late April 1972. After his split with Nancy, he'd taken some time off from school and gone back to live with his parents. He took a job at a bookstore, where he'd found a boss willing to look the other way when he needed a drink to get through the day. His stay under his parents' roof had ended badly, and he'd packed up and left after an argument, heading to the street to find a ride back to college. He hitchhiked from Arizona to Kansas City, along the way meeting a series of drivers who offered him one kind of illicit substance or another. It was outside of Kansas City when he encountered the Eckhart family and took the fateful trip to Bethany, Missouri, and spent those few moments on Big Creek Bridge.

When he finally arrived on campus, he had a story to tell. Bob Stall was the first to hear about the fatal car accident. Denis told his friend about the events of the night from start to finish—the family, the crash, the beer bottles strewn across the road, the hospital—and how, after the incident had washed over him like a dream, he had made his way back to campus. Stall thought the story provided another remarkable piece of evidence that Denis's life was touched by experiences that went way beyond those of ordinary people.

Denis also told a friend, Maury Barr, about the crash. Barr was an alumnus of the Carolyn Maisel poetry salons from Denis's undergraduate days and had worked for Paul Engle alongside Denis in the International Writing Program. Barr had also recently returned to Iowa City after an extended break in his studies. He'd been in a long-term romantic relationship with Susan Fletcher, Denis's undergraduate classmate from Bell's poetry workshops. Fletcher was a strikingly beautiful Catholic school graduate from the small town of Albert Lea, Minnesota, near the Iowa border. She had come to the University of Iowa on the advice of a nun and writing instructor after winning a national poetry contest while in high school.

Barr and Fletcher had spent the previous year together in Berkeley, California, both as an adventure and as part of a strategy for Barr to avoid military service. Barr had spent some of his childhood in Berkeley. He and Fletcher moved there from Iowa after Barr learned that he was to be drafted and sent to Vietnam. He initially attempted to avoid the war as a conscientious objector but decided to instead tell recruiters that he wasn't mentally fit for service. After confronting the draft board and being sent to a psychiatrist, Barr began to question his own sanity, but he was eventually allowed to avoid the military and the war.

He and Fletcher lived in Berkeley, where he worked as a janitor at the California College of the Arts and Fletcher worked as an international operator for Pacific Bell.

Barr and Fletcher came back from California around the time Denis got back to town in 1972. Denis was drinking heavily, sleeping on friends' couches, and often seen around town dragging a big plastic bag of his clothes behind him, searching for somewhere to spend the night. Things weren't going all that well for Barr and Fletcher either, at least as a couple. During one particularly animated fight, Barr suggested that Fletcher could use some downers to help her calm down and told her that she should go see Denis to get some. Fletcher took her soon-to-be-ex-boyfriend's advice. Denis didn't have any downers, but he had some pot, and he soon asked Fletcher if she wanted to go out for a drink. It was the beginning of a relationship between Denis and Sue that was to last several years in reality, and eventually have a second life much later, as fiction, on the page and the big screen.

But first Denis wanted to make sure that Barr would not object. He and Sue drove to Barr's house on Jefferson Street. Denis parked and told Sue to wait in the car. He walked up the steps to Barr's top-floor apartment and found his friend. He told Barr that he wanted to start a relationship with Sue and asked Barr if that would be all right with him. Barr gave Denis the green light. "I was just so impressed that he would actually ask me that, that he was a man of honor," Barr said.

*

When the fall semester of 1972 got underway, Denis was, once again, broke. He was living in a residence that he referred to as "a tenement," but even that arrangement was short lived. In September, the tenement was condemned. Housing officials arrived to inspect it, deemed it to be "unfit for human occupancy," and told Denis to get out. He wrote to his parents asking for a loan. Sue had tallied up the money she'd spent to keep him fed and decided to cut him off, he told his parents in the letter. His only meal the previous day had been a frozen sirloin steak that his ex-sister-in-law had given him out of pity. She had also given him some shirts that were too small in the neck. He asked

Al and Vera for $300. "I'll really pay you back, half on October 1st and the other half on November 1st." In the margin in ink, he added one more "really!" to seal the deal.

As would happen throughout his life, just when he was in the most desperate of financial straits, an opportunity would come along to save Denis from starving to death. Nancy had a new boyfriend and had moved, along with Morgan, to a nearby farm. Before relocating, she had been living in a small home provided by the state welfare office, at a reduced rate of only $30 a month. Nancy offered the home to Denis. There was just one catch: the welfare office must believe that Nancy and Morgan were still the occupants of the house, or the reduced rent and the use of the house would be revoked. Denis agreed to the terms, and he and Sue decided to take the opportunity to move into the welfare house together.

Denis had recently made the acquaintance of Scott Walker, another aspiring poet who had been drawn to Iowa City by the Writers' Workshop. Walker had come to town from Spokane, Washington, had not yet enrolled in school, and was looking for a place to stay. Denis and Susan offered him a bed in the welfare house. Again, there was a catch. Since the house was supposed to be occupied by a single mother, Walker would be staying in a child's bedroom, sleeping in a child's bed. "The bed was like three-quarters length," Walker said. "I could never stretch out, I had to sort of curl up and make the best of it."

Officials from the welfare office could appear unannounced at any time, so the shades had to be drawn, and the house had to be kept dark. Almost every day, somebody from the office would come and start banging on the front door, shouting, "We know you're in there!" Denis and Susan slept through many of the attempts, waking late in the day to start drinking, and occasionally shooting heroin. "We never talked about it," Walker said. "I knew what was going on, and they just sort of agreed not to talk about it."

There didn't seem to be much time in the schedule for writing, or for attending class. On occasion, however, something would awaken the writer in Denis. Usually it was the potential for money. He learned about a $3,000 fellowship for which he was eligible. "When he found out about it," Walker remembered, "he didn't do anything, and he didn't do anything, and then, the night before everything was due, he wrote some poems, and he won the fellowship." To Walker, the ease with which he created poetry on deadline was more proof of Denis's brilliance as a writer.

Denis and Sue's relationship was fiery from the beginning. Periods of bliss were apt to shift to angry exchanges with little warning. Whether they were enraged at each other or enamored, the intensity level was turned up several notches when they were together. After he and Sue began living together, Denis told Al and Vera about the relationship. His parents had relocated to Scottsdale, Arizona, so Denis used the opportunity to take Sue to meet them in their new home while the university was on holiday break. During the visit, Denis argued with his father. Al was clearly frustrated with his son and told him he was being irresponsible and needed to start acting like an adult. Vera pulled Sue aside to talk about Denis as well. Vera said she was aware that Denis had a drinking problem, and she and Al were concerned about his ability to be a good father to their grandson. Sue acknowledged the problem and tried to reassure Vera.

The welfare house provided some relief from financial pressure, and, when Denis resumed working for Engle in the International Writing Program office translating Russian poetry, the pressure eased further. Sue won a poetry contest put on by *Mademoiselle* magazine, a national publication that paid well and offered to publish more of her work in the future. Life, Denis wrote to his parents, was boring, but comfortable.

The sanctuary of the welfare home was not to be a long-term solution, unfortunately. State officials discovered the ruse. Denis and Sue suspected a neighbor had ratted them out. Whether it was due to a nosy neighbor or a resourceful state investigator, they were soon out on the street again, looking for new arrangements.

"Those are really, probably, my best memories with Denis, our time in that little house," Sue said. "That was our honeymoon period."

DOUBLE LIFE 9

Each of us needs to take a look at each other and see that we're all people. There's a big gap in understanding—that the police are people, but the freaks are people, too. —**Dave Osmundson, manager of the Vine Tavern, Iowa City**

To many of the graduate students in the Writers' Workshop, Denis was a bit of a phantom. The workshop formed its own community, and those within it went to class together, drank at the same bars, and went to the same parties. While most of those connected to the workshop knew of and revered Denis, his appearances were rare enough that when he did show his face, it was cause for celebration. Though the world around him was beginning to move on by 1972, Denis remained a strict adherent of the tenets of the '60s. He was a "stone hippie" with hair to his shoulders who always looked like he'd just finished off a joint. He walked the halls of the English-Philosophy Building in ragged clothes and bare feet, even in the dead of winter. Often Morgan would be trailing along naked, in true child-of-a-hippie fashion. Denis was wiry, with tight musculature, about five feet, nine inches, but he moved with a swagger and projected confidence. Perhaps because of his infrequent appearances, many of his fellow graduate students sensed an air of mystery around him. He was quick with a smile, but it was also difficult for someone who wasn't in his inner circle to get beyond a short greeting or a wave. It seemed, to many of the students, that Denis was hiding a secret and waiting to find the right person to share it with. "I thought he was very, very shy, and he was always kind of twinkly and foxlike," remembered Tess Gallagher. "He had a lot of self-amusement. He was kind of twinkling in the corner. He seemed like he was sitting on a lot of unhatched eggs."

He also occupied an odd slot in the workshop pecking order. He was one of the youngest students in the program, an *enfant prodige* surrounded by mostly older yet less accomplished writers. The workshop at that time had a clearly defined ranking system that was based entirely on whom the faculty chose to bestow fellowships and other paid teaching opportunities. The gold standard was to be granted a teaching/writing fellowship and acquire the glorious title of "twiff." Twiffs taught undergraduate fiction or poetry workshops and received the largest stipends. Below twiff were two levels of teaching assistantships, then came the research assistantship, and at the very bottom the dreaded designation of "no funding." It was a punitive system that bred intense competition among the students and incentivized kowtowing to the faculty.

Denis was a twiff and had, in some cases, known members of the faculty for as long as five years. He was unmistakably a VIP. Occasionally his behavior would slyly acknowledge that he enjoyed his veteran status. He developed a standard response whenever a visitor or newer student would ask directions around campus or town. No matter what destination they were inquiring about, Denis would offer the same answer: "You go seven blocks, make a left, you can't miss the sign."

His offbeat sense of humor was expressed in other ways. In the fall of 1972, presidential politics and Richard Nixon's attempt to secure four more years in the White House was on everyone's mind, including the students in Denis's undergraduate workshop. Denis was caught up too. Al was a hard-core New Deal Democrat dating back to the 1930s, so the Johnson house had been a Democratic stronghold. Denis had also become intrigued with Gus Hall, the candidate running on the communist ticket. While presiding over his undergraduate workshop, he took a more active approach to the election: he announced that he, himself, was running for president. He installed his students as his campaign committee and began hanging signs all around campus heralding his candidacy. Eventually, he said he was throwing his support behind the Democratic candidate, George McGovern, and downgrading to a campaign for Congress.

To some of the older students, Denis retained an innocent quality and seemed quite impressionable. Stuart Dybek was in his late twenties when he arrived in Iowa City. Denis sought him out and told him that, despite his reputation as a poet, he was a fiction writer as well, and he wanted to talk to Dybek about writing fiction. Later, they had a beer together and were discussing the art of the short story. Denis proposed the shopworn idea that short stories are closer in form to poetry than they are to novels. Dybek informed Denis that the idea was commonplace, and that Denis, had not, in fact, invented it. Denis stuck to his guns. It was his idea, he maintained. Dybek left the conversation still unsure whether Denis was serious or not. "He was really one funny guy, in a kind of a weird low-key way," Dybek said. "And he was a sweet guy. There was something about him, a humanity about him, that I felt was always there from the start."

The writing community on the University of Iowa campus was in a particularly vibrant phase as Denis undertook his graduate studies. George Starbuck, Denis's fellow Vietnam War protester, had left the workshop in 1969. His replacement was Jack Leggett, a fiction writer who had a background in publishing, having been an editor at Houghton Mifflin and Harper & Row. Leggett's New York City connections brought a steady stream of agents and editors from large publishing houses to campus, looking for new talent and filling the young writers with dreams of book contracts.

The visiting faculty was a revolving door of well-known writers arriving in town to bless the workshop and its inhabitants with their literary renown, which they did with varying degrees of effort and success. Novelist and short-story writer Richard Yates, best known for his novel *Revolutionary Road,* did a long stint at the Writers' Workshop. One semester, he taught just a single class before succumbing to an alcoholic breakdown and being relieved by a graduate student, but he fared better on other occasions. John Cheever, by then celebrated as the author of some of the best-known short stories of the era, brought an even higher level of fame with him to campus. William Price Fox, the screenwriter, novelist, and essayist, was a favorite of students in the workshop. In addition to faculty members, there were regular readings given by the hot literary names of the day, always followed by parties that went late into the evening.

Engle's International Writing Program, where Denis was still employed, helped to increase the level of intellectual firepower on campus. The program had by then been in existence for nearly a decade, its reach and reputation steadily growing. Readings by foreign writers, often of a political bent, were apt to fill Shambaugh Auditorium or the Memorial Union. Czech expatriates such as Miloš Foreman and Arnošt Lustig were brought in by Engle. When somebody like poet Joseph Brodsky, who had been thrown out of the Soviet Union the previous year, came to campus to speak, the entire writing community would turn out and the place would, to the young writers, feel like the modern epicenter of global literature. The literary celebrity emanating from Iowa City grew to the point that *Playboy* magnate Hugh Hefner would regularly drive down from Chicago to pick up the latest visiting writers and bring them back to the Playboy mansion, where he would wine and dine them for a weekend—just another perk of an invitation to the Writers' Workshop.

The visiting writer who had the greatest effect on Denis arrived in Iowa City in the fall of 1973 behind the wheel of a beat-up Ford Falcon convertible with a jug of grapefruit juice and ice beside him and a half gallon of vodka behind the seat. Raymond Carver was returning that year as somewhat of a conquering hero, arriving flush with his first burst of literary success and fame at the place where he had tried and failed to earn a degree a decade earlier. Carver was a product of the Northwest, the son of an alcoholic mill worker and a waitress who grew up in working-class poverty. He was married with children by his early twenties and spent that decade of his life in dead-end blue-collar jobs in California. A fiction class at Chico State taught by Iowa grad

John Gardner put him on the path to a writing career, and years of rejection and the occasional small-journal publication followed.

Carver caught his break in 1970 when his friend and occasional collaborator, Gordon Lish, talked his way into the position of fiction editor at *Esquire* magazine. *Esquire* had been known throughout the twentieth century as the periodical home to many greats of American literature, but in the late '60s, the magazine had moved away from fiction and instead spent its literary capital on New Journalists like Gay Talese and Tom Wolfe, who wrote deeply reported, novelistic works of nonfiction. Lish had promised Harold Hayes, then the top name on the masthead, that he would find the most current, fresh writers of "new fiction" and restore *Esquire* to its previous glory. He got the job, and exhibit number one was his friend Ray Carver. Although at that point Carver had not yet had much success on a national scale, he had developed a minimalist style and a focus on working-class subject matter set in the trailer parks, diners, and factories of small-town America that would, with the help of Lish, eventually set him apart. *Esquire* published a story entitled "Neighbors" in the summer of 1970, and, as they both had hoped, Carver's career took off. His stories and poems ran in *Esquire* and many other magazines and journals, and he began to receive teaching offers from prestigious institutions.

His newfound success earned him a job at the Writers' Workshop for the 1973–74 academic year. The Ray Carver of those days was in his midthirties, a tall, husky figure with hair that fell across his forehead and a face that was always red. He seemed to always be eating, drinking, or smoking a cigarette—often all three at once. Although his writing career was on the upswing when he arrived in Iowa City, he was in a troubled marriage—troubled mostly because of his drinking habit. He had always been a heavy drinker, but by then, he had advanced into hard-core alcoholism.

John Cheever had long been an idol of Carver's. Cheever, then in his early sixties and coming off a stay in the hospital for complications related to alcoholism, was even further down the road toward ruin. The two writers became friends and drinking buddies immediately. Carver took Cheever on semiweekly alcohol runs to the state liquor store, they drank together in their rooms at the Iowa House, and they passed the days at the Mill, one of the local writers' watering holes. The first time Carver stepped in the English-Philosophy Building to conduct class, he looked around at the sterile academic setting and announced he would be conducting his classes at the Mill as well.

Carver was an extremely charismatic figure, and a good number of the graduate students, including Denis, gravitated toward him. He dressed like a "hulking cowpoke," favoring jeans, work boots, and western-style shirts. He had one sweater that he wore throughout the semester, and students watched a small hole in the sleeve progress as the weeks went by. Eventually Carver's entire elbow was visible. He related to the students on a one-to-one level without even a hint of elitism, was a good listener, and rewarded a good story with an enthusiastic and reverberating laugh. Dan Guenther, a student in the workshop at the time and a classmate of Denis, found Carver to be devoid of the ego that accompanied interactions with most writers at the workshop. "There were some people there who had a certain formality in their tone, and implicit in that was that they were holding themselves slightly apart from you, or above you in some way," he remembered. "Ray didn't have any of that. If the shit hit the fan in a bar, and you needed somebody back-to-back, Ray Carver would be back-to-back with you. Ray was really interested in our writing, but Ray was a guy struggling with his soul."

Denis was not a student in Carver's workshops. His mentorship instead took place in bars and at card tables, usually well after classes had concluded for the day. And it was through Carver that Denis met Gordon Lish. In the three short years that Lish had been at *Esquire,* he had gained an outsize reputation in the publishing world—and an ego to match. He had taken to signing his letters "Captain Fiction." He had also began editing the work of writers heavily. Carver would often bristle at Lish's editing suggestions, but he usually accepted them, making the calculation that getting his stories into *Esquire* was worth this Faustian bargain. Many other writers balked and withdrew their stories. (Later, after his fame had far eclipsed that of his editor, Carver's stories would be published in their original form, and much debate would take place over Lish's influence and impact on Carver's work.)

Carver invited Lish to campus during the spring semester. As part of the visit, Lish came to Carver's fiction workshop, where he did not make a good impression in the room. He talked about himself for an hour and harshly criticized the stories of some of the students. His behavior didn't quell the students' interest in making a connection, however. Lish solicited stories from several of the writers he met. Allan Gurganus, another workshop graduate student, sent Lish a batch of stories after the visit and had them returned with extreme revisions, including large sections marked out and sample replacement sentences written in the margins. Gurganus rejected the changes and told Lish to "write your own stories, not mine." Denis had a similar experience. He sent four stories to Lish in New York and later had them returned with editing suggestions. Lish made major changes, including asking Denis to break one of the stories into two separate pieces. Denis agreed to some of the changes at first, but after several rounds of editing, he became upset over the process and ultimately rejected the edits and withdrew the stories. He told Maury Barr and Scott Walker about the experience later. Both were impressed that Denis, who was desperately in need of money at the time, would tell a famous editor to "get lost."

Workshop parties often ran late into the night, and sometimes many attendees would surpass even Carver's level of intoxication, with outlandish results. Tom Meschery hosted one such party. Meschery and his wife, Joanne, also a student in the workshop, rented a large house near campus and occasionally agreed to host get-togethers for visiting writers. That night, Michael Ryan, a poetry student who would later go on to win the Yale Series of Younger Poets award, got into an argument with a German poet from the International Writing Program who specialized in the form known as concrete poetry. Each poet ridiculed the other's chosen poetry form. At this particular party, insults regarding one's poetry were akin to questioning the virtue of someone's mother. The dispute became increasingly heated until finally punches began to fly. Meschery and his wife had just served the dessert for the evening. Dozens of dishes of Baskin-Robbins ice cream of all flavors were lined up on the dining-room table. Ryan rushed the German poet and knocked him through the back door. This time, it was Carver who acted as the calming presence. Carver grabbed Ryan from behind, picked him up, and held him in the air, allowing the German poet to clamber to his feet and get away. As the untouched ice cream melted into soup, people surrounded the combatants in the street, while the usually mild-mannered Meschery bellowed from the steps, "This is my house! How can you do this in my house?"

Sometime during the evening, Carver might have seen or even bumped into Denis's classmate, Tess Gallagher. But his year as a visiting professor at the University of Iowa passed without so much as an introduction to Gallagher. In the next few years, his alcoholism would grow steadily worse, until his physical condition would began to deteriorate. Extended blackouts would become a regular part of his life. He would find himself working at a bookstore in Sausalito, California, for $2.35 an hour—a job from which he was fired for stealing books. Several attempts at rehabilitation would fail, until, finally, on June 2, 1977, he would quit drinking for good. As his personal life was crumbling, the success of his writing life would steadily grow. The short stories he had crafted during his years in the bottle would be published in book form under the title, *Will You Please Be Quiet, Please?* The appearance of that book, along with subsequent stories and books, would eventually lead to his name being associated with a movement in American fiction known as dirty realism, a movement that would become, a few years later, the dominant form of literary fiction published in America. Carver would become known as America's Chekhov. But it wouldn't be until after he achieved sobriety that he would finally meet and fall in love with Gallagher, with whom he would spend the last dozen years of his life, a bond formed and cultivated through the love of and dedication to poetry and writing that he would enjoy until his death from lung cancer at only fifty years of age.

The name "Raymond Carver," in fact, would loom so large over the literary world of the late twentieth century that Denis's limited association with him would, once he finally began to publish fiction of his own and gain a small following, become the single fact of most interest about him to the reading public. A few years later, Denis would find himself peppered with so many versions of the question "What was Raymond Carver like?" that he would feel the need to escape a literary conference he was attending in Croatia by hiding, for an extended period of time, perched on a toilet seat in a bathroom stall.

*

The students of the Iowa Writers' Workshop had their own little world within the larger university community, and it had two centers of operation: the classrooms and offices of the English-Philosophy Building, and the pubs that ringed the campus. The heart of Iowa City's tribal life was in its bars. Often, if students didn't have a chance to have their poem or story evaluated in class, the same participants would regather at one of the acceptable drinking establishments and take up the critique over a round or two. "Iowa City was set up perfectly for a bunch of writers," recalled Bill Herz, a poetry student at the time and friend of Denis's. "As you walked down the street, you'd pass a drugstore, and then a bar, then a post office, then a bar, then a grocery store, then a bar, and a bar, and a bar. And at those watering holes, you'd always see other people from the workshop. You'd stay up late shooting pool and just talking junk, and eventually everybody would join you."

There were several stops on the regular writers' bar crawl of Iowa City in those years. The Deadwood, a hole in the wall with a dozen booths, was the top choice for most workshop denizens. There was Donnelly's, the town's Irish pub, where the poet Dylan Thomas was forcefully removed after consuming an ungodly amount of Guinness, or whiskey, or some other concoction—an incident that just about everybody associated with Iowa City seems to have their own version of. (Donnelly's lasted until the city's infamous urban renewal project in the early 1970s. When it came time to demolish the building that housed it, the demolition was scheduled for a Sunday morning, because that was the only time it could be accomplished without an uprising from enraged and inebriated clientele.) There was Joe's Place, a sizable bar and restaurant that sported assorted pinball machines and pool tables—two of Denis's favorite pastimes. Large sums of money were put on the line at the pool tables, sometimes leading to hand-to-hand combat. Denis's friend Dan Guenther, who bartended at Joe's, first met Denis at one of those pool tables, when he had to step in to prevent Denis from being flattened by a 260-pound Iowa Hawkeye offensive lineman of whom he had run afoul. The favorite bar of the writing faculty was the Mill, which had a small bar reserved for the literary elite of Iowa City. Kurt Vonnegut, John Cheever, John Irving, Vance Bourjaily, and many others claimed their own personal seat at one time or another.

Though he spent countless hours in all of the above, a bar called the Vine was Denis's true home away from home. The occasional workshop student would stop in, but the population of the Vine was usually weighted toward hard-core hippies and elements of Iowa City's recreational drug industry. Local law enforcement viewed the Vine as an essential stop on any search for suspected criminal drug-related activity in Iowa City. In fact, relations between the police and the Vine became so entwined that the bar and the Iowa City police department began to hold softball games, called "The Pigs vs. The Freaks," to allow the participants to settle some of their disagreements on the playing field instead of the streets.

The original Vine was on Clinton Street, perfectly situated amid the other bars for those who wanted a pit stop. The building was a converted retail space, with a large picture window and a couple of tables looking out on an import shop and a large bank across the street. It had a long, L-shaped bar, with the bottom of the L facing the window, and a partition that separated the front room from the back area, which comprised a row of booths often called the "halls of hell." Denis had his own favorite booth in the back and could sometimes be found asleep at the table. The Vine had no jukebox, but the speakers played a repeating playlist of classic country and western music.

The owners of the Vine knew their clientele. At one time, they ran ads in the *Daily Iowan* that read: "If you can live on four hours sleep, the Vine can take care of the other 20." On another occasion, the owners decided to have a promotion where they offered customers pitchers of whiskey. The questionable idea attracted a large crowd, and, later in the evening, many of those who took the Vine up on the offer could be seen vomiting on the sidewalk in front of the bar.

Denis and Sue spent much of their time in the Vine. "He basically lived there," Sue recalled. Denis consciously tried to keep his life among the crowd at the Vine separate from his life in the workshop. In class, he went by Denis, but at the Vine, he was strictly Johnson. Among the students and faculty of the Writers' Workshop, Denis was a star writer approaching legendary status and a man of mystery. Inside the walls of the Vine, however, he was way down on the social ladder. "He was considered kind of a nerd at the Vine," Sue said. "People were always asking me, 'What are you doing with this guy? You should get rid of him.'"

Denis and Sue were constantly low on funds. Once, Denis decided that a drug deal he'd concocted with some people at the Vine might alleviate their money problems. Sue argued against it. She didn't trust the people involved, and she didn't think Denis was ready for their level of criminality. Denis went ahead with the deal anyway, and, as Sue had predicted, he was ripped off, costing them money they couldn't afford to lose. It happened, she thought, because nobody in the Vine viewed Denis as a threat. "In their viewpoint, you could rip off someone who wasn't going to come back on you, and shoot you, or kidnap your children, or something, and they knew Denis was harmless," she said.

A more successful application of Denis's skill set at the Vine was the collecting of stories and characters. Tales of money and passion and of crimes gone wrong flowed through the crowd in the bar and the halls of hell, and Denis loved them all. (His favorites would end up playing out once again two decades later in *Jesus' Son.*) Heroin use was rampant, so many of the stories had tragic endings. There were regular deaths from overdose—deaths that served as a constant reminder that the people Denis and Sue associated with were living dangerously close to the edge. According to one story that circulated, a girl named Jane Russell took an overdose of pills and left a note for her boyfriend to revive her when he came home. The boyfriend arrived later that night, drunk, and passed out directly on top of the note, which he had not seen. When he finally woke up, Jane Russell was dead. "Denis loved that story because it was so bizarre," Sue said. Another character who made it into the notebook was "the Widow Lawson," a young woman with a series of boyfriends who all overdosed while they were with her.

Yet another Vine tale that would resonate with Denis and be stored in his memory involved Jeff Hottel, the drummer friend with whom he'd spent time at the farmhouse. Hottel robbed and assaulted some people and was arrested. He spent a few weeks in jail before posting bail, but when the incident eventually went to trial six months later, he told the judge that he had beaten and robbed the men because they had been selling drugs to his little brother. The judge believed him and found him innocent. Afterward, he returned to the Vine in triumphant celebration, happily relating his story to the assembled crowd.

In the version of the incident that made the local newspaper, Hottel and another man, David Huffman, entered the home of William Kragie and Alan Kasik, pointed a gun at them, and took their shotgun, along with $125. They were arrested, and Hottel's case went before a judge the following summer. His younger brother, Mark, was to be called as a witness, but as he waited outside the Iowa City courthouse to testify, he was arrested because he had a switchblade. Regardless, three days later, the case went to a Johnson County jury, which took just an hour and fifteen minutes to find Hottel innocent of the charges. Denis theorized the content of the jury's deliberations twenty years later in the story "Out on Bail": "Completely confused as to who the real criminals were in this case, the jury had voted to wash their hands of everybody and they let him off," he wrote. "We had that helpless, destined feeling. We would die with handcuffs on... and yet we were always being found innocent for ridiculous reasons."

The denizens of the Vine shared stories and would also, on occasion, share vehicles. Maury Barr had acquired a 1963 Chevy Impala that was known in the bar as White Trash. It had no ignition or key, and the floor had rusted out to the point that whoever sat in the driver's seat could see the highway below them when the vehicle was in motion. Anybody was allowed to drive it, as long as they agreed to put it back in the parking lot near the Iowa Old Capitol Building when they were done.

Ownership of White Trash went from Barr to another friend of Denis's, Don Smith, a doctoral student in European history who preferred Wild Turkey and, on many nights, drank it until he was unconscious. Smith was divorced and raising one of his three daughters. From time to time, Sue would babysit Smith's daughter in their apartment in married housing, and when Sue and Denis were fighting, Smith's apartment was a welcome refuge. For his trouble, Smith would earn himself a place in Denis's notebook on the way to future fictional infamy.

Denis continually made efforts to keep his life at the Vine separate from his life as a grad student and writer at the university, but sometimes one world would bleed into the other. Once, a Vine denizen who had literary interests decided to go looking for "Johnson" at the English-Philosophy Building. He showed up at the EPB wearing dark sunglasses and a leather jacket and proceeded toward the International Writing Program office. Denis managed to head off the interloper before he ran into Engle, but he was shaken and angered by the episode.

The mingling of his separate lives could work the other way as well. One night at the Vine, one of the regulars began to question why Denis spent so much time there. "You're only hanging out with us so you can write about us later, aren't you?" he asked.

It was an astute observation. Denis was indeed already in the process of writing about them and their stories. He was hard at work on a novel about a group of junkies and their favorite bar. Indeed, he had promised the novel to an editor at Houghton Mifflin. The stories he heard and the lives he witnessed at the Vine were, he would write later, "the stories that would fill the Old Testament if God had written it after the invention of gunpowder."

*

Dealing drugs at the Vine was just one of Denis's many schemes, albeit one of the least successful, in his ongoing effort keep afloat financially. Other money-earning plans had more positive outcomes. He found he could make money by selling plasma to the local blood donation center. He took a paper route, but this job only lasted two weeks because he learned quickly that he was not suited for a job that required waking up before sunrise. He gained a reputation around the workshop as an expert typist, and he made money typing the final, error-free version of some of his fellow students' master theses. He found a job as an orderly at Mercy Hospital, where he had experiences that would lead to some memorable stories and characters down the road.

The job at the International Writing Program for Engle was still a steady form of income. The problem was, whatever level of income he was able to achieve, Denis would spend the money faster. Soon Denis was going into Engle's office each month to ask for an advance on his salary. Engle would admonish Denis to be more responsible, but eventually he would acquiesce and hand over the money. "We never had enough money, and Denis was just a free spender," Sue said. "He would just spend money as fast as he could, and if there was no dope in town to buy, we'd go drinking or find some other way to spend it."

Some friends learned that when Denis and Sue were short of money, it was a good idea to safeguard their belongings. Once, Denis's friend Alan Soldofsky lost some money to Denis in a card game. Soldofsky agreed to pay Denis with a few of his Rolling Stones records. Instead of waiting for payment, Denis came to Soldofsky's apartment and took his entire Rolling Stones collection. "Sometimes they were really not nice people to be around, because they were using," Soldofsky said. "And every once in a while, he and Susan Fletcher would literally, on the fly, show up at your door, and I sort of thought they were looking for something to steal."

Denis was not always able to keep his drug habit from affecting his academic life. One semester, he enrolled in the poetry workshop taught by Donald Justice. Justice and Marvin Bell were the two full-time poetry professors in the graduate workshop at the time. Justice had received his doctorate from the University of Iowa in 1954 and begun teaching in the workshop shortly thereafter. Where Bell was involved in his students' personal lives, Justice was more reserved, but he was still known to students as a deeply committed teacher. One day, Denis made a surprise visit to Justice's office.

"I'm sorry, but I have to withdraw from your class," Denis said.

Justice was shocked. Denis was one of the most talented students he'd ever taught. "Why?" he asked.

"It seems I've become addicted to heroin," Denis answered.

The withdrawal would not be the only episode in which Denis did not complete a course he'd started. For a while he abandoned the Writers' Workshop completely; he got a ride to Berkeley, California, where he spent several weeks on the streets near the university. He lived off handouts, worked whatever odd jobs he could find, and used the meager returns to buy drugs. He wasn't alone. Hundreds of "destitute youngsters without any idea how to take care of themselves poured up and down Telegraph Avenue in a state of semi-crazed exhaustion." Denis occasionally had enough money for a bed in a hostel, but most nights, he camped in the hills above the city. He and his fellow wanderers were "drinking up the dregs of the sixties," he would write later, and he imbibed until he couldn't anymore. Then he went to his parents' house in Scottsdale, and soon back to his life in Iowa City.

*

Despite such setbacks, Denis was approaching graduation in the spring of 1974. The potential for a more respectable form of income—one that could enhance his academic career—arrived in the form of a temporary teaching job at Cornell College. A professor was going on leave for a semester. Denis learned about the opening and applied to be his replacement. He drove to Mount Vernon for what was supposed to be lunch with the head of the English department, but it turned into a meal with the entire English faculty. As he tried to eat, Denis was presented with "numerous ridiculous classroom situations" and asked for theories on teaching and literature. Though he never got a chance to take a bite of his hamburger, he survived the interview and received the contract for the job the next day.

Despite its religious affiliation, the students at Cornell College had absorbed the culture of the '60s and sported the long hair and wardrobe that fit with the times. Denis, though, arrived on campus properly fitted in the attire of a young professor—a stiff blue Oxford shirt, chinos, a nice leather belt, his own long hair tied in a fat ponytail. Elizabeth Evans was a poetry student at Cornell and had been studying with Robert Dana, the professor for whom Denis was filling in. Evans remembered Denis showing up for one of their meetings holding a copy of *The Collected Poems of W. B. Yeats.* The two discussed the work of Yeats, and Denis told Evans that his favorite Yeats poem was "When You Are Old." To Evans, Denis seemed confident, even a bit full of himself, but helpful and friendly. He told her about his childhood overseas and about his father's important post in the State Department. The two worked together through the semester, an arrangement that resulted in one of her poems being published in the Cornell anthology and eventually earning Evans an award.

The job ended up entailing more than just the class time Denis had signed up for, but he committed to the responsibilities. He edited and designed the school's literary magazine, organized a student reading, and hosted a dinner for the students. It was too much work for the money he was getting paid, he told Al and Vera, but it was worth it to fatten his résumé. At the end of the semester, the department was pleased with Denis's contributions and even discussed offering him a full-time position after he graduated.

Denis and Sue began to plan their next move. Many options were on the table. Sue was applying to graduate schools and had already been accepted by Columbia University in New York. They began to investigate the possibility of a move to New York City, despite Denis's profound distaste for New Yorkers. I've never met one that was normal, he wrote to his parents. Several other destinations were in the running, depending on where Sue received offers. Denis continued his dalliance with Houghton Mifflin, and the editor who had agreed to evaluate his novel. He was extremely dissatisfied with her, however. She was only interested in comparing who knew more famous writers, Denis wrote. He considered requesting a male editor.

When spring graduation approached, Denis submitted his thesis to his examining committee. Bell was his thesis supervisor, with Justice and Engle filling out the rest of the group. He entitled the thesis *The White Fires of Venus,* after a poetic meditation on loneliness he'd composed as a graduate student. The manuscript comprised forty poems, about half of which came from *Man among the Seals,* now five years behind him. Many of the other poems had been published as well—nine different journals were cited in the submission. It was a dazzling collection of poetry for a young writing student, but it also reflected what Bell called a "period of stasis" that had occurred during Denis's years in the MFA program.

Graduation failed to push Denis and Sue to leave Iowa City. Sue did not enroll in graduate school in the fall of 1974. Instead, the couple remained in Iowa City, sometimes together, sometime apart. Denis devoted himself to his novel, charting his progress day by day. Another grant, this one for $5,000, helped keep him afloat. He told his parents that he'd conquered his battles with alcohol. The key, he said, was working. When he wasn't working, he used alcohol as a "temporary suicide"—something he'd now figured out how to avoid.

Near the end of 1974, another tragedy among the Vine community occurred that would be part of the impetus to finally drive Denis out of Iowa. Jeff Hottel had left town after his acquittal and taken a job as a forest ranger in Truckee, California. He came back to Iowa City for what he told friends was just a pit stop on the way to another adventure in another part of the country. He never made it out of town. On November 25, 1974, police found him dead in an apartment on Iowa Avenue. It was ruled an overdose.

Hottel was a well-liked member of his social group, and his death hit everybody hard. His move to California had been an attempt to escape the drug scene. Hottel died on a Saturday night. The following Tuesday, Denis, Sue, and several other friends went to St. Paul's Lutheran Chapel for the funeral service. They took a seat in the balcony.

Toward the end of the service, Hottel's parents walked to the front of the church and stood at the casket. From the balcony view, Hottel's mother, a petite blonde woman, appeared to be sobbing, her body heaving, overcome with grief. The sight of a mother in such distress had a profound effect on Sue. "All of the sudden, I had this thought that it could be me, and that could be my mother standing there. I thought how absolutely ashamed she would be. I was just completely rattled by it," Sue said. "I remember walking home, by myself and thinking, for once and for all, 'I have to get out of this scene.'"

10 ADRIFT

Smooth seas do not make skillful sailors.

—African proverb

A year or so after he left Iowa City, Denis's friend Maury Barr was in Miami when he decided it was time to pay his old pal a visit. He had heard Denis and Sue were in Chicago, so he pulled onto the highway and headed north. On the road, he picked up a few hitchhikers, part-time orange harvesters who agreed to help pay for gas. Barr drove for hours and hours, finally arriving in Chicago well after dark, hitchhikers in tow. He found Denis and Sue's apartment, knocked on the door, and asked Denis if it would be all right if he and the hitchhikers came in and stayed the night. Denis was visibly annoyed and declined the request. A year earlier, a group of random unannounced strangers sleeping on the floor would have been no problem, but no longer. The orange pickers spent the night in the car.

Inviting a group of hitchhikers into his apartment was not, at the time, the environment Denis wanted to create. He and Sue were indeed back together, but it hadn't been easy. After she left Iowa, Sue had gone back to her hometown of Albert Lea, Minnesota, to live with her mother. Denis had relocated as well. After nearly seven and a half years in Iowa City, he found a job as an adjunct English professor at Lake Forest College in suburban Chicago. Lake Forest was an exclusive private school near the shores of Lake Michigan with a student body made up largely of the children of the moneyed Chicago business class. Many of the students were at Lake Forest because they had not been extended admission in the Ivy League. Faculty members at the time sarcastically transformed the meaning of the school's abbreviation, LFC, to "last fucking chance," because of the large percentage of students biding their time, trying to get a degree while waiting to go into the family business.

He settled in downtown Chicago. The parents of a friend from Iowa owned a duplex, and Denis occupied the top floor. The job at Lake Forest was only part time and did not pay much, so he often took factory work to supplement his income. He would get up before sunrise and take a train to an office building, where state employment officers hired laborers to work on a day-to-day basis. The labor pool consisted largely of alcoholics and people without housing, and Denis, still battling his demons, saw his future in their faces. "I sensed I'd be living here, too, someday, and I observed electrically and sadly my future all around me… a bum woke up in the gutter right beside where I stood. He felt in the waist of his pants and came up with a pint bottle, half full. He tipped it up and gurgled it steadily until he'd emptied it all down into him. I was only twenty-four or -five, but already I could have told you how important it tasted."

He was still heartbroken from his latest breakup with Sue. He began calling her and begging her to come back to him. Things will be better, he told her. Things will be different—you'll see. Sue was reluctant at first, but Denis was persistent. He would go to a phone booth every night after work, dial Sue's number, and tell her about how exciting their lives would be in the city together. She finally agreed, and the two were back together again in the duplex. Sue signed up with a temp agency and found a job at the Cook County electricians union.

Denis did not dedicate himself to the work of teaching English as he had at Cornell College the year before. Something about the job ignited his rebellious impulses. He wore his hair down to his shoulders and did not fit in with the conservative bent of the faculty. When Barr came to visit him at his apartment, the semester was nearly over, and Denis had only graded a few weeks of his students' writing submissions. He told one of his students that he'd found a way to solve the problem. Instead of grading each essay by hand, he would throw the entire pile of essays down the stairs at his apartment, then assign grades depending on where each essay fell on the staircase.

Barbara Guenther was another young faculty member at Lake Forest at the time. Guenther got the feeling that Denis wasn't very committed to the profession. She and Denis would ride the train from Evanston to Lake Forest and chitchat about work. At the time, a train rider could buy ten-pass tickets instead of purchasing a single ticket every day. Doing so would save a considerable amount of money on fares. Guenther bought the pass every week and told Denis about the value. Denis declined. That was farther in advance than he was willing to plan, he told her.

They rarely talked about their personal lives on the train, but once a comment about Denis's homelife slipped out. Guenther had recommended to Denis a potential change to his schedule and asked how he would feel about it. He couldn't even consider it, Denis told her. If he wasn't home at a certain time, there would be "hell to pay" with his girlfriend.

Sue and Denis were still drinking heavily. They didn't have connections in Chicago like they did in Iowa City, so drugs were hard to come by. Alcohol became the recreational drug of choice. Sue thought Denis's alcoholism was worsening. She had written to Vera the year before about the situation when she thought it was getting better. Her father had been an alcoholic, so she knew the signs intimately. Denis "has made certain promises," Sue wrote, "and you can be sure he won't be an alcoholic if he lives with me."

In Chicago, however, Denis's drinking was steadily increasing. The promises of change that he had made to entice Sue to come back to him did not materialize. She was drinking too, but not to the degree that Denis was, and she did not drink to the level of madness that he reached on a regular basis. Life moved from crisis to crisis. Sue got pregnant and decided to have an abortion. Denis was not supportive, and the incident further damaged their relationship. The situation led to an argument between them that soon became physical. The sounds of violence went on long enough for the neighbors on the floor below to call the police. During the confrontation, Denis pushed Sue's head into the wall. She was bleeding and in tears when the police arrived. Denis calmly talked to the officers, showing little sign of the fight that had preceded their arrival. He told them that Sue was out of control. According to Sue, the officers told Denis to "take a walk next time," then left. "Denis could be really glib. He could talk his way out of anything," she said. Later, she went to the hospital, where a doctor stitched up her wound. The incident was yet another sign that Denis was becoming more and more helpless to fight his addictions, as well as the impulses that came with them. It would be years before he would be able to clearly make the connection between addiction and his behavior, or do anything about it. Many years later, he would reckon with it through his fiction. "Nothing I could think up, no matter how dramatic or completely horrible," he would write, "ever made her repent or love me the way she had at first, before she really knew me."

At the end of the academic year, a job listing for an adjunct professor of English appeared on the bulletin board in the English-Philosophy Building at the University of Iowa. Denis's former classmate, Mary Swander, was nearing graduation, so she inquired about the job. Wasn't that where Denis worked? she asked. Another grad student told her that indeed it was the same college, but Denis had been "kicked out." That's strange, she thought. She asked for further details, but none were forthcoming. "Oh, that's just Denis," she was told. She eventually took the job at Lake Forest, and when she arrived on campus in the fall, she found that "Denis had left a trail of stories behind him on the way out."

*

Denis turned twenty-seven on July 1, 1976, just three days before the United States of America turned two hundred. It was America's bicentennial summer, and all around the country, patriotic celebrations were planned to celebrate the history and achievements of the world's greatest democracy. It was also, in actuality, the final, conclusive end of the '60s. Richard Nixon had resigned over the Watergate scandal and climbed into a helicopter on the White House lawn in 1974. In April 1975, the last Americans had climbed into another helicopter, this one on the roof of the American embassy in Saigon, in view of North Vietnamese tanks that were rolling over the gates of the presidential palace, bringing the interminable Vietnam War to a conclusion for the United States. Gerald Ford was president now. In a few short days, he would be flown by yet another helicopter onto the USS *Nashville,* part of a 225-ship armada that would sail the Hudson River in New York to toast Independence Day and the bicentennial of the great democratic experiment. Hundreds upon thousands would "jam the shores of lower Manhattan, some dangling from trees like so many Christmas decorations, to watch the dazzling fireworks explode over the harbor and the Statue of Liberty."

Denis and Sue had recently attended a celebration as well. The previous month, Nancy had gotten remarried to Jack Settle, a divorced father of two whom Nancy had met shortly after she split with Denis. The wedding had taken place on a farm owned by Nancy's sister outside of Iowa City. Every remaining hippie in Iowa came to the party. Denis, perhaps channeling his father's State Department protocol, was the only person there in a coat and tie. There was a big tent, a live band playing rock 'n' roll, and an enormous cloud of marijuana smoke hovering above the festivities. When it came time for the actual nuptials, Settle made a half-hearted attempt to quiet the crowd. Then he, Nancy, and Morgan got together in the center of the gathering, and a skinny girl with glasses waved her arm over them, causing the entire audience to hoot and whistle, and bringing the marriage ceremony to a decisive conclusion.

The wedding was a short break on a cross-country trip toward a planned relocation for Denis and Sue. Their friend and former roommate from Iowa City, Scott Walker, was living in Port Townsend, Washington, and had recently gotten into the publishing business. He contacted Denis with the idea of publishing another book of Denis's poems. Come on out to Washington, he told them. Even if you're broke, you can live off the land. "Living on 1,000 bucks a year is always difficult, but less so here," Walker wrote to Denis. "The garden grows, the water waits, and there are always food stamps."

Denis and Sue were indeed broke. To earn a little money, though, Denis agreed to drive someone's van from Chicago to Washington for a fee. They drove the vehicle to Nancy's wedding, and, as a present to the newlyweds, agreed to take Morgan with them to Washington and watch him for the summer. Once the three of them got on the road, Denis explained the van delivery agreement to seven-year-old Morgan, who promptly spilled a milkshake all over the floor. It was an ominous sign for the summer to come.

Port Townsend, Washington, is a small city on the tip of Quimper Peninsula, looking out over the water of Puget Sound, an hour's ferry ride from Seattle. Denis and Sue rented a small house in Port Townsend and settled in. The cost of rent had left them with little money for food, so Denis tried to follow Walker's advice to live off the land. He brought Morgan along on his attempts to hunt for clams to feed the household. Denis tried to make a father–son game out of it, but at night, Morgan would go into the kitchen and see several children's buckets filled with dead and dying clams, which, a little later, would be served to him for dinner.

Childcare was not priority number one for Denis and Sue, and Morgan suffered because of it. Early on in their stay in the rental house, Morgan discovered a stack of porn magazines that had been left by the previous occupant. He showed them to his father. Denis told his son to use the magazines to make friends. Morgan dutifully went around the neighborhood and started passing out the magazines to any willing children. Parents in the neighborhood began to find their six- and seven-year-olds with pornography, and when the kids pointed the finger at Morgan, his choice of playmates dwindled to nothing. As a result, he spent the entire summer isolated and alone.

*

A few buckets of clams were not going to be enough to sustain them, so Denis needed to find a way to generate income. His friend Maury Barr had also migrated to Washington state and was living nearby in Seattle. Denis called him up and asked him to come to Port Townsend and help him make some money. They lived near the water, so their first plan was to get into the fishing business. Neither knew the first thing about commercial fishing, but that did not seem at the time to be an insurmountable obstacle. They found what they thought was a suitable boat to start their business lying in somebody's yard in town with a "for sale" sign on it. It was a typical Puget Sound fishing boat, about eighteen feet long, with a cabin in case of bad weather. Somehow they came up with $300 and bought the boat. Soon after the transaction, they began to realize the amount of work it needed to make it operable, which was considerable. "I think the guy who sold it to us really was just unloading his piece of junk," Barr recalled. The boat never made it into the water, and the business never got off the ground.

Another money-making scheme revolved around poker. As a graduate student in the Writers' Workshop, Denis found he enjoyed playing cards and had an aptitude for it. Poker was a popular pastime around the English-Philosophy Building while he was there, and Denis spent considerable time at the poker table with fellow grad students and sometime even with faculty members such as Don Justice, a noted gambling enthusiast, and Ray Carver. His success at cards led him to write home to ask Al for books to improve his game. Al obliged and sent Denis *The Complete Guide to Winning Poker* by Albert Morehead. "Poker is a game of skill. If you aren't beating the game, you're being outplayed," Morehead declared on the book jacket. Denis absorbed the book and became a Morehead disciple. "He had that one famous poker book, and he carried it with him everywhere he went," recalled Walker. "He was always memorizing the odds and practicing ways to remember cards. He was really into it."

In Washington, Denis hit on cards as a possible solution to his financial problems. He and Maury, Denis decided, were going to become professional poker players, free themselves from the nine-to-five life, and live off their winnings. It was time to put the Albert Morehead system into action. Denis found a card room near the naval base in Bremerton. He brought Maury with him to the card room, gave him $50, and told him to follow the system. Also, Denis said, whatever you do, don't drink. Maury followed the system, and soon the chips began to accumulate. The plan was working. Once Maury got significantly into the black, he thought he could relax the no-drinking rule that Denis had put in place for their poker partnership. He ordered a scotch. And then another. And another, and soon, the winnings were gone, and eventually, the $50 that Denis had given him was gone. The poker partnership did not last much longer either.

*

There was a fledgling literature community forming in Port Townsend around the time that Denis and Sue came to town. A group of poetry enthusiasts had started a publishing house called the Copper Canyon Press in Colorado in 1972 and had relocated to the area in 1974. Copper Canyon began working with Centrum, a nonprofit arts agency formed around the same time and operating out of Fort Worden State Park. The social life of this new literary community revolved around an establishment called the Town Tavern.

Clientele at the Town Tavern was a mixture of fishermen, loggers, and people associated with the arts community. The tavern boasted a thirteen-by-six-foot painting of a nude woman, back provocatively arched, with a half dozen demon-like creatures leering at her from above, the creation of a local artist in exchange for beer and a few nights' lodging in the room above the bar. In fact, Town Tavern employees were often paid for their labor with access to the rooms on the floor above the barroom.

Jim Heynen, a poet from Minnesota who had studied at the University of Iowa, had recently moved to the area to take the position of literature director for Centrum. He remembered drinking with Denis at the Town Tavern on numerous occasions. One night, the two were having a beer together when an extremely drunk customer came over to their table and began to threaten them, menacingly waving around a beer bottle. Denis showed himself to be both fearless and a veteran of similar barroom confrontations, Heynen recalled. Denis looked up at the drunk and said, "I bet you couldn't break that bottle over your own head." The drunk took him up on the challenge: he brought the bottle down hard on his skull, and the resulting commotion of shattered glass and head wounds brought the argument to a conclusion.

The bar fight was not the only outcome of Denis's association with Heynen. Through Centrum, Heynen was organizing a workshop for gifted high school writers and was looking for instructors. Denis agreed to participate and looked forward to the much-needed paycheck.

In his homelife, though, conditions were slowly deteriorating. The volatility in Denis and Sue's relationship that existed in Iowa and Chicago continued in Port Townsend. This time, there was a child around to witness a lot of it. Denis's young son was the unintended victim of much of the warfare between the two of them. "There was a lot of fighting and drinking, and then makeup sex, then screaming again," Morgan remembered. "It was just a whole summer of that."

Near the end of the summer, Nancy learned of the circumstances her son was living in, and she decided it was time for Morgan to come home. She sent her new husband to retrieve her son. The vehicle that arrived in Port Townsend seemed like a mobile version of the hippie wedding from earlier in the summer. The car door opened and several empty Olympia beer cans fell out, along with Morgan's stepfather, a couple of women in full '60s regalia, and a cloud of pot smoke. Jack Settle said a few words to Denis, Morgan was told to get in the car, and shortly, his summer vacation in the great Northwest had reached its sad conclusion.

Denis did not remain a resident of Port Townsend much longer than his son. The pattern of breaking up and getting back together with Sue continued. Sue began to feel that Denis was mentally unstable. All the drinking of the past few years had led to significant changes in his personality. In the past, she had thought some of his more outlandish behavior was an act—a performance as a brilliant alcoholic writer awash in his own genius. But now she began to "realize that there was some real craziness there." She feared for her own safety. When an argument between them would grow intense, Denis would withhold food from her. There were more breakups. For a while she went to live with Walker and his girlfriend; then she moved back in with Denis. Finally she felt she could not remain with Denis any longer, and for the last time, in Port Townsend at least, she packed up her belongings and moved out.

Soon after Sue left, Denis was walking down the street, confused and inebriated. For some reason, on this outing he had put an alarm clock in his pocket before he'd gone out, perhaps thinking he wouldn't make it home and would need the clock to wake him up in the morning. He saw a pickup truck filled with teenagers. In his disoriented state, Denis thought a woman in the front seat was Sue. He called out to her by name as the truck drove by. The driver of the truck heard the shout and turned the truck around. Denis, thinking he was about to come under attack, took the alarm clock out of his pocket and threw it at the truck, breaking the windshield. The woman was not Sue, and now, Denis believed, the teenagers were coming after him. He managed to evade them.

Denis showed up at Heynen's house later that evening, desperate to get out of town. He explained the situation to Heynen, telling him about the violent teenagers out for revenge, and the two planned Denis's escape under the cover of darkness. They drove to Denis's house and packed up what they could of his belongings. In their haste, much of Denis's writing was left behind. Heynen accompanied Denis on a late-night ferry from Port Townsend to Seattle and on to a friend's house, who agreed to let Denis stay for a while. Then Heynen took the ferry back to Port Townsend.

Soon after, it was time for the first class of the Centrum workshop for gifted high school writers that Denis was supposed to participate in. Heynen began the class and let the students introduce themselves. One of them had a story to share. Just a few nights earlier, he and a few friends his had been driving in their pickup truck when a deranged person had shouted at them, and then, for no discernible reason, had thrown an alarm clock through their windshield.

UNPREDICTABLE WEATHER

11

An alcoholic is someone you don't like who drinks as much as you do. —**Dylan Thomas**

Scott Walker had taken his own meandering journey from Iowa City to Port Townsend since he had been the third roommate in Denis and Sue's secret welfare apartment back in Iowa City. He had left the Midwest and gone on an extended camping trip through the wilds of Canada. Then he had slowly made his way back down into the United States, working in logging mills and restaurants, first settling in Gig Harbor, near Tacoma, Washington, then finally landing on the Quimper Peninsula. Walker had studied religion and philosophy as an undergraduate at the University of Oregon, but it was his love of poetry that had brought him to Iowa City years before, and now he decided he would put his fascination and knowledge with the craft to work and become a publisher.

He started a small poetry magazine called *Twelve Poems,* which featured the work of a variety of poets. Soon, however, he found that he was more suited to books and liked the idea of working as an editor with a single author on a full-length book project. Resources and infrastructure are needed to become a book publisher, though, and Walker had little of either. He had heard a quote by the poet Ezra Pound years before: "The key to economics is low overhead." That would be his motto as he entered the publishing business at the ground floor.

He bought an old printing press and got it in working order as cheaply as he could, searching for scraps and discarded parts wherever he could find them. Because the letterpress he had acquired was obsolete, he could get the equipment he needed for next to nothing. Once he was operational, he christened his new publishing business Graywolf Press, after the nearby Graywolf River and Graywolf Ridge in the Olympia Mountains.

The next step was to decide whom and what to publish. He resolved that he would use this new entity to discover outstanding young poets and introduce them to the world. Many of them had been floating around Iowa City while he was there. One of them happened to find him before he could find her. Tess Gallagher heard about Graywolf and went to see Walker at Imprint Bookstore in downtown Port Townsend. Gallagher had accepted a teaching job in upstate New York after Iowa City but was back in the area, visiting. She had been working on a book of poetry since she left Iowa City and now thought it was ready. Graywolf's first book, they decided, would also be Tess Gallagher's first book, and it would be called *Instructions to the Double.*

The production process for the first Graywolf release would not be a lightning-quick affair. Walker worked with Gallagher on her poems, section by section. Gallagher revised and revised, and then revised again. Before the manuscript was even deemed ready, Walker began the physical printing process. He was Graywolf's sole employee, though his girlfriend agreed to help out occasionally. Graywolf operated out of the tiny burg of Irondale, just south of Port Townsend. With the help of a chicken-farming neighbor, he constructed a small building that was called the "print shack," where the production would take place.

Each copy of *Instructions to the Double* had to be hand printed on the ancient press. The process was laborious. The letters were set by hand; then each page was printed and folded, and gathered into sections. Then they were sewn together with a needle and thread. "On quite a few of those little books, the buyer would find the blood of the binder smeared in the center seam," Walker said. The process was followed for nine long months, ten hours a day, seven days a week, book by book, until, finally, he had 1,500 copies ready for sale.

Walker released *Instructions to the Double* into the world in 1976. It was eighty-six pages of deeply personal poetry, including poems about Gallagher's childhood, family tragedies, elegies to the region where she was formed. The entire run of 1,500 copies sold out in less than two months, a level of sales unheard of for a collection of poetry—even more so for an unknown publisher with no connections or distribution mechanism.

For his next release, Walker decided it was time to resurrect the career of his old friend Denis Johnson. "Denis hadn't had a book published in a long time. It had been seven or eight years or something since his first book, and I just thought he deserved another one," he remembered. Letters were exchanged, publishing plans were made and remade, Denis and Sue moved west, and Denis's next book was soon in the Graywolf pipeline. Still aggravated and reeling from the agonizing production process on Gallagher's book, Walker decided the printing of this one would be outsourced. He found a designer and printer in Portland to handle the production. The editing process was smooth as well. "His poems didn't need much editing, frankly, I didn't think," Walker said. "We had some editorial back-and-forth, but my involvement was much lighter with Denis's work."

The poems required little to no editing perhaps because almost all of them had been part of Denis's master's thesis and had been thoroughly reviewed by Marvin Bell, Donald Justice, and Paul Engle. Denis included only one poem that had been written since he left Iowa, the title poem, "An Inner Weather." The short author bio that Denis contributed alluded to the causes of the dry spell: "After spending a year in the stark realism of Evanston, Illinois, Johnson reports powerful dreams of South America and the West."

Denis's verbal contract with Graywolf did not include monetary payment. "Pay will include, of course, fame and sultry women," Walker told him. Walker did, however, expect Denis to be involved in marketing the book. He suggested some readings and book signings, and he floated the possibility of a book-launch event at Epstein's

Books in Iowa City. "You've got to do at least half the work in hustling this thing," Walker wrote, "though that's a distasteful side of the business."

Inner Weather did not have the success in the marketplace that Graywolf had seen with *Instructions to the Double.* Gallagher had thrown herself into the promotion of her book, and it had paid off. "Tess was very aggressive in getting her name out there," Walker said. "She saw the business side of poetry." Denis, as might be expected given what else was going on in his life, did not participate in book marketing or hold any events. He rejected Walker's ideas for signings and readings. His dislike of the promotion process, which he would harbor for most of his writing career, had already taken hold. He told Walker he preferred a "put it out in the world and see what happens" approach. Walker took that into account and printed six hundred copies of *Inner Weather,* of which he was left with a good portion after the initial release.

Graywolf Press almost didn't survive its first year. Despite Walker's efforts to follow Ezra Pound's low-overhead dictum, he was severely in the red and on the brink of collapse. "Every day was a wild, pressure-filled, anxiety-producing adventure," he said. As a grasp at national exposure, he went looking for prize contests he could enter. Fortuitously, 1976 was the first year of a new national contest, the George Elliston Book Award, sponsored by the University of Cincinnati. Only small nonprofit presses were eligible. Walker packaged up his two books and mailed them off to Cincinnati, where they became two of the 340 volumes of poetry published in 1976 to go before the judges. When the judging was complete, Graywolf had swept the competition. *Instructions to the Double* had won the grand prize, and Denis's book was one of only two honorable mentions.

The prizes and the reaction to those first two books were enough to keep Walker in the publishing business despite ongoing financial peril. Within a few years, the press was publishing between ten and fifteen books a year, aggressively marketing them, and competing successfully with more established small presses. In 1985, Walker moved the press to St. Paul, Minnesota, and by 1993 Graywolf had achieved a $1 million budget. Walker left Graywolf in 1994. As of early 2024, Graywolf Press is one of the leading independent publishers in the United States; publishes thirty to thirty-five books a year of poetry, fiction, and nonfiction; and has an annual budget of more than $4 million. Its authors have won Nobel prizes, Pulitzer prizes, Booker prizes, and all sorts of other prizes, but Graywolf also has the distinction of being the press behind the only book that Denis Johnson would publish during the entire decade of the 1970s.

*

Denis and Sue continued to stay in each other's orbit around western Washington, like two asteroids on separate but adjacent trajectories. Denis moved in with Maury and his girlfriend, Carol, for a while in Seattle, then got his own apartment in the First Hill region of the city. He took a job as a temporary typist, capitalizing on the secretarial skills he'd honed at Iowa. Maury had taken a job bartending. Sometimes Denis would come in when his friend was working. One night, Denis was particularly smitten with a young woman in the bar who told him she was a belly dancer. He was also, as usual, completely drunk. Maury knew the woman, and he also knew that she was a prostitute and was working with another bartender, who happened to have a dangerous and violent history. Despite Maury's repeated attempts to talk Denis out of pursuing her, Denis continued. "I kept trying to tell him, and here he's a few sheets to the wind, and I'm trying to tell him she's just going to take all your money, or whatever else you have," Maury said. Denis left with the woman, and Maury did not see him for several days. Denis never filled in the rest of the story for his friend, but the belly dancer would live on in fiction, in *Jesus' Son* twenty years later: "I liked her the minute I'd seen her for the first time. She was resting at a table between numbers in the Greek nightclub where she was dancing. A little of the stage light touched her. She was very frail. She seemed to be thinking about something far away, waiting patiently for somebody to destroy her."

Denis soon packed up and moved again, this time to Gig Harbor, a small town on Puget Sound about twenty-five miles south of Seattle.

He rented a house and started a relationship with a female guard from the local prison. His alcoholism continued to get worse. Maury came to visit him and found Denis to be drunk nearly all the time. He appeared, to Maury, to have become a classic alcoholic. Denis showed his friend where he had hidden bottles of liquor in the hedges around his house. He also told Maury that he had begun to experience blackouts, something that had not happened to him before.

Sue lived off unemployment in Port Townsend for as long as it lasted, then moved to Seattle and took a job as a waitress at the Hotel Sorrento, an iconic Seattle landmark. She lasted one day. Soon she found a more stable job. Her attraction to Denis remained alive and well. She found out where he was living in Gig Harbor and began to go down to visit him. "We kept hooking up," she said. "It was like we couldn't live together but we couldn't live apart."

The desperation was growing, and alcohol was having less and less of the desired numbing effect. Still, Denis could not get himself to stop drinking. He would later describe a "crawly" sensation that appeared when he hadn't had a drink for a while. He constantly felt the need to escape his environment, to do anything to change his circumstances. But he once again found himself without enough money to effect change. He traded his typewriter for cash in Tacoma pawnshop. Despite his previous near-death experience, he decided to try hitchhiking again and headed down the coast. He told Maury mournfully that the world was different now. The '60s and the days of love, peace, and togetherness were long gone. Hippies were being murdered in sleeping bags, and Denis was afraid he'd be next.

Alan Soldofsky, Denis's friend and classmate from the University of Iowa, was working in Cody's Books in Berkeley, California, at the time. One day, he looked out the front window of the store and saw Denis on the sidewalk, panhandling with a sign. He appeared to be, Soldofsky thought, just as bad as, or even worse than, the strung-out drug addicts, relics of the previous decade who had then populated the streets of Berkeley. "He was really ashamed and embarrassed. He needed money but he wouldn't take any from me, or any favors," Soldofsky said.

Somehow, Denis made it back to the state of Washington. At some point, he spent time in a rehabilitation center, but after release, he resumed the same lifestyle. One day, he showed up at Sue's door and told her he had blacked out again and did not remember the last four days. He had woken up, he told her, on the floor of somebody's apartment in Tacoma, with no memory of anything and the deep-seated feeling that something terrible had happened. The physical effects of alcoholism were clearly visible. He was bloated and pale, his speech was slurred. He told Sue that now he kept drinking even though it wasn't fun anymore. He couldn't stop, he said. He begged her for help. She agreed to let him stay if he promised to look for a job. He moved in but did not fulfill his promise. Instead, he stole from Sue and went out drinking. She told him, for what would truly be the final time, that it was over between them and that he had to leave.

*

There began to be an awareness within Denis that he was falling so deep into a hole that it was becoming impossible to return to the surface. The lifeline that was his writing was nearly gone as well. His typewriter was sitting on the shelf in the pawnshop in Tacoma. He'd lost some pages of his writing along the way. He began to contemplate suicide. Once, he secured some pills that would do the job and walked out to the beach, holding the bottle in his hand. He sat on a log, looked over the water of Puget Sound, and thought about how his life had collapsed, and how his lifelong project of forming a literary career had not come to fruition. He couldn't write. Even his ability to write poetry, something that he'd felt was part of him since he was a teenager, had abandoned him. The sense of failure was palpable. Years later, he would view those moments on the beach as a turning point, but at the time, he struggled for the will to go on. Eventually, he talked himself out of taking the pills by convincing himself to try, one last time, to write what was inside him, this time with no interference from the outside world.

In the meantime, word of his condition had traveled from Washington down to Scottsdale, Arizona, to his parents. Vera decided it was time to retrieve her wayward son. She contacted Sue's mother in Minnesota, who in turn called Sue in Seattle. Where was Denis? she wanted to know. How bad was it? Sue told her about the blackouts and the stolen money and the constant drinking. She told Vera that she had kicked Denis out, and that after he left, he'd continue to call her, so regularly that she'd had to unplug the phone. Vera told Sue that it was time for Denis to come home.

It had been a year and a half since he left Chicago and three years since he'd completed graduate school in Iowa. As soon as it could be arranged, a ticket was purchased and sent to Seattle. Denis packed up what remained of his belongings and climbed aboard a bus to begin a journey that would take him from the ocean to the desert, and from the bottom of the hole back up to the surface.

Denis and Nancy Jo Lister cut the cake at their wedding in August 1968. The couple was married in Nancy's hometown of Dallas Center, Iowa. Photo courtesy of Nancy Lister-Settle.

Denis and Nancy Jo stand with their son, Morgan, in Nancy Jo's hometown of Dallas Center, Iowa. Morgan was born while Denis was a sophomore at the University of Iowa. Photo courtesy of Nancy Lister-Settle.

Denis and Nancy Jo celebrate Morgan's first birthday. The couple made their first home in the University of Iowa's married housing complex on Hawkeye Drive. Photo courtesy of Nancy Lister-Settle.

Paul Engle, director of the Iowa Writers' Workshop from 1941 to 1965, speaks with students at the University of Iowa. Engle was a mentor and father figure to Denis during his years in Iowa City. Courtesy of Frederick W. Kent photograph collection, University Archives, University of Iowa Libraries.

IOWA CITY PRESS-CITIZEN

14 PAGES — IOWA CITY, IOWA, SATURDAY, AUGUST 9, 1969 — 10 CENTS

3 Arrested, Drugs Seized in Raid Here

Seized in Drug Raid

Seven bags of processed marijuana, kilo molds, machetes and other drug paraphernalia were confiscated in a raid early this morning at a farm southwest of Iowa City. Johnson County sheriff's deputies, aided by a state narcotics agent and Iowa City police, arrested three persons at the farm house.

Marijuana Sale Value Of $36,000

By ROBERT R. ROSS
Of the Press - Citizen

Three persons were arrested and more than 150 pounds of processed marijuana were confiscated early this morning on a farm about four miles southwest of Iowa City.

Johnson County Sheriff's Department raided the farm after obtaining a search warrant signed by Justice of Peace T. E. Lyon.

Those arrested were Barbara Blair, 21, of Iowa City, Timothy Griffith, 18, of Ames and Steven McCurdy, 19, of Oskaloosa. They were charged with possession of marijuana with intent to sell.

Violent Storms Rage Across Iowa

Basic Income for the Poor In Nixon's New Welfare Plan

WASHINGTON (AP) — President Nixon wants a "New Federalism" that will ship tax dollars and job programs out of Washington and nationalize the welfare system and give every poor family a basic income.

Reaction: Page 4B

Long Quarantine For Astronauts May End on Sunday

Proposals At a Glance

Strict Limiting On Nerve Gas Seen

What's Where

On Inside Pages

Local Weather

The front page of the *Iowa City Press-Citizen* reports the raid of a farmhouse outside of town where arrests were made and drugs were seized. Denis spent time with friends at the farmhouse, and it was later the setting for several stories in *Jesus' Son*.

Susan Fletcher was a student in the first poetry workshop Denis took at the University of Iowa. The two would become a couple a few years later and live together in Iowa City, Chicago, and Washington state. He later fictionalized aspects of their relationship in *Jesus' Son.*

Denis and his son, Morgan, enjoy a swim in the pool at his parents' home in Scottsdale in the late '70s. Denis moved to Phoenix from Seattle to enter a rehabilitation facility in 1978 and spent two years there reviving his writing career. Photo by Jane Krause.

Denis and Jane Krause pose at the Phoenix airport in the late '70s. Denis met Jane at an Alcoholics Anonymous meeting in 1978, and the couple lived together until Denis moved to Provincetown in 1980. Photo courtesy of Jane Krause.

Denis reads on the front porch of the Robert Frost house in Franconia, New Hampshire, on June 14, 1983. Denis was the poet in residence at the Frost house in the summer of 1983. He lived in the famous poet's home for the summer and worked on the novel *Fiskadoro*. Photo by Ruben Perez for the *Boston Globe*. Courtesy of Northeastern University Archives and Special Collections.

Denis stands next to the artist Sam Messer. The two met at the Fine Arts Work Center in Provincetown, Massachusetts, in 1981, where they became friends and collaborated on projects. Photo courtesy of Sam Messer.

Denis poses with his dog in Wellfleet, Massachusetts. Denis and his second wife, Lucinda, moved to Wellfleet after they got married in 1982. Photo courtesy of Lucinda Johnson.

Denis stands with Morgan on a visit to Iowa in 1984. At left is the Datsun sports car, painted with the words "Maniac Drifter," a phrase from Denis's first novel, *Angels*. Photo courtesy of Nancy Lister-Settle.

Denis rides in a boat with Sandinista rebels in Nicaragua in the early '80s. He became an international correspondent and reported in war zones around the world for several magazines. Photo courtesy of Richard Pearce.

Actor Billy Crudup starred as Fuckhead in the movie adaptation of *Jesus' Son*. Photo courtesy of Sam Messer.

In a scene from the movie *Jesus' Son*, Denis played Terrence Weber, a character from his short story "Emergency." Jack Black (left) gave Denis acting advice during filming. Photo courtesy of Evenstar Films.

Denis speaks with attendees at a book signing in Santa Fe, New Mexico, in 2007. He became much more comfortable in public appearances later in his career. Photo by Don J. Usner.

In the early '90s, Denis moved to the northern tip of Idaho and lived on a ranch near the town of Bonners Ferry. He spent much of his time in Idaho for the rest of his life. Photo courtesy of Sam Messer.

Denis speaks with James Magnuson, the director of the Center for Writers at the University of Texas. Denis taught writing at the University of Texas and several other universities over the course of his career. Photo courtesy of Jim Magnuson.

The Eckharts still have photos of what was left of the cars involved in the fatal crash. Photo by Ted Geltner.

The crash took place on Big Creek Bridge on Highway 69 outside of Bethany, Missouri. In those days, it was the most dangerous stretch of highway in the state. Photo by Ted Geltner.

A PLACE FOR PEOPLE LIKE US

12

But what about the real alcoholic? He may start off as a moderate drinker; he may not become a continuous hard drinker; but at some stage of his drinking career, he begins to lose all control of his liquor consumption, once he starts to drink. —**Alcoholics Anonymous, *The Big Book***

The Maverick House was a twenty-two-unit rehab center housed in a dilapidated motel on East Van Buren Street in Phoenix. It was run by fifty-two-year-old W. L. (Skip) Carter, a man who had drunk himself into the gutter in his younger days, then discovered Alcoholics Anonymous in middle age and decided to dedicate his life to saving discarded old alcoholics like himself. Carter founded the Maverick House in 1967, and when Denis arrived in 1978, it treated about thirty men and women at a time on a short-term basis, and kept another dozen for long-term treatment. The Maverick House preached the gospel of Alcoholics Anonymous. Before treatment could begin in earnest, patients had to admit to their addictions. Then they would begin the long, excruciatingly difficult process, first laid out for the public fifty years before, of giving an honest account of their condition, submitting to a higher power, and starting out on their lifelong journey to recovery.

The term *Alcoholics Anonymous,* or any other addiction with the word *anonymous* placed after it, long ago became shorthand for a group of people telling each other stories of their worst experiences related to their vice of choice as a kind of group therapy. The idea was born during the Great Depression when a doctor named Bob Wilson decided he could help maintain his recently achieved sobriety by helping another man, Bill Smith, get sober too. The idea at the heart of the program was that alcoholism was not a personal weakness on the part of the drunk; it was an actual malady that had to be cured through treatment, something that could be accomplished with the help of others who had gone through a similar process. The two men, who had beaten their addictions with the help of Christianity, formed an alcoholics-only fellowship. Through the experiences of the men in the fellowship, a twelve-step recovery method developed. The history, method, and theories of the group were crystalized in 1939 with the publication of a volume entitled *Alcoholics Anonymous,* also referred to as *The Big Book.*

When Denis started the program in earnest, Alcoholics Anonymous had been around for nearly five decades. There were twenty-eight thousand Alcoholics Anonymous groups in ninety-two countries. More than two million copies of *The Big Book* had been sold. The organization claimed to have cured over a million alcoholics, many of whom became devoted to the program, serving as sponsors for new arrivals.

Graduates of the Maverick House were told to begin a daily program to keep clean and sober. Denis embarked on his journey after release. He threw himself into the daily program with the gusto that he had previously reserved for his pursuit of drugs and alcohol. He attended AA meetings daily. Shortly his physical appearance began to change. The overweight, blotchy, watery-eyed zombie who had stepped off the bus from Seattle began to show pink in his cheeks and a bounce in his step. He moved in with Al and Vera at their home in Scottsdale. Around the same time, his grandmother, Maggie Childress, had moved in with the family from her home in rural Surrey County, North Carolina. Maggie, an eccentric woman with a strong southern accent, provided a counterpoint to Denis in his struggles to recover from his years of self-abuse. "I was going crazy in a new way," Denis said. "And she was crazy in a pretty standard way."

Denis soon began to reconnect with Morgan, whom he'd spent very little time with during his years in the Northwest. To Morgan, his dad was like a new person. "He was way different. I remember him looking completely different," Morgan remembered. "He started hanging out with me more and talking to me more, interacting with me more in all ways. He was just a more pleasant person."

In the sixteen days he spent at the Maverick House in 1978, Denis became a strict adherent to *The Big Book*. The second step in the program was to "believe that a Power greater than ourselves could restore us to sanity." This belief in a higher power would become a central tenet in his worldview and set him on a lifelong search to find the form and location of his own personal higher power. He had, during his struggle to get sober, a "strong experience of the presence of God," an epiphany that he could not explain but that propelled him to commit further to the spiritual aspects of AA. The cure, he would say later, began to take hold when he saw clearly that he had been deceiving himself all his adult life. "It was increasingly necessary for me to be dishonest with myself in order to keep doing something that was clearly harmful to me," he said. "And I think eventually a person gets to the point where up is down and black is white, and night is day."

The search for spirituality, or for a religion in which he could explore his own spirituality, had begun years earlier for Denis. Al and Vera had not been churchgoers, so as a child Denis had little experience with organized religion. In Manila, he had attended the ritual crucifixion ceremony that was performed annually on Good Friday. Devout Christians carried wooden crosses, and some were willingly crucified in imitation of the death of Jesus Christ. The image affected Denis deeply. He'd flirted with Buddhism as a teenager because of its close association with the Beat movement. Once, while he was still living in Iowa City, he had come back from a forty-eight-hour-long stretch of partying and imbibing and, arriving home, decided it was the perfect time to take Morgan to church. Morgan, a toddler at the time, went along willingly, but once inside the sanctuary, he began to scream curse words uncontrollably. Denis, still under the influence of LSD, said he thought Morgan had become possessed.

In Phoenix, Denis became interested in Catholicism. He began to attend church occasionally and study the precepts of the religion. He took several classes and eventually brought Morgan to a ceremony during which he officially converted to the religion. On another occasion, he convinced a group of monks to allow him to join their monastery for several weeks. Denis followed the practices of the monks, following their rituals and abstaining from sex. He told friends it was part of his exploration of religion and theology, a preoccupation that would continue throughout his life.

Morgan regularly attended AA meetings with Denis when he was in Phoenix visiting his father and grandparents. Denis didn't have the money for a babysitter, so Morgan would tag along and listen to the stories of the other AA members. "I thought that all the stories sounded cool, like fun, and I remember thinking... that you could do all this shit and still come out okay, like all these people did," he recalled.

Number nine in the twelve-step Alcoholics Anonymous program is to "make direct amends to [people we have harmed] wherever possible, except when to do so would injure them or others." Denis approached this step cautiously. One day, Vera showed up at Scott Walker's house in Port Townsend. She told Walker she wanted to apologize for the harm that Denis had caused him. "We had a cup of tea... and she offered her amends, and I sent her on her way. I don't know how many places she stopped. Denis had no reason to offer me amends, he was nothing but nice to me," Walker said. "I was puzzled by the visit, though. I'm not sure that's how it's supposed to work." Denis did not make personal visits to apologize to most of the people he was close to while he was an addict. He would, however, issue a blanket apology "to the people I have lied to" as the dedication on the first book he published after he had achieved sobriety.

*

Though he was dedicated to AA and quickly made meeting attendance a regular part of his life, Denis violated one of the rules of the organization early on. To "thirteen-step" someone, in AA parlance, is to become romantically involved with a member who isn't as far along in the recovery process as you are. Shortly after he left the Maverick House, Denis attended a meeting in Scottsdale. He took a seat in the front row. Once the meeting started, he noticed a young woman in the back of the room. The attraction was immediate. "He stared a hole in me," Jane Krause remembered.

Jane was a college student from Dayton, Ohio, who had come to the desert to study in the fine arts program at Arizona State University. She got caught up in the party scene, and took a trip to Mexico involving too many drugs, too much alcohol, and too few dollars in her bank account. After her return, she decided that AA might be the way to get back on track. The meeting in Scottsdale was only the second or third she had attended.

After the meeting was over, Denis introduced himself. He was, she remembered, exceedingly confident. Denis told Jane he didn't have a car and asked her for a ride home. Perhaps because he was embarrassed to be driven to his parents' house, Denis went out of his way to impress Jane. He managed to slip into their conversation the fact that he had a 162 IQ. When they got to the house, he told her to wait in the car, then came back out and proudly presented her with some of his poetry books.

They quickly became a couple. Within a few weeks, Denis moved into the Phoenix apartment Jane shared with a roommate. Jane asked him to contribute to the rent, so Denis found a job in a Mexican restaurant in nearby Tempe as a dishwasher. Jane worked at various restaurants as a waitress and continued her studies.

They shared an apartment in a working-class neighborhood on East Holly Street in Phoenix. A nearby lesbian bar called the Incognito Lounge with an attractive neon sign, on Thomas Street across from the 7-Eleven, was a neighborhood landmark. The complex that housed their apartment was a cheaply constructed two-story box of a building with a small pool in the middle. The walls in the complex were so thin that it was easy to learn about the lives of neighbors just by listening. Denis, always looking for material, observed and took notes. The other tenants were generally poor and down on their luck. Burglaries were common. Soon after he moved in, somebody broke in and stole the television. Denis laughed off the incident, saying he was better off without it, and expressed gratitude to the robber for leaving his typewriter.

Denis and Jane spent a lot of their free time together. They shared a love for movies and went to the cinema regularly. They made a point to go to the first showing in the Phoenix area of *Apocalypse Now,* the highly anticipated Vietnam epic from director Francis Ford Coppola. Often, they would go to Al and Vera's house in Scottsdale to have dinner and watch television. Al heard Jane was interested in fishing, so he bought her a fishing rod. Denis and Jane took day trips to lakes around the area to use the new rod. They went biking regularly as well, once taking their bikes to the North Rim of the Grand Canyon for a camping vacation. Both had decided that marijuana was not on their banned substances list, so they got high together regularly.

They developed a domestic routine. Each morning, they would wake up and do exercises together. Denis would check books out of the library on theology or physics and talk about them with Jane. He had developed the habit of writing down phrases and ideas on bits of paper and matchbooks and leaving them around the apartment. Jane would collect them, organize them, and place them on his desk for him.

As his previous girlfriends had discovered, Jane learned that being in a relationship with Denis could be a roller-coaster experience. "He could be incredibly romantic, and wildly sexual, and so charming. But there was a flip side to that stuff," she said. "He could also be volatile, and cruel, and unpredictable."

Impulsive acts were frequent. They could be romantic or vindictive. Once, they were driving through Phoenix, with Denis at the wheel. They reached a stoplight at a four-way intersection in a heavily trafficked area of the city. Without warning, Denis set the parking brake and jumped out of the car. He ran to the middle of the intersection and gestured with his hands for traffic to stop in all directions. Then, with horns honking all around him, he pointed at Jane and screamed, over and over, "I love this woman!"

He also hopped out of the car in traffic on another drive with Jane. This time, he had picked up a hitchhiker earlier in the ride. It was an impetuous move. He had not told Jane he was going to do it. After they dropped the hitchhiker at his destination, Jane told Denis it had scared her, and asked him not to do it in the future. Once again, Denis slammed on the brakes and stopped the car. "You don't know what it's like to hitchhike!" he screamed at her. "You don't know what it's like not to have anything!" Then he jumped out of the car and ran off. Jane had to climb over the console with the engine running and drive the car home. Later, Denis returned to the apartment and didn't mention the incident.

*

He threw himself back into his writing with the same zeal that he had shown in his submersion into Alcoholics Anonymous. Even before he had moved out of Al and Vera's house, he had begun to submit poetry to journals. He collected rejections. In his mind, his literary career was now, finally, beginning in earnest. The previous books of poetry were part of a different life. Where once he had seen them as his greatest accomplishments, now he underplayed their importance. "My poems have been included in two limited edition books," he wrote in the cover letter of one submission, "but I haven't yet had a regular book published."

He joined a local poetry group. Several area writers of varying levels of skill and experience would meet at the home of one of the members and read poems to each other, then offer critiques. The members would often go out to bars afterward to listen to country and western bands from the area. Denis would tag along, order a club soda, and enjoy the music with his fellow poets. He wouldn't volunteer any information about his battles with addiction or his past, but he didn't hide those experiences either.

Once again, his secretarial wizardry came in handy. He found a job as a clerical assistant at the Arizona Department of Education. He was still low on funds most of the time, but now at least he had enough regular income to pay his share of the rent. When he couldn't use Jane's car, he woke up earlier and took the bus downtown to the Department of Education office. Writing had to be wedged into the schedule, sometimes early in the morning, other times late in the evening.

His new life, it seemed, was a complete break from his past. Still, he occasionally longed for his previous existence. In his weaker moments, he pined for Sue. His relationship with her had lasted the better part of a decade. Now she was a thousand miles away. Sue had remained in Seattle for a while after Denis left, then had moved back to Minnesota, and soon she too had joined Alcoholics Anonymous. They started to correspond. They sent each other their newest poetry for critique. Sue told Maury that she was over Denis—a claim that, according to Maury, she made on multiple occasions. Sue also flirted with the idea of seeing Denis again, but she remained conflicted. "I miss you very much like I always do," she wrote. "I would like to be able to see you, but you can't stay here because I'm a nervous wreck."

Denis told Sue he had a fantasy about them getting back together, and he even sent Sue a clipping about Hollywood movie icons Elizabeth Taylor and Richard Burton, who had famously rekindled their romance and remarried after a much-publicized divorce. Soon, though, Sue had a new boyfriend, and Denis's relationship with Jane became more serious. Their correspondence no longer mentioned getting back together. Instead, the letters began to include supportive messages about their respective recoveries.

*

Gradually, the circumstances of Denis's existence began to improve. Acceptance letters began to find their way into his pile of rejections. *Poetry*, a prestigious national journal, took four of his poems. One of them was yet another entry poached from his MFA thesis, but the batch included new work as well. In his author's note for *Poetry*, Denis described himself as "an educated clerk typist."

His penchant for financing his life by applying for and winning grants returned as well. For the first time, the Arizona Commission on the Arts and Humanities announced it would be giving out a $3,000 creative writing fellowship. Denis heard about the competition and submitted two chapters of his long-dormant novel about the woman on the bus. He also included fourteen poems. Of 265 entries, Denis was selected as the sole winner. He learned that he won the fellowship at his desk at the Department of Education and "let out a whoop that could be heard for blocks."

Thanks to the publicity department at the Commission on the Arts and Humanities, a local columnist from the *Arizona Republic* decided that the grant and its winner warranted news coverage. Denis's photo appeared in the newspaper above the headline "Big Writing Award Lets Office Worker Develop His Talent." Denis told the newspaper writer that he had already used some of his winnings to buy a new IBM electric typewriter. "It's been my dream to own a really fine machine and believe me this one is so great and classy, it's not the kind you'd ever see in a hock shop," he gushed.

He decided to use the rest of the money from the grant to extricate himself from the nine-to-five office life and free up more time to devote to his writing. He gave notice at the Department of Education. Instead of taking the bus downtown every day, he planned to work intermittently as a substitute teacher in various Phoenix area secondary schools and subsist on that income, along with whatever other part-time gigs he could conjure up through the commission. Jane joined him in the Phoenix area substitute-teaching pool. They requested jobs at schools near their apartment so they could bike there, and they used the car when they were assigned to more distant schools.

An area school district hired him to teach poetry to gifted writing students at Litchfield Elementary School for $9 an hour. "I'm trying to introduce poetry to the kids," he said at the time. "While they are more open than adults, you can even see in some of the 10-year-old boys the idea that liking poetry might not be a masculine thing to do." Sometimes, working with the kids would be an invigorating experience. Other times, he would find it draining. Once, after a fight with Jane, Denis told the students they could do whatever they wanted all day so he could put his head down on his desk and mope.

He took a job teaching weekend creative writing classes at the Scottsdale Center for the Arts. Anybody interested could take the class for $25; Denis would pocket 80 percent of the take. Before his first class, he began jotting down his thoughts about teaching in one of his notebooks. The job of the writer, he decided he would tell his new students, was to withhold judgment. "Start where you are," he scribbled. "Don't wait for a great idea. Being creative means being willing to be creative. Let the ideas come." They wouldn't all be winners, but to be a writer, you had to try them all. To illustrate, he wrote to himself, he would tell them that Shakespeare wrote a bunch of dull sonnets and Babe Ruth led the league in strikeouts.

With the increased flexibility in his schedule, more time was available to pursue his writing projects. By now, he had learned that his entire life had to revolve around the act of writing for him to find real satisfaction and to write to the level he required of himself. He would start poems, then put them aside until experiences had given him the material needed for him to resume the work. "Over the years, I have realized that I need to work and create and worship and play and share myself with people—and all these things happen when I'm writing poetry," he said at the time. "So even though I haven't touched a poem in three weeks, it is still mostly what I'm doing: working on the poem. I don't even have to think about the words."

Along with his poetry, Denis returned to the novel that he'd started in Iowa with the short story "There Comes After Here" from the *Atlantic*. The story, which had been through dozens of iterations in his mind and on the page, had begun to coalesce into something he could finally articulate. He even settled on a title. The book would be called *Angels*, the name of a hardware store on McDowell Road, near his apartment. Each time he drove by the store, the sign would remind him that he should be working on his novel. *Angels* was to be "a country-western story with the kind of characters in it that are sung about in country-western songs. Ex-convicts, losers, cowboys—the kind of guys who aren't really angels," he said. He agreed to let some Phoenix area magazines publish early chapters of the work in progress and received positive feedback once they were released to the public.

The characters and the motif were set, but the actual plot and direction of the book were not. Soon, though, an opportunity arrived that would finally solve that problem—a problem he had wrestled with for a decade. Through his association with the Arizona Commission on the Arts and Humanities, he learned about a program in which writers taught fiction and poetry in state correctional facilities. The key to unlock *Angels* had arrived. The story, which began as a bus ride to nowhere, would now be a journey that would end in prison. Denis decided that for his characters to go to prison, he would also have to spend some time there himself—and now the chance to do so was right in front of him. He applied to be part of the program. "I practically held the interview committee hostage until they gave me the job," he said. The commission finally relented and hired him for the position. Contracts were signed. Denis now had another source of income. For fifty bucks a class, plus another twenty for travel, Denis was to be the creative writing teacher in the South Unit of the Arizona state maximum-security prison in Florence, Arizona.

THE SOUTH UNIT 13

I was born a poet one noon, gazing at the weeds and creosoted grass at the base of a telephone pole outside my grilled cell window. Through language, I became the grass, speaking its language and feeling its green feelings and black root sensations. Earth was my mother and I bathed in sunshine. **—Jimmy Santiago Baca, inmate, Florence State Prison**

The heat drifted up in waves off the pavement of Highway 87 as Denis drove south toward his new job for the first time in May 1980. All around him, the endless desert expanded into every shade of beige. The highway blurred into a kaleidoscope of light and heat as it stretched before him on the seventy-mile trip from Phoenix to the tiny town of Florence, population three thousand, which existed in the shadows of the state prison complex. He searched for a radio station in Jane's beat-up car, which he was using to transport him on the lonely trip through the desert.

Once he arrived in Florence, he drove by the Pinal County courthouse, a large Victorian structure that towered over the town's fading downtown, then past blocks of ancient adobe houses that lined the dusty streets. He continued on, beyond the town of Florence, down a drive lined with palm trees that led to a high wall, behind which lay a huge neoclassical structure and several other buildings that made up the town's dominant industry: the state of Arizona's maximum-security prison complex, one of the most dangerous penitentiaries in the country. Just a few years before, a massive riot had shut it down for days and put both guards and prisoners in the hospital. In 1977 alone, seven men were murdered and twenty-four stabbed as gang violence, coinciding with the rise of the Aryan Brotherhood, erupted regularly. Behind the prison lay a graveyard of forgotten deceased convicts. Until only a few years before, the graves had been marked only with license plates.

Denis parked and went up to the main gate of the prison, a huge archway covered with black metal bars that could be opened electronically. It was the same iron gate that had adorned the territorial prison used to lock up outlaws and horse thieves in the nineteenth century, before the Florence facility was built. Through the gate, he could see into the prison yard, and behind it the various buildings that housed the prisoners. He was body searched and told to pass through a metal detector. Then he was led through the yard to a room that, for the next year, would serve as his classroom.

*

The prison poetry program at Florence had been born ten years before, when a convict on death row named Charles Schmid sent a letter to an assistant professor in the University of Arizona English department requesting feedback on his poetry. Schmid was an infamous teenage criminal who had been convicted of the "thrill killings" of three young girls in the mid-'60s in a case that had garnered widespread media attention. The professor who received the letter was Richard Shelton, a poet in his early thirties, who heretofore had no connection to or interest in convicts or their poems. Though he remembered the case and shuddered at the thought of interacting with Schmid, he still agreed to critique the convicted murderer's writing.

At first, the two men corresponded via mail. Once Shelton realized that Schmid was indeed a talented writer, he began visiting his new student in person. Schmid turned out to be exceedingly gifted. Shelton took an interest that went beyond Schmid's poetry. He met Schmid's mother and learned about the difficult life Schmid had led before his crimes. Soon other convict writers were corresponding with Shelton.

He brought the idea for a regular workshop that would be held inside the walls of Florence prison to the Arizona arts council. Officials were enthusiastic, and in the summer of 1974, Shelton and a fiction writer named Tom Cobb taught the first class to a group of nearly thirty convicts.

The workshop achieved a level of success that Shelton could not have imagined. One convict, Jimmy Santiago Baca, who had been sent to prison for drug dealing and had taught himself to read and write in isolation, began to attend. Shelton worked closely with him to help him discipline his writing, and soon Baca was a published poet. After his release, Baca would publish several collections of poetry and win multiple national and international writing awards. Another convict named Stephen Dugan joined shortly after the workshop formed and garnered attention while still in prison. Dugan won the National Endowment for the Arts Creative Writing Fellowship, the first time the award was given to somebody behind bars. The entire workshop won a special prize from PEN America, a prestigious international literary organization.

Shelton was a seasoned teacher and had taught poetry to extremely passionate students at the University of Arizona. But now he had a group of students who were, quite literally, dying for their art. Gang violence was greatly increasing during the early years of Shelton's workshop. The first workshop member to be murdered was Shelton's very first student: Charles Schmid. In 1975, Schmid had symbolically broken with his violent past by legally changing his name to Paul David Ashley. He also began to publish poetry in journals and had received word that a collection of his poetry would be published as a chapbook. Before it was published, Schmid/Ashley was stabbed forty-seven times in the face and torso. He died ten days later. Two members of the gang that would become the Aryan Brotherhood were convicted of the killing, but no motive was ever determined.

The death of member "Little Ray" Arvizu could be more definitively connected to his participation in the workshop. Racial tension had continued to increase throughout the prison in the late '70s, along with the growth of ethnic gangs. The leader of the Mexican mafia ordered all Chicano prisoners to leave the creative writing workshop or face deadly consequences. Arvizu was the only one who remained. Gang members caught him in a stairwell, held him down, and stabbed him to death.

Deaths in the workshop began to become almost commonplace. Another poet in the class, a white-collar criminal named Tony Serra, was targeted for violence because of the knowledge and connections he had outside of prison. He pleaded with the prison administration for a transfer and was denied. He asked Shelton to deliver a message to his wife that he was in danger. Before a transfer could be arranged, he was attacked by a group of convicts, who subdued him and drilled through his forehead with an electric drill.

Shelton questioned whether his presence was contributing to the violence. Still, the workshop persevered in the face of the dangers. A prison riot broke out while class was in session on one occasion. The convicts, who had planned for such an incident in advance, blocked the door and kept Shelton out of harm's way until the riot was under control. It was glimpses of the humanity of the convicts such as this that kept him from abandoning the project in its darkest hours.

Like many others then and now, Shelton believed societal circumstances beyond their control had created most of the criminals and convicts living behind the walls of Florence prison. Many felt this way during this era, and many also felt that providing convicts with intellectual stimulation, confronting them with philosophical questions such as "Why do I exist?" and "Why am I what I am?" was not only key to their salvation but also a gesture that was owed to convicts by a society that, in many ways, had failed them. It was a way of thinking that would eventually lose favor, as American political and societal forces trended away from rehabilitation and toward retribution for those living in the country's ever-expanding prison system. Shelton, though, had created something viable and had allies on the Arizona Commission on the Arts and Humanities, and with their help the program was expanded statewide. Shelton taught his last class at Florence in 1980, the same year that Denis's prison teaching career was just getting underway.

*

For his first class inside the prison walls, Denis prepared a lecture on the significance of writing and literature. He told his new students to look around at their surroundings. They were incarcerated for various crimes against their fellow citizens, he said, but they lived in a society in which the written word was rarely one of those acts for which they could be locked up. In most other countries around the globe, he told them, that was not the case. In those places, writing often was a dangerous act. Taking pen to paper alone could land you in a jail cell.

Then he transformed the small room off the courtyard into a creative writing workshop reminiscent of the ones he attended years before in the English-Philosophy Building on the campus of the University of Iowa. Class members, sitting around a table, read their work and then listened quietly to the critiques of their fellow students.

Ed Montini was a young reporter from Pennsylvania who had just joined the staff of the *Arizona Republic* a few months before. He had been an English major in college, and like many young journalists of the era, he was enthralled by what was at the time known as New Journalism: deeply researched articles filled with evocative details and elegantly crafted scenes by writers such as Tom Wolfe and John McPhee. Montini heard about the prison workshop program shortly after arriving in town and thought it might be the perfect subject for just such an article. He tracked down Denis, called him up, and asked if he could tag along on one of the trips to Florence. Denis agreed. He'd like the company, he told Montini. He was getting tired of driving into the desert alone.

One morning in July, Montini drove to the apartment complex, parked, greeted Denis, and climbed into the passenger seat of the little sedan. He looked at the worn-out vehicle, which did not have working air conditioning, and wondered to himself how many more times it would be able to take Denis to Florence and back. Together, they drove the seventy miles, first listening to the classic rock radio station out of Phoenix. Denis extolled the "poetry" of Eric Clapton's guitar solos. As they got farther outside of the city, the radio station turned to static and then silence, and the two men were left to listen to the wind rushing through the open windows.

They arrived in Florence and stopped to have breakfast at a shabby little diner, in view of the barbed-wire fences that were the last line of defense surrounding the prison. Montini asked Denis why he was spending his time teaching prisoners to write. "He said how much he liked the nitty-gritty kind of stuff," Montini recalled. "You could tell for him it was research. It wasn't just teaching a class. It was learning about the guys who were in that class and learning about their lives, and about the prison, and... about that kind of lifestyle."

Montini brought along a letter that had been sent to the *Republic* by an angry reader after the newspaper had published an article that mentioned the prison workshop program. "It doesn't matter in the least to me whether a convict paints, writes poetry, or exhibits any other type of creativity while in custody for taking someone's life, money or property," the letter read. Montini planned to contrast the sentiment in the letter with what he saw inside the prison walls.

During breakfast, Denis told Montini about his life before Phoenix and how he'd come back to Arizona to get sober. Montini asked Denis what his parents thought about his teaching in prison. They're glad I'm teaching in prison rather than living in prison, Denis replied.

After breakfast, the two passed through three separate fences rimmed with barbed wire, each higher than the next. They were escorted by heavily armed guards across the prison yard and to the assigned meeting room. Just a few weeks earlier, a prisoner had been beaten and stabbed to death in another section of the facility. Inside the classroom, the inmates sat around a cafeteria-style table, bathed in fluorescent light. A dilapidated air conditioner wheezed in the corner of the room, doing next to nothing to relieve the stifling heat. Eight convicts, wearing blue jeans and denim shirts, greeted Denis warmly and agreed to sign forms allowing Montini to observe the class.

A student named Chuck Hadd Jr. had submitted a first-person story called "Meditations on John Walker," about a drug dealer who learns about the death of a narcotics agent while in jail awaiting trial. It was, like many of the stories submitted, lived experience. Hadd was a former navy recruit who had graduated from the University of Arizona and then begun smuggling marijuana across the border from Mexico, for which he eventually received a five-year prison sentence and a cell in Florence. Denis read the first paragraph out loud, then signaled for each student to follow suit, a paragraph at a time. Afterward, critiques ranging from grammatical corrections to philosophical inconsistencies were offered. Denis participated but did not dominate the conversation.

Almost all of the students interacted enthusiastically during the class. One student, however, remained in the back of the room and did not speak. The student stood out in other ways. He had his shirt buttoned all the way up to his neck, and his sleeves were buttoned up as well. His hair was perfectly cut and combed. Everybody else in the room was sweating profusely, but the silent student was like a lizard, Montini remembered, dry as a bone, as if he were in a room air conditioned to sixty degrees.

The class went on for a couple of hours. A few other stories were read and dissected. Afterward, on the drive back to Phoenix, Montini asked Denis about the student in the back of the room. That, Denis told him, was Robert Benjamin Smith, the best writer of the group by far. Smith was also a mass murderer, serving time for one of the most heinous crimes in Arizona history.

On November 12, 1966, Smith, then a quiet, lonely, mentally disturbed eighteenth-year-old high school student, had gone into a Mesa, Arizona, beauty shop and executed four women and a three-year-old girl, shooting them in the head at close range. When the police arrived, he surrendered and calmly showed them what he had done. Under questioning, Smith told police he had researched the murders committed a few months earlier by Charles Whitman on the University of Texas campus in Austin, where fifteen people were killed and thirty-one wounded as Whitman fired his rifle from atop UT's clock tower. Smith pleaded innocent by reason of insanity, and after a thirty-two-day trial the following year, was convicted and sentenced to death by the jury in under two hours.

Smith lived for years in the death-row wing of Florence prison. During that time, he became close friends with Charles Schmid, the original Florence prison poet. Smith's parents brought him bundles of books every week. He tore through books about psychology, history, and science fiction as well as technical military volumes.

Then, in 1972, a U.S. Supreme Court decision in the case of *Furman v. Georgia* found the death penalty to be cruel and unusual punishment, invalidating 630 death sentences around the country. Shortly before the Furman decision, Robert Smith was granted a new trial because of questions surrounding an informant who had been a witness in his first trial. Before a second trial took place, Smith pled guilty to all counts. A judge sentenced him to two consecutive seventy-five- to ninety-nine-year sentences. The death sentence was no longer an option. Smith had a new address in Florence prison and was eligible, eight years later, to attend Denis's class.

Montini went back to the *Arizona Republic* newsroom and crafted his work of New Journalism all about creative writing behind bars. He wrote about the convicts, the writing, and the new teacher who led the class. He also included what he had learned about Robert Benjamin Smith. It was a lengthy article by newspaper standards when he put the finishing touches on it and turned it in. Soon after, his editor called him into his office and told Montini he'd have to cut the material about Smith. Though it had been fifteen years, the editor feared a backlash if the *Republic* published a story in which Smith was portrayed as admirable in any way.

After the article appeared, Montini wrote a letter to Denis, thanking him for the access, apologizing for the lack of depth in the article, and hinting about his editor's decision. "I wish I could have attended three or four more classes before having to write a story," he said in the letter. "Several inches of the story never appeared in the paper because I had to comply with an editor's wishes. Such is life."

Denis called Montini after he received the letter. He told Montini that he liked the article. "This is the most famous I'm ever going to be," Denis said. Then Montini told Denis the truth about the editor's decision and the removal of the section about Robert Benjamin Smith. Denis took the news in stride. "That's okay. Now that you've written it, you should hang onto it," he told Montini. "Maybe you can use it in a short story."

*

As the class progressed, Denis began to share more of himself with the students. He found common ground with many of the men by telling them details of his drug and alcohol use and his battles with addiction. In turn, the convicts, both in their submissions to Denis and through classroom discussion, offered details about their crimes and their daily lives in prison. In one class, Denis talked about the blackouts he began to have when his drinking was at its worst, and he told them about taking Antabuse, a medication prescribed to addicts that causes an adverse reaction to alcohol.

For another class session, Denis handed out copies of "There Comes After Here," the story from the *Atlantic* that had by now become the first chapter of *Angels*. The students offered their critiques. In the story, the character who meets the young woman on the Greyhound bus was named "Leather Bill" Houston. The class members fixated on that particular detail. How, they asked Denis, can you name a character Leather Bill and offer no explanation whatsoever? Denis took the critique to heart. Soon, in the manuscript that was *Angels,* Bill Houston's nickname had been permanently removed.

Denis's notebook filled up with details and anecdotes from the lives of the men. They told him about themselves, but also how their crimes affected their relatives on the outside. Themes began to develop for Denis. Some relatives of the convicts suffered, while others found that the notoriety of the convicts and their crimes gave their lives meaning. One member of the class said that his mother had been a nobody, ignored by society, until he had gone on trial. Only then did his mother receive attention and feel important.

Occasionally, class discussion veered into directions that, if anybody in authority had been paying attention, might have caused an immediate end to the entire workshop program. Once, the class discussed the best techniques for robbing a store. Theories were suggested and then critiqued as if they were poems. One seasoned thief came out heavily in favor of armed robbery. When you burglarize a store, he explained to the class, you have very little control of your surroundings. Too many things can go wrong. When you commit armed robbery, however, you have complete control. You know how many people are there, you know who has a gun and who doesn't, and you are solely in charge of the situation. Denis might not have been convinced of the wisdom of the theory, but he took note of it nonetheless.

Of the rotating cast of attendees in the workshop, Denis became closest with two of the men, Robert Smith and Chuck Hadd Jr. Hadd shared an interest in history with Denis. The two talked about a famous Arizona Wild West story, the "Power's Cabin Shootout," and how as a result the outlaws involved spent many decades in Florence. Hadd wrote essays and short stories, but he also kept a journal of his time behind bars with detailed personal reminiscences of all aspects of prison life. Denis wrote Hadd letters of recommendation for reductions in his sentence, and when Hadd was transferred to another prison in the Arizona system, Hadd corresponded with Denis and continued to send Denis his writing.

Robert Smith attended the workshop religiously. Interest in the class waxed and waned. Sometimes Denis would arrive at the prison, go through the security gate, and arrive at the room to find Smith sitting alone, waiting for him. They would discuss writing but would also talk about whatever else was on their minds. Denis would talk to Smith about his attempts to find publishers, his love life, or his relationship with Morgan. "Denis was great company," Smith remembered. "A more affable person I have never met, soft-spoken, gentlemanly and always a genuine pleasure to talk to."

One day, Denis arrived with some exciting news to share with Smith, who once again was the only one in attendance. Denis had applied for and received a small grant that allowed him to purchase postage stamps so the class members could send out their work. Then Denis reached into his pocket, pulled out a $5 bill, and attempted to hand it to Smith. Smith quickly waved him off. Denis, unknowingly, would commit a felony by giving money to a prisoner. "I could have pocketed that five and sold it on the yard for twice its face value, yet I respected Denis and our friendship far too much to think of such even for a second," Smith said. Denis sheepishly put the bill back into his pocket and made a note to purchase the stamps himself.

Smith became not only the workshop's most consistent attendee but also its publicity chairman. He made sure the class was advertised in the prison bulletin, personally invited convicts to attend, and provided a link for Denis to those who attended intermittently. He even made coffee for the members before every class session. After they'd gotten to know each other well, Smith asked Denis for a favor. He was petitioning for minimum custody status, which would grant him many more privileges within the prison. He asked Denis to support the request. Denis said yes and penned an enthusiastic letter to the director of the Arizona state department of corrections. "More than any prisoner I have met," Denis wrote, "Robert Smith seems to regard himself as a member of a society that does not end at the boundaries of Florence prison. He maintains the attitude of a citizen, never slipping into a 'them–us' mode of thinking. I am privileged to work with Robert Smith."

*

One day in January, Denis and Jane had returned from a trip to the theater to see the movie *Invasion of the Body Snatchers*, when Jane received a phone call that would upend both of their lives. It was her father on the other end of the line, calling to say that her mother had been murdered. The killer was the ex-boyfriend of Jane's sister, Patty. Patty had come to visit Jane in Arizona months before and had told Jane about the boyfriend, Phillip Blake. Patty had later broken up with Blake, but he had continued to menace her. Around Thanksgiving, Blake had sexually assaulted Patty and shot himself in an attempt at suicide. He'd spent time in the hospital, then once again pursued Patty, eventually breaking into the home of Jane's mother, Glenna, and bludgeoning her to death with a wooden sculpture.

Denis and Jane traveled back to Dayton for the funeral. Jane's parents were divorced, and her father had remarried. The family, including several of Jane's siblings and their partners, gathered at the home of Jane's father and stepmother. They suffered through the episode as best they could, just beginning to understand the ramifications of an event that would change the course of all of their lives and rupture relationships among the family.

Denis returned to Arizona, and Jane followed a few weeks later. At first, going through such a harrowing event together seemed to strengthen their relationship. Denis wrote to Jane's father and step-mother shortly after Jane's return. "I'm overjoyed I got a chance to meet you, even under the worst possible circumstances," he wrote. "[Jane is] a strong lady and I'm crazy about her, I have to admit it. Someday I'm going to marry her and make honest in-laws of you."

In the long term, however, the incident was another complication in an already volatile situation. Jane's grief was compounded by the outcome of Blake's trial that spring. As a result of a variety of circumstances, Blake was offered a plea bargain without the family's consent. The extent of his punishment was the four months he had already served in jail and a $1,500 fine. Denis was supportive throughout, but he also urged Jane to move on from the incident in a way that she would come to resent. After the trial, he told Jane that the law had spoken, and it was time to put it behind her. "He told me to stop thinking about it," she remembered. "Well, I'm thinking about it to this day."

The murder was one of a number of incidents that hampered the relationship between Denis and Jane. His occasional outbursts of anger scared Jane. On two occasions he punched a hole in a door in their apartment, and on another he threw a tray at Jane. For a while they separated, mainly because Jane, still psychologically shaken from her mother's murder, objected to the regular stream of phone calls Denis was receiving from convicts at Florence prison.

Denis continued to make the trip to the desert for the year-long term of the contract. He did his best to keep up interest among the prison's writing community and supplement his research. As the end of the contract approached in the spring of 1981, the volume of material for his novel was plentiful. Little progress had been made toward the actual writing of the novel, however. "I have plans to work on this novel that I have been planning to work on for about a year," he told Montini. "It's fast becoming a joke among my friends."

Instead, he was devoting most of his writing efforts to poetry. In the spring of 1981, as his prison job was concluding, he received notice that his commitment to verse had paid off. He had submitted his manuscript of new poetry to an open call for the National Poetry Series Award. Out of nearly two thousand entries, his submission was one of two selected for publication. The series editor was Mark Strand, poetry professor and pseudo recruiter for the Iowa Writers' Workshop. As a selection for the series, Denis was now going to publish, for the first time, what he believed to be "a real book." He had entitled his submission *The Incognito Lounge,* after the bar with the striking neon sign in his neighborhood. Along with the $350 advance from Random House, his new publisher, he thought that the contract for publication allowed him to stop revising the poems in the submission, freeing him to work on other projects.

Another piece of life-changing news came in the mail around the same time. A few months before, his old friend from Iowa City, Carolyn Maisel, had called Denis and told him about the Fine Arts Work Center in Provincetown, Massachusetts, where she was currently living as part of a fellowship. On her advice, Denis applied to the same program. The acceptance letter that arrived in the mailbox in the summer of 1981 informed him that he was to report to Provincetown in the fall for a seven-month stay, where he would be given a room, $250 a month for living expenses, and all the time in the world to write his novel.

Denis asked Jane to come with him, but by that time, the relationship had run its course. A new, more stable job in Phoenix that she liked and a wariness about the tempestuous nature of life with Denis made up her mind. She declined his offer.

Living in New England was not something Denis had really expected or longed for, but he was beginning to think that he was being guided by forces beyond his control. "It's funny. I didn't think I was going to turn out like this, but the more I do turn out like this, the more I like it," he told Montini. "Things have just fallen into my lap lately. I haven't had much to do with the course my life has taken."

LIFE ON THE CAPE 14

There is a charm about Provincetown from its mixture of the old fishing life and the new artistic impulse. The fishermen's sturdy crafts and nets lie side by side with the painters' easels and the sculptors' tools.

—Joseph C. Lincoln, *Cape Cod Stories*

In the fall of 1980, right around the time that Denis was getting comfortable in prison, a young painter on the other side of the country was preparing to make the move to Provincetown as well. Sam Messer had gone to Yale for a semester with hopes of earning an MFA but had dropped out and was living at home in Brooklyn, spending his days working in a frame shop. He submitted some paintings to the Fine Arts Work Center's fellowship program and was accepted into the class of 1980.

One day, just before he was supposed to leave for Massachusetts, he was in the frame shop, teaching a replacement how to use the freight elevator. He showed his protégé the elevator and then, without looking, stepped into what he thought was the elevator but was actually now just an opening to the elevator shaft. As a young child, his mother had told him a story about somebody in her apartment building in Queens dying from just such a fall. Now, as he plummeted through the dark, he believed he was falling toward his death. By a stroke of luck, he landed on a piece of wood that broke his fall. The impact knocked him unconscious. His arm was shattered. The owner of the building was the first one to find him. He looked Messer over, saw he was alive, and said to him, "It looks like you're okay."

Messer, now awake and feeling intense pain, stared up at the building owner. "Fuck you," he said. "Get me an ambulance."

The fall, though it debilitated Messer for a year, had the additional effect of postponing his fellowship in Provincetown until the fall of 1981, allowing him to enter the program at the same time as a poet from Arizona who would eventually become his collaborator and lifelong friend.

The origin of the Provincetown Fine Arts Work Center can be traced back to 1911, when a man named Frank Days bought some property at the address of 24 Pearl Street with plans to build a lumberyard. The building that was eventually erected included ten small studios for working artists, separated by thin boards, with a single toilet in the hall. Days, and later his son, Frank Days Jr., became benefactors for the art community in Provincetown, hosting painters, poets, and sculptors through the twentieth century, offering them a place to create their art at little cost. In 1968, a group of local artists launched a cooperative, named it the Fine Arts Work Center, and began to offer residency fellowships to artists. The group purchased the property at 24 Pearl Street in 1972, and in 1976, fellowships for writers were added. That year, the center offered residencies for ten artists and ten writers, a tradition that, as of the fall of 2024, was still alive.

The little enclave of Provincetown was a thriving beach community located on the tip of Cape Cod, with dozens of shops and eateries there to collect the money of the summer tourists from New York and Boston. In the fall, when the fellows arrived, the town had already cleared out, most of the restaurants and bars had shut down for the season, and only the year-round residents remained. There wasn't much to do in the town's off-season, making it the perfect place for artists and writers to focus on their work.

Denis and Messer became friends almost immediately after arrival. Each was intrigued by the other's art. They found they worked similarly, so they quickly began to operate in tandem. They would write and paint for an hour or two, then take a break to stroll around town or go down to the beach, learning about each other's work and life history. "He always would say I was the first living artist he met, and he certainly was the first living writer I met," Messer remembered. "I loved literature, but until then, I just thought all writers were dead. So, we just kind of bonded in that way." At night, they would attend readings or potluck dinners with the rest of the fellows in the Work Center common room, or they would go out to Crown & Anchor on Commercial Street, one of the few bars that remained open. Denis told Messer he didn't drink because he was an alcoholic, but he liked to go to bars to get a contact high.

The $250 monthly stipend didn't go far, so the two fellows were always short on funds. They began to pool what little money they had. When Messer received a payment from a settlement related to his fall down the elevator shaft, he gave half to Denis. When Denis got a small payment from Random House for the approaching publication of *The Incognito Lounge,* he returned the favor. Soon after, another one of the writing fellows, Tama Janowitz, signed a publication contract for her novel, *American Dad.* She showed off the $10,000 check she had received for her advance. "Denis looked at me and said 'Fuck this. I'm writing a novel,'" Messer said.

The fellows at the Work Center were expected to give readings and showings of their works in progress. Denis and Messer decided they would present their work together. Denis planned to read a poem he was working on called "Red Darkness." The creation of the poem involved Denis writing numerous phrases and lines on scraps of paper and taping them to the wall of his apartment. Later, at an AA meeting, he asked the other attendees to pick the lines out of a hat. When Denis had completed the lines in "Red Darkness," they appeared in the order in which they were chosen at the meeting.

While they were preparing for the big night, Denis asked Messer to drive with him around Cape Cod. He brought along a cassette recorder and turned the trip into a quasi-journalistic mission. Denis would stop the car and go with Messer into stores, restaurants, and bowling alleys, turn on the tape recorder, and ask people, "What do you think of the work of Sam Messer?" Nobody had heard of Messer, of course, but Denis continued asking the question and recording the confused answers. It was, Messer thought, Denis's first real attempt at the act of journalism. Eventually, Denis brought the recorder to Messer's mother's house and asked her what she thought of the work of her son. "I don't understand it," she said. "I wish it wasn't so sad." Messer, whose father had died three weeks before he came to Provincetown, was struck by the poignancy of his mother's words.

Their joint presentation was held February 22, 1982, in the Work Center gallery. Denis had handwritten "Red Darkness" on thick oaktag pages and displayed them in the gallery, and Messer's paintings were shown using a slide projector. They handed out copies of the poem. Denis read it to the audience as the paintings appeared on the movie screen. "Sam and Denis were like the absolute perfect example of what the Work Center can do," remembered Bert Yarborough, the center's visual coordinator at the time. "It really was an amazing collaboration."

*

One of the attendees at the event was Lucinda Johnson, a recently divorced artist who was in her second year as a fellow at the Work Center. Lucinda was originally from California. She studied at the University of California at Davis and earned degrees in Spanish literature, ceramics, and painting. She married one of her art professors and moved with him to Massachusetts, where the couple had a son, Matthew, and then split soon after. Lucinda lived in the studio directly above Messer. Denis was immediately captivated by Lucinda, but at first she was not particularly interested in Denis romantically. She was coming off a broken relationship that was damaged by alcohol abuse, and she knew Denis's history. But life at the Work Center kept the fellows close to one another with communal dinners, readings, and parties. Lucinda's defenses eventually weakened. Before the seven-month residency was complete, they were a couple. "Denis was a character," Lucinda remembered. "He was very charming, very funny, and pretty crazy."

Though he had not actively been looking for a long-term relationship,

Denis quickly became deeply committed to Lucinda. He spent time with Matthew, who was three when the fellowship began. The two became close. "It was a romantic time for him," said Catherine Gammons, another fellow in the program and a close friend of both Denis and Lucinda. "He was in a relationship with this beautiful woman.... He was head over heels, and there was something romantic and happy about it."

On a bright, sunny day in the late spring of 1982, as the tourists were just starting to return to the area, Lucinda and Denis were married at Town Hall in Provincetown. Lucinda's family, including Matt and her parents, sister, and brother-in-law, were in attendance, as were some of the couple's friends from the Work Center. Messer and Gammons served as witnesses. After the ceremony, the entire wedding party, which consisted of about a dozen people, gathered on the picturesque front lawn outside, took pictures, then headed back to the Work Center gallery for a reception. What Denis had initially thought would be a seven-month interlude before he resumed his life in Arizona had turned into a long-term commitment. Pretty soon, the newlyweds were making plans to start their married lives in earnest in their newly adopted hometown.

*

Earlier that year, Gary Fisketjon, a young editor for Random House, was waiting to have dinner with novelist Richard Ford in a Manhattan restaurant. Ford was late. Fisketjon had brought with him the manuscript of *The Incognito Lounge*, which he was in the process of preparing for publication. He decided he would sit at the table, have a drink, and read the manuscript one more time. It was, he thought, the best poetry collection he had read in years. Random House was one of several New York publishers participating in the National Poetry Series, and Fisketjon oversaw it for his company. "It was far and away the best of the books that had been shown to the participating publishers," Fisketjon recalled. "I mean, it was the best book, I'm sure, that was published in that whole series."

When Ford arrived at the restaurant, Fisketjon couldn't stop talking about his new discovery. Have you ever heard of Denis Johnson? he asked. Ford happened to be a good friend of Raymond Carver. He told Fisketjon that he knew of Denis through Carver but had never met him. Fisketjon, also a friend of Carver's, was intrigued. He asked Carver to lunch a few days later. Carver told Fisketjon of his friendship with Denis in Iowa. Denis, Carver said, was magnificently talented and incredibly original. Soon after, Carver wrote Fisketjon a letter about Denis. "The best poems in *The Incognito Lounge* are examples of what the finest poetry can do—bring us closer to ourselves, and at the same time bring us in touch with something larger," Carver wrote. Fisketjon took portions of Carver's letter and excerpted them on the back cover of the book.

The Incognito Lounge reached bookstore shelves in May 1982. Around that time, Denis came to New York City to meet with Fisketjon and to give a public reading. On the day of the reading, Denis arrived at the Random House offices, which were on the eleventh floor of a building in Manhattan. He took a seat in the reception area and waited. Fisketjon greeted him and motioned for him to follow through the door that led to the offices. Denis saw the floor-to-ceiling windows that looked out over the New York skyline, said "Wow," and stopped short. Fisketjon wondered about the reaction and asked Denis about it. "I've never been up this high in a building before," he said.

It was, in fact, the highest Denis had climbed in the world of publishing, and not just physically. *The Incognito Lounge,* as a book of poetry, was never going to make a dent in the bottom line for Random House. "I don't even think in terms of money," Fisketjon told Ed Montini for an article about the book's release. "What I do hope is for the book to be reviewed seriously and widely, which is hard enough. I only hope the people who read poetry find it a book they must have."

Fisketjon's hopes were answered, to a much greater degree than he could have anticipated. *The Incognito Lounge* received raves from every publication that reviewed it, and there were many, from literary journals to big-city newspapers. Reviewers from Chicago, New York City, Boston, Memphis, and dozens of other cities across the country heaped praise on the book. *Publishers Weekly* said Denis combined "graphic realism and strikingly original metaphor in a sensitive voice." KUSC, the National Public Radio station in Los Angeles, dedicated a lengthy segment to the book. Howard Moss, a poetry editor at the *New Yorker,* wrote Denis a personal letter, lauding the book and asking for submissions. "If I had a chance to publish a great many poems in your book, I would have done so after a first reading," he wrote. Denis even appeared in *People* magazine, which published two photos of him and said he "writes a rock 'n' roll kind of poetry, casual, loose-limbed, and full of allusions to sex and self-discovery." Denis clipped the pages from *People* and, as he had done as a college student thrilled by his first journal publications, put them in an envelope and sent them to his mother.

It was an extraordinary reaction to a book of poetry by an unknown author. Reviewers noted Denis's technical achievements in his writing. They commented on the bleak imagery, interrupted by moments of hope and poignancy, his "virtuoso wordplay and manipulation of syntax."

The beauty and style that he had created had been a function of his method, which he had been honing since he was a teenager. He observed, took notes, and then, when he felt himself laden with the imagery, ideas, and characters he required to write, he began to craft the poems. His method was to empty his head onto the page in long, free-flowing paragraphs. Phrases would be repeated, over and over, reordered and refined until he was satisfied. Then he would sift through the paragraphs, cut the excess, and break what remained into lines to form the poem.

Out of a year of this work, he had created *The Incognito Lounge,* a world of language populated by characters from his apartment complex, his numerous bus rides to and from work, diners in his neighborhood, people from the streets of Phoenix. Decades later, he would cite the book as the work of poetry he was most proud of from a lifetime of creation.

*

In the spring of 1982, the publication of *The Incognito Lounge* and the resulting attention took up much of Denis's time and energy. Another project was percolating under the surface, however. His life still revolved around AA. He attended meetings daily. Step nine, apologizing for past wrongs, was still on his mind as well. For a while, he attempted to craft letters to the people he felt he had injured while he was an addict. He did not complete and send the letters, but through the process, he began to spend more time thinking about the people he'd known during his dark years, and the incidents that had happened to him and the people around him.

He also used some of his time at the Work Center to jot down anecdotes from his years as a junkie, a period that had now begun to recede into his past. He began to fiddle with the stories and search for the right voice. He thought about how the material—material that he had not really concentrated on in these terms for years—could be turned into literature. Outlines of stories started to develop. Eventually, however, the notebooks devoted to the project went into a drawer, and his attention turned in other directions.

The subject on the main burner was still *Angels*. He had been making progress on the book through his months at the Work Center. Beyond the writing, he began to think more deeply about the path to publication. Again, his friend Mark Strand came through for him. Strand sent the novel in progress to an agent he knew named Bob Cornfield. Cornfield picked it up one night, read thirty pages, and was entranced. Cornfield was a close friend of Robert Gottlieb, then the top editor at the publishing house Alfred A. Knopf and, thanks to a string of successes, one of the most influential editors working in publishing at the time. Gottlieb happened to call Cornfield as he was reading the manuscript. Cornfield told him he was on page thirty of a manuscript and was "terrified to read further because so far the book was so magnificent." Gottlieb advised Cornfield to sign Denis immediately. Cornfield followed the advice, and Denis gained an agent who would become one of his closest and most trusted confidants for the next two decades.

The end of the long road for *Angels* was beginning to come into view. By now, in the manuscript, his country and western characters had been through many of the troubles that he himself had experienced in his twenties. The horrors of extended alcoholic blackouts, heroin addiction, and stays in uncaring mental hospitals were all experienced by one character or another. The settings, Chicago and Phoenix, mirrored some of Denis's travels as well. He began to feel, however, that his own experiences would not be enough to get him all the way across the finish line. To write the novel that he truly wanted to write, he was going to need an assist from his friends back in the South Unit.

GOING UP THE PIPE 15

These death sentences are cruel and unusual in the same way that being struck by lightning is cruel and unusual.... I simply conclude that the Eighth and Fourteenth Amendments cannot tolerate the infliction of a sentence of death under legal systems that permit this unique penalty to be so wantonly and so freakishly imposed. —**Justice Potter Stewart, *Furman v. Georgia*, U.S. Supreme Court, 1972**

When their fellowships were over, Denis and Lucinda needed a place to live as a couple. They found a tiny, cramped apartment for $100 a month and moved in together, with little Matt in tow. They also needed money. Provincetown had its share of former Work Center fellows who had stayed in town once their stipend ran out. Several of them ended up working at the local newspaper, the *Advocate*, to supplement their income. Lucinda followed suit and began taking regular hours there. She worked in the production department pasting up pages of the newspaper, and in the darkroom developing film. Denis went back, one more time, to the well of government money set aside for writers, a strategy that never seemed to let him down. He landed a $12,500 creative writing fellowship from the National Endowment for the Arts.

Despite Denis's financial contributions, Lucinda grew irritated when she would drag herself downtown to the newspaper office, work all day, and return to the apartment to find her husband still lounging around the apartment. After one particularly rough day, she came home and saw Denis sitting at the kitchen table in front of the typewriter. The irritation boiled over.

"When are you going to get a real job?" she demanded.

Denis looked up at her from the typewriter. "Never," he said flatly. "This is my real job."

It was a moment in which Lucinda was beginning to grapple with the fact that the man she had started a life with was a thirty-something ex-junkie with limited employment opportunities. "I had a sinking feeling that, oh my god, I just married a completely down-and-out poet who's not going to make any money, and I'm going to have to support him the rest of my life," she said.

Indeed, the notoriety that came with the publication of *The Incognito Lounge* enhanced Denis's reputation, but not his bank account. As he'd learned from Tama Janowitz at the Work Center, though, there was money to be made in novels. He threw his energy into the completion of *Angels,* which was now entering its second decade of existence.

As the story currently stood in Denis's manuscript, Jamie, the young mother, and Bill Houston, the alcoholic drifter, travel together for a while after meeting on the bus, then split up. Bill goes to Chicago, where he robs a hardware store and drinks away the money he steals from the store. Jamie goes to Chicago looking for him, gets drugged and raped, and finally finds her way back to Bill. The couple, along with Jamie's children, go to Phoenix to live with Bill's Bible-thumping mom, where they fall in with Bill's brothers, James, a repo man, and Burris, a heroin addict. James works for Dwight Snow, a hardened criminal, who has concocted a plan for a bank robbery.

The reasoning behind Dwight's armed robbery plan would have been familiar to anybody who had attended a certain poetry workshop in the South Unit of Florence prison. Snow lays it out, just as Denis heard it from his convict/student in Florence a few years before:

> Burglary is insanity.... You walk around on tiptoe and you have absolutely no control over your environment, no idea what's waiting for you in there. You could walk your face right up some vigilante's

> twelve-gauge.... I feel much more comfortable doing business in the daytime with my neighborhood savings and loans association, or my local jeweler's. I know who has the firepower—me—and I know exactly who's there, where they're located, and what they're doing, before I even make a move. The environment is one hundred percent mine—or I go home.

In Denis's typewriter, the monologue he heard in Florence convinces the Houston brothers. They sign up for the bank robbery, which goes spectacularly wrong. James is shot in the stomach by a security guard. Bill in turn shoots and kills the guard, at which point the story moves behind the walls of Florence prison.

Denis had kept up correspondence with both Chuck Hadd and Robert Smith. He had written letters of support for both men to prison administrators to improve their circumstances. Now he asked for a favor in return. He wrote to Hadd and asked if he could see Hadd's personal journal, specifically the pages dedicated to his first nights in Puma County jail, where Hadd was incarcerated immediately after his arrest. He wanted to use them to help him write the scenes that Bill Houston spends in Maricopa County jail after the robbery and arrest. Hadd agreed to transcribe the pages for Denis, but not to send the journal. "I am too paranoid to let the actual journal out of my hands," he wrote to Denis. "Parts of it are very personal, though, if we are ever together on the streets, I'd let you look at portions of it."

From Robert Smith, Denis requested a description of life on death row. He had decided that Bill Houston would be convicted of first-degree murder for killing the security guard and would be sentenced to die in the gas chamber. Smith, he knew, had lived on death row for years in the late '60s and early '70s. The letter he received from Smith in response to his request far exceeded anything Denis could have hoped for or imagined.

Smith wrote Denis a ten-page treatise that explained life on the row in amazingly granular detail, including the pastel-green bars on the cells, the light bulbs housed in little cages to prevent prisoners from breaking them and using them to cut their own throats, and the broom handles the men used to reach through the bars to turn the channels on the black-and-white TV sets outside their cells. Smith covered all aspects of a condemned man's existence, creating vivid scenes. The men were allowed into the exercise yard every third day, and from the yard they could easily view the building that housed the gas chamber, distinguishable by a tall pipe towering over it. "That pipe will carry the used-up gas after the man is dead. Hence to get gassed is to 'go up the pipe,'" Smith wrote. Once every six months, the gas chamber would be tested on a pig. The guards would make sure the prisoners knew of the test and would leave the windows open so the prisoners could listen to the "great terrified squeal" of the pig in its final moments. "Think it's painless? Come listen to the pig sometime."

Of particular use to Denis was Smith's descriptions of the actual execution. He provided Denis with a minute-by-minute schedule of death by gas chamber in the state of Arizona. The Last Supper, as the men on the row called it, was served. Then the condemned man was shaved and stripped to only his shorts, causing him to shake uncontrollably in the freezing gas chamber. The warden asks the prisoner for last words. "Regardless of preparation, few can manage more than strangled 'no' or a shake of the head." The man is strapped down, the gas pellets are dropped with a thunk on the concrete floor, and gas begins to fill the chamber. "The man in the chair sees it plainly as it swirls and rises, inch by inch. The prison doctor has invariably advised him to take a deep breath of the gas in order to end it more quickly: some do, some don't. The end result is the same," Smith wrote.

Denis thanked Smith and praised the letter. He told his student that the writing within it was worthy of publication and sent it back for that purpose. Then he went about composing the final scenes in the life of Bill Houston. In the final pages of *Angels,* Denis's protagonist would be put through the harrowing scenes that Smith had described. Details, such as the sweat stains on the straps used to lock down the prisoner, were taken from Smith's letter. "He stood there handcuffed, shorn nearly bald, wearing only his white underpants," Denis wrote. Then Denis took Houston into the chamber and all the way to his final breath. "A visible vapor was curling up over his knees.... He felt he could hold his breath forever—no problem. Boom, boom, boom. Even as his heart accelerated, it seemed inexplicably that his heart was slowing down.... He was in the middle of taking the last breath of his life before he realized he was taking it."

Like much of his finest work, Denis had created a scene that is almost unbearably bleak, yet he managed to instill it with a glimmer of hope. Bill Houston's death in the gas chamber was actually, to Denis, triumphant. "I think that book ends happily," he said later. "The guy gets executed.... But at the moment of his death, and to some degree in the days before he goes to the gas chamber, his spirit seems to wake up inside him. And right at the end he thinks of praying for other people. Then, his life has sort of come full circle, and he's being born as he dies."

Denis deemed the manuscript ready for publication at the end of the summer of 1982. The production process began the next year. For the cover, Lucinda painted an ominous black-and-white image of lightning in the sky over a desolate, cactus-covered desert. On the book flap was a photo that included a leather jacket that Maury Barr had given Denis while the two were in Port Townsend. The following summer, the Knopf publicity machine kicked into gear. Ads featuring the biggest names in the book world began to appear. "Johnson is a first-class writer," Robert Stone said in the copy of print advertising that ran in newspapers across the country. "He shows us peculiar skewed beauty that makes desperate souls a subject for the bravest art," Don DeLillo added. "Prose of amazing stylishness," wrote Philip Roth. For Denis, the appearance of literary stars and legends shilling for him—including Stone, one of his idols—was another of the moments aspiring writers dream about.

When the reviews began to appear a short while later, the general consensus echoed the pronouncements in the advertising. It was a debut novel that introduced a prose stylist of incredible talent. Many noted that Denis was also a poet and said this fact was reflected in his ability to create striking images. "He is the sort of craftsman that does not regularly appear in the marketplace of American fiction writers," wrote novelist George V. Higgins, reviewing *Angels* for *Newsday.*

Many singled out the death-row section for its power. "In what must be one of the most remarkable scenes in recent fiction, Johnson takes us through Bill's execution in a prison gas chamber step by step, and finally heartbeat by heartbeat," one reviewer noted. The dour subject matter and the antiheroes who drive the plot also stood out to most reviewers. Denis's failure, either purposeful or not, to create sympathy for his morally compromised characters was the single negative note that appeared regularly in the slate of reviews.

In his acknowledgments section in the back of *Angels,* Denis thanked the Fine Arts Work Center and the National Endowment for the Arts. After ten years of writing the book, only two people merited a personal mention: his friends from the South Unit. "The author is most grateful... to Charles Hadd, Jr., and Robert Smith, without whose contributions and assistance there would be no story." He mailed copies of the book to both men in prison. "It's an amazing, amazing piece of work," Smith wrote after he received his copy.

Chuck Hadd proved to be a reviewer with a more critical eye than any of the professional writers who reviewed *Angels* for newspapers and magazines. "Though you haven't asked me for my opinion," he wrote to Denis, "I do have a few comments which you can have for free." He then proceeded to offer Denis eight free pages of detailed notes, commenting on minutiae ranging from the Denis's choice of model of Harley-Davidson motorcycle to his decision, in one scene, to give a character a machine gun rather than a standard rifle. He repeated back to his one-time instructor the advice Denis had given him in the workshop—the importance of using concrete images over abstract ones. He said he thought the novel dragged in the beginning and picked up in the Arizona section. He ended his review on a positive note, however: "I think you've written a really good novel to be proud of," he concluded. "And I'm proud to be acknowledged in it."

A few months later, *Angels* was still in Hadd's thoughts. He wrote Denis again on the subject. This time, he had been going over some of the workshops in his mind. Now he was not just sizing up the novel but beginning to understand his role in the process of its creation. "As I recall, the novel was in progress when you first took the job here,"

Hadd wrote to Denis. "I wonder, did you take the job here in order to learn about prison?"

*

The widespread positive attention meant that Denis's proclamation to Lucinda that he did indeed have a real job was vindicated. It also meant that his seemingly endless battle to graduate from struggling artist to working writer was complete. His legendary typing skills would no longer be needed to bring in more income. He was entering a new phase of his career, one with expanded opportunities but also a loss of anonymity and an increase in demands on his time.

Some of the immediate benefits were financial and material. After a lifetime of driving junkers, Denis decided he had earned himself a nice ride. He used some of his earnings to buy a Datsun 240Z sports car. It wasn't brand new, but it was the most expensive vehicle he'd ever owned by far. Still, he wasn't satisfied. The car needed to be distinct. He took it to a body shop and had it painted bright orange. Then he asked Lucinda to put the final touches on it. Toward the end of *Angels,* a character on death row writes a poem that includes a phrase that had particular meaning to Denis. Now he decided to find a new use for the phrase. At Denis's request, Lucinda painted, in large neon-blue letters, the words MANIAC DRIFTER on the side of her husband's new acquisition.

Denis and Lucinda exchanged the $100-a-month apartment in Provincetown for a new residence just down the Cape in the town of Wellfleet. Their new hometown was a slightly smaller version of their old one—another tourist destination that filled up in the summers and emptied out when the weather turned. Their new living arrangement would be a family affair. Denis and Lucinda, along with Lucinda's parents, her sister, and her brother-in-law, pooled their money and bought a large house in town that had been formerly owned by a well-known sea captain. The house had living quarters for each couple, as well as room for an art gallery in front. Denis and Lucinda moved into the top floor.

Lucinda's father was an oceanographer who had moved his family to Japan for a time years before. Both Lucinda and her sister were well acquainted with Japanese art, which would become the focus of the enterprise. It was christened the Soroban Gallery, after a Japanese abacus. The gallery became the center of Lucinda's existence in Wellfleet. It was open for business during the summer months. Lucinda would buy and sell Japanese art, and the gallery would host Work Center artists for shows. In the off-season, she would go to work creating her own art. She took welding classes at Cape Cod Community College and began to work that skill into her sculpture. In addition, she served as visual director at the Work Center.

For Denis, life revolved around writing and Alcoholics Anonymous. He began using a spare room in a friend's house as an office. His schedule was consistent. Each day, he would clock in at his office around 11:30 a.m. and never stay past four in the afternoon. The evenings were for AA. He had dedicated *Angels* to the Higher Power and to his fellow AA disciples. Every evening, he would say good-bye to Lucinda, jump in the Maniac Drifter, and cruise up Highway 6 for a meeting in one of the neighboring towns. When the opportunity arose, he saw it as his place to share what he had learned in the program with friends whom he thought needed guidance.

His friend Catherine Gammon had moved to New York after her fellowship was over. She would regularly visit the Johnsons in Wellfleet. She also was developing an unhealthy dependence on alcohol. On one visit, she drove from Wellfleet to another town on the Cape to spend the evening with an old boyfriend. The date went badly, and Gammons arrived back at the Johnsons' home late that night, drunk and upset. She poured her heart out to Denis. He talked with her about her romantic problems and her drinking. He offered her a solution, culled directly from his AA experience. When you go to sleep tonight, he told her, I want you to pray to have your compulsions lifted. "I went to bed . . . and started a fire, and snuggled into my sleeping bag, still drunk and miserable about the old boyfriend, and with great sincerity, I did what he told me. And when I woke up in the morning, the first words in my head were 'maybe alcohol really is the problem,'" Gammons remembered. A day later, she had her last drink.

The success of *Angels* continued to reap benefits. *GQ* magazine chose Denis as one of "tomorrow's literary lions" and ran a profile of him along with three other young first-time novelists. *Angels* was translated into multiple languages and found readers across Europe. He traveled to London to publicize the book. Soon after, his Italian publisher invited him to the country for a three-week tour. Lucinda accompanied him on the trip. Together, they started in Rome and traveled across Italy, giving readings in bookstores and at universities, staying at four-star hotels and receiving celebrity treatment along the way. Denis's aversion to public appearances was still with him, but as he and Lucinda were feted from Milan to Sicily, he managed to relax, enjoy the rewards of his work, and sink into his new role as a famous international author. "It really was quite amazing. It was a grand tour," Lucinda remembered. "And he was a big hit over there."

A TRIP TO TWICETOWN

16

It would be wonderful if we could restore our balance with the Soviet Union without increasing our own military power.... But let's not fool ourselves. The Soviet Union will not come to any conference table bearing gifts. Soviet negotiators will not make unilateral concessions. To achieve parity, we must make it plain that we have the will to achieve parity by our own effort. —**Ronald Reagan, radio address, April 17, 1982**

The genesis of Denis's next novel, and of one of his most iconic poems, can be traced to another trip that he took during the period when he was finishing *Angels*. The accommodations on this particular journey did not include posh villas in the Italian countryside. Instead, it involved sleeping in a car on the side of a South Florida highway.

After his fellowship in Provincetown, Sam Messer had moved back to New York. He had a little money left from his elevator settlement, so he decided he would spend it on new vehicle. His mother was now living in Florida. She convinced Sam that the Sunshine State was a cheaper place to buy a car. He went down, picked up a Toyota wagon in Broward County near Fort Lauderdale, and then called Denis to see if his friend would keep him company on the drive back north. Denis agreed, but he had a specific itinerary in mind that would not be a direct route back to New York.

The first stop was in the other direction. Like many writers of his generation, Denis idolized Ernest Hemingway. Back in Iowa City, he and Maury Barr had read and reread Hemingway's classics and discussed them frequently. Now he wanted to go to Key West and see where his hero had lived. The house where Hemingway spent most of the 1930s had been turned into a shrine to the writer, complete with the supposed descendants of his famous six-toed cats, and eventually designated a national historic landmark in 1968.

Denis and Messer drove the Toyota wagon south, across the many bridges that connect the Florida Keys. Once they got to Key West, they created their own Hemingway expedition. First, they took the tour at the Hemingway home. It was the minutiae of Hemingway's life that intrigued Denis—minor details, like how he kept his phone in the bathroom. Then they walked around town, going to the bars and restaurants that Hemingway frequented, and observing the topography and landscape of the island. Denis, Messer thought, was gathering what he needed for a future project.

Then the long trip north began. When they tired, they pulled to the side of the road near a marsh and went to sleep in the Toyota, leading to a night in which they were feasted on by the mosquitoes of South Florida. The next stop was Kennedy Space Center at Cape Canaveral for a launch of the space shuttle. In Jacksonville, they went to a jai alai fronton, placed their bets, and won $1,000. With their trip funds now replenished, Denis found them the most expensive room in town. They slept in style, mosquito-free, for the night.

Another reason Denis had been anxious to take the trip had to do with a specific work of art that had become an obsession for both him and Messer. The work that had captivated them was a piece of street art called *The Throne of the Third Heaven of the Nations' Millennium General Assembly,* created by an unknown artist named James Hampton. Denis and Messer had learned of it from Messer's wife, Eleanor, who was researching self-taught artists. A native of Elloree, South Carolina, Hampton built the massive, intricate structure out of discarded junk—light bulbs, whiskey bottles, tables, eyeglasses, anything he could find—between 1950 and his death in 1964. Hampton reported seeing visions and wrote in an invented language about his artwork. It was found by his landlord after his death, became a phenomenon, and eventually ended up in the Smithsonian American Art Museum in Washington, D.C.

The work became the focal point of the next stage of the trip north. Denis and Messer drove to Elloree. They walked the streets of the small town of less than a thousand people. As he had done in Provincetown, Denis went into convenience stores and restaurants with a tape recorder, this time asking locals if they knew of James Hampton and recording their answers. Nobody had heard of Hampton. Then they drove to Washington to see the *Throne* for themselves. They went to the Smithsonian and found the piece, which took up an entire room in the gallery. They spent hours there, observing and talking to other visitors. Messer began to feel that Denis was becoming overwhelmed by the experience.

Afterward, they got a room for the night in a small motel near the museum. They showered, turned on the TV, and were watching the evening news when Denis turned to Messer and said, "I've got to go."

"What do you mean?" Messer asked.

"I have to get out of here. I can't take it. I have to go," Denis said. He packed up, asked Messer for a ride to the airport, bought a ticket, and flew back to Massachusetts, leaving Messer to drive the final leg of the journey by himself. The combination of the trip and the visit to the museum had apparently given Denis sensory overload. The observations he had accumulated along the way, however, were beginning to be processed in his mind and would become source material once he made it back to the safer environs of his office, his desk, and his blank pages of paper.

*

Much of the work of transforming his experiences from the trip with Messer into literature would take place at an ideal location for such work. Denis had applied for and been chosen as the poet in residence at the Frost homestead in Franconia, New Hampshire, the house where the poet Robert Frost had lived in the early part of the twentieth century. He had learned of the opportunity through his friend from the Work Center, Cleopatra Mathis, who had held the position the previous year. A few months after he learned that he was chosen, he packed up his typewriter, a new word processor, and clothes and personal items, and got a ride from Lucinda and Matt from Wellfleet to New Hampshire.

The stay at the Frost house was to be a solo affair. The house where he was to spend the next two months was a classic wooden New England structure, with a long front porch that offered a striking view of Mount Lafayette and the Franconia mountain range. Inside, the house was relatively spartan. The seven rooms contained much Robert Frost memorabilia, but little else. A reporter from the *Boston Globe* was on hand to write about the new poet in residence on his arrival in Franconia. The reporter described Denis as "curly haired and boyish looking." Denis paid tribute to the name on his new home. "The first time I came here [on the porch], I got shivers thinking this is where the great man stood," he said.

Frost, best known for the poem "The Road Not Taken" and the lines "Two roads diverged in a wood, and I— / I took the one less traveled by," was a prolific poet who lived to the age of eighty-eight and won four Pulitzer Prizes. Denis focused on another aspect of Frost's life. He had researched Frost, and he took the *Globe* reporter into the room where Frost had apparently threatened his wife with a gun. The reporter asked if Denis saw any similarity between Frost's work and his own. "Particularly with the darker side," Denis told him. "Particularly with death. There was a time when I was acutely concerned with it."

Denis settled in and used the isolation of the Frost home to forge ahead. He was spending the summer in a shrine to a version of the past, but his subject matter was far in the future. For his next book, he had conjured up a world that existed many years after a nuclear apocalypse. The setting was a new rendering of the landscape he had observed on his trip to the Florida Keys with Messer. In the work in progress, Key West was now called Twicetown, so called because of the two unexploded nuclear bombs that had allowed the island to survive a world war. The scenic highway he and Messer had driven on their way from the tip of Florida to Key West was, in Denis's fictional world, covered with hulks, skeletons, and ashes. The history of America and the world were a faded memory.

The protagonist and title character, an adolescent boy named Fiskadoro, owns a relic of the civilized world, a clarinet, and he takes lessons on the instrument in one of the many attempts by characters to recreate the past in the postnuclear world. Denis said the idea was initially "for a book about a person left after the nuclear holocaust, living in sort of a savage state. It was much more primitive than this, and very tribal." In the writing, the vision expanded to a world complete with worshippers waiting for the return of Bob Marley, pidgin dialects, a postapocalyptic fishing-based economy, a ragtag symphony orchestra, and allusions to another of the totems from his road trip with Messer: the great Hemingway. One of the only remaining books to survive the nuclear war is a copy of *The Sun Also Rises,* leading many inhabitants of Twicetown to name themselves after the protagonist, Jake Barnes.

Growing out the world of *Fiskadoro* was on his mind at the Frost house, but so was the writing of verse. "Since I'm in a place of poetry, I want to try to devote more of my time to that than anything else," he said. One such effort came directly from the road trip. He began to craft a paean to James Hampton's *Throne.* The poem that began to emerge included images he and Messer saw and discussed as the Toyota made its way north—Cape Canaveral, the Elloree Stop n' Go, his abrupt escape from Washington, D.C., to Massachusetts. The poem, in the end, was to be about Hampton and, like so much of Denis's poetry, loneliness. "To think he died unknown and without a friend," he wrote. "But this feeling isn't sorrow. I was his friend."

*

The small steps Denis had been taking since Provincetown on the path toward journalism became much larger in 1984 when he set off on what at the time was his first attempt at a true reporting trip. He said later, "I wanted to experience what real chaos was like... places where the authority has broken down, somehow or another." The closest place to Cape Cod in the mid-1980s to find that type of environment in the world was Nicaragua, where a fight for control of the country had been raging since the beginning of the decade. The small Central American country had been run by the Somoza regime, which was supported by the U.S. government, since the 1930s. In 1979, the Sandinista National Liberation Front, backed by the Soviet Union, toppled the Somoza government, opening up another Cold War skirmish, this one not too far from the southern U.S. border. In 1984, an election was approaching in Nicaragua. Fighting between the contras, heavily financed by United States at the behest of the administration of President Ronald Reagan, and the Sandinistas was heating up. Denis booked his flights and headed to the chaos zone.

The idea was to report on the conflict with the goal of eventually writing nonfiction magazine articles. Denis went to Costa Rica and crossed the border into Nicaragua to begin his reporting. Very shortly after arriving, he began to doubt his ability to make the transition to journalism. The thought of his analysis of politics and ideology being widely read and believed by the magazine consumers of America was, he quickly decided, untenable. Still, despite no experience or contacts, he tried to forge a career as an international war correspondent. He began to contact editors at U.S. publications, offering his services to whoever would take his call. All rejected him. His money quickly began to run out. He toured the hotels of Managua, first staying at the nicer establishments where he observed actual journalists drinking cocktails and casually exchanging war stories. Then, as his funds dwindled, he moved down the chain, to smaller hotels, and finally to boardinghouses in the slums of the city.

If he couldn't quite be a foreign correspondent yet, he determined he would instead step into the shoes of another of his literary idols, Graham Greene, the English writer famous for setting his novels in politically and morally ambiguous locales. Denis began observing and taking notes with the idea of crafting a fictional account of Nicaragua, a task he was far more comfortable with. He also discovered he felt at ease in the midst of the anarchy that he had taken the trip to find. In fact, the dangerous environment he had landed in was thrilling to him. The echoes of his youth, spent outside the U.S. border, living as an outsider, flooded back. It was a lesson about himself that he would take to heart, and one he would remember when the opportunity to return to similar destinations presented itself.

Shortly after Denis returned to the States, he was scheduled to give a reading at Warren Wilson College in Swannanoa, North Carolina, which housed a prestigious MFA program. He had been invited by his friend and classmate from the Writers' Workshop, John Skoyles. On arrival, Denis talked excitedly about his recent excursion to Central America. He gave Skoyles a Nicaraguan coin he'd brought back from his trip. The poet C. K. Williams, who was a decade older than Denis and of another generation, was another invited guest that week at the college. Williams overheard Denis and Skoyles talking and approached. What was it like down in Nicaragua? Williams asked.

"It's rock 'n' roll, man," Denis replied, channeling the '60s. "It's all rock 'n' roll!"

Williams shook his head disgustedly, turned, and walked away.

*

Fiskadoro began appearing on the shelves of bookstores in the late spring and early summer of 1985. For the cover, Knopf used "The Departure of Quetzalcoatl," a section of the painting *The Epic of American Civilization*, by early twentieth-century Mexican artist José Clemente Orozco, which featured a bearded godlike figure standing in the surf as serpents and snakes swirl around him. Denis's second book had gone from just an idea to an actual, published book in a mere two years—the blink of an eye compared to his experience with *Angels*. His debut had heralded the arrival of an important new author on the literary scene, and, like all writers who make a splash with their first offering, the appearance of book number two came with anticipation and potential pitfalls. It could establish for him a permanent place in the literary landscape or mark him as a one-note writer destined to fade quickly from view.

The consensus of the reviewers of North America was the former. Denis, they all agreed, was a writer of singular talent, and his new book, while it had its flaws, was a work of extraordinary imagination and linguistic dexterity. The headline of the story, they all decided, was Denis's brilliance; the subhead was that he hadn't quite hit the mark. "It's the sort of novel a young Herman Melville might have written," wrote Michiko Kakutani for the *New York Times,* "had he lived today and studied such disparate works as the Bible, *The Waste Land, Fahrenheit 451* and *Dog Soldiers,* screened *Stars Wars* and *Apocalypse Now* several times, dropped a lot of acid and listened to hours of Jimi Hendrix and the Rolling Stones." By the end of the book, she added as a proviso, the prose becomes "increasingly windy." The writing is "so well internalized as to approach poetic magic," but it "sometimes falters in an excess of eclecticism," the *Philadelphia Inquirer* declared. "Johnson's exquisite prose and flawless sense of structure don't fully compensate for the passion his story lacks," declared the *Austin American-Statesman.*

He had avoided the young writer's trap of trying to duplicate himself. As his career would progress, it would become evident that he was immune to such a trap, because the personal style that was to emerge was one in which each new novel had only the barest traces of the one that came before. The through line was talent and imagination. The critical reaction to *Fiskadoro* meant his work was respected and his standing was secure. Another bonus was the fact that the book sold well, going into a second printing in the fall of 1985. Denis rendered a slightly less affirmative judgment of *Fiskadoro* later that year, in a letter to Maury a few months after its publication: "Actually it's kind of a weird book," he said. "But who cares?"

The reception cemented his position as a rising star. When *Esquire* released its collector's issue of 1985, featuring "America's New Leadership Class: Men and Women under Forty Who Are Changing the Nation," Denis was on the list, among such other young American up-and-comers as Bruce Springsteen, Cyndi Lauper, Eddie Murphy, and Larry Bird. If he had survived the perils of the release of his second novel, though, he was having less success with the hazards of his second marriage. Increasingly, he was finding it difficult to navigate the effects that his newfound status was having on his personal life. There was a downside to his success that would, sooner rather than later, begin to have an impact on his emotional well-being and that of the people around him.

HIDING OUT 17

And there is an approach to this section of the Mendocino coast...that thrills the soul, beauty too wonderful to seem real, to be remembered as long as memory lasts. —*Ukiah Daily Journal,* May 18, 1934

The problem with undiscovered paradises is, of course, that the word always gets out, and they always get discovered. The world at large had begun to discover the sleepy, hidden little beach town of Wellfleet, Massachusetts. Denis wrote to Maury Barr and described the conundrum he was facing. More people were coming up, so real estate prices on the Cape were rising, which meant that the sea captain's house was worth a lot of money—much more than they paid for it, which meant that it was getting really crowded in town, "which means we have to get out of here."

Denis himself was no longer undiscovered. Like Cape Cod real estate, he was in demand and his price was going up. There were now Denis Johnson fans out there, and some of them began to find their way to Wellfleet and to the Soroban Gallery on the first floor of the sea captain's house, looking for their hero at all times of the day and night. This was a development that Denis did not appreciate.

Invitations to readings and appearances were constant. Denis ignored many of them, but some were too good to pass up. He was invited to an event in New Orleans during Mardi Gras. Lucinda came along. They went to one of the Mardi Gras parades and began to participate in the age-old New Orleans custom where costumed performers atop the floats throw beads and trinkets to the adoring crowd. Denis became obsessed with obtaining and collecting the trinkets. Among a crowd of stumbling, inebriated bead pursuers, he was the lone sober attendee engaging in the battle. His intensity led to several near scuffles. Lucinda pulled him aside and tried to calm him down. "Hey, it's not that important," she said. "And these people are going to kill you."

More often, though, Denis took the trips by himself while Lucinda stayed in Wellfleet to run the gallery. On the road, he was the center of attention, and much of that attention came from young women. He had trouble passing it up. "He had a million affairs, because who doesn't want to have an affair with a famous poet author?" Lucinda said.

The same sequence of events began to repeat itself. Denis would take a trip for an appearance, meet a young admirer at the reading, and end up in bed with her. He'd return to Wellfleet, mope around for a week or two, and eventually, wracked with guilt, confess his infidelity to Lucinda. Lucinda would throw him out of the house for a while, eventually relent, and take him back until the next episode.

Denis related the problem to Sam Messer. Shortly after hearing about Denis's situation, Messer was watching the evening news and saw a report about a new organization he hadn't heard of: Sexaholics Anonymous. It was a twelve-step program that revolved around confessional meetings, similar to AA, only for sex addicts. Immediately he called Denis to offer the solution to his problems. Denis cut him off. "I've been going to the meetings for months," he told Messer.

Still, the issue persisted. Lucinda began to feel that Denis saw a loophole in the AA code—one that existed in Catholicism, his current chosen religion, as well. These beliefs allowed Denis to give in to his addictions, apologize, and be forgiven, until the next time, when he would do it all over again. "I remember getting really tired of it," she said. "You [confess], and you're pardoned, it's like, okay, are you just going to keep doing the same thing over and over? How many times can you say you're sorry?"

CHAPTER 17

In the summer of 1985, Denis and Lucinda separated. This time, they lived apart for several weeks. To Lucinda, the marriage had run its course. Denis didn't think so and made one final appeal to her. What their relationship needed was a new start, he told her. They should sell the sea captain's house, find some land in the country somewhere, and leave behind the temptations and distractions that were driving them apart. Reluctantly at first, Lucinda agreed, and soon they were together again and searching for their next paradise.

By this time, they had three cats and two Great Danes, one of which weighed 180 pounds, and Lucinda wanted to add a few more species to their brood. As they hunted for their new home and the location for their new life, they shared an inside joke: there was to be no talking about poetry and no talking about painting, but a lot of talk about pig farming.

At first, they set their sights on New England and began taking trips to New Hampshire and Vermont, so Denis could be a car ride away from his agent and publisher. They found a ten-room house in Corinth, Vermont, with forty acres and a stream filled with trout that seemed right. Then Lucinda decided she wanted to look in California, to get closer to her roots. She and her mother took several trips driving around Northern California, until they settled on the town of Point Arena in Mendocino County. It was an isolated little burg that required a long, winding drive up Highway 101. They found a thirty-acre ranch on top of a mountain with a breathtaking view of the Pacific. The nearest town was thirty minutes away. "It was one of the most beautiful places in the world, actually," Lucinda recalled. "It was gorgeous."

The sea captain's house sold easily for a big profit in early 1986. Lucinda and Denis had bought out her sister and parents earlier, so they settled their affairs and got ready to relocate. Denis bought a Chevy minivan to transport the animals. By the summer of 1986, the Johnsons were residents of Mendocino County.

Shortly after they moved into the ranch, Denis invited Maury Barr down from Washington to see the place. Maury was married by then and had a baby son. He brought his family to Point Arena. Maury found Denis to be in high spirits. In college, Denis had told Maury that his one true goal was to be able to live off his writing. Now he was doing just that, and he was living well, with money to spare. Denis took his friend to his garage and showed Maury a sparkling Corvette sports car he had just purchased on credit. He told Maury to leave his wife and baby at the ranch with Lucinda, and the two of them would try out the new car. Denis took the wheel and immediately began to test its limits. "First he started doing doughnuts in a field, and then all of the sudden he took off down the highway," Barr remembered.

With Denis's foot on the gas pedal, the Corvette went faster and faster down Highway 101, until finally Maury cracked. "Slow down! I've got a baby and I don't want to leave him fatherless," he begged.

Denis looked over casually, as if the car were standing still.

"Oh, am I scaring you?" he asked with a smile.

*

At first, life on the ranch was exactly as they had pictured it. There was an old barn on the property. Together, they turned one side of the barn into a studio for Lucinda's art, and the other side they made into a study where Denis could write. Lucinda had loved horses as a child, so now she bought some for the ranch and began to return to her childhood passion. The isolation of Northern California and the invigoration triggered by his new environs allowed Denis to slip into an easy routine. He would rise early, head over to the studio in the barn, take in the morning view of the Pacific Ocean washing out over the horizon, watch the osprey and herons diving for their breakfast, and then sit down at his desk to write. He would stay in the studio until one or two in the afternoon. It didn't matter if the words were flowing or not; he put in the time every day. In the afternoon, he would drive to an AA meeting in one of the tiny towns that dot the Northern California coast, then come back and spend what time was left in the day working on the ranch.

Mendocino County was an ideal place for the Johnsons to disappear from public view. It was full of old hippies and wayward musicians who were doing the same thing. The population was sparse, and the economy was fueled by illegal marijuana growers. "There were a lot of people hiding out up there," Lucinda recalled. Years later, when he was ready to turn this part of his life into fiction, Denis would write that the region was a "place a person could disappear into" and the towns "felt like little naps you might never wake up from."

As he had done at his previous stops, Denis found friends among the other attendees at AA meetings. He became a sponsor for Jim Hodder, a recovering addict who had been a drummer in the pop-jazz band Steely Dan in the '70s. Hodder became a good friend and gave Matt piano lessons for a while. A few years later, Hodder went off the wagon and drowned in his swimming pool at the age of forty-two.

Another friend Denis met through AA, one who would become one of his closest confidants for the remainder of his life, was giant of a man named Bill Winkelholz, whom everybody called Wink. Winkelholz grew up, all the way to six feet, nine inches tall, in Glendale, California, where he played basketball and was a star center for Glendale Hoover High. He played for legendary UCLA coach John Wooden in 1965 on a team that went 28–2 and won the national championship. Winkelholz finished his college career at Humboldt State, married, and migrated to Northern California, where he became a successful building contractor for many years, until he discovered cocaine and other drugs. By the time Denis met him, Winkelholz had lost his business and family thanks to his addictions and was living in a local junkyard. The two bonded during AA meetings. Denis would help his new friend through several recoveries and relapses during his years in California.

It wasn't long after Denis and Lucinda had settled into life on the ranch that the next Denis Johnson novel was published. The failed reporting trip to Nicaragua of two years before had turned into a success once it moved into the realm of fiction. A manuscript was completed in less than nine months, then published in the fall of 1986. "I felt rushed because I wasn't really steeped in the locale," he told a reporter from the *New York Times* at the time of publication. "The feeling of the locale was leaving me rapidly, so I wrote it fast. I wanted to give it the kind of sensation it had left in me."

The story that he had created was straight out of the Graham Greene oeuvre. Denis entitled it *The Stars at Noon,* after a line from another of his literary heroes, poet W. S. Merwin, and he also excerpted several Merwin poems in the text. The novel featured a first-person female narrator, a nameless American expatriate and part-time freelance writer who dabbles in prostitution. Just like Denis was on his trip two years earlier, she is in Nicaragua ostensibly for journalism, but actually she is there because she wants to know "the exact dimensions of hell." The plot follows her through her attempts to escape the country, her wrangling with third-world bureaucracy, her nights in seedy Managua hotels. She meets and falls in love with a shadowy English businessman for an oil company. They bounce from bar to bar, hide from indeterminate government officials, plot their escape, are tested with Greene-inspired moral dilemmas. The book had the architecture of a political thriller, but at its heart it was, as one reviewer put it, "a labyrinthine passion play, with the requisite overtones of spiritual torment and betrayal."

Reviewers were split on *The Stars at Noon.* Some found it to be mystical and poetic, while others viewed it as pretentious and incoherent. The release of the book and the subsequent requests for publicity were not enough to draw Denis off the ranch. Another demand for his presence, one that had a significantly greater impact on his bank account, would eventually be the enticement that would lure him back to the city.

Elliott Lewitt was a young documentary filmmaker from New York City who moved to Los Angeles in 1979 with the idea of writing and producing a Hollywood feature. He spent the next five years working toward that goal. In 1984, he was on the set of a movie he had developed called *At Close Range,* starring Sean Penn and Christopher Walken, when an assistant brought him a copy of *Angels*. He read it during the brief lulls on the set of his movie and quickly decided that it would be his next project.

Soon after his decision, Lewitt flew to San Francisco and drove up to Mendicino County. He and Denis spent an afternoon in the bar at the

Gualala Hotel discussing *Angels,* the movie business, and life in general. Lewitt immediately was drawn Denis. He could sense that Denis had some experience with the type of characters that appeared in his first novel, and that he was somebody for whom there was "no time or reason for bullshit." Lewitt decided, despite Denis's lack of experience, that the writer of the novel was the person who should write the screenplay. The writer didn't need much convincing. Lewitt purchased temporary rights to *Angels.* Denis and Lucinda happily accepted the six-figure boost to their income, and Denis sat down to write his first screen adaptation.

Shortly after the contract was signed, Denis began traveling back and forth between Point Arena and Los Angeles, attending occasional meetings to discuss his progress on the script. The process of writing a screenplay was new to Denis. He had little experience with the cooperative process that was filmmaking. Now, he was receiving notes from other readers of his work. And because he was beholden to those who would eventually produce the movie version of the book, he was required to at least listen to suggestions, and perhaps make the changes outlined in the notes. The idea of losing complete control did not sit well with him.

Once *At Close Range* was finished and released, Lewitt began in earnest working the town in an effort to get the financial backing he would need to make his next movie. For *At Close Range,* he had served as writer and producer. *Angels,* he decided, would be his directorial debut. Actors and actresses were approached for the roles of Bill Houston and Jamie. Both lead roles were dream parts that would be showcases for young stars-to-be who were looking for a route to stardom. For Lewitt, though, it was a classic Hollywood catch-22: he needed the actors to buy into his project so he could get the money from the studios, but he needed the money from the studios before he could offer the actors contracts.

Still, Lewitt's vision of *Angels* on the big screen looked like it would become a reality. It was enough of a sure thing to merit a mention in the *Cinefile* column in the *Los Angeles Times.* The film was budgeted at $5 million. Lewitt told the *Times* he was "very close to having all the financing." Young actresses on the rise were slotted into the role of Jamie. Meg Ryan, then twenty-six years old and best known for her role in *Top Gun,* was attached. Then Holly Hunter, coming off a star-making debut and an Academy Award nomination for *Broadcast News,* was to be the big-screen Jamie. Arliss Howard, best known for the recent Stanley Kubrick–directed Vietnam epic *Full Metal Jacket,* would be the killer, Bill Houston. At another point, Ed Harris, who had already been in several successful movies including *The Right Stuff* and *Places in the Heart,* and who was known as an accomplished stage actor as well, was slotted into the Bill Houston role. Readings were held. The script circulated around the industry.

Throughout the process, Lewitt was protective both of Denis and of his own vision of what *Angels* should look like on-screen. But the process was immensely frustrating for both of them. Executives, who had likely only read treatments of the script, told Lewitt they loved it and would definitely finance it—if only it had a happy ending. Such suggestions were made with no promise of a contract, of course. At other times, actors or actresses with bigger names who were known to draw the moviegoing public to the box office on opening weekend, but whom Lewitt thought were completely wrong for the parts, were floated by studio suits. Well-known directors, with the clout to get the needed financing, expressed interest, but said it was conditional: they wanted to rewrite Denis's script. Lewitt turned them all down.

The only such rejection he would later regret was when he received a phone call from a representative of Ethan Hawke. The young actor had read *Angels* and decided he wanted to direct the movie version. A meeting was suggested. Hawke was a highly sought-after presence in the industry at the time—someone who, if attached to a project, could give that project the boost necessary to get it made. But Lewitt still, at that point, could not envision anybody directing the movie other than himself. He said no to Hawke.

The dance continued for several years and through several iterations of the script. Via Lewitt, Denis heard all the ideas that various studio executives offered to make his book into a blockbuster—ideas that inevitably would mean waving the Hollywood wand over the story and changing some aspect of it from the tale Denis had created. Eventually, several years after he first contacted Denis, Lewitt could no longer afford to keep paying for the rights to *Angels.*

One day, Denis returned from a trip to Southern California and arrived at his home in Point Arena even more dejected than usual. It's over, he told Lucinda. Somebody else wanted him to change the ending. He had told them he wouldn't be coming back.

"I was proud of him," Lucinda said. "He stood his ground on that one."

*

If his first foray into Hollywood did not result in his work being projected on the big screen, it did introduce Denis to the world of filmmaking and the community of artists and executives who operated it. Through the process, he made numerous contacts that would pave the way for a steady stream of film-related paychecks, which he would use to supplement his income for the rest of his life.

One opportunity that came soon after his *Angels* experience put him back into the middle of the Nicaraguan jungle. He had become friendly with a filmmaker named Richard Pearce. Pearce had started out as a cinematographer in the '70s, working on award-winning documentaries including *Woodstock* and *Interviews with Mai Lai Veterans,* before moving to directing and helming successful feature films in the '80s. He had been interested in the rights to *Angels,* but once he learned the rights were unavailable, he began looking for other projects he could work on that involved Denis. The hostilities in Nicaragua had become a cause célèbre among a certain element of the Hollywood community, and projects that centered around it held a modicum of cachet in the mid-'80s. Soon, Pearce had convinced HBO to finance a trip to Nicaragua so that he and Denis could update *The Stars at Noon,* with the end goal being a screenplay, and eventually an HBO movie.

They arranged to fly to Costa Rica, where they planned to travel by land into Nicaragua to meet up with Susan Meiselas, a documentary photographer who had been operating in Central America on and off since the late '70s. Before they connected with Meiselas, however, they had an adventure of their own in Costa Rica.

The small country to the south of Nicaragua was formally neutral in the battle between the contras and the Sandinistas, but the contras, with the help of the CIA, operated clandestine operations on the Costa Rican side of the border. A shadowy figure by the name of John Hull was a large part of the CIA–contra plan. Hull, a World War II veteran from Indiana who had taken on the role of anticommunist crusader, owned a 1,600-acre ranch in the region. With CIA assistance, Hull operated secret air bases on his ranch where weapons, and later drugs, were funneled to the contras. Hull had five CIA-financed bodyguards and a reputation as the godfather of northern Costa Rica.

Pearce had somehow obtained a phone number for Hull. He dialed the number, told the voice on the other end of the line that he and Denis were Hollywood filmmakers scouting locations, and, to his surprise, received an immediate invitation to Hull's ranch. He and Denis were told to travel to a small town near the border, find a particular table at a café in the town, and wait. The voice on the phone told them they would be met by one of Hull's drivers and taken a few hours through the jungle to the Hull ranch. All went according to plan, and on their very first night in the country, they arrived at the ranch and were greeted by Hull and his wife, served an elaborate Costa Rican dinner, and then invited into Hull's study, a small room filled with maps and filing cabinets that the godfather of Costa Rica used to strategize his war efforts.

Pearce had told Hull nothing about his and Denis's background, other than that they were from Hollywood. If Hull had known anything about him, Pearce would have received a decidedly different reception. He was as far as you could get on the opposite side of the political spectrum from his host. He had been the cinematographer on a 1974 anti–Vietnam War documentary called *Hearts and Minds* that had won an Academy Award. The director of that film was Peter Taylor, another darling of the left who had gone on to be involved in pro-Sandinista projects related to Nicaragua. As Hull excitedly showed Denis and Pearce his grand plan for defeating the Sandinistas and bringing glory to Reagan's America, Pearce noticed, in one of the open file cabinets, a file labeled "Peter Taylor." He realized, as he leafed through it, that Hull was actively tracking his friend.

Just as Pearce was becoming truly anxious about his situation, Denis came over to him with a twinkle in his eye. "He told me that he was having a fantasy about pulling John Hull aside and telling him that he was currently harboring a communist spy," Pearce remembered.

Denis decided against ratting out his friend, and they made it safely off the ranch. A few days later, they were traveling with the Sandinistas. They met up with Susan Meiselas and hired a pilot to take them to the town of San Carlos on the Nicaraguan side of the border. The pilot brought his tiny four-seat propeller plane in for a landing on a runway that, its occupants could see, was on a mesa and came to an abrupt end at a cliff, over which was a ninety-degree drop into the waters of the Gulf of Mexico, hundreds of feet below. As the plane approached the end of the runway, the pilot began screaming in Spanish for them to open the doors in order to slow the plane down and avoid a quick trip off the edge of the cliff.

From there, they traveled in canoes, accompanied by machine gun–toting Sandinistas, down the San Juan River, which separates Costa Rica and Nicaragua for a portion of the border. "You have to understand that at that time, traveling down that river was very scary, because that was the divide, that was exactly where the contras were crossing over," remembered Meiselas.

Throughout their adventures, both Meiselas and Pearce marveled at the joy Denis was getting out of the entire experience. He was in the middle of a war, Pearce recalled, and he was like "a kid in a candy store.... His kind of enthusiasm for the sheer adventure of it, was just matchless," Pearce said. "I've never been with anybody who had that sense of just wanting to throw himself into it."

Like nearly all of Denis's efforts related to filmmaking, nothing much came of his second adventure in Central America. HBO lost interest in the project, and it faded away. "Looking back, arguably we'd have had a better film if I just filmed everything that happened to us on that trip, and then made a documentary about it," Pearce said. It did, however, serve as another step on the road to journalism for Denis. He understood clearly now that he thrived in the chaos of political upheaval and armed warfare. He had developed a taste for it. He had found that he had the constitutional makeup to be a war correspondent. Now all he needed was a job.

LOOKING FOR ZEALOTS 18

I say to myself, "Oh, no, you can't say that! It isn't done."... But you reach a point where you realize, of course you can do it. You can do anything. You just have to issue yourself a license to do those things. And then you do them. **—Michael Herr, on covering the Vietnam War**

When Denis walked into the Manhattan office of *Esquire* magazine at 1790 Broadway in early 1988, he held in his hands a copy of his favorite book, Walt Whitman's *Leaves of Grass*. Though transcendental poetry may have been on his mind, he was at *Esquire* to talk about journalism—specifically where on the globe he would find his first story for the magazine. A few months before, Denis had been contacted by a young editorial assistant named Will Blythe about writing some text to accompany a photo essay *Esquire* would be publishing. Blythe had joined the staff of *Esquire* only months before. He also happened to have read and loved both *Angels* and *The Stars at Noon*. Knowing *Esquire's* history of transforming novelists into magazine writers, he tracked Denis down, called him, and offered him the job. Denis wasn't interested in writing the text for the photo essay, but he certainly was interested in working for *Esquire*.

The plan was to walk down to Patsy's, an Italian restaurant that was a favorite of Frank Sinatra's, and plot out Denis's first assignment for the magazine. They took the elevator down to the street and began the walk along Broadway to the restaurant. A few steps into it, Denis pulled up.

"Did you see that?" he asked.

Blythe looked around. All he saw was what he always saw on the streets of Manhattan: people, cars, stores, city life.

"What was it?"

"You didn't see that?" Denis asked again with a pleasant laugh. "I guess in New York you get so you don't notice that kind of thing."

Blythe didn't inquire further, but he thought that perhaps Denis was talking about a man they'd passed, an aging gentleman suffering from some ailment, battling, step by step, to make his way down the street. It was an example of what Blythe would come to understand about Denis: that he had an eye for the "subtle glories of infirmity" that the majority of civilization blithely ignored.

At Patsy's, Denis's attire didn't meet the restaurant's dress code, so he borrowed a blue blazer from the waitstaff to gain entry. (From then on, Denis and Blythe always dined at Patsy's, and each time the staff would be ready for Denis with a blue blazer to borrow.) At that first meal, they discussed *Esquire's* war correspondence history. Famed *Esquire* editor Harold Hayes had an eye for the kind of literary talent that would be able to bring foreign conflicts to life in the way that traditional journalism never could. Hayes had been the editor of *Esquire* during the '60s, an era in which the magazine encouraged literary innovation. Hayes, along with another influential editor, Clay Felker, helped create the school of New Journalism—magazine writing that combined in-depth reporting written in the style of literary fiction, but based on fact. *Esquire* published groundbreaking nonfiction writing by Gay Talese, Norman Mailer, Tom Wolfe, and others whose names would become associated with this style of writing, which flourished during the era. (It was Wolfe who coined the phrase.) Blythe and Denis talked about Michael Herr, a then-unknown young writer whom Hayes had hired and sent to Vietnam, where he penned vivid first-person accounts of the war for *Esquire,* and later wrote a book-length account entitled *Dispatches,* which was widely considered the seminal nonfiction work on the Vietnam War.

This was exactly the type of reporting Denis was interested in, and he had an idea for where such reporting might take place. He pitched Blythe a story about Muslim guerillas in the Philippines. He proposed a trip to the Arakan Valley, the southern region of Mindanao Island, where Muslim revolutionaries had been fighting a secessionist war since the mid-1970s. More than forty thousand armed fighters were on the island, at war with the Philippine government and with themselves, as the separatist movement had broken into factions. It was just the type of chaos that Denis was drawn to, and it had the added bonus of being a trip back to the land of his childhood. Shortly after their lunch at Patsy's, Blythe got the green light, and Denis was on his way across the Pacific.

When Denis climbed onto a plane to the Philippines in June 1988 looking for chaos, he was escaping another kind of chaos: the domestic type. Life at the ranch had been going steadily downhill since he began his commute to Los Angeles to work on the *Angels* screenplay. His propensity toward infidelity had returned. Once again, Lucinda was threatening to end the marriage. She also did not approve of his plan to risk his life on the other side of the world.

Soon after arriving in Mindanao, Denis made contact with some of leaders of the Moro National Liberation Front, one of the Muslim separatist groups, and began negotiating with them to be allowed to visit their camp. Communication with the outside world was hit or miss. He told Blythe to contact Lucinda and tell her that he was all right. He added that because of the tenuous status of his marriage, Blythe should try not to mention machine guns, guerillas, or other details that would imply he was in danger.

His adventure in Mindanao was to be hot, drenched in sweat, and filled with long intervals of waiting—waiting for developments that were frustratingly beyond his control. Before his trip, he had been in contact with the mayor of a small jungle town called Damulog, who had implied that he could take Denis to meet some of the rebel fighters. Denis traveled to the town, checked into a seven-room plywood hotel with no running water, and began negotiating for a trip into the jungle to meet the rebels. His stay in Damulog, envisioned as a single night, extended into several days, then several weeks. His contacts kept postponing the trip into the jungle and adding stipulations. The trip would be more likely to happen, Denis was told, if he took some pictures for them of a schoolhouse in another town, which they would use to apply to the government for assistance. Denis hiked hours to the town to take the pictures, then took an eight-hour bus trip to get the film developed. Still, his hosts were not ready to take him to the rebel camp.

He passed the time drinking coffee and eating rice in a ramshackle eatery with intermittent power called People's Sunshine Café, and taking notes. The residents of Damulog sipped rum and watched Denis. "A lid of clouds pressed the heat down so hard it crushed the flowers and forced its way inside everybody's head," he wrote of the experience. "Nobody moved. It was ax-murdering weather." He also consciously analyzed his own reporting techniques. "From out of vague intuitions, my rules emerge," he wrote in his notes. "Travel without the solace of other American companions. Don't disengage myself from personal encounters; go with them, if they want to talk, talk, if they want to eat, eat."

Denis also laid out his thought processes as he struggled to understand what he was, in fact, searching for in Mindanao. It was not a better understanding of this particular persecuted religious group that he was after, or even the desire to meet people who were willing to give their lives for their beliefs. What he was there for, he wrote, was to have his own faith tested. To be in the presence of true religious zealotry, he thought, would provide such a test. Denis believed his faith was predicated on his ability to predict and control his environment, but he feared that the ability only existed in his own narrow reality, and once he pierced the walls of his life, his faith would crumble.

After weeks of waiting, his contacts finally agreed to take Denis through the jungle to the rebel camp. They hiked for hours through the heat and mud, camped for a night, then hiked for another day. "I perspired in torrents. My clothes were sopping. My pockets were full of sweat. I couldn't seem to drink enough water to quench me, but I knew I was drinking too much. I filled my jug at every creek, but still it was empty," he wrote.

They reached the camp, where they found a couple dozen undernourished warriors armed with outdated weapons and a few children. Denis feared he would be held for ransom, but his hosts were welcoming. He spent several days in the camp, ostensibly waiting to meet with a regional chief who, he was repeatedly told, was "a handsome, handsome man" but who would never materialize. The thatched-roof hut he slept in with the fighters allowed the torrential Philippine rains to soak them each night. Denis spent most of his time with a one-eyed boy named Mosa, who asked Denis to adopt him and take him back to the United States.

In the end, he completed his reporting and traveled back to America without adopting any young Muslim guerillas. Instead, he brought back a parasite; he had acquired his new friend by being bitten by malaria-infested mosquitoes as he hiked through the jungle and forded streams. On his arrival back in Mendocino County, Lucinda told him he was not welcome on the ranch, so he went to stay with his friend Bill Winkelholz. His physical condition quickly deteriorated. Despite warnings, he had taken no preventative medicine before his trip into the jungle.

He began experiencing recurrent fever spikes and chills. His skin turned yellow, as did his eyes. He began to hallucinate. He called Morgan and told him that he was watching a chicken the size of a house land on the lawn outside his window. He called his brother, Randy, who was a herpetologist, and described his symptoms. Randy told him it was obvious that he had malaria, and perhaps he should call a doctor instead of a specialist in lizards and amphibians.

Still, Denis chose to wait it out. The disease progressed, and finally, when he was barely conscious, he called Lucinda. It took just one look at him for Lucinda to pick up the phone and call an ambulance. The EMTs wheeled him, comatose, out of Winkelholz's house. He spent the next nine days in the hospital, in and out of consciousness. Once he was safely on the road to recovery, doctors told him the disease had nearly been fatal.

It would be several months of recovery from his bout with malaria before Denis could write the article that he had promised *Esquire* about his trip to Mindanao. He finally sent the manuscript to New York late in 1988. The story he submitted had just a few paragraphs about the plight of the Muslim separatists and their political concerns. The rest of it was made up of Denis's observations about Damulog and its residents, the details of his efforts to meet the rebels, and his personal motivations for traveling there in the first place. He infused the story with vivid detail, and, as he had in *The Stars at Noon,* found humor in the pace and spirit of life in the third world. He described one of his many evenings in Damulog, as residents organized a dance party outside his window:

> I was heartbroken and pissed off to hear a "disco" show striking up again on the basketball court. Meanwhile there was a meeting, right outside my door at the hotel, of barangay Captains from Cotobato, and they preferred to listen to a Neil Young tape loudly and ignore the "disco." Eventually, the folks on the basketball court got their act together, more or less, and played some songs all the way through. I looked out my window and beheld the scene, and sure enough, not a soul was on the court, nobody was dancing, they only ringed the dance floor as if it were sacred ground they'd traveled here as a tribe to revere. It struck me, not for the first or last time in the Philippines, that you really get an appreciation of how ridiculous we humans are, when you see someone being ridiculous in a way that you are not.

It was a meandering tale that mirrored Denis's own experience—heavy on narrative buildup, but with very little payoff. Blythe read it and understood at once that he had been correct in his initial belief that Denis's writing would translate to narrative journalism. He was particularly taken with the religious themes in the story, which focused not on the plight of the Muslims but on Denis's own search for personal meaning in his analysis of their plight. "He had a great gift for writing about religion, not in a doctrinaire fashion, but in a very idiosyncratic way," he said.

Blythe thought the piece, which came in at more than ten thousand words, needed to be trimmed if it were to make it into the magazine. One section he targeted for cutting involved Denis lying silently with the separatists at night, wondering what they were thinking. Denis wrote that he himself was thinking about "Lucinda, who was kind of divorcing me." Blythe thought the reference, which was the only mention of Lucinda in the piece, was superfluous. He called Denis, told him he planned to remove the section, and knew immediately that he had hit a nerve. "It was one of the few times I actually saw a flash of anger from him. He actually sounded like he was crying, and he said, 'No, no, you can't take her name out.'"

In the end, it didn't matter whether it was left in or not. *Esquire* chose not to publish the article. Once he thought it was ready for publication, Blythe sent the piece to Lee Eisenberg, *Esquire's* editor in chief at the time. Eisenberg sent it back to him requesting changes, then, on seeing another version, rejected it outright. "Will, realistically, I don't see much chance of running this. So, we'll have to pass. It is better than before, but still seems rather pointless to me," Eisenberg wrote.

Blythe was heartbroken, but he understood the decision. Denis had written a few critically lauded novels, but he wasn't a household name in the publishing business, and he definitely had not acquired the level of literary fame that would sell magazines if his name was put on the cover. The story Denis had written had no real action or conclusion and was about a conflict that nobody had heard of—one that wasn't receiving any press coverage whatsoever. Still, Blythe thought Denis had produced a tremendous work of personal journalism, and he didn't want his new discovery to be disappointed and give up.

Denis took it in stride. He told Blythe that the kill fee and the expense payments he'd gotten from *Esquire* had helped to repair his relationship with Lucinda. He'd given her the money so she could buy another horse.

*

Blythe thought it was important to offer another journalistic assignment to Denis quickly. It wasn't long before he found one that he knew would draw Denis out of Northern California again. Blythe clipped a photo out of the *New York Times* that had run with a story about the civil war in Liberia. In the photo, a young fighter wore a wedding dress and a wig and held a machine gun. Liberian soldiers apparently believed such outfits inoculated them against enemy bullets. He sent the photo to Denis, then called him up.

"Would you like to go this wedding?" he asked Denis.

"Who do I RSVP to?" Denis replied.

Unlike the Muslims in Mindanao, the Liberian civil war was a story that had the attention of the international media. The West African country of approximately five million people, founded in the nineteenth century by former American slaves, had seen varying levels of political unrest for a decade, beginning in 1980 when a soldier named Samuel Doe had led a popular rebellion and toppled the government. Doe gave a sneak peek of his leadership style a few days later, when all of the cabinet members of the former government were taken down to the beach, stripped to their underpants, tied to telephone poles, and executed by a drunken firing squad as television cameras rolled. Doe's reign proceeded as such a beginning would predict, with cruelty and incompetence. In 1989, an exiled politician, Charles Taylor, organized a rebel force in neighboring Ivory Coast and invaded. To add to the confusion, one of his followers, Prince Johnson, broke from Taylor and formed his own rebel force, so by the summer of 1990, three armed factions were fighting for control of the Liberian capital of Monrovia, refugees were fleeing to all borders, and reports of civilians being brutally murdered came daily from across the country. It was almost complete anarchy.

If it was true chaos Denis was after, then the city of Monrovia in September 1990 was about as close as he could hope to get. It was also an extremely dangerous place for a heretofore unpublished war correspondent. In August, Michael Goldsmith of the Associated Press, Michael Roddy of Reuters, and Mark Huband of United Press International had been detained, beaten, and threatened with execution by government forces. Denis traveled to Freetown in the neighboring country of Sierra Leone to book passage on a Nigerian freighter called the *River Oli,* which was in port, preparing to bring two hundred tons of rice and a peacekeeping force of five hundred soldiers from some West African countries into Monrovia. He arrived in Sierra Leone and found himself in the same situation as he had faced in Mindanao—waiting powerlessly for a trip he'd been promised to materialize. Day after day drifted by as one obstacle after another prevented the *River Oli* from setting sail. After a week had passed and he was still languishing in Sierra Leone, Denis called Blythe and said he didn't think he could wait any longer. Yet he remained, and after eight days of waiting, the ship finally began the journey to Liberia.

Between the time he accepted the assignment and when he arrived in Monrovia, Samuel Doe had been tortured and executed by Prince Johnson's soldiers and by Prince Johnson himself. It was that kind of war. The *River Oli* took two days to make the trip, arriving on September 28 with Denis and a few European journalists in tow, including Patrick Robert, a photographer who was working for *Esquire.* The ship's captain steered the vessel directly into the dock, gouging a wedge out of the pier. When its passengers finally disembarked, smoke was visible from burning buildings, and sporadic gunfire could be heard in the distance.

The Monrovia Denis walked into was a true version of hell on earth. Starvation had overtaken the remaining population. The shops were empty, having all been looted and looted again. Dismembered corpses lay in the streets and floated in the surf on the city's beaches, where murder squads from the various factions deposited fresh bodies. The city's remaining residents searched through piles of rubbish for any morsel of nourishment. Everywhere, dogs scavenged and feasted on corpses. Denis and the other journalists found their way to a neighborhood called Mamba Point, where embassies lay abandoned and a handful of remaining foreign diplomats waited for evacuation.

Unlike what Denis had experienced in Mindanao, the leader of the rebels in Liberia entered the story quickly. The day after they arrived, the journalists from the *River Oli,* along with a French film crew who had been on the ship, were invited to Prince Johnson's headquarters, which had been set up in the home of a Christian Lebanese Palestinian that Johnson and his forces had borrowed. Soldiers with machine guns and gas masks milled around on the lawn outside, among the many parked Mercedes sedans. Inside, Prince Johnson, the self-declared brigadier general, acting president of Liberia, and commander in chief of the Independent National Patriotic Front of Liberia, was leading his personal reggae band in a rendition of "Rivers of Babylon" as young rebel soldiers swayed to the music.

Denis and Mark Huband, another journalist covering the war, were led to chairs set up in front of a large desk. Prince Johnson joined them, dressed in fatigues and drinking a can of Budweiser wrapped in a paper handkerchief. Denis and Huband began asking the acting president of Liberia questions as the French crew filmed the interview. The conversation turned to the fate of the late president, Samuel Doe. Johnson casually told the journalists that during the course of Doe's interrogation, he had cut Doe's ears off and made him eat them. The stunned journalists asked Johnson to repeat what he had just said. He did, and then he offered to show them the video.

Soon they were led out to the veranda and given folding chairs. Soldiers wheeled in a large color television. More Budweiser was served. Johnson's wife cued up the tape. For the next hour, as the reggae band continued to play and the young rebels stood behind them and watched the video with them, hooting and cheering, Denis and Huband viewed the brutal torture of the former president of Liberia. They watched as Doe, bleeding and stripped nearly naked, begged for his life while soldiers interrogated and tortured him. Halfway through the viewing session, the driver who had brought the journalists to the compound approached fearfully. They needed to leave shortly, he told them. After 1 p.m. all the soldiers would be drunk, and anything could happen.

They stayed long enough to watch the rest of the tape and eat rice and drink more Budweiser with their hosts. Then, after Prince Johnson had given the journalists T-shirts emblazoned with the name of his reggae band, they headed back to Mamba Point. As they listened to the distant gunfire from outside while sitting in the abandoned luxury apartment of an American diplomat, Denis knew that this time, his story would be published. What he had witnessed was as gripping as it was gruesome. Seasoned war correspondents could go an entire career and not observe the kind of true mayhem that Denis had seen at Prince Johnson's compound. And he had not blinked in the face of the danger and madness. In fact, when the tape of Doe's torture had cut off as a result of technical difficulties, he had pressed his hosts repeatedly to fix the problem so he could view the tape in its entirety. Along with a riveting story, he had found something that he'd also felt in Nicaragua and the Philippines: the tremendous adrenaline rush that can be accessed only in war zones—a rush that lures a certain type of thrill-seeking personality into life-threatening situations, again and again.

A short while later, Blythe was in the eleventh-floor offices of *Esquire* when pages from Denis began to roll off the fax machine. He had heard nothing but silence since the phone call from Freetown where Denis nearly called off the trip. Now Blythe stood by the copier and read the story, page by page, as it came out of the machine, in a trance. He would say much later that it felt "closer in form to a poem composed in the midst of a gun battle."

The pages Denis sent this time differed significantly from the story he had composed after his trip to the Philippines. This time, there was no self-reflection, no examining of his own motivations. The lens of this story was focused firmly outward. In fact, it was, for the most part, devoid of analysis. Blythe noted that it lacked the gloss usually found in the work of seasoned correspondents but instead felt like a raw recitation of the experience.

Denis opened the story by laying out the grisly scene in Monrovia, describing the factions fighting for control amid the "gutted landscape of unrelieved starvation," where the dwindling remains of the legitimate Liberian army "robs and loots and burns as the skeletal citizens wander, dying of cholera and hunger." He offered a quick history of Liberia leading up to the current conflict, then structured the piece around his own journey—the monotonous wait in Freetown, the voyage of the *River Oli,* the trip through heart of Monrovia, where "people will eat anything. Here and there, a figure pauses by the street, vomiting up something that didn't work as food." He described the horror, slowly building the tension, leading up to the final scene at Prince Johnson's rebel compound and the viewing of the tape of Doe's torture. Only in the last few sentences of the story did Denis write anything that could be interpreted as authorial judgment. The ending was a fatalistic coup de grâce that pointed out the world's indifference to the type of suffering he'd witnessed:

> Everywhere on Earth, the people are at war, or preparing for war, or trying to extricate themselves from war—civil war, tribal war, even, in the Middle East, at long last, World War III; border disputes, factional clashes, punitive strikes, holy campaigns; and these must be photographed, catalogued, monitored, brought to light, but there isn't space in the papers to tell about them all, not even half of them.... The question is: Where is Liberia? Does anyone out there care?

Blythe read the story and declared it ready for publication without a single word of editing. *Esquire's* new editor in chief, Terry McDonell, who had taken over for Eisenberg in 1990, agreed with Blythe's assessment and scheduled it for publication. "The Civil War in Hell" ran in the December 1990 issue of *Esquire.* The story was accompanied by Patrick Robert's photographs of child soldiers holding machine guns, strands of bullets around their necks and women's wigs on their heads to protect them. It was Denis's first published work of journalism. It was also his masterpiece of the form.

Later, after he was safely home on American soil, Denis unpacked his bags from the trip and found the T-shirt that the self-proclaimed acting president of Liberia and reggae band leader had gifted him as he left the rebel compound in Monrovia. He put the shirt in the laundry, and when it emerged from the washing machine, he saw that the name of Prince Johnson's band had been washed away. His host had printed the band's name over what was originally a Coca-Cola shirt.

OUT OF THE DRAWER 19

My task which I am trying to achieve is, by the power of the written word to make you hear, to make you feel—it is, before all, to make you see. That—and no more, and it is everything. —**Joseph Conrad**

At a particularly vulnerable moment during his headlong pursuit of a career as a war correspondent, Denis unwittingly made a decision that would eventually change the trajectory of his career as a fiction writer. It was made for the same reason that many of Denis's fateful decisions were made: he needed money.

As he lay in his hospital bed recuperating from his bout with malaria on his return from the Philippines, his financial situation appeared dire. Lucinda wanted a divorce. His next novel was far from complete and without a contract. He knew that because of his illness, it would be a while before he could write about his trip to Mindanao or make progress on his fiction. In desperation, his thoughts turned to a set of short stories he had written years before, the ones about his life as a junkie, which were still languishing in his files. They had been composed in the early '80s, while he was a fellow at the Fine Arts Work Center in Provincetown, then deposited in the drawer and kept hidden because he decided they were too autobiographical. The stories embarrassed him—not because of their contents but because he felt the act of writing and publishing them was somehow unbecoming. To allow them out into the world, he thought, would be a blatant grab for attention. "I didn't want people to say 'Oh, look at this guy!'" he said later. But his fiscal crisis, and the change in outlook caused by a near-death experience, altered his perception. "I think after going through the common humiliations of a human life, I realized it just doesn't matter," he said. "There's nobody who can disguise himself. Eventually we're all outed in one way or another."

When he was released from the hospital, he dug out the stories and began to reexamine them. He was now a decade removed from his last contact with most of the characters who populated the stories. But here they were, brought back to life on the page in a barely altered form: Sue Fletcher and John Dundon and the farmhouse gang and the rest of the crew from the Vine. They had evolved from the accomplices in his early life of mischief to punch lines in anecdotes he told to friends and acquaintances; now they were characters in fiction. He read the stories again from a new vantage point. It was, he saw now, the kind of writing he would have loved at sixteen, when he was enchanted with coming-of-age stories like J. D. Salinger's *Catcher in the Rye.*

Denis's own Holden Caulfield in the stories was a first-person narrator without a given name, only a derisive nickname invented by his friends. In Iowa during the time in which the stories took place, the real Denis Johnson had been called Denis by fellow students and professors on campus and Johnson inside the walls of the Vine. In the fictional account, his narrator became known as Fuckhead. If the stories were born out of actual experiences that had happened to Denis or to his friends, the character of Fuckhead was to be only a portion of who Denis actually was during those formative years. In this interpretation of his existence, the person at the center of the stories that had happened to Denis was an innocent drifter, an addict floating from episode to episode in search of drugs and hypersensationalized experience. The other side of Denis's experience from those years—determined artist, always hunting for material; ambitious young poet, navigating the world of the Iowa Writers' Workshop with an eye toward literary success and fame—had been excised from Fuckhead and his environment. What was left was an older man's hazy reminiscences of his drug-infused wayward days as a youth, set among the cornfields of Iowa and the waterways of Washington state.

Denis's process for writing the stories when he composed them back in Provincetown had been similar to the way he wrote poetry. He compiled notes for each of the anecdotes that he wanted to include, writing his thoughts in bursts of language, sometimes putting single lines on slips of paper, then taping them to the wall or putting them in a box for later use, as he had done with his poetry for years. He was at the time an unpublished novelist but an accomplished poet, and his poetic method morphed into his short-story writing process. Once enough material had been captured, he would stitch everything together and turn them into semicohesive narratives. Lines and phrases that felt right were placed in the story, then moved around until he was satisfied.

Most of the stories comprised two separate anecdotes that, when fused, created something that he considered a more fully formed work of art. The stories slipped seamlessly from present action to remembrance, creating the feel of blurred vision from a narrator whose memory was formed by the experiences and by the substances he'd consumed during those experiences. Often the narrator would remember an incident, then retell the same incident differently, as if the fog in his brain was momentarily lifting.

Denis had come to believe writing short stories should be like going to a party—arrive late and leave early—and the Fuckhead stories were written with that thought in mind. He wrote not necessarily toward a conclusion but to the point where the energy lapsed. Then he would type in the rest of the notes he had made for the story—sentences or phrases he believed to be worth saving. In some cases, those phrases or sentences remained where they were and became the actual ending of the stories in the final version, producing the feel of poetry. It was the reason a line like "Your husband will beat you with an extension cord and the bus will pull away leaving you standing there in tears, but you were my mother" could serve as the ending of a story, despite being seemingly unrelated to the entire account that had preceded it. These final, haunting, poetic lines, when placed in the context of a narrative, would be some of the most memorable he would ever write.

With his newfound outlook, Denis revised and revamped the stories until he considered them ready. Then he called his agent, Bob Cornfield, and told him he had a bunch of stories that might be publishable. Cornfield asked to see them and quickly decided they were indeed worthy of publication. As he had done when he first read Denis's manuscript of *Angels,* he sought out his friend Bob Gottlieb for how advice on how to proceed.

Gottlieb had moved into a new role in the intervening years. In a development that became the publishing industry's version of Johnny Carson stepping down from *The Tonight Show,* with a comparable media frenzy, Gottlieb had been hired to replace William Shawn, the legendary editor who had served as the top name on the masthead at the *New Yorker* for the previous thirty-five years. Gottlieb, an outsider to a venerable magazine rife with traditions, wanted to maintain its august status while also shaking off some of the dust that had formed in its sixty-plus years of existence. One of the ways to do this was to bring new young writers into the fold. He asked Cornfield to send him all of Denis's stories. (Denis was ambivalent about pitching the stories to the *New Yorker.* "I figured they would never take 'em," he said later. "I was pissed off in advance.")

The *New Yorker* published fiction in every issue and had done so since it first came into being in 1925. To have a short story published in the magazine was the mark of a particular level of success for any writer of fiction. The standard practice in the fiction department at the *New Yorker* was for writers, either through an agent or independently, to submit short stories to the editors, one by one. Writers might be rejected a dozen times before finally having a story accepted for publication. The best of them would eventually sign a contract with the magazine, where they would offer the *New Yorker* first rights to all of their stories and receive bonuses for publishing a certain number of stories in a calendar year. Gottlieb broke convention when he read Denis's stories. He called Cornfield and bought the rights to several of them all at once.

The stories made their way to the fiction department, eventually arriving on the desk of Chip McGrath, who had been at the magazine since 1972 and a fiction editor since 1977. Under Shawn, a stereotype had developed around the type of fiction the magazine published. A *New Yorker* short story was "a piece of suburban ennui that had neither a beginning, a middle or an end." McGrath fought against that premise and looked for writers who broke from the magazine's bourgeois reputation and dealt with working-class concerns in their fiction. He took pride in having brought writers such as Alice Munro, Richard Ford, and Denis's old friend, Ray Carver, into the magazine. Still, he was surprised when he read the stories that Gottlieb had purchased, filled as they were with junkies and thieves and degenerates. "I had a sense that in the Shawn era, Johnson's stories would never have flown," he remembered. "[Shawn's] term for them would have been that they were 'too rough.'"

But it was a new day, and the stories were going into the magazine. McGrath began to prepare them for publication. Another convention in the *New Yorker* fiction department was that stories would go through a rigorous editing process, during which they sometimes would be changed significantly, in both sentence-to-sentence composition and content. It was a process that Denis, who had published a grand total of two short stories in his lifetime and none in the past fifteen years, was not prepared to undergo. "Editing was not something that he had had much experience with, and it was like pulling teeth," McGrath said. "Even changing a comma to a semicolon was a crisis." Denis wasn't argumentative and did not get angry, as some other writers McGrath edited did, but he was staunchly resistant to almost all changes.

The experience of editing Denis helped McGrath formulate a theory about writers. They could be divided into two types. One type comprised those who were hyperaware of the effects their work produced in readers and how they had achieved those effects. Writers such as John Updike, the quintessential *New Yorker* contributor of the late twentieth century, loved to work with editors on the nuts and bolts of a piece of writing to achieve the desired effect. The other type comprised writers who operated on inspiration and feel. McGrath thought this type of writer believed that because their genius was born out of unexplainable impulse, something as minute as the change of a comma might ruin the overall effect of a story and reduce the entire structure to rubble. Denis, McGrath believed, was the writer most closely identified with this second type.

The stories began appearing in the *New Yorker* in the fall of 1988. The first one, "Two Men," read like a fictional account of one of the nights during Denis's undergraduate years that ended up being chronicled in Iowa City police reports and in the crime section of the *Iowa City Press-Citizen.* Fuckhead is simultaneously running from and hunting a character named Thatcher after a drug deal gone bad, all while avoiding what he's truly afraid of: the six-month-old baby and angry wife awaiting him at home. Less than two months later, the *New Yorker* published "Work," another tale of petty crime committed in the pursuit of drugs on the outskirts of Iowa City. In "Work," the narrator teams with a man named Wayne, whom he knows from the Vine, to steal copper wire from an abandoned house that turns out to be the home of Wayne's ex-wife. Later, they return to spend their earnings at the bar in the Vine, where Wayne provokes a fight with the "biggest, blackest man in Iowa" during a poker game. Wayne was a fictionalized version of a real denizen of the Vine. The provocateur at the center of the poker incident, however, had in reality been Denis himself.

The publication of "Work" dropped another hot pepper into a sauce that had been cooking in the *New Yorker* fiction department for several years. The hot pepper was in the form of the word *fuck,* which had been verboten at the magazine for most of the Shawn era. The first use of it in a short story had been three years before, in a story by Bobbie Ann Mason called "In Country" that ran in June 1985. For that one, McGrath went to Shawn's office to argue his case that the language was vital to the overall effect of the piece—an argument that had been rejected many times before. But Shawn had caved on his long-held, magazine-wide ban against *fuck* a few months before when it appeared in a police report relevant to a nonfiction article, so McGrath successfully ended the fiction *fuck* ban once and for all. Once

Gottlieb took over, the rule remained relaxed, but only to a point. "He opened the gates a bit, he didn't open them wide open," McGrath said. Around the same time, McGrath had been forced to have a similar argument with Gottlieb over a story by Richard Ford. "Gottlieb said we could only have so many 'fucks,' and we couldn't have a 'fuck' on every page." All of Denis's *fucks* managed to make it into the pages of the *New Yorker* unscathed.

Another story in the group that Gottlieb purchased had a less successful outcome, at least for the *New Yorker.* This one concerned the night that Denis had hitchhiked his way into the fatal car accident on the Missouri highway in 1972. Denis initially decided to write a poem about the incident. He submitted it to a journal and received an acceptance, only to pull the poem back when he realized it should be written as a short story instead. The story version resulted in another dispute over language between writer and editors. This time the issue had nothing to do with obscenity. The point of dispute involved the final line of the story, which was a second-person, direct address statement—"And you, you ridiculous people, you expect me to help you"—following an account of the accident rendered entirely in the first person. Denis was told that the line was gratuitous and would be cut. He rejected the edit. The *New Yorker* stood firm. Nobody blinked. So Denis, for the second time, pulled "Car Crash While Hitchhiking" from publication. Years later, after the ending to the story became perhaps the single line most associated with his entire body of work, and after he'd seen someone with the words tattooed on her arm, he would use the incident as an example of the need for writers to trust their own instincts. The story appeared, with the line intact, in the spring 1989 edition of the *Paris Review.* Denis's paycheck on the story was one tenth of what the *New Yorker* had initially offered to pay.

Over the next few years, the stories Denis had written in Provincetown appeared in a number of different publications. Denis discussed the stories with Blythe, and a short time later, at Blythe's behest, *Esquire* bought two of them. The two stories were published in the March 1989 issue of the magazine under the headline "The Bullet's Flight." One of the stories *Esquire* published, "Dundun," was a fictionalized account of the day that John Dundon shot Steve McCurdy at the farmhouse in the summer of 1969. Dennis barely changed the names of the key participants, changing just a single letter in the fictional last name of his friend John. The rumor that had circulated around the Vine at the time of the incident was that Dundon had shot McCurdy because McCurdy's young child had urinated on Dundon's bullets, and that McCurdy had been saved because the urine had disabled those bullets and blunted the impact of the shot. Denis deemed that version to be too outlandish, even for fiction. In his fictional account, everybody at the farmhouse seems to be too stoned to tackle the question of the motivation behind the gunshot. Fuckhead takes Dundun and his victim, McInnis, to the hospital, and the tale that was told to the actual police officer in 1969, that the shooting was an accident, is concocted on the way. Denis did change one important fact. In the story, Dundun's bullet is fatal. McInnis dies on the way to the hospital. The narrator ends the story by sympathetically chronicling what he believes to be the demise of Dundun, describing him as imprisoned in Colorado for series of violent crimes. "If I opened up your head and ran a hot soldering iron around in your brain, I might turn you into something like that," Denis wrote about his long-lost friend. The real John Dundon had indeed been serving time in Colorado when Denis lost contact with him after grad school.

The remaining stories in the set continued to appear in publications large and small for the next few years. "Emergency," inspired by Denis's time as an orderly at Mercy Hospital in Iowa City in the summer of 1973, and "Dirty Wedding," set in Chicago and revolving around Fuckhead's girlfriend, Michelle, having an abortion, both appeared later in the *New Yorker.* "Out on Bail," based on the exploits and overdose death of Denis's friend Jeff Hottel, appeared in a journal called *Epoch.* "The Other Man," set in Seattle, appeared in the journal *Big Wednesday,* and "Beverly Home," set in Arizona and the only story in the group starring a sober Fuckhead, was published in the *Paris Review.*

The secrets he harbored for years were now out there for all to see. That offhand comment made one insignificant night in the Vine twenty years before—"You're just hanging out with us so you can write about it later"—had proven prescient. He had indeed written about them, and now it was all on record. In his mind, though, it wasn't really the actual people from the actual incidents who were on the page. They had been filtered through his understanding and had come out on the other side as fiction. It was now part of the wider "human experience," and Denis believed he had a calling to write stories from that human experience. The imagined versions of his friends had fared, in Denis's fictional world, even worse than their real-life counterparts. Denis the writer had killed Susan Fletcher, he'd killed Don Smith, and he'd killed Steve McCurdy. In the fictional account of those long-lost years, it was only Fuckhead who made it out alive.

NEW LIFE 20

"Oo-ooo-oo-o." A ghastly noise like a gasp issued from the mouth of the man, and those country people who are superstitious were terribly frightened. Skaggs' fingers began to twitch. —*New York Times,* **September 1, 1870, on the execution by hanging and resurrection of murderer John Skaggs**

Just a few weeks after the first of his Iowa short stories landed in the pages of the *New Yorker,* Denis received another piece of good news. His current writing project, a novel set in Provincetown that he had started in 1983 and been working on steadily since he moved to California, would soon be published. After the publication of his last book, Denis had grown disillusioned with Knopf. He asked Bob Cornfield to find him a new publisher. Cornfield complied and took the manuscript to his friend Jonathan Galassi, an editor at Farrar, Straus and Giroux. Galassi was a fan of Denis's, having made a bid for *Angels* years before, when he was in the acquisitions department at Random House. Galassi was impressed with the new novel, which Denis had decided to call *Resuscitation of a Hanged Man.* "I loved that book," he recalled. "It wasn't an easy book, because it is a religious allegory. But it was incredibly beautiful writing." Galassi also saw an opportunity to bring in a writer whom he viewed as enormously talented and who he thought had a long career ahead of him at FSG. The contract was drawn up. FSG would pay Denis $125,000 for *Resuscitation of a Hanged Man* and an untitled novel, which Denis committed to deliver two years later.

Though the setting of the book was Provincetown and the beaches of Cape Cod, the true seed had been planted many years before, when Denis was an undergraduate at the University of Iowa. In the course of doing research for a class assignment, he'd come across an article from the *New York Times* from the nineteenth century with the headline "The Resuscitation Horror." The article described the hanging of a murderer, John Skaggs, on August 26, 1870. Skaggs was hanged, his pulse stopped, and he was cut down. Then a doctor used a galvanic battery to bring him back to life and keep him alive for fifteen hours. Denis was intrigued, xeroxed the article, and kept it in his files for years, waiting to find a use for it. That use turned out to be both as the title of his fourth novel and a clue to the mystery in the book.

After the contract was signed, he went to work preparing the manuscript for publication. *Resuscitation of a Hanged Man* was the story of Leonard English, a former medical supplies salesman who comes to Provincetown to be a disc jockey and the assistant to a private investigator after surviving a suicide attempt. Denis drew from his experiences at WOMR, the public broadcasting radio station in Provincetown, where for a time he'd had a regular show that consisted of his playing songs from his personal collection of rock 'n' roll records. In the novel, English is a lapsed Catholic, and his spiritual struggles lie at the heart of the book. The plot centers around his relationship with Leanne, a beautiful lesbian whom he pursues romantically after surreptitiously recording her with another woman. It also follows English's obsessive investigation into the disappearance of a missing artist, Gerald Twinbrook, whom he believes to be at the center of a conspiracy that involves his boss, a priest, and a secret Massachusetts militia. (English finds the ancient *New York Times* clipping about the nineteenth-century hanging in Twinbrook's files during his investigation.) The character of Lenny English—sensitive, confused, searching for spiritual redemption—was the closest Denis had come to placing a personal avatar at the center of a novel.

He sent the final version to his new publisher in the spring of 1990. "I've gone over the manuscript again and found it, if anything, more extraordinary the second time around," Galassi wrote to him. FSG published it a year later, just a few weeks after "The Civil War in Hell" came out in *Esquire,* and shortly after the publication of *The Best American Short Stories of 1990,* which included "Car Crash While Hitchhiking," the story of that deadly night on the Missouri highway. Many of Denis's Fuckhead stories had appeared in the interim as well. In a period of eighteen months, some of the best writing he would produce in his entire life appeared in print. The omnipresence of Denis Johnson in American publishing was hard to miss, and many reviewers noted one or more of the contemporary stories and articles. "Mr. Johnson is, as they say, on a roll," wrote one reviewer.

Resuscitation of a Hanged Man received a similar critical reception to his previous novels. The consensus was, once again, that Denis was the Mozart of the sentence, but he was closer to Salieri when it came to the complete books that were made up of those glorious sentences. "Denis Johnson is an artist," wrote Mona Simpson for the *New York Times Book Review.* "He writes with a natural authority, and there is real music in his prose. Yet in this book he has not found the subject to match the scale of his talent and intelligence." "His style blends dramatic, high-flown rhetoric and colloquial usages to great effect, but the progress of his narrative is sloppy and off-hand," wrote Douglas Seibold in the *Chicago Tribune.*

The reading public, specifically the section of it given to purchasing newly released novels, came down even harder on Denis than the critics. They didn't buy his book. More than a year after publication, Cornfield sent Denis a royalty statement that showed $62,790.40 of his advance was still unearned. Less than a year after publication, *Resuscitation* was selling about ten copies a month worldwide. Denis told an interviewer that the book had sold so poorly that he had ended up owing his publisher money.

The fact that he was with a new publisher did not change Denis's penchant for sitting out the publicity campaign. FSG arranged an interview with *Publishers Weekly* to promote *Resuscitation of a Hanged Man*. Denis didn't show up for the interview. "I just didn't feel like talking to somebody," he said. "I didn't realize it was some big deal not to."

*

The arc of the relationship between Denis and Lucinda was now at the phase that Denis's previous romantic relationships always tended to arrive at eventually. He had successfully begged for and been granted forgiveness over and over. Each episode chipped away at Lucinda's patience. Without fail, Denis would confess to an affair, and Lucinda would throw him out of the house. His response to his expulsion often would be to find a spot somewhere among the towering redwood trees on the ranch, pitch a tent, and wait to be let back into his home. Once he made a sign in Lucinda's workshop, painted it with the words "Camp Bozo," and hung it from his tent. Matt, by then an adolescent, would sometimes bring his sleeping bag out and spend the night with his stepfather at Camp Bozo. "[Denis would] make a joke about it, even though it was pretty serious stuff," Lucinda said.

He tried to charm his way back into her good graces and used humor to lighten the situation most of the time. But sometimes the levity would disappear, and in its place were dark moods that stretched into weeks. "He could be almost bipolar," Lucinda said. "I mean he was very funny, and fun to be around, then he'd get into these deep, deep funks."

The pattern of marital bliss followed by disharmony, caused by fluctuations in Denis's moods and behavior, had been going on for the majority of their marriage. All of the years of it had worn Lucinda down. By now, the periods of harmony were becoming extremely rare. The final blow to the relationship came shortly after Denis returned from Liberia. Lucinda came to believe that during his trip, he had been having sex with African prostitutes. It was, to her, yet another outrage, one more piece of evidence that the pattern of their life would never change if she and Denis stayed together. Now she thought the marriage was putting her life in danger.

The AIDS epidemic had been causing widespread panic in the United States since the early 1980s, and by the end of the decade, fear of the deadly disease was pervasive. By the late 1980s, media reports signaling Africa as the epicenter for the spread of AIDS were prevalent. In some Central African countries, researchers believed, nearly a quarter of the population of the urban areas were infected with HIV, the virus that causes AIDS. It was known to be transmitted primarily through unprotected sexual contact.

Lucinda was well aware of the developing situation in Africa and what it meant to her own health. She was in fear for her life. She went with a friend to Oakland to get tested for the disease. While waiting in line at a free health clinic, she had a moment of clarity. "I asked myself: 'What am I doing?'" she said. The wait for the results was agonizing but came back negative. The experience had a powerful effect on Lucinda, however, and shortly thereafter, she made the decision to file for divorce.

Their marriage of almost a decade was over. During that period, Denis had gone from unemployed poet to successful writer, thus achieving his lifetime goal, but was unable to find lasting domestic happiness. The causes that led to the dissolution of his first marriage may have been different this time, but the outcome, the heartbreak associated with a broken family, was the same. Lucinda stayed at the ranch. Denis moved out, this time for good. "The hardest thing about the divorce for me was that my son was very, very attached to Denis," Lucinda remembered. "Denis, in some ways, was kind of like a big kid, he was fun to be around, and Matt really liked him. But when we split up, boom, that was it."

*

When Denis and Lucinda had been searching the continent for the perfect place to start their life of isolation after Wellfleet, one of the possibilities they had discussed had been the northern tip of Idaho. They had surveyed the area at the time. The region intrigued Denis and stayed in the back of his mind. When it came time to relocate and start a life by himself, Idaho soon became his preferred destination.

He told friends that he had chosen northern Idaho because he learned that it was the very last place on the continent of North America at which the Soviet Union would aim a nuclear missile at when World War III began. Even Montana, he said, wasn't isolated enough for him, and, besides, too many writers lived in Montana.

He went back to Idaho after his split with Lucinda and kept driving north until he found his utopia, only a few miles from the Canadian border. He bought a cabin and forty acres of land, mostly up the side of a mountain, on Meadow Creek Road, a twenty-mile, mostly unpaved artery in sparsely populated Boundary County. From the cabin, he could peer out the window and see the tips of the trees in the valley below, with the mountains standing majestically behind. The nearest town of any consequence was Bonners Ferry, a small enclave of around two thousand inhabitants founded during a gold rush in the mid-nineteenth century. Good Grief, Idaho, the closest notation on the map, was really just an intersection and a bar of the same name on the side of a highway. For someone looking for a place to be left alone, Good Grief was perfect.

When it came time to make the move, Denis called his friend Sam Messer, who agreed to help. Messer came out to California and stayed at the home of Bill Winkelholz, where Denis had been living since leaving the ranch. The plan was for Denis to drive his Nissan and for Messer to follow behind in Denis's other vehicle, a truck with a camper that would serve as their moving van. Denis had christened the truck Ida, short for Idaho. At Denis's request, Messer painted a giant eyeball on each side of Ida. They packed Ida with Denis's belongings, including several file cabinets with past and present writing projects, and got ready to depart.

Just before leaving, Denis took Messer into the back of Ida and showed him some of his files. The cabinet was arranged alphabetically. Denis pointed out some of the papers related to the Iowa City stories, including one folder filed under "F" and marked "Fuckhead." Then he told Messer that if anything went wrong on the journey, he was to open the back of Ida, go to the file cabinet, and look in the file under "A" labeled "Answers."

Once they were on the road, Denis immediately pulled ahead and sped away, leaving Messer and Ida struggling to get up the steep inclines of Northern California's highways. Messer found himself alone on a nearly deserted road when the inevitable happened: a tire blew out. Now he was stuck in the middle of nowhere with a disabled vehicle and without the money to get it fixed. He did as Denis instructed and looked in the files under "A" for "Answers." There he found an envelope with a thick wad of bills in it. Denis had planned for disaster. Messer used the cash to get Ida back in shape and was soon back on the road.

Another reason for the road trip was for Denis to introduce Messer to his new girlfriend. Denis had met Cindy Burke when he gave a reading at Mount Hood Community College in Gresham, Oregon. She worked in the publicity department of the college and had seen his photo before the reading when preparing flyers for the event. She took one look at the photo and immediately inquired if this latest visiting writer was married. When Denis and Cindy met in person, her attraction was reciprocated, and they began a relationship. Cindy was divorced, a young mother with two children, a boy and a girl, both under the age of five. She had also had previous struggles with alcohol—another shared experience that helped her bond with Denis. On the trip to Idaho, Denis introduced Cindy to Messer. "You could tell right away there was something special there," Messer remembered.

Denis, Messer, and Ida made it the rest of the way to Idaho, where Denis settled into his new home. The hidden outpost on Meadow Creek Road in the Purcell Mountains turned out to be the perfect place to land. In it, he could be safely away from the incursion of humanity for as long as he liked. His own personal safe haven had been established. "His personality... was very diametrically opposed from itself," said Messer. "On the one side, he would go across the globe to interview people and experience things. But he couldn't stay in New York City for more than two days, because it freaked him out to be around that many people.... He wanted to be on his own, and the purpose of moving to Idaho was to get as far away from anybody as possible."

RELUCTANT JOURNALIST 21

If you don't know which port you're sailing to, no wind is favorable. —**Ram (The Hijacker) Barahama, Filipino pirate**

On the night of January 16, 1991, Denis was in his room at the Carlton Hotel in Dhahran, Saudi Arabia, when what everybody believed to be World War III officially began. He had quickly graduated from covering minor-league conflicts to what was most definitely the Major Leagues of War. In Monrovia, he'd been part of a press corps that numbered in the single digits. In Mindanao, it had numbered one. Now, he was one of more than seven hundred journalists, an international media behemoth that had been amassed in the desert, waiting for the biggest story in decades to unfold. The tension, built from six months of heated rhetoric, anticipation, and dread, had reached a crescendo in the Middle East and around the world.

Near midnight, the journalists heard the first of the planes taking off to begin the American bombardment of Iraq. Journalists watched as pairs of F-15s roared into the desert night, on the way to sow destruction on the cities and bases of Iraq. A few hours later, Denis was on the phone with Cindy when sirens began to ring out through the city. The phone line went dead.

Military officials and journalists were expecting a deadly counterattack from the mighty Iraqi air force. For weeks, the media members had been warned of the impending barrage of Scud missiles filled with chemical weapons that they could expect to rain down on Saudi Arabia when the war started. Now, with the invasion in its third hour, they were told to put on gas masks and go down to the basement of the hotel for safety. When Denis opened his door, he was met with pandemonium as terrified reporters and hotel employees in masks and full-body protective suits dashed by. One of them stopped at Denis's door.

"Steve! Steve! Get your gear on!" he screamed at Denis through his mask.

"But I'm not Steve," Denis said.

It was the first official act of aggression from the United States in the confrontation that had been brewing since around the time Denis had taken his trip to Liberia. The conflict that is now known as the First Gulf War had started when Iraq, under dictator Saddam Hussein, soon to be American Enemy No. 1, had invaded its smaller, richer neighbor, Kuwait, in August 1990. George Bush (the first), the occupant of the White House at the time, had marshaled a coalition of Western allies against Iraq, hundreds of thousands of troops had gone to the Middle East to prepare for the inevitable war, and thousands of journalists had followed.

Denis had been back in the United States only a few months when Blythe asked him to go to the Middle East for *Esquire*. The magazine would also be sending John Sack, who had covered Vietnam during the Harold Hayes era. Sack had authored some of the magazine's most searing coverage about that war.

Unlike his previous reporting experiences, Denis was now part of the pack. To cover the war, he had to go where he was assigned, with hundreds of other journalists who were ostensibly doing the same thing. The Gulf War was America's first war since Vietnam, so everything was framed against the shadow of that experience. U.S. officials hadn't forgotten that journalists like Sack had roamed free across Southeast Asia, reporting on the U.S. military's failures—in their view damaging the American war effort. So now the red tape was thick, and so was the censorship. Reporters were told where they could and couldn't go and were forced to rely on pool reports for much of their information. "The rules and restrictions are an abomination," Sack complained.

Denis followed along, as both part of the pack and as a disassociated observer. He joined the press on an excursion to view the supply lines, watched quietly as officers in the Saudi Arabian army dined in the Carlton Hotel restaurant, and listened to the journalists debate whether or not the conflict they were attending was indeed a world war. He observed and wrote it all down in his notebook. As he worked, the same ambivalence and insecurity he'd felt in Nicaragua and the Philippines began to creep back in.

He filed a story about his experiences in January that described the scene in Saudi Arabia and the beginning of the air campaign. The article ran in the March issue of *Esquire* under the headline "Dispatches from World War III." It was a short piece of a single page, filled mostly with description and anxiety for what was to come. "The [soldiers] see themselves as having to fight boredom, as having to maintain a sense of humor, a state of readiness. I see them and these million others as having finally found something more enormous than their own deaths," he wrote.

Once the air war began, new tension coalesced around the beginning of the ground campaign, when American foot soldiers would have to come face to face with the enemy. This, as the common wisdom throughout the media had it, would be when the real carnage would begin for American troops, and when the true "next Vietnam" would occur. Denis also saw the war in terms of Vietnam. The great offense that had been at the center of the protest movements of his youth—heartless warmongers sending young boys off to die—still framed his view of war. "American boys with everything to live for, with the equivalent of ten lifetimes of opportunity, joy, abundance ahead of them by most of this planet's standards" were being sent into battle for oil and for money.

In what would become a characteristic of Denis's behavior that would later be accepted as a defining part of his personality, he was unable to hide his emotions. The thought of all the impending death and suffering brought him to tears. He did not feel the need to live up to the stereotype of the battle-hardened, detached war correspondent. Instead, he wept openly. Sack took note of his colleague's behavior. Denis could become the modern-day Ernest Hemingway of war reporters, Sack told Blythe, if he didn't cry all the time.

The seeds of doubt continued to grow as the weeks dragged on in the desert. Soon it was accompanied by a contempt for many of his fellow journalists. They were "pimps for war in burgundy velvet suits," he would write later. The contempt went both ways, he thought. The full-timers saw Denis as a cheap adventurer taking up the spot of a legitimate journalist. All of it fed into his uncertainty about what it was he was actually doing all these weeks in the desert. Was he one of the velvet suits? Was he just a voyeur to mayhem and death?

Back in New York at the *Esquire* offices, there was no ambivalence. The April issue was in production, and Terry McDonell, the editor in chief, had saved several pages in the middle of the magazine for Denis's story. The photos had been chosen. His name was on the cover, right over it-girl actress Ellen Barkin's right shoulder. All that was needed was Denis's story. That story, Denis informed Blythe, would not be forthcoming. Denis had decided not to write it.

"It was a very passionate conversation, or conversations, that we had," Blythe recalled. "I think that it was such an emotionally rending experience that he just did not want to write that piece. He did not think he could write the piece. [He thought] that the piece was gratuitous, and that it seemed to him small-minded compared to what was actually happening."

Blythe reported the development to McDonell. There was no backup plan, McDonell told him. A story by Denis Johnson must appear on those pages. So Blythe got back on the phone with Denis. "Send anything," Blythe pleaded. "Anything will do." After much negotiating, Denis agreed to send his notes through express mail. When they arrived, Blythe began to read them and felt immediate relief. The notes were so well crafted that much of the material could be published as written. The outline of a story was already there. Blythe went to work, adding transitions where needed and crafting an ending, trying to mimic the Denis Johnson sound where he could.

The story made it into the issue, under the headline "Knocking on Heaven's Door," a cynical twist on the Bob Dylan song, which Denis mentioned in his notes when cataloging all the songs with macabre double meanings that played regularly on Armed Forces Radio. The Blythe–Johnson piece made no mention of the fact that the ground campaign had been a seventy-two-hour rout by the United States and its allies. Instead, the story was structured around a book that Denis had borrowed from a reporter from Cleveland called *How to Make War,* written by James F. Dunnigan ten years before. The book analyzed the ways in which politicians and military leaders brainwashed foot soldiers to kill and risk their lives. The story included quotes from the book, then found those very techniques used on the young soldiers on the ground in Saudi Arabia. "The picture emerges of a vast machine for destruction, a horrendous device whose operation can be entrusted only to those people too young to have any appreciation of how long a person stays dead," read the story that ran under Denis's byline.

After the magazine came out, a media writer for the *Village Voice* published a review of the piece. In it, the writer noted that there was something slightly different to Denis's writing that was hard to pinpoint. Blythe read the article, clipped it, and sent it to Denis. Then he asked Denis about the end result of all the toil and angst in the desert.

"What do you think?"

"Not bad," Denis said. "But I do an even better Denis Johnson."

*

For the next several years, Denis was a writer for hire. The Liberia piece had put him on the short list of correspondents that magazine editors could choose from when they had an international story that needed a literary touch. The era of massive profits, infinite pages of advertising, and unlimited expense accounts at national magazines was coming to an end, but there was still a little cash left in the system. Famous bylines still equaled newsstand sales. There were no smartphones to scroll through, so the idea of sitting down to read five or ten thousand words of finely crafted prose remained a reasonable consideration to much of the reading public. *Esquire* promised its readers stories by literary stars of the previous decades like George Plimpton, Hunter S. Thompson, and Richard Ben Cramer.

Magazines came calling, and for the right assignment, Denis could be convinced to come down the mountain in Good Grief and climb onto a plane. The more dangerous the assignment, the better. His passport read like a map of the danger zones of the late twentieth century: Somalia, Iraq, Afghanistan, back to Liberia, the pirate-infested waters of the South Sulu Sea.

A Denis Johnson story with an international byline usually came with a few defining characteristics. For one, it was likely to be structured in classic Hunter Thompson gonzo style: it was really a story about the writer getting the story, so the writer was at the center of it. In a Johnson piece, the reader was apt to learn about the ineptitude and bureaucratic rot that made life in the third world excruciatingly slow and comically frustrating—a phenomenon Denis had been riffing on since *The Stars at Noon*. Finally, at the heart of the story the reader would find a slightly bumbling, ill-prepared American fish out of water, a persona Denis used both to navigate his environment while reporting the stories and as a relatable protagonist on the page. Also, it was likely that somebody would call him by the wrong name.

In 1992, the *New Yorker* hired Denis to make a return trip to Liberia, this time with the goal of writing a profile of warlord Charles Taylor. Since Denis had been there two years before, the political situation had grown even more confusing. Taylor had consolidated power outside of Monrovia and, by signing and breaking numerous cease-fire agreements, now controlled half the country. Prince Johnson, the reggae rebel, had joined with forces aligned with the previous government. The situation was just as volatile as before. None of this deterred Denis. His editor at the *New Yorker* arranged transportation into Liberia, working through Taylor's U.S. lawyer to provide contacts and a schedule for an interview, all of which fell through shortly after Denis stepped off the plane in the Côte d'Ivoire with forty U.S. $100 bills stuck in the seams of his pants.

The experience followed the pattern of Denis's previous third-world excursions. During his attempts to cross the border into Liberia, he was told over and over, by multiple contacts, that "everything has been arranged." Of course, each time, nothing had actually been arranged. Cars broke down, drivers didn't show up, drivers showed up but drove somebody other than Denis. Finally a driver took Denis into the country and to a rubber plantation with luxury accommodations. "In this place I remained for several days before I understood that I'd been taken prisoner," he wrote.

Days stretched to weeks at the compound. He was treated well and could even call the States, but he could not leave. Finally, he was taken to meet Taylor at his compound. There, he encountered the Small Boys Unit, adolescent orphaned soldiers who viewed Taylor as a father figure and were trusted completely by the rebel leader. Some of the boys took Denis to meet a prisoner of war who had been tortured repeatedly and was bound and bleeding. Denis watched and recorded as they interrogated and beat the prisoner. Finally, he could take no more. "At this point, I made a bizarre gesture," he wrote. He took his press credential and put it around the prisoner's neck. He made a show of saying, out loud, the name of the prisoner, the United States, and the *New Yorker,* as if "the magic from these names would stand around him against his misfortunes." The ruse worked. The prisoner was untied. Then he was led away by the boy soldiers to an uncertain fate, which Denis would spend much effort to determine after the trip, to no avail.

His meeting with Taylor yielded nothing. The warlord spoke in platitudes. The wind caused the tape of the interview to be nearly unintelligible. Then Denis went through an even more convoluted experience trying to escape the country, during which he and several of his contacts were arrested, released, and rearrested, time after time. Once he made it out of Africa, he made a call to his editor at the *New Yorker* that was similar to one he'd made to Blythe after his trip to Saudi Arabia. No article, he told the editor, would be forthcoming. "As far as I could see at the time and as far as I can see now, I accomplished nothing," he wrote. He would not publish anything about the trip for ten years. "Why did I go to Liberia? What was I thinking, why did I do it, why? I don't know. I don't know."

*

Such a pronouncement would seem to preclude further excursions. It did not. The experience of parachuting into the perilous situations stimulated a nerve in him that could not be reached in civilization. Only the proximity of actual combat and fresh death could deliver it. Once he was asked the obvious question for someone who voluntarily put himself into life-threatening situations: Do you have a death wish? He denied it. "I think there's more of a life wish, in a way, in wanting to be where there's a little bit of danger and chaos," he said. "There's a feeling of being more alive, more fully alive, when that sort of thing is happening."

If he did not wish to die, neither did he believe he was ever really at risk of being killed in a war zone. He had complete confidence in his survival skills. Those skills amounted to what he felt was a nonthreatening, guileless persona that he could use to disarm people in even the most tense of situations. A well-timed laugh or smile could get anybody to lower their machine gun. "There was just this aura about him, that he was not going to hurt anyone," said Sam Messer. "He just had this kind of naïveté [about him], thinking nothing bad was ever going to happen, because his intentions were so open. I think people understood this."

It was 100 percent effective. It worked when he tracked down Rambo Barahama, the murderous kidnapper and pirate of the South Sulu Sea who had been unsuccessfully hunted for years by the Filipino army. Ram the Highjacker invited Denis onto his boat, told him about all of his crimes, and then let Denis go. All he took was Denis's Australian hat. It worked when he traveled to Kabul just days after the Taliban had taken the city and executed the president and his brother. Their bodies still swung from scaffolds, cigarettes and paper money stuffed in their nostrils. Denis was the only paying customer at the Hotel Intercontinental in Kabul. He smiled at the Taliban soldiers when they came into the hotel, draped in bandoliers. And it worked when he traveled to the Horn of Africa to witness the end of the American involvement in Somalia. He impersonated a German and dined with Somali fighters high on *chaht,* the warrior's drug of blood and ecstasy. He waited for days, then finally made it into the wreckage of Mogadishu, another devastated African capital. He was on the beach when the last Marines and U.N. peacekeepers left the country. Gunfire broke out before the Marines' transport was even out of sight. One of Denis's African contacts told him, "You're not the last journalist left in Somalia, but I'm happy to tell you that you're the last American."

The thrill of it kept him coming back for one more story. Eventually, though, the experience did not deliver the juice as it once did. In addition, the moral implications of the act of international journalism, which he'd wrestled with since his first trip to Nicaragua, weighed on him more and more. He couldn't shake the feeling that, as he'd written in his notes on that first trip to Africa, he was just another American sissy who wanted to be Indiana Jones. The internal argument wore him down. "It's the same thing over and over again," he said years later, after he'd retired from the war correspondent business. "You figure out some way of getting into a place, finding somebody to show you what's going on. This person is risking their life to get the word out about their cause, or their country, or the plight of their people. Then after two or three weeks, you just say, 'So long, buddy,' and just flush them down the toilet and go home. It just got old, and I couldn't do that sort of thing anymore."

*

He began to take more magazine assignments that allowed him to remain on American soil. In some of these stories, he turned the lens on U.S. brands of extremism. Antigovernment sentiment was on the rise during the early years of the Bill Clinton administration. The siege at Ruby Ridge, a high-profile confrontation between a rancher and the FBI that resulted in several deaths, occurred just miles from Denis's outpost on Meadow Creek Road. Less than a year later was the siege of the Branch Davidian complex in Waco, Texas, a similar, even more deadly confrontation involving federal law enforcement. Conspiracy theorists who believed the U.S. government, an international cabal, or some combination of the two was preparing to trample on the Bill of Rights now had evidence. Many of them were Denis's neighbors.

Denis had wrestled with the question of whether the U.S. government was a force for good or evil since he first became sensitive to world events. Of course, he was no stranger to antigovernment activity, dating back to his days as a Vietnam War protester. Now the fault lines in the fight were shifting, and he found himself straddling both sides of the argument. He sympathized with the sentiment among the population of Boundary County, Idaho, that the government, which existed to protect the freedom of its citizens, had begun to do the opposite in too many cases. But as a '60s hippie whose politics started with the New Deal Democrats and progressed to Students for a Democratic Society, he found himself swimming in uncharted waters.

He dealt with the contradictions in an article for *Esquire* headlined "The Militia in Me." The story ran through a series of incidents, some from the news and some from his personal experience, that had led to an evolution in his understanding of the meaning of his citizenship. He attended an America First Party rally, led by Bo Gritz, the war hero turned 1992 presidential candidate who ran with the slogan "God, Guns and Gritz." Denis was intrigued by the message but bothered by the undertones of racial animosity buried in its core. He talked politics with Boundary County residents and found common ground in suspicion of government authority, but then dug a little deeper and struck a vein of rampant homophobia. He chronicled the competing messages he continued to receive: pamphlets pushing anti-Semitic theories arriving in his mailbox, police locking down a local middle school and searching the grounds with drug-sniffing dogs. He had difficulty reconciling the evidence before him.

> Why should I be talking about resisting government? Take it all around, we Americans are the freest people on the planet. Our riches afford us mobility, variety, and opportunity enough to drive us crazy as well as the time to go crazy in—more and more of all these as time goes on. Like other systems descending from English law, ours offers

> certain protections from government intrusion—fewer and fewer of these as history marches forward. If I'm not on either side when the shooting starts, and I don't like being in the middle, then where do I belong?

The story ran in *Esquire* shortly after the bombing of the Alfred P. Murrah Federal Building in Oklahoma City, a tragedy on a mammoth scale that brought the issues Denis was dealing with into sharper focus. "The piece was very prescient about what has happened in American politics and culture in America since the '90s," Blythe said.

*

"The Militia in Me" was followed by several other assignments that took Denis deep into red-state America. He went to North Carolina the write about the hunt for Eric Rudolph, the antiabortion bomber who was hiding out in the caves of Nantahala National Forest. He went to Texas for a Bikers for Jesus rally.

Another trip to Texas gave him the opportunity to once again appear in the magazine that had so greatly enhanced his reputation in grad school. The same assignment allowed him to write about a subject that had long fascinated him but that, at that point, he had only written about in fiction. *Rolling Stone* hired Denis to travel to Huntsville, the execution capital of America, to watch five prisoners die at the hands of the state of Texas over the course of two weeks.

He arrived in Huntsville in early May 2000 wearing his *Rolling Stone* press credentials proudly. Another bonus was an association with a writer whom he much admired. "Texas is sparsely dotted with subscribers to this magazine, many of whom believe that Hunter S. Thompson still writes long, crazy articles for it and seem also to believe that I may actually be Hunter S. Thompson," he wrote.

But his *Rolling Stone* credentials, it turned out, would be more hindrance than help in getting Denis into the death chamber. He spent the rest of the month interviewing the condemned men immediately before their final appointment with the state and negotiating with Larry Fitzgerald, head of public information for the Texas Department of Corrections, who had decided to prevent Denis from seeing anybody die. To do so, Fitzgerald invented a rule that barred journalists who came into Texas from outside the state from viewing executions. "He's got me snookered, won't let me inside the Walls Unit in downtown Huntsville to watch and tell the world what it's like in there at the moment the state deals death," Denis wrote. "It's Larry Fitzgerald's job to prevent that, to protect the machine from non-Texas scrutiny, but I really wish he'd just fuck off."

The article that appeared in *Rolling Stone* a few months later did not include a first-person account of an execution by lethal injection (though Denis included a scene in the death chamber described to him by others). Fitzgerald could not be budged. As each of the five prisoners was put to death, Denis stood across the street and watched despairingly while Fitzgerald led the approved witnesses to the death chamber. But Fitzgerald had given Denis one valuable thing: the needed ingredient to write the quintessential Hunter S. Thompson article, which was a story about a journalist's experiences in reporting a *Rolling Stone* piece.

Spliced throughout the narrative of his battles with Fitzgerald were observations about every other aspect of life in and around the Texas death machine. He attended the executions outside the walls, with the sparse crowds of anti–death penalty protesters, some of whom had been on site for the deaths of dozens of men. He mingled with ex-cons, who, on release, went to the Huntsville surplus store to exchange their prison garb for the latest shipment of Ban-Lon golf shirts and checkered pants before boarding a Greyhound to their former lives. He went to the prison museum to peruse the contraband weapons and view photos of the bullet-ridden corpses of Bonnie and Clyde. He spent two of the last twenty-four hours of the condemned men's lives asking them about their final meals and if they were prepared for death. He went to the Rita B. Huff animal shelter, which also performed its executions using lethal injections.

The climax of the story would turn out not to be the last breaths of the final executed prisoner but a conversation with Fitzgerald at Murski's Icehouse, a Huntsville bar where Denis bought his enemy scotch after scotch in one last futile attempt to buy his way into the death chamber. Fitzgerald thought he had managed to prevent the story from ever being published, but Denis had other ideas. "It's vendetta journalism now," he wrote. "The Tale of Stonewall Fitzgerald, hero of Huntsville." As Fitzgerald allowed Denis to buy him drinks and casually talked of watching men die—"you'd probably feel more emotion putting down a dog"—Denis was able to convey the essential point of the entire enterprise: the utter callousness of the Texas death machine and the men who controlled it.

His output and interest in reportage would decrease as the years went by. Still, he relished the occasional opportunity to come out of seclusion and interact with people, safe in the knowledge that it was for a limited period of time. And, over time, his understanding of his own personal form of journalism crystalized. "I'm here only to enjoy one of the great freedoms, that of having no choice but to trust the moment and everyone in it. I'm here to taste the giddy joy of understanding that any other moment is inaccessible... I'm making a story. And I get to be in it."

JUST A SHORT LITTLE BOOK 22

You never know what cultural context something is going to be published into. You never know what's going to resonate with people. —**Jessica Bruder, author of *Nomadland***

The Fuckhead stories were now all in print, in various magazines and journals, and Denis's world remained intact. The ghosts from his past had not reappeared to unmask him. On the rare occasions that he came down off the mountain to appear before an audience, he began to choose a few of those stories to read. The reaction of the crowds, filled with wonderment and laughter, pleased him. He began to understand more clearly how the stories worked. At a reading in Iowa City, the Shambaugh Auditorium, a large hall at the University of Iowa usually reserved for the most famous of names, was standing room only. There was a buzz in the crowd because many of the attendees knew the stories were set in and around Iowa City and were ready for them. The applause, once Denis took the stage, was tremendous.

The publishing contract he had signed with Farrar, Straus and Giroux in 1989 called for Denis to produce two novels, *Resuscitation of a Hanged Man* and an as yet unwritten novel to be named later. Now two years had passed, and it was time for Denis to hand over that second novel—a novel that did not exist. In the ensuing years, there had been a divorce, property sales and acquisitions, and speaking engagements and writing assignments large and small. When the revenues and expenditures were all counted up, Denis learned that the calculations did not come out entirely in his favor. He owed the Internal Revenue Service $10,000 in back taxes.

For every problem there is a solution, and for Denis, the solution to financial issues usually was that money would arrive from some unanticipated source to save the day. Bags of cash did not fall from the sky this time. Instead, he came on an idea that could eliminate his indebtedness to both the IRS and to FSG. He would send his publisher a story collection made up of the Fuckhead stories and use the advance to pay off the tax debt.

Bob Cornfield pitched the idea to Jonathan Galassi at FSG. Galassi knew about the stories and was quickly on board with the plan. Soon the eleven stories were in the FSG offices. Galassi loved them, captivated by how they fused poetry and prose to create something he thought was altogether new. He also recognized that together, the stories could form a narrative arc that would essentially turn the book into a novel. He requested Denis put them in chronological order, which, for the most part, was how they were eventually published.

Galassi's only other concern was that the stories were brief and there were only eleven of them. If FSG published the collection as is, it would be a very, very short book. Galassi contacted Cornfield and asked if there were any more stories that could be included in the collection. If not, perhaps Denis could write a few more, he said. Cornfield relayed the question. Denis was not pleased. This was the collection, he said. Take it or leave it. He gave Cornfield the job of delivering the news to Galassi. "Denis was not very direct about those type of things," Galassi said. "That's what an agent is for." Though it was an ordinary everyday request for Galassi, Denis took it as a personal insult. It was an offense that he would not forget when it was time to look for his next publishing contract.

But for now, Denis was with FSG, and his next book was on the way. For a title, he chose a phrase from the song "Heroin," which singer Lou Reed had written for his band, the Velvet Underground, in the mid-'60s, right around the time when Denis had his first experiences with the drug. "When I'm rushing on my run, and I feel just like Jesus' son" was the line Denis's title was referring to. The Reed song is a seven-minute ode to the drug that falls somewhere between condemnation and endorsement—probably closer to endorsement. The song could be a musical version of Denis's book, with lyrics that render the experience of shooting heroin from the point of view of the user and music that mimics the experience as well—a soothing melody to imitate the drug's intermittent calm, and the rush of the high interpreted through up-tempo drums and guitar spliced throughout the song. Reed said later that he stopped performing "Heroin" because of the number of fans who told him they experimented with the drug for the first time after hearing it. Reed agreed to allow Denis and FSG to use the lines from the song as an epigraph for $250.

When he was sent a copy of the galleys for *Jesus' Son,* Denis was in Iowa City, where he'd taken a year-long teaching residency at the Writers' Workshop. He had recently made the acquaintance of a young writer named Chris Offutt, who was living in Iowa City at the time and had just published his first collection of short stories. The two would become lifelong friends. At first, though, Offutt was intimidated by Denis. "He was already a fabled creature in Iowa City," he said. But they hit it off, often the only two sober writers in the bar. Denis asked Offutt, as a fellow short-story writer, if he'd like to see the galley for *Jesus' Son.* Offutt agreed, and Denis handed him the book. The question from Galassi—are there any more stories?—seemed to still be echoing in Denis's head. "He referred to it as a CD," Offutt remembered. "He was a little embarrassed by the size of it." FSG had chosen to produce a book of 7 ¾ inches—two inches smaller than the standard size, in an effort to increase the page count.

Regardless of the size, Offutt immediately saw the book as a masterpiece and told Denis so. When book was released to the public on December 27, 1992, the reviewers of North America began to write their own version of Offutt's declaration. This time around, there were rarely any of the caveats that tended to come with the critical reception to a Denis Johnson book. The reviews shone with praise from beginning to end. "Mr. Johnson managed to extract a harsh, lovely poetry. In the violent, seemingly random life [of the characters], he is able to find modern-day parables that glow with a strange, radioactive light," wrote Michiko Kakutani for the *New York Times.*

Many reviewers noted the fact that this book was a step forward for Denis that they believed would be rewarded with increased book sales. "His previous titles have been met with uncommon critical praise, but as yet not equivalent commercial success. That may soon change," wrote Kate Moses in the *San Francisco Examiner.* "His fans speak of his writing with hushed reverence, as if reporting miracles," wrote Vince Passaro of *Newsday.* "His time, if it's coming, has come."

Praise for *Jesus' Son* came in other ways as well. Some of the biggest names in American literature took note of the book and extolled Denis, both in person and in print. In the *New Yorker,* John Updike compared Denis's style to a young Ernest Hemingway. The book is "astonishing, worth four novels from somebody else," Barry Hannah wrote to Denis in a letter. Awards with impressive names, and even impressive dollar figures, followed. The Lannan Foundation chose him for their 1993 literary fiction award, recognizing him as "an accomplished writer who has made a significant contribution to English-language literature," and gave him a check for $50,000. The American Academy of Arts and Letters gave him the 1993 Academy Award in literature. And, unlike his experience with *Resuscitation,* his publisher was pleased with how the book was being received by the book-buying public. Within a few months of the publication date, FSG had ordered a second, then a third, printing. Soon efforts began to get some of Denis's old titles back into print.

It was, at this point in his writing career, the strongest response he'd yet received to a single publication. There was a slot reserved for him on all the best-of-the-year lists. The critics, the booksellers, and the literary establishment had made Denis one of the hot names of 1993. But 1993 would not prove to be the year in which his book truly hit its mark. The most important audience for book, the people who were going to read it, and then read it again and again until it flowed through their veins—those people were only just beginning to discover *Jesus' Son.*

*

During the time that passed between when Denis lived the Fuckhead stories and when he finally published them, American culture had passed through several transformations. The tales that made up *Jesus' Son* were written during the Vietnam era, a time when, as the story goes, the values and mores of a new generation, the children of the baby boom, was rebelling against the crew-cut conservatism of the 1950s that had come before them. The '60s, though, were being viewed through the lens of nostalgia when they were barely over. The hopeful wave that was the counterculture movement of the 1960s, as Hunter Thompson wrote, crested and crashed back to shore before the '70s were out of the gate. The last vestiges of the '60s were swept away with the landslide election of Ronald Reagan in 1980, ushering in a decade during which the pursuit of wealth and power became the only pursuit worth pursuing. American culture had reacted to the reaction, and by the early 1990s, the pendulum was beginning to swing back once again.

When the stories that Denis had first scribbled into his notebook in Iowa City in the '60s appeared on the shelves of bookstores twenty years later, a new generation was grabbing for the steering wheel of American culture, one with a new sensibility. The old rebellion had been against the army, the government, and the flag. The new rebellion focused on corporations, greed, and the singular pursuit of money and status. The young baby boomers of Denis's early years wanted to come together to fight the evil and corrupt forces that held power. The kids who gobbled up Denis's stories in the early '90s were an alienated, nihilistic species who wanted to separate themselves from the entire structure itself.

Sometimes a book comes around at just the right time to pulse directly into the heart of the national zeitgeist. Joseph Heller wrote *Catch-22* on the basis of his experiences in World War II, but when it was published in 1961, the antiauthoritarian impulses that drove the narrative struck the perfect nerve as America emerged from the postwar, conformity-and-prosperity era of the 1950s. Countercultural readers latched on to Heller's message at the dawn of the Vietnam era and helped turn it into a best seller and American classic. *Jesus' Son* followed a similar trajectory, filling a hole in a new generation searching for touchstones. Fuckhead's mantra—that there "was something wrong with us, and we didn't know what it was"—merged nicely with the new ethic.

For those forming their identities in those years, the search for meaning led to a discovery of the emptiness and decay of late twentieth-century America—divorce, scandal, nuclear war, spiritual rot. For many, the path forward was detachment and disengagement, finding a way of operating on the fringes. "Our attitude had everything to do with withdrawal, contemplation, and seeking the margins—albeit with the volume knob cranked to eleven," wrote Douglas Coupland, author of the novel *Generation X,* another book that found its way into the zeitgeist in those years.

The dropout ethic was the engine that drove the narrative in some of the innovative art that emerged during the early years of the decade. A no-budget, plotless independent film called *Slacker* by an unknown twenty-six-year-old director from Austin, Texas, became a prophetic window into the artistic vision of the time. Richard Linklater's underground movie celebrated a certain type of oddball character who had decided, consciously or not, to drop out and exist on the margins.

In the narrative nonfiction aisle of the bookstore, a little book from an unknown author, *Into the Wild,* told the story of another dropout: Christopher McCandless, an upper-middle-class kid who withdrew from society by throwing away his money, belongings, and identity and hiking to his demise deep in the Alaskan outback. (Jon Krakauer's piece for *Outside* magazine, which led to the best-selling book, hit newsstands just weeks before the publication of *Jesus' Son.* It would cause the largest reader response in the history of the magazine.) For the consumers of these new flavors on the cultural menu, Denis's creation fit right in.

The portrayal of illegal drug use and abuse was also receiving a cultural reevaluation. The war on drugs, a political creation of the Reagan era that took aim at the latest enemy of the state, had placed substance abuse at the center of the cultural conversation, where it was examined in black and white, with little room for shading. The idea that illegal narcotics were rotting America from within began to dominate the entertainment of the era. Drug narratives of the 1980s hit all the same notes: the catastrophic effects of drugs always looming, disaster inevitable in the final act. There was a vacuum for a more nuanced interpretation of illicit drug use and the drug culture. Films such as *Drugstore Cowboy,* which mirrored elements of Denis's book, began to fill the vacuum. Young director Gus Van Sant adapted the film from an unpublished novel by a convict that told the story of addicts who rob pharmacies in the Pacific Northwest. *Drugstore Cowboy* provided a completely different depiction of addiction and the lives of addicts and became a success, first on the film festival circuit, then finding a more mainstream audience.

Like a bead of food coloring dropped into liquid, *Jesus' Son* appeared and then gradually spread into the veins of the youth culture of the early '90s. Twentysomethings, who probably weren't reading the *New York Times Book Review* regularly, might hear Denis or his book casually referenced in *Spin* magazine or in their local alternative newspaper. Or they might hear the title name-checked by their favorite VJ on MTV as he or she riffed between videos by the Butthole Surfers and the Meat Puppets. Denis had become relevant in an entirely different universe.

Sales of the books that surrounded it on the best-of-the-year lists slowed to a drip the next year, but *Jesus' Son* had a long tail. The media ecosystem was still a print-and-analog operation in the early '90s, which meant that the audience for a certain type of movie or album or book could be built progressively, person to person, a mention here or there, until it reached and began to circulate among its true congregation.

Chuck Klosterman, author of *The Nineties,* a cultural history of the decade published in 2022, remembered hearing about *Jesus' Son* time after time from a variety of sources before actually picking up a paperback copy and reading it a few years after its initial publication. "You bought the book not knowing much about it, only that it was supposed to be good and/or cool," he remembered.

For many, the book so directly tapped into the vibe of the era that it became a defining marker. People's cultural choices were increasingly a way of telling the world who they were. "You wouldn't be cool by reading *Bridget Jones's Diary,* but you could be cool by just carrying around a Denis Johnson book," Klosterman said. "There were certain books... that sort of had these coded things in them. If you saw people with the book, you would think, maybe this person smokes marijuana, or whatever. It was like it was signal. *Slacker* was another great example of that. If you were into the movie *Slacker,* that told people a lot about who you were."

In the early '90s, the worst insult that could be leveled against artists was that they were sellouts. If it could be ascertained that a musician or a filmmaker was in it for the money, then they were rotten to the core and not to be trusted. It was yet another reaction to the "greed is good" ethic of the decade that had come before. The reason to create art, for the Gen Xers, lay in the creation itself. Any attempts to commodify a work of art cheapened it and disclosed the avaricious motivations of its creator. Those who bought into this ethic were searching for authenticity and repelled by any hint of commercialism. It was a high bar for acceptance. The characters in the *Jesus' Son* stories had no such motivations, and their ethic, by some readers, was assigned to the creator. Because the MTV generation had no history with Denis and he avoided the publicity machine, he was a blank slate; readers could, and did, grant him the status of total and complete artistic virtue.

The stories in *Jesus' Son* shared another characteristic with popular art of the era: part of their allure was that they seemed as if they had been created with very little effort. (As an added bonus, the stories themselves took minimum effort on the part of the reader—it was a book that could be digested in a few hours, even if it took a few times through to truly understand what was happening.) Just as Denis had conceived them, the openings to the stories sounded like the beginning of an anecdote delivered at the bar after the third or fourth drink. "I went out to the farmhouse where Dundun lived to get some pharmaceutical opium from him, but I was out of luck," reads the first sentence of "Dundun." There doesn't appear to be an iota of "literature" in that sentence. Denis, of course, had been rewriting the stories for a decade in an attempt to perfect the voice when the book came out, but the illusion was there. Klosterman compares it to the music of bands such as the Talking Heads or Pavement, which produced sophisticated music, with the sophistication used to create a primitive sound. "It's very strategically amateurish in some ways, which means it's not amateurish at all," he said.

If *Jesus' Son* touched a nerve among a large slice of the youth culture, it scored an even more direct hit on the writers of Generation X. Just as the Velvet Underground's debut album was said to have sold thirty thousand copies and spawned thirty thousand new bands, *Jesus' Son* would have a similar effect in the creation of an army of aspiring writers. The academic creative writing industry that had proliferated over the course of Denis's life now was filled with young writers, and *Jesus' Son* became both textbook and totem to a great many of them.

Nathan Englander was one of the many up-and-coming writers who fell under Denis's spell in those years. Around the time he arrived in Iowa City to study in the Writers' Workshop, a friend gave him a xeroxed copy of "Car Crash While Hitchhiking." The title was cut off so that it read only "Car Crash." The author's name was absent. He absorbed it and emerged with an altered vision of his future as a writer. Then he went looking for the rest of the collection. "This book, for my friends and me, became sort of a young writers' bible," said Englander, who would become a celebrated short-story writer and novelist himself by the end of the decade. "[It showed us] the kind of thing that could be done, that we were allowed to do." Jenny Offill, a future award-winning writer then studying the craft at the University of North Carolina, felt the same effects. "It's one of these permission books, where you see things in it that you didn't know you could do," she said. "We all read it and then we all wanted to write it." Through the '90s, the same scene was playing out across the country.

"Everyone who started writing seriously in the 1980s or 1990s can tell you where he or she first consumed the morsels that eventually made up *Jesus' Son*," said Rick Moody, another writer who got his start in those years and went on to a successful career in fiction. Michael Cunningham was a fellow in the same class as Denis in the Fine Arts Work

Center in Provincetown, and he had been among the small group that attended Denis's wedding to Lucinda outside the Barnstable County courthouse. By the mid-'90s, he was a prolific writer who also taught in the creative writing program at Yale University. He witnessed first-hand the effect his old friend's book had on his students. As young writers often do, many related so deeply to the stories and the writing within that their work read like a bad imitation. "This book seems to inspire the desire to write this book," Cunningham said. "There are a lot of good books, but this one has a particular, mesmerizing, I'm-going-to-write-like-that effect.... My thought was 'Oh, here comes a new generation of fake Denis Johnson writers.'"

Ironically, *Jesus' Son* is credited by many writers of the generation as breaking the spell of Denis's own mentor, Ray Carver, whose work was, at the time, the instruction manual to contemporary literary fiction. The Raymond Carver–Gordon Lish combination that had produced the stories that made Carver famous in the '70s had also been the blueprint for what would be understood as literary fiction in the decade to follow. Through the '80s, the codes of Carver's Kmart realism were in place. Minimalism was the guiding principle. When Chuck Palahniuk, who would touch the nerve of Generation X with books such as *Fight Club* and *Choke,* was studying fiction, the Carver rules were still being strictly enforced. Young writers often felt uncomfortable breaking outside the boundaries of Carver's pared-down writing. *Jesus' Son* was a revelation to him. "Suddenly, Johnson was lapsing into these poetic, writerly flourishes, that we were being grilled not to do," Palahniuk remembered.

Whether it was just the right balance of poetry and minimalism or the perfect concoction of the '60s and the '90s, *Jesus' Son* struck a nerve that made Denis an icon across U.S. culture. It was a phenomenon he didn't quite seem to understand, but one that he increasingly enjoyed. "It's had a longevity that does kind of amaze me," he said a few years later. "And there are always young writers who come up to me and say 'I read this book and that decided it for me. I want to become a writer.' Does that mean it looks easy? I don't know. Because, you know, it is just a short little book."

KNIFE IN THE EYE 23

What defeats most men in life? Probably the fact that they make false gods for themselves and strive to attain things that don't have an enduring value for them. —**John Huston**

Denis's third wedding was much more elaborate than his second, but not quite the traditional black-tie affair of the first. Around a hundred people made the trip to northern Idaho for the outdoor ceremony. Tony Brown, owner and bartender at the Club Bar in nearby Troy, Montana, performed the extremely abbreviated ceremony. Denis's old friend Maury Barr was among the attendees and recalled a relaxed atmosphere that matched the bucolic milieu. "Denis just seemed really, really happy," he said.

Denis and Cindy's honeymoon was to be a trip into an even more remote locale than where they hosted the wedding. They decided to fly into the Bonanza Hills of south-central Alaska to try to pan for gold, which they planned to use in the making of their wedding rings. The trip would also double as a magazine assignment for Denis.

The original idea was for the newlyweds to meet a friend from Montana who would take them prospecting. When they got to Anchorage, the friend was nowhere to be found, so they went hunting for somebody who could fly them into the mountains on their quest for gold. They found Richard Busk, a charter pilot with several crash landings in his flight history. On their trip into the backcountry, it seemed as if he was about to add another line to that list. The engine on the four-seat propeller plane he was flying began to cough and wheeze. Denis tried to reassure Cindy while at the same time he scribbled in his notebook: "Random clattering and thundering noises... gray smoke coming out of the floor."

That flight ended in an emergency landing an hour short of their destination. Another, less crash-prone pilot took them the final stretch and dropped them off on an isolated mesa, seventy miles from the nearest human, promising to return in nine days to pick them up. Cindy, no doubt imagining an extremely short marriage that would end with a gruesome death in the Alaskan wilderness, pleaded with the pilot to write down the return date and location.

Despite the inauspicious beginning to the honeymoon, the couple settled into the remote fantasy that Denis had imagined for them—"the only new part left in the New World! The Last Frontier!"—and created both a memorable experience and the plot for a magazine article. Denis panned and panned but did not find gold. At least in print, he still declared the trip a success. "The newlyweds spend days wandering through the solitude, discovering things you can't buy but can only keep inside," he wrote. "They find a certain peace and a certain magic, and to some extent they begin the process of finding each other."

Denis was once again a married man, now one part of a family unit that included two small children of barely elementary-school age. His biological son, Morgan, was ready to go to college, and, though they hadn't spent much time together in recent years, he idolized his father and decided that he too would go to the University of Iowa to become a writer. As an undergraduate, Morgan initially chose not to tell people who he met on campus the name of his famous father. One undergraduate writing teacher, after reading a story he had submitted, pulled Morgan aside and told him that his work was excellent. "There are two writers who you remind me of," the professor told Morgan. "I'm not sure if you've heard of them, but I think you need to go out and get a few books by Denis Johnson and Robert Stone."

Morgan also shared his father's tendencies toward substance abuse and addiction, and Iowa City was, for those reasons, perhaps not the best place for him to spend his postadolescence years. He drank in some of the same bars Denis had inhabited twenty years before. Sometimes he was even served by the same bartenders who had poured drinks for Denis. "I remember, one of my favorite things was when somebody would say 'Man, you drink just like your dad,'" Morgan recalled. "I would be so proud."

Soon it was not just the shadow of Denis who was walking the same streets as Morgan while he was in college. Denis was offered a year-long teaching stint in the Writers' Workshop, and the family decided to relocate to Iowa for a year. Morgan, who by that time was doing less writing as he was pulled deeper into a life of drugs and crime, found out where his dad would be staying. "He was getting a professor's house, who was leaving, and it was a super nice house," Morgan said. "I went beforehand and broke into the house with a couple of my friends. We crashed it. We were there for two weeks." Parties, property damage, and phone calls to the police from irate neighbors followed. Before Denis and Cindy even arrived in town, they received multiple calls from law enforcement. Each time, Denis had to explain to the officer that one of the partiers was indeed his son, provide assurances that he would get everything under control, and ask politely that Morgan not be arrested.

That semester in the Writers' Workshop, Denis decided to offer a seminar about his favorite poet, Walt Whitman. He added his own personal innovation to the seminar process. In his class that semester, there were to be no assignments, no analysis, not even any discussion among the students of the poetry of Whitman. The entire seminar was to consist of the students reading selections from Whitman's *Leaves of Grass,* one by one, while Denis and the rest of the class listened silently.

Each time the class met, Denis had the students pull the desks into a horseshoe so everybody could see the face of the reader. Often he would recline, put his head back, close his eyes and let the words of Whitman flow over him. Mike Judge, one of the dozen or so poets in the class, said he thought the entire exercise was just an excuse for Denis to be read "Song of Myself" over and over. The act of reading, however, could be deeply affecting. "Sometimes it would just be so moving that everybody would stop. You could feel Whitman's presence in the room," Judge said. "It was an overwhelming experience, and it happened on a regular basis." The class would usually conclude not at the scheduled time, but whenever Denis was overcome with emotion, began to tear up, and, with his voice cracking, said to the class, "Let's end it there."

*

In his own writing, Denis was slowly making progress on an idea that had been born in 1984, when he struck up a conversation at a literary event with a poet he admired by the name of Bill Knott. Denis was intrigued with a work entitled "Poem Noir," which Knott had written years before. The poem was the story of a murder-for-hire scheme. It read like the plot for a 1940s Humphrey Bogart movie—indeed, Knott had even included a cast list at the end of the poem. In his conversation with Knott after the reading, Denis casually mentioned the idea of using the poem as an outline for his next novel. Knott laughed and, in Denis's memory of the exchange, tacitly agreed to the plan.

It would be several years before Denis got to work on the novel based on the Knott poem, and many more years before he had a completed manuscript in hand. As would be the case throughout his career, a certain amount of time needed to pass before Denis felt enough distance to write about a period and place from earlier in his life. This new book was to be based on his years in Northern California. The bones of the novel would be from Knott's film noir poem. The characters and setting would grow out of his experiences in and around Mendocino County, California, in the late 1980s.

In *Poem Noir,* an angry husband sees a mysterious young man trying to drown himself in a lake near a cottage. The husband saves the man. Then, when he learns that the man is suicidal, he asks him to kill his wife. As the audience immediately understands when presented with this type of setup in a Bogart movie, the simple plan will not go accordingly. Around this structure, Denis placed characters clearly based on people from his life. The wife who is the target of the murder plot is a sculptor named Winona; a friend of the mysterious man from the lake is Wilhelm Frankenheimer, a six-foot, nine-inch muscle-bound metal worker. He built plots on top of plots: a drug deal gone wrong; a pair of hapless hit men; a family marijuana business; a jaded police officer wading through the evidence; a character practicing witchcraft and talking to the dead. All are told by shifting points of view, between first and third person, with occasional lengthy, multipage forays into nonsensical diary entries and letters from one character or another. When he was finally done, it was longer than any three of his previous books combined. He told Will Blythe that he had created such a complicated, layered plot that he himself could not remember who killed whom and why.

The book, which Denis entitled *Already Dead: A California Gothic,* was nearing publication in the spring of 1996. He had not contacted Knott in the intervening years to inform him that he was indeed novelizing the poem. Knott heard about it through a friend who attended a public reading in which Denis read a section of the novel and told the audience about the connection to Knott's "Poem Noir." The poet did not take it well.

Bill Knott was a notoriously thorny character who spent much of his life attacking what he viewed as the poetry establishment. In his twenties, he circulated a letter that said he'd committed suicide, then published his first book under a pseudonym, Saint Geraud, a name he'd found in a pornographic French novel. The poetry community was nonplussed when he turned up alive a short time later. Though he was a tenured professor at Emerson University whose books were acquired by major publishing houses and who won major awards including a Guggenheim fellowship, he behaved as if he were a pariah, blogging about his litany of rejections, claiming to self-publish his poems out of necessity, and editing positive reviews of his work into pans. Some thought it was a lifelong prank. Galassi, who edited some of Knott's books at FSG, said, "I think he had a kind of phobia about the establishment. Belonging was not his thing. It made him uncomfortable."

Whether it was a put-on or not, he responded to the news of *Already*

Dead as if he were the victim of a felony. He wrote to Galassi threatening legal action. As the publication date approached, he sent a letter to Denis that said that if Denis had contacted him at the beginning of the project, he would have happily given his blessing. "But to be presented with a fait accompli; to be taken for granted; to be ignored until practically the last minute; to be an afterthought in your considerations is humiliating. It leaves me degraded and in a position to be ridiculed by everyone . . . a nobody like me never has any rights. You and Galassi can roll right over me and crush me and never twinge a hair." A day later, he sent a second letter, relenting somewhat, but continuing to paint Denis as arrogant and thoughtless. "For what it's worth (nothing!) you can have my 'blessing,' if you still want it. . . . You've always been the star. And I've always been the opposite. Always. You can't understand, you could never understand."

It was a deflating addendum to the release of Denis's first book in over five years. The bad karma seemed to bleed into the reception of *Already Dead.* The critical reaction ranged from "ambitious but flawed" to "a heaping pile of garbage." Those in the garbage camp argued their point forcefully. The characters were all detestable and the plot was a jumbled mess, they said. "The reader might reach the point where he doesn't care who lives or dies," wrote the Associated Press. "A lot of it is a mess," said the *Boston Globe.* And Michiko Kakutani, a champion of Denis's previous books, unloaded both barrels on *Already Dead* in the *New York Times:* "a virtually unreadable book that manages to be simultaneously pretentious, sentimental, bubble-headed and gratuitously violent."

Years later, Denis would acknowledge that his critics had a point. Perhaps his brilliance with the language and his infinite imagination, which produced beautiful poetry and taut novels, could be a little much if allowed to experiment and expound unchecked. It would be another decade before he attempted a second novel the length and breadth of *Already Dead.* And when he did, he would have a much better understanding of the pitfalls that can accompany such an undertaking.

*

In the 1990s, the decade when American independent cinema grew from an underground movement to a wing of the movie business christened "Indiewood," it was inevitable that a transformational work like *Jesus' Son* would be a hot commodity for young filmmakers. Three of them, Elizabeth Cuthrell, David Urrutia, and Lydia Dean Pilcher, got their hands on the rights to the book and convinced Denis to let them take a shot at a screenplay. Denis liked the first draft and agreed to come to New York to meet with them in person.

The producers arrived for the meeting and waited for Denis. When he finally arrived, he ambled into the room wearing a vintage aloha shirt, red cowboy boots, and Elvis Presley glasses held together in the middle with tape. At the meeting, he lauded the filmmakers with praise for their script, and then presented them with a single demand for his green light on the movie. He wanted to play Terrence Weber, the unfortunate hospital patient who arrives with a hunting knife sticking out of his eye, from the story "Emergency." The filmmakers agreed, and Denis found himself in a new role in the movie business.

His previous experience as a cog in the Hollywood machine had been generally painful and unsuccessful. Since his days as a screenwriter for hire working for the producer who had acquired the rights to *Angels,* he had written hundreds of pages of screen dialogue, almost none of which had ever wound up in the mouths of actors. Sometimes the failures would be punctuated with an insult. In the early '90s, he was hired to write a screenplay for a hot book called *Barbarians at the Gate,* about the hostile takeover of RJR Nabisco. After he handed in a draft, an executive pulled him aside and said the script read like poetry.

"Exactly!" Denis replied.

The executive had not meant it as a compliment. By the end of the day, Denis had been fired.

His association with HBO and efforts to create a movie out of *The Stars at Noon* was similarly fruitless. He was also hired to write a screenplay for a novel called *Up Above the World* by novelist Paul Bowles—another attempt that never reached production. In 1998, a screenplay that he had written as an adaptation of the novel *A Swell-Looking Babe,* by Jim Thompson, actually did get produced. The movie, entitled *Hit Me,* opened on the first weekend in October of that year and made $3,478, well on its way to its final gross revenue of $12,500. It "looks like outtakes from a badly done Coen Brothers movie," wrote one of the few reviewers who chose to write about it. Years later, in an interview with a literary journal, Denis said the screenplay for *A Swell-Looking Babe* had never been produced. The film had apparently been erased from his memory.

It didn't always require a producer with a checkbook to get Denis into screenwriter mode. He decided that his experiences covering the civil war in Liberia were fodder for the big screen and went about creating a treatment to offer to Hollywood. As he imagined the movie, an international group of journalists ride a cargo ship from Freetown, Sierra Leone, into the hell that is Monrovia during the civil war. At the heart of the story is a reporter derisively known as C.Q. by the other journalists because he writes for a monthly magazine and is only interested in "color and quotes." As the narrative proceeds, the chaos of the war uncovers for C.Q. facts about himself—his attraction to violence, his infatuation with the dark side, his buried prejudices, his need for stimulation. It had the elements of a political thriller, but, like the rest of his scripts, it languished in purgatory.

Like many successful writers, income generated from flirtations with the movie business paid many bills for Denis over the years. His friend Chris Offutt said he and Denis would occasionally discuss the dangers of writing for the movies and how the process could sap their energy—energy that they felt should be reserved for writing fiction, the art that they viewed as their true calling. "We were both on our guard about it, but we just saw it as, this is where the money is," Offutt said. "It's like that old saying—'Why'd you rob so many banks? Because that's where they keep the money.'"

Denis understood that his value in the eyes of Hollywood executives rose and fell with the success of his books and learned to capitalize when his name had sizzle. Later, he became a hot commodity after winning a major national award and hitting the best-seller list. For a short while, he became a popular guy in Los Angeles. Producers were fighting for the chance to work with him. Denis told friends that movie executives would take him to pitch meetings and excitedly try to profit off his newfound notoriety by introducing him around, though they barely knew who he was or why he was in demand: "This is Dave—he just won the National Book Award," they would say.

Richard Pearce, who worked on several aborted projects with Denis, thought if there had been one screenplay that became a successful movie, it might have changed the trajectory of his career. "The real question is, is Denis really as gifted a screenwriter as he was a novelist and short-story writer and poet and everything else? That's an arguable question," Pearce said. "That's the name of the game for screenwriters, though. They spend a lot of time working on things that never get made."

So when Denis saw the momentum beginning to build behind the film version of *Jesus' Son,* he was more than happy to jump on the train. He chose, through the entire process, to provide input only when asked. The screenplay he had okayed was filled with dialogue and narration pulled directly from the book. The writers had kept their copies close by during the writing process. An initial draft was over two hundred pages—extremely long for a screenplay. Denis gave the three young producers some notes that were respectfully received.

Later in the process, they came back to him with a request: they wanted to add material about the relationship between the protagonist, Fuckhead, and his girlfriend, Michelle. The love story between the two would be a driving narrative force—something that didn't exist in the book. The producers were, Denis said later, too reverent about the material and not comfortable going beyond what was on the pages of the book. He wrote three pages of dialogue between Fuckhead and Michelle, which would be the extent of his direct contributions to the screenplay. He also sent the filmmakers a tape of music that he said "Fuckhead was carrying around in his young and very messed up head." Some of the songs, such as "Sweet Pea" by Tommy Roe and "The Ballad of the Green Berets" by Sgt. Barry Sadler, made it into the final soundtrack.

When the producers settled on a director, it turned out to be someone with whom Denis was well acquainted. Alison Maclean had worked with him previously on yet another failed attempt to get *The Stars at Noon* to the screen. Maclean was a Canadian who moved to New Zealand with her family as a teenager, where she became a filmmaker. Her first feature film, a psychological thriller entitled *Crush,* had garnered praise and attention from the American film industry. Though she was so enchanted with *Jesus' Son* that she regularly gave out copies as gifts, she had not imagined it as a movie. However, when the producers contacted her about directing the film version, she eagerly agreed.

It was an ideal time in Hollywood to be casting for an independent film with dozens of juicy parts and the cachet of a cult book behind it. The success of movies that came from outside the major studios had led to a stampede of well-known actors who were willing to take small parts, and small paychecks, in exchange for the career boost that came with an appearance at independent film festivals like Sundance or Toronto. A cast that was sure to attract the attention of the *Hollywood Reporter* and *Premiere* magazine was assembled. For the role of Fuckhead, Maclean wanted, and eventually landed, Billy Crudup, a young actor who had already had his name above the title in several movies, including *Inventing the Abbotts, The Hi-Lo Country,* and *Without Limits.* British actress Samantha Morton signed on to play Michelle. Morton was to be nominated for an Academy Award for *Sweet and Lowdown,* released just a few days before *Jesus' Son.* Several other well-known actors signed on and agreed to take small roles and work for scale, including Jack Black, Dennis Leary, Holly Hunter, and Dennis Hopper, who played the rehab patient with the immortal line, "Talk into my bullet hole and tell me I'm all right." (Denis sent the producers a tape of himself reading the lines for the Hopper part.)

The film had a $2.5 million budget, financed by independent investors to reduce studio meddling. The six-week production took place in various rural outposts in Pennsylvania, New Jersey, and Arizona and was a decidedly bare-bones affair. The hospital and hotel scenes were filmed in a deserted section of Philadelphia in a pair of abandoned buildings. It was true independent filmmaking—extremely long hours with a young crew, average age in the twenties, who were devoted to the process and the film. The actors were not pampered. "They ate horrible food, nobody had a trailer, and I swear to god nobody complained," Cuthrell told a reporter later.

A twenty-five-year-old actor with just a few bit parts under his belt named Michael Shannon was brought in to read for the role of Dundun. He got the part. On the set, Shannon remembered, everybody was extremely reverent of Denis, and his first rumored appearance was anxiously anticipated. "None of us had every read anything quite like the material in the script," he said. "We were expecting someone exuberant, with a feather in his hat, or something."

When Denis finally arrived, he was unexpectedly ordinary. He was clearly delighted by the experience. He offered little guidance to the actors, instead going out of his way not to affect the performances. "You could tell he kept a lot of secrets and not everything was for everybody," Shannon said.

For Denis's scene in the emergency room as Terrence Weber, the film's makeup team did its best to replicate the description that Fuckhead tossed off in the pages of the book: "The blade was buried to the hilt in the outside corner of his left eye. It was a hunting knife kind of thing." Nicky Lederman was a young makeup artist on the crew. The prosthetic used to serve as the eye and knife on the head of Terrence Weber was the first one she had ever used in a movie. On the day that the knife-in-the-eye scene was to be filmed, the prosthetic was glued onto Denis's face. Lederman painted it as Denis sat in a chair in a room off the set and prepared him for filming. Joy was radiating from Denis. "He was in awe of the process, and really appreciative of what everybody was doing," Lederman remembered. "He was really interested and observant and having fun while we were doing it. He was the perfect person in the chair." Denis immediately felt a kinship with the young technicians and artists on the set. "He just blended in, he was like one of the crew guys," she said.

The actual filming was to be a surreal experience in which Denis was wheeled into a hospital room where Crudup, dressed as the fictional version of Denis, awaits. Denis told a reporter that during the scene he asked Jack Black, a rising comic actor just a few years away from leading roles, for acting advice. "Jack said acting is all about your facial expressions and you don't have to worry about that. You've got a knife sticking out of your head!"

On-screen, Denis played Weber just as deadpan as he had written the character when he first created him, barely acknowledging that he has a hideous wound, while the actors around him react with shock. The lines he speaks in the scene are exactly as he had written them a decade before. "We'd better get you lying down," says a nurse. "I'm certainly ready for something like that," Denis responds without a trace of discomfort.

The film was ready for audiences in the fall of 1999. Spurred by the big-name cast and the popularity of the book, the producers were able to take it to the cream of the international film-festival circuit: Telluride, Toronto, Venice, London, and Paris, where it was widely praised. Crudup won best actor at the Paris film festival. In Toronto, the producers secured distribution for North America and Germany. In a nod to Denis, the film even appeared in the Sunburst Resort Scottsdale Film Festival, where his parents could see it. And Denis himself made a trip to Santa Fe, New Mexico, where a sneak preview was held at the College of Santa Fe.

Jesus' Son went into wide release in the United States in the summer of 2000. If critical acclaim translated into box-office revenue, then its backers would have been rolling in cash. Glowing reviews appeared in all the right places. Roger Ebert, celebrity film critic and TV personality, granted it his stamp of approval both in print and on his syndicated television show, *At the Movies*. "It surprised me with moments of wry humor, poignancy, sorrow and wildness," he wrote. The majority of reviewers at major newspapers across the country had similar reactions. At the box office, however, it made little mark. Its theatrical release failed to make back its slim budget.

Though it wasn't destined to be a money maker, the positive critical response helped many of those involved in the ways they likely had hoped for: notoriety, artistic cred, name recognition. And for Denis, the process was peppered with moments of joy. When he visited the set in New Jersey, he felt he was gazing into a one-way mirror on the

Iowa City of his youth. "I was astonished. The actors looked like they had strolled right in from my past," he said. And when it was done, the filmmakers had managed to make a movie that successfully conveyed the mood and tone of his book, something many had not thought possible. They had even intentionally changed details from scene to scene to show how Fuckhead's clouded brain had misremembered them from one retelling to the next. Crudup's Fuckhead was very close to the bumbling searcher Denis had written. His seminal character had not been transformed into something polished and made to be hip for movie audiences. In interviews during the publicity for the movie, Denis told all reporters who asked that he was pleased. Maybe he was just doing his part to add to the hype, but during the rollout he did make one concrete decision that reflected his true feelings. He gave the producers the movie rights to *Resuscitation of a Hanged Man*.

PLOT IS CHARACTER, CHARACTER IS PLOT

24

There are places where acting is writing and writing is acting. I'm not interested in the divisions. I'm interested in the way things cross over. —Sam Shepard

Agreeing to take part in a Hollywood publicity campaign was not the only sign that Denis's hermit tendencies might be easing. The idea of living off the grid in the wilds of northern Idaho was no longer as appealing to him as it had once been. "I just like to be up here in the summer now," he told an interviewer about his mountain retreat. "It's tough to go thirty-five miles to get a quart of milk." As Al and Vera aged, he began to spend more time in Arizona to be near them. A regular teaching opportunity at the University of Texas at Austin was presented to him, and soon he was splitting his time between Texas, Arizona, and Idaho. The simple pleasures of proximity in city life were not lost on Denis. "It's so nice living in Austin," he said. "I don't even have to put on my shoes, I can just go barefoot down to the 7-Eleven and get some milk. That really makes a difference in your life, your whole day. Plus, I can go to plays, I can go to movies, all that suddenly became a lot more fun. I don't know why."

Another factor in drawing Denis out of the woods was a change of direction in his creative process. A few years before his experiences during the making of the movie of *Jesus' Son,* he was invited to an event at the MET Theatre in Los Angeles. A group of actors, including

Ed Harris, Arliss Howard, Amy Madigan, and Holly Hunter, were involved in a series of performances that combined author readings and actors performing scenes from popular works of contemporary literature. Howard, who had been involved with the failed production of *Angels* a few years earlier, invited Denis and hosted him at his house.

Authors Fran Lebowitz, Barry Gifford and Hubert Selby Jr. were on the program at the MET, as were actors Laura San Giacamo, Forest Whitaker, and Ed Begley Jr. Denis gave a reading of "Car Crash While Hitchhiking" while accompanied by a timbale player that electrified the crowd. Then he took a seat in the audience to watch the actors Howard and Hunter perform a scene from *Resuscitation of a Hanged Man*. The experience was transforming. He bathed in the laughter of his fellow audience members. Humor had always been an important element of his work, and he was used to getting laughs when reading in public. Seeing the words he had written brought to life and given new meaning by the choices of the actors, however, was something new to him. It wasn't long after the experience that he started writing his first play.

His new identity as playwright took a while to develop. He gave up on his first attempt when he was unable to find a theater group willing to work with him. Soon, however, he found his partners. A troupe called Campo Santo in San Francisco would become the vehicle Denis would use to bring his plays into the world. The group was founded in 1996 by several Bay-area artists. The following year, Campo Santo started working in association with Intersection for the Arts, a non-profit organization that supported the San Francisco art community.

Early in the existence of Campo Santo, the group began to collaborate with another San Francisco theater group, Word for Word, which, as its name suggests, chose short stories and performed them verbatim. Soon after the two groups had formed a working relationship, the idea of performing stories from *Jesus' Son* was floated and accepted. The actors began staging and rehearsing a performance of two stories, "Dundun" and "Emergency."

Through the process of clearing the rights to the stories, the group had been given the phone number to the Johnson household in

Meadow Creek. Sean San José, one of the founders of Campo Santo, was offered the job of calling Denis to invite him to the show. San José made the call and was shocked when it was Denis himself who picked up the phone. He told Denis his name and who he was, and what followed seemed to him like something out of a Cheech and Chong routine.

"What did you say your name was?" asked Denis.

"Sean."

"Sean. Sean. Sean Penn is that guy who's in *Dead Man Walking*. Right?"

"Right."

"But you're not him?"

"Definitely not, sir. No."

"Oh, okay," Denis said. "And you're from San Francisco?"

"Right," San José said.

"Hey, did I speak to you after a meeting? Are you from the rehab group?"

"No, sir."

The two eventually came around to the point of the conversation, and Denis agreed to attend the show, provided there was no fanfare around his appearance. Denis made the trip to San Francisco in early February 1999, watched the show quietly and with little reaction, and then left town, but not before a member of the troupe asked him to write a play for them. That sounds interesting, he told them. No further arrangements were made.

San José called him again soon after to close the deal. He asked Denis how he liked the performance of the *Jesus' Son* stories. Denis told him that he thought the troupe had injected humor into the performance that wasn't there. You didn't trust the stories, he said. Still, he agreed to write an original play for the group. Once again, however, no commitment was made. San José thought the group's short involvement with Denis had come to a close.

A few months later, an envelope arrived with the postmark Coeur d'Alene, Idaho. San José had been hoping, at best, for a two-page idea for a future script, but instead, Denis had written an entire play, entitled *Hellhound on My Trail*. "It wasn't like, oh, he had dabbled in screenplay, so it's a version of a screenplay," San José recalled. "It was, boom, boom, boom, everything from technical things, stage directions, the setting and the mood, the tone, even the lighting."

Campo Santo went about staging and rehearsing *Hellhound*. When they had made enough progress, Denis flew to San Francisco to observe. He attended a private table reading where the actors went through the script from beginning to end. When the last words were spoken, San José looked over at Denis. He was leaning over the table, head in hands, and San José could see that he was weeping. The actors looked at each other, thinking they had misread the work, or gone too broad, or done something else to offend the creator. They sat in silence for a moment. Then Denis raised his head to the group.

"That was so beautiful," he told them. "I've never imagined a world where people would read my words like this."

The reading cemented what was to become a long-term association between Denis and Campo Santo. "That was our 'you may kiss the bride' moment," San José said.

Hellhound on My Trail was a psychological drama composed of three two-person scenes set in the offices and bars of Houston, Texas. (It was published in the late winter 2000 issue of the literary journal *McSweeney's*. Denis gave the fledgling journal the rights to publish the play in exchange for the promise that somebody on staff would come to his home in Idaho and build a shed on his property.) The play premiered on July 26, 2000, at Intersection for the Arts in San Francisco. *Hellhound* introduced characters and themes that Denis would return to, including the pill-popping criminal drifter Mark Cassandra. Cassandra, Cass for short, would become a kind of stage version of the narrator from *Jesus's Son*, with a family and a more fleshed-out backstory. Denis's collaboration with Campo Santo accelerated. Shortly after *Hellhound* made it to the stage, the troupe asked him to be their writer in residence. He accepted.

Two more plays, adding to the first to make up a sort of trilogy, followed shortly: *Shoppers Carried by Escalators into the Flames* and *Soul of a Whore*. *Shoppers* was loosely based on the time Denis spent living with his parents and grandmother in Scottsdale before entering the rehab clinic; *Soul,* which arrived as 220 pages of blank verse, centered around the trip Denis took to Huntsville, Texas, years earlier for *Rolling Stone* magazine to cover a series of executions.

The spirit of collaboration involved in preparing a play for the stage, something that he'd struggled with artistically in the past, was now the draw for Denis. He began spending more time in San Francisco and among the members of Campo Santo. "What changed is that I want to get these plays to the stage," he said. "I began to enter, cautiously, into collaboration with people. When I got to the point of being able to tolerate people, enjoying their company and working with them, then I thought, 'Why can't I live in the big city? What's the big deal?'" The Campo Santo crowd, he said, reminded him of the artistic community from Iowa City in his younger days.

Denis found that the act of writing plays often happened quickly, unlike his experiences with novels, which could take decades to take shape. He described his writing style for the stage as "trancelike" and much closer to his process of creating poetry. Sometimes the material for a play would come out of the air. For one of his first plays, he went regularly, by himself, to a coffee shop inside a Borders bookstore in Austin. He got a table, ordered a "Writer's Chai," and listened to the people seated at the tables around him talk, taking notes as he sipped. Characters, dialogue, and situations formed in his mind and flowed easily to the page. "I had very little memory of writing it at all," he said about one of the plays. "It just kind of appeared one day."

Though he was usually hands-off and understood the writer's role in the collaborative process, Denis was deeply attached to his personal vision of his plays, so when he saw something that compromised that vision, he could be compelled to act. "Denis was fierce about protecting his work," said Elizabeth Cuthrell, one of the producers of *Jesus' Son* who went on to work on several plays with Denis. "If someone tried to change or wrongly interpret his writing, he would be crushed, but he would also do what he could do to protect it."

Once, one of his plays was being readied for the stage by a different theater troupe in Chicago when Denis learned that the director planned to use a theremin, a musical instrument that would add eerie-sounding background music to the production. Denis was passionately against the idea. He pleaded his case with the director and then the producer, but he was told that the theremin, and its eerie sounds, would remain in the play. Left with no recourse, he took matters into his own hands. He came back to the playhouse after everybody had gone home, grabbed the theremin, took it to a bridge over the Chicago River, and tossed it into the water below. The next day he was told he wouldn't be allowed in the theater during rehearsal.

In all, Campo Santo produced and performed ten plays with Denis, most of them original works for the stage. In time, some of the plays traveled out of San Francisco and were performed by other troupes in Chicago and New York. In San Francisco, the openings became something of a literary event, with famous writers and Johnson fans from far and wide joining the audience to see what Denis was up to. San José was amazed by how beloved Denis was by other writers, even those of great stature. Denis, however, was always unfazed.

Late in his association with Campo Santo, Denis told San José he wanted to resign his position as writer in residence to let somebody else have a chance. San José reluctantly agreed. Soon after, Denis called again with an idea for another play; the theater had apparently not lost its grip on him. He told San José he had an idea: maybe there could be two writers in residence.

"It was like a love affair that never ended," San José said.

*

One of Denis's projects that been percolating for years was a book of novellas. Three separate works, all started in the early to mid-'90s, were in their final stages as the end of the decade approached. The original plan had been for the three separate works to be published as a single volume entitled *Name of the World*.

In 1995, Denis had started taking notes for a work of historical fiction about the American West. The story was to take place in the Moyie River Valley, beginning in the late nineteenth century—the same valley where he was spending most of his time in the late twentieth century. In his vision, the tale would incorporate the history and myths of the region, many of which he had learned about during his time in Bonners Ferry. The home on Meadow Creek Road was partway up the side of a mountain, and a train line traversed the valley below. The Burlington Northern Santa Fe and the Union Pacific lines ran through Boundary County, so the whistle of the engine as trains passed through was unavoidable. The character who began to speak to him and became the protagonist of the story was an itinerant laborer who was present when the railroads of Boundary County were first built.

The manuscript was ready to submit in October 2001. During its writing, the rail worker who had been conjured up while Denis listened to the train whistles scream through the valley was now Robert Grainier, an orphan who arrived by train in northern Idaho circa 1893. The story Denis wrote followed Grainier from the dying stages of the Wild West all the way through the era of Elvis Presley. (Grainier nearly has a chance meeting with Elvis, with whom Denis harbored a lifelong near obsession. Elvis managed to make an appearance, however unlikely, in many of Denis's books.)

Grainier eventually marries and has a daughter. His wife and child perish in a fire that destroys much of the valley, perhaps a version of a real forest fire that burned through the Idaho panhandle in 1910 and became, to that point, the largest forest fire in U.S. history. After the deaths, the book follows Grainier's life in episodic fashion, as the character becomes increasingly hermetic and haunted by his past. Denis had found another key in which to write, one that was built on spare and exacting language, and real or imagined western dialect—just the right flavor for the story he had chosen to tell.

By the time *Train Dreams* was ready to be shopped around, Will Blythe had taken the job of literary editor at *Men's Journal*. The managing editor of the magazine was Mark Bryant, who had come from *Outside* magazine. Under Bryant's leadership, the magazine began to expand beyond its fashion-and-fitness mission. Blythe asked Denis if he'd like to write about the playwright Sam Shepard. Denis, who had been studying Shepard's work as he progressed in his own theater writing career, enthusiastically agreed. The story fell through, however, when some of the actors said they felt uncomfortable with Denis observing rehearsals.

Blythe also commissioned a work of fiction from Denis for *Men's Journal*. It was left to Denis what type of work he would submit. *Train Dreams* arrived on Blythe's desk a few months later. "It was such a unique piece," Blythe recalled. "It was so different from the fiction he'd written before."

He sent the manuscript to Bryant with his blessing. The publisher of *Men's Journal* at the time was media mogul Jann Wenner, of *Rolling Stone* fame. Whether Bryant thought Wenner wouldn't approve *Train Dreams* or whether Wenner rejected it himself, Blythe was not told. Either way, it was rejected. Blythe left the magazine soon after. Instead, *Train Dreams* found a home at the *Paris Review*, another favorite landing spot for Denis. It ran on fifty-nine pages of the summer 2002 issue of the journal. The following winter, Denis was awarded the Aga Khan Prize for the best short story of the year in the *Paris Review*, along with a check for $1,000.

Another of the works originally destined for the book of novellas was a story about a character named Michael Reed, one more protagonist whose wife and child had been killed, this time in a car accident. In the story, Reed is a former political speechwriter now sleepwalking through a job as an associate professor of history at an unnamed midwestern university. As in *Train Dreams*, the story unfolds episodically as Reed goes to cocktail parties where he endures academic chitchat, becomes infatuated with a graduate student and part-time stripper named Flower Cannon, and gets punched out in a Native American casino.

Together with his editor Robert Jones at HarperCollins, Denis chose to publish *The Name of the World* as a single volume and drop the three-novella plan. The book was out in the summer of 2000. Its release created another blip in time, like the moment ten years earlier, when Denis seemed to be everywhere and available in all mediums.

Jesus' Son was still in the theaters and soon to be available on VHS; his first play was on stage and soon to be in print; and a new and well-reviewed novel was on the shelves of bookstores.

For the ending of *The Name of the World,* Denis again tapped directly into his own personal history. The conclusion centers around the end of Reed's academic career as well as his affair with Flower Cannon. He finds himself in a baseball field thinking of Flower when a group of teenage boys drive by and jeer at him. Then Denis recreated that night in Port Townsend, Washington, in 1976, when, imagining that he saw Susan in a passing truck full of teenagers, he hurled an alarm clock at the truck and broke the windshield. In the book, Reed throws a bottle at the boys' truck, breaks the window, fights with the teenagers, and, just as Denis had done fifteen years before in Port Townsend, packs up and leaves town before dawn.

In the space of one more page, Reed, now awakening from his four-year spiritual hibernation, becomes an international correspondent and takes an assignment to cover the Gulf War:

> I flew in a helicopter above blazing tank battles in the desert in the night, through black smoke overclouding a world pocked by burning oil wells like flickering signals of distress, of helplessness, floated like prey in the talons of a hawk above a bare brown planet with nothing in it but two or three roads and a war; and continued day after day in a life I believe to be utterly remarkable.

ANOTHER APOCALYPSE 25

Vietnam has haunted America. It's been its bastard stepchild since the '60s, and the people that try to deny it or ignore it are covering up America's soul.

—**Oliver Stone**

As the years drifted by and the narrative of his life came further into focus, it became increasingly clear to Denis that the place where his time on earth intersected with the contours of human history was in his relationship to the story of the Vietnam War. The shadow of it hung over his entire existence. He was a small child when Vietnamese forces drove the French colonists out of the country and the Cold War dance between the United States and Soviet Union began to gather steam in Southeast Asia. Through his childhood living overseas behind the gates of the U.S. government, he watched as his father and his friends' fathers, and then the rest of the world, became consumed with the geopolitical conflict in Vietnam. The vague notion that Alfred was part of the great American war machine alternatively attracted and repelled him. He was a baby boomer, which meant that he lived through the center of the cultural upheaval that flowed directly from America's quagmire. When he came of age and officially became a part of the Vietnam generation, he observed, then joined, then quit the protest movement. He maneuvered to avoid the draft and saw friends who weren't so lucky go off to war. He chose a life in the arts and lived in a time when much of the great art that defined the era, in cinema and literature, grew out of the tragedy of Vietnam.

And somewhere along the journey, he was compelled to make his own contribution to the story of the Vietnam War.

Earlier in his development as a writer, while still a student in the Writers' Workshop plotting the creation of his fiction debut, he crossed "Vietnam novel" off the list of potential subjects. Too much research, he told Al and Vera. Also, everyone around him was already writing one, veterans and protesters alike, and the shelves of bookstores were beginning to pile up with them. He held firm to that decision through graduate school and stuck to it when he finally published his debut volume a decade later. But within *Angels,* whether he knew it at the time, were the seeds of his Vietnam book.

For a writer whose projects often materialized over many years, the Vietnam novel would be his ultimate marathon. He began taking notes for a work of fiction set in Southeast Asia on a pair of trips back to the Philippines in the late '80s, one when he traveled to Mindanao for *Esquire,* and a second trip soon after. Initially, the research was aimed for inclusion in a novella set in the Philippines entitled *Door in a Blank Wall.*

Denis always worked on multiple projects at various phases of development. Certain projects jumped to the front of the line on the basis of factors he often had little control over. "Every once in a while, one takes off and I stick with it," he told an interviewer. "The world of [the Vietnam] novel was building, and I was just making notes, and I kept getting interested in other projects."

In the fall of 2003, it was the Vietnam novel's turn to take off. Over the course of its multiyear gestation period, his initial vision had expanded into a story with multiple threads in several countries that spanned the years of the war and beyond. It was to be an epic. Two of the threads would fill in the military backstory of the Houston brothers, Bill and James, the unfortunate bank robbers from *Angels.* These sections would follow James through four tours as a grunt in the jungle and Bill's struggles to function on the streets of Phoenix after his discharge from the navy. Another thread would follow an uncle–nephew team of CIA operatives through the Philippines and Vietnam. In this story line, Denis would mine some of the real-life experiences of Alfred Johnson, United States Information Agency official and CIA liaison. The relationship between the two characters, a World War II hero and his protégé, was to be at the heart of the book.

Through the mid-2000s, the novel, initially entitled *The Years,* began to take shape. It was now organized chronologically, starting with the assassination of John F. Kennedy and moving through the duration of the war, even following some of the characters into the 1980s. It was a lot to cover. The chapters began to pile up, and the word count grew beyond anything he'd written previously. "I had a number of characters, and I just wanted to follow each one until everyone's story has been told," he said. "The rule I made for myself was let everyone in who wants to come.... Basically all were welcome."

His years spent in Asia gave him a feel for the material, but still he wrestled with the fact that he was writing about a war that he did not attend. His best work had always grown out of lived experience. Now he was attempting to chronicle something from afar, something based only on research and imagination. The classics of the genre already in existence were all written by men who had been in Vietnam as soldiers or journalists—Tim O'Brien, John Herr, David Halberstam, Robert Stone, Philip Caputo. "It has been troubling me," he said to an interviewer when he was in the final stages of writing, "to what extent am I appropriating the experience of other people who have been traumatized—veterans and so on? I'm not sure I have a right to do that." The trauma he had experienced, along with most of his generation, had not been through direct contact with violence but from the resulting cultural upheaval, which had spared no one.

The manuscript was in the hands of his publisher in early 2007. He was now back with Farrar, Straus and Giroux. His years with HarperCollins had not been as successful as he had hoped. Jonathan Galassi, his editor at FSG, came to Phoenix for a sales conference while Denis was in town. The damaged feelings over the number of stories in *Jesus' Son,* in hindsight a laughable controversy, had apparently healed. "We met, and we decided to work together again," Galassi recalled. "It was an enjoyable reunion."

The Years had by then been given the title *Tree of Smoke.* Denis had heard the phrase from a painter of religious themes, Norbert Cox, who had told him of its existence in the Bible. Later, he heard it again in Bob Dylan's song *Angelina:* "Beat a path of retreat up them spiral staircases / Pass the tree of smoke, pass the angel with four faces / Begging God for mercy and weepin' in unholy places." In his book, it took on new meaning.

The rollout for *Tree of Smoke* began in the late summer of 2007. The willingness Denis had shown to promote his plays had not resulted in a reversal of his long-standing boycott of book publicity. He read an excerpt from the book at an appearance in Santa Fe, New Mexico, and afterward told the audience that the reading would serve as his book tour. "My publisher has been trying to get me to do some publicity and I've been resisting," he told them. "If you run into anybody from Farrar, Straus and Giroux, tell them what you heard here."

As it turned out, his presence was not needed for the publicity campaign. Sometime during the preceding years, he had achieved the status of American literary nobility and joined the ranks of those authors who, on the release of a new work of fiction, merited front-page coverage and career reexamination. A media consumer in the late summer of 2007 would have had to work hard to miss the fact that a new Denis Johnson novel was now available. In perhaps one of the most notable elements of his coast-to-coast coronation, the *New York Times Book Review* devoted the cover of its September 2, 2007, issue to *Tree of Smoke,* in the process gifting Denis with an enviable nickname: the Revelator. A line drawing of the Revelator himself, his face creased and wizened with age, stared from the front page wearing a disapproving expression that likely mirrored the one that appeared on Denis's face when he picked up the issue and first laid eyes on the sketch.

The critical establishment reacted to *Tree of Smoke* as the attendees at a child's birthday party react when the lights are turned off and the cake is brought out. Praise was heaped on both Denis and the new book. The word *masterpiece* was prevalent. "Good morning and please listen to me: Denis Johnson is a true American artist and 'Tree of Smoke' is a tremendous book," opened the *New York Times* review.

Similar sentences could be found in almost all North American publications with a book section and a working printing press.

Though it was less prominent, there was a parallel reaction that bubbled just below the surface of much of the coverage: Denis was late to the party. Popular culture had been saturated with Vietnam for nearly four decades. Everybody knew about the jungle and the tunnels and the pot-smoking, rock 'n' roll privates and the incompetent, bumbling officers. They'd seen *Apocalypse Now, Platoon, Full Metal Jacket,* and all the Rambos. Though *Tree of Smoke* was a different experience, and the Denis Johnson imprint gave the story a new flavor, it was impossible to avoid the tropes. Many of them were in the book. Colonel Sands, the war hero / career soldier driven to madness, was interchangeable with Marlon Brando's Colonel Kurtz in *Apocalypse Now.* Scenes of brutal violence against captives and villagers were reminiscent of Oliver Stone's *Platoon.* The stoned nights with the bar girls of Saigon, the broken vet's alienation on returning to the States—it had all been shown before, times ten. Because Denis did not have firsthand knowledge of the war, the scenes and characters he created owed much to previous interpretations.

If reviewers buried the question of timeliness, the headline writers of the world clearly picked up on this idea. "Apocalypse Again," ran the bold type over the review in the *South Florida Sun-Sentinel*—not the only publication to settle on that idea. "The Things They Carried," read the headline in the *Boston Globe,* stealing the title of Tim O'Brien's collection of Vietnam stories. An article in *Esquire* by Tom Chiarella entitled "Denis Johnson Killed the Sixties" faced the issue head on. "I won't read another book about the sixties because *Tree of Smoke* is old material," Chiarella wrote. "So many books. So many movies. I can't tell the difference between what I remember and what I've been told. Worse, I don't care anymore."

Still, the appetite for material about Vietnam, or maybe the thirst for another Denis Johnson masterpiece, was strong enough to make the popular reaction to *Tree of Smoke* the greatest of his career. In 1981, he said in the *Arizona Republic* that it was his goal "to write a best-seller someday." He would probably be dead when it happened, he added. Denis was still drawing breath on September 23, 2007, when the goal was finally achieved. There it was, all the way up at No. 6 on the *New York Times* Best Seller List for Fiction, *Tree of Smoke,* right between *Playing Dirty* at No. 7 and *The Elves of Cintra* at No. 5. By September 30, one week later, Denis had quietly slipped off the list, never again to return.

He had been collecting awards all his life, but the most prestigious of them, the Pulitzer Prize for fiction and the National Book Award, had eluded him. He was a cult writer or a writers' writer, with books that didn't make that much money. Now that he had been admitted into the literary aristocracy and written something approximating a pop novel, he was finally eligible for the top prizes. Soon after its release, *Tree of Smoke* appeared on the finalist list for both the Pulitzer and the National Book Award.

On November 14, 2007, the night of the ceremony for the presentation of the 2008 National Book Awards, Denis was approximately six thousand miles away from the Marriot Marquis Hotel in Manhattan. He was, in fact, staying at the Erbil International Hotel in Kurdistan, on assignment for *Portfolio* magazine, researching an article about the Iraqi oil business. His presence was conspicuous in the Marriot Marquis ballroom, though. The *New York Times* reported that he was "widely favored" to take home the prize, a difficult-to-verify statement for an award that was chosen by a panel of five judges and did not have a Las Vegas betting line. The favorite status was likely because the pool of people who cared about the outcome of such an award was made up of people who now felt Denis deserved such an award—and in fact felt it was an outrage that he had not already received one.

The handicappers proved to be right. In a room full of bow ties and champagne, author Francine Prose strode to the stage and told the crowd that Denis was indeed the winner. Nobody was surprised that he did not attend. Cindy, accepting for him, alluded to his reputation for avoiding such events. She told the audience about her husband's trip to Iraq, noting that she'd been asked if he was actually in the Middle East solely "to duck this fancy award ceremony." Then she opened an envelope Denis had given her on which he'd written "Just in case." "I'm very sorry to miss this one chance to dress up in a tuxedo," Denis had written, "in front of so many representatives of the world of literature and say thank you to the people who have given me my life."

The applause was long and deep, and the feeling that a wrong had been righted was palpable in the ballroom. But it also might have been true that, if there existed a higher, more fair-minded body than the National Book Foundation to bestow honors on literature, and if awards were not handed out months after publication based mostly on hype campaigns from multimillion-dollar publishing companies, then when Denis arrived back home in Idaho and found his prize, he would have picked up a quarter and begun to scratch along the etching on the plaque, and the words *Tree of Smoke* would have flaked away to reveal the name of Denis's creation that the gods of literature had actually chosen to preserve for eternity: *Jesus' Son.*

*

Morgan Johnson worked his way through the 618 pages of *Tree of Smoke* in the same place he'd read the last phonebook-sized creation written by his father: in a jail cell. The same addictions that had brought down Denis in Iowa City had come for Morgan. Substance abuse led to small crimes, then larger ones, and finally a life that sometimes was devoted mainly to the acquisition of drugs by any means possible.

His relationship with his father was sporadic throughout his life. He had spent his youth in the care of Nancy and her second husband, spending many nights in bars with his stepdad and, for a time, his days in a hippie commune where drug use and sexual assault were common. His infrequent contact with Denis had only caused him to idolize his father more. "For years, I wanted to be exactly like him," Morgan said.

By the late '90s, he had gone from a student with a recreational drug problem to a life lived almost fully on the streets. On one occasion, Nancy contacted Denis to tell him that Morgan's situation had spiraled out of control. The two, who had navigated the difficult waters of teen parenthood together, had little contact at that time. But Nancy was deeply concerned about their son and asked Denis for help. They traveled to Seattle, where they'd last heard from Morgan. Somehow they ended up on the same street corner where their son was currently conducting a drug deal. Morgan, who at the time had fiery red hair and was outfitted in Seattle punk-grunge attire, turned and saw his parents together for the first time since early in childhood. "They looked right at me, and that's how messed up I was, because they did not know who I was," he remembered. "They both looked right at me, and I thought, 'Oh shit, I'm going to have to go to treatment.' But then they just walked away."

His descent into a life of crime continued, leading to several stints in prison. He went long stretches without contact with Denis, but his father, whom he continued to idolize, was rarely far from his mind. He read the books and saw himself in some of Denis's writing. Once, he was on the outside, discussing a possible crime with some other aspiring felons. Burglaries, he told them, were bullshit, because you don't have control. With armed robbery, you're in control and you know who's there, who's got a gun and who doesn't have a gun. His coconspirators didn't know it at the time, but he had stolen the logic directly out of *Angels*. What had originally been an exchange between Denis and an inmate in a writing workshop inside Florence prison twenty years before had been turned into a work of fiction, published in an acclaimed novel, and then extracted by author's son and reintroduced back into the real world of crime.

If Morgan stole fictional material from Denis to use in his real life, then his father could reverse the proposition and steal from his son's life for fiction. While serving time in Washington state, Morgan was extradited back to Iowa to face some outstanding charges. He was chained to other inmates and put on a van, which proceeded to traverse the country, dropping off and picking up prisoners along the way. It was a grueling trip but also a great setup for fiction, one he recognized while still in shackles. Morgan wrote a short story about the experience and showed it to his father. Denis also saw the possibilities. He lifted the entire episode and used it for a monologue in one of his plays. Morgan later confronted him about the offense, but Denis just laughed it off.

Eventually, Morgan found his way to Alcoholics Anonymous like his father. He sobered up, married a woman, Penny, whom he'd met while still a student in Iowa City, and the couple started a family. His maturation allowed him to view his relationship with his father in a different light. Lifting the fog of hero worship helped Morgan to better understand his father, as did his own experiences in AA. He understood that at times Denis felt it necessary, for the sake of his own fragile sobriety, to stay away from his son, to steer clear of behavior that could reignite his addictions.

He also came to think that Denis had been at times callous and insensitive. On one occasion, Morgan cut his wrist in a drunken incident in Iowa City. The wound required nine hours of surgery and led to a stay in the hospital's psych ward. Denis, who was in Iowa teaching at the time, never came to see his son in the hospital. Years later, when Morgan and Penny got married, had kids, and bought a house, Denis did not come to visit and rarely saw his grandkids.

Morgan believed Denis struggled not only with his addictions but with another part of the AA remedy: the need to control one's ego and focus on others. "A lot people think that recovery is just about not drinking, but that's just the beginning," he said. "The rest of it is just trying to learn how to deal with life like a normal human being, and it's really easy to relapse behaviorally, without ever relapsing on a substance.... You just do that by getting back into your own [world], worrying more about yourself than anybody else." Denis, he said, lived in an environment where he was surrounded by people who worshipped him. It played into his weakness for ignoring the needs of those around him.

The fight to remain clean was an hourly battle for Denis that never let up. His reliance on AA was strong and consistent. No matter where he was, he would find the time and location for a meeting if he felt the need. On trips to remote locations for writers' conferences, he would sometimes resort to attending meetings via shortwave radio.

His proclivity toward substance abuse was fierce and could awaken at any time. He would occasionally illustrate his own unquenchable thirst for alcohol with a joke: A guy walks into a bar. The bartender tells him it's his lucky day, because the bar is running a special: all you can drink for just one dollar. The guy opens his wallet and pulls out two bills, and says, "I'll have two dollars' worth, please."

In the late '90s, Denis went to Oregon with his high school friend Joe Cohen to participate in a Rainbow Gathering, a latter-day celebration of the hippie lifestyle in the Ochoco National Forest attended by thousands of current and former flower children and their descendants. (Denis would later chronicle the trip in the *Paris Review.*) Drugs were everywhere at the event. The '60s vibe pierced Denis's thin defenses against all mind-altering activities, and he bought a bag of hallucinogenic mushrooms for himself and his friend. He was preparing to split the bag between the two of them, but then his true nature kicked in. "Here is why I can't permit myself even to try to coexist with these substances: I said I'd split it, but I only gave him a quarter. Less than a quarter," he wrote. "Yeah. I never quite became a hippie. And I'll never stop being a junkie."

Relapses like the Rainbow Gathering were rare. One occurred on a research trip he took to Vietnam for *Tree of Smoke.* He hired a driver to take him around Hanoi. He asked the driver to get him some pot, then moved on to heroin. At first he told himself the hunt for drugs was part of his research, but soon he was using what he acquired. The resulting drug spiral didn't end until friends from the United States made the trip to Vietnam to rescue him.

Morgan said that Denis told him about several other relapses involving various drugs. Sometimes an extended break from attending AA meetings would contribute to the weakening of his resolve. Morgan thought his father to be somewhat hypocritical, choosing to protect his reputation rather than admit publicly to the episodes. "There was an image, and part of that image was the recovery," Morgan said. "You know, the guy, Fuckhead from *Jesus' Son* who came out of it and is a success now. So, he didn't really want to fess up that Fuckhead was still around, and Fuckhead still was using sometimes."

The relationship between father and son was rocky at times but improved incrementally in later years. Before committing to AA, Morgan spent time in Idaho, often to escape from the clutches of substances and to regain his health. During one of those occasions, father and son took a road trip from Idaho to Canada, where Denis was planning to buy a cabin in the Yukon Territory. They drove hundreds of miles, just the two of them, camping out under the stars and talking about the past.

Still, although he gradually grew more accepting of his father's fallibility, it was hard for Morgan to kick the feeling that he was always seeking something that Denis was unable or unwilling to provide. The scars from his childhood remained. Therapy helped heal some of the wounds. It was in a therapy session that Morgan had a moment that told him he had finally broken free of the chains of his father's influence. He had gone a lifetime believing that his father's writing was infallible, that everything that came out of Denis Johnson's typewriter was a work of pure genius. But now the mist had cleared, revealing a new reality, and he was able to say, out loud, that he didn't really care for *The Stars at Noon*.

THE REVELATOR IN REPOSE

26

All the battle, murder, and sudden death any fictioneer can imagine are here, a homicidal carnival that leaves nothing unsaid and nobody unshot. —**Review of *Fast One* by Paul Cain, *San Diego Sun*, November 15, 1933**

Because Denis had neither interest nor proficiency in financial issues, Cindy assumed the role of chief of staff. Denis stayed away from the business side of the operation. Once, he accompanied Cindy to cash a royalty check. When Cindy presented identification to the bank representative, Denis asked if he should also provide ID. "You don't have an account here," Cindy told him.

Denis was constantly in demand. Offers could come from anywhere, in all sizes and shapes—television, movies, plays, speaking engagements, even album liners. "Hey," opened a letter that arrived at the house in Bonners Ferry one day in 2003. The sender was David Byrne of the Talking Heads. His band was releasing a box set and thought it would be a great idea for Denis to whip up a little something. "It doesn't even have to be about the band, per se," Byrne pleaded. "Just thought I'd ask." If Denis happened to be in the office when the phone rang, and somebody presented him with a proposal that promised a new challenge or somehow engaged his creative juices, he was apt to agree to it before he hung up the receiver. Often the deal he struck would not be in his best interests. It happened often enough that Cindy placed a note prominently on his desk that read, "No agreements over the phone."

One entity that seemed to have the knack for getting past Cindy's defenses was *McSweeney's*. The literary journal had already secured the rights to publish one of his plays in return for the promise of assistance in building a shed—certainly a deal with questionable fiscal merit. A few years later, Eli Horowitz, a new staffer at *McSweeney's*, called to ask for another submission from Denis, unaware of the previous deal. Sure, Denis replied, I'll submit something. But your magazine still hasn't built me the shed. An addendum to the deal was struck: Denis agreed to give Horowitz an unpublished chapter from *Tree of Smoke*, and Horowitz agreed to make the trek to northern Idaho to work as a day laborer.

The resulting gathering was the beginning of an annual event that was christened the Week of Chaos. Denis and Cindy would invite relatives, former students, friends, and friends of friends who happened to have carpentry skills to their home in Meadow Creek for an extended, weeks-long get-together that could include woodworking, hiking, firing automatic weapons, or any of a dozen other activities that suited Denis's interests. Invitations would go out to an exclusive list of his inner circle:

> TO ALL FRIENDS OF CHAOS:
> Last week in July
> Same deal: All who arrive will get shelter from rain and three meals a day and nothing else
> MUSICIANS WILL RECEIVE SPECIAL TREATMENT
> poets will be treated like slaves
> NEWLYWEDS WILL BE FETED (perhaps that means "eaten")
> BABIES BORN HERE WILL BE AMERICAN CITIZENS AND HAVE GOOD LUCK ALL THEIR LIVES
> ALL WHO ARRIVE WILL BE WELCOME ESPECIALLY BABIES BORN HERE
> Same place as last year, same directions
> If you fly and you're too cheap to rent a car from the airport, come anyway. Maybe someone can pick you up.
> See you last week in July—D.J.

Visitors who made the long journey might be picked up by Denis in his jeep, which pulled a camper with the word "Evolve" on the back. They would be ferried to the house, see the carved wooden sign with the words "Doce Pasos North" (twelve steps) carved into it, and be introduced to the dog, Colonel, and the cat, Hunter S. Thompson. Some stayed in the house, some in cabins, others in tents. The days could be filled with actual work, or with hiking trips, soccer games, or other activities at the whim of the host. Sometimes there would be poetry readings at night on the deck under the star-filled Idaho sky. The Week of Chaos continued until the project, which had evolved into the construction of a cabin, was completed, and for years afterward. The summer that the cabin was deemed ready for use, Denis and several of the original construction crew decided to put their signatures to the work. Denis went first. On an exposed beam, he wrote, "We will defend this house for a thousand years."

*

Time spent with friends was appreciated, but Denis could be just as fulfilled spending time in his own head, in the worlds of his own invention. Once, on a night out with Marvin Bell, he told his mentor that he couldn't wait to get home so he could be with his characters. It could take weeks, months, even years until those characters began to truly speak to him. "I get up every day, I sit at my desk, and I write," he told his friend Sean San José. "If I can come out of my office and have one fully formed sentence, that's a good day." He sometimes kept a handwritten note taped to the wall in front of him at eye level with a quote from Ralph Waldo Emerson's essay "Self-Reliance": "God will not have his work made manifest by cowards."

He was more than willing to devote the time and energy that was required for whatever writing project was in front of him. That was less true if he was working at the behest of someone else, or for the money. "One of the things we had in common," said his friend Chris Offutt, "was a deep resentment at the preposterous notion that we were expected to have jobs."

He was also always on the hunt for new, thrilling experiences, even some that might seem far-fetched. Once he typed out a letter to the National Aeronautics and Space Administration, asking to be accepted into the one-year astronaut-training program. And preparation was not always part of the plan when he was ready for an adventure. He might put on his fishing vest, grab whatever supplies could fit in the pockets, and set off on a camping trip, confident he'd find someone or something to guide him safely through the experience.

He could go out of his way to be thoughtful to both friends and strangers. He kept a note on his computer that reminded him to do something nice for a fellow writer every day. When he spent time in San Francisco with the Campo Santo troupe, he was regularly approached by homeless people asking for money. He went to the bank and got out three hundred $1 bills and kept a bunch of them stuffed in his pants pockets at all times so he could buy a cup of coffee for anyone who approached. Later, he did the same thing in Austin, but he was approached much less frequently. The dollar bills piled up. He told a friend about the problem. "I didn't want to risk being ungracious," he said. "So, you and I may need to drink about 150 cups of coffee."

When he heard his friend Jim Galvin's house had been vandalized in Iowa City, he drove to the little Amish town of Kalona, about a half hour south, to go shopping for him. He showed up one day unannounced and gave Galvin a stained-glass window. "I heard you needed some glass," he said. Denis also liked to go shopping for gifts before the opening nights of his plays. Then, on the night of the first performance, he would present them to all the members of the cast. Once everyone received engraved money clips and wallets. For the opening of the play *Soul of a Whore,* which featured a character walking with a cross on his back, he had a woodworker create miniature crosses for the Campo Santo performers.

On other occasions, when in a different mood, small gestures or courtesies could prove to be too much for him. One writer friend asked for a blurb and was told: I don't write blurbs anymore, but I'd be happy to put one of your books in my library and tell anybody who comes over how great you are. Small, perceived offenses could get under his skin. After a literary event at the University of Texas, he went out to dinner with Ron Hansen, another classmate from the Writers' Workshop. At dinner, Hansen remembered that Denis had been a lightning-fast typist who had supplemented his income by typing the theses of other students. Hansen was perplexed when Denis, for some reason, fervently denied the story.

In 2014, Denis was elected as a member of the American Academy of Arts and Letters, an honor society for artists, composers, architects, and writers. It was a prestigious distinction, and enough to draw Denis to the event in New York held to honor the recipients. During cocktail hour, Denis was chatting with an old friend from the Writers' Workshop, Allan Gurganus, when another attendee approached and joined the conversation. *Jesus' Son* is the best book of short stories in the last thirty years, he told Denis emphatically. The interloper made the unfortunate mistake of pronouncing a second "s" in the title. "It's *Jesus' Son,*" Denis replied curtly, not even looking the man.

"I thought it was really interesting, that someone, at the peak of his recognition—there's only 150 positions in the American academy, architects, composers, and you're being admitted to Valhalla—at the same time, you're telling people they're mispronouncing things. That might be a clue to whatever contradictions there were within him," Gurganus remembered.

He continued on his quest to put himself through all possible literary experiences. Offers that allowed him the opportunity to walk in the shoes of some of his heroes were particularly appealing. In 2008, he took on one that granted him the status of a modern-day Charles Dickens and Raymond Chandler at the same time. He signed a contract with *Playboy* magazine in which he would write, on deadline, four 10,000-word installments of a novel to be called *Nobody Move.* "I've always admired Charles Dickens, who wrote big, involved novels in monthly installments," he was quoted as saying in *Playboy's* press release announcing the deal. "I wanted to find out what it was like. It's a little nerve-wracking."

The germ of the novel was a trip he took to Bakersfield, California, to participate in a competition of barbershop choruses. The event was overflowing with Denis Johnson characters. "They were all sort of sleazy musicians even though they were insurance salesmen," he said. "They gambled and whored, and their wives went with them, and they interested me, and I wanted to write something about people like that."

To prepare for his adventure in nineteenth-century serial writing, he read the Raymond Chandler collection, then moved on to Hemingway to learn about "writing tight." He also became interested in a writer named Paul Cain. The name was a pseudonym for Peter Ruric, a screenwriter who worked consistently in Hollywood in the 1930s on movies such as *Grand Central Murder, One for the Money,* and *Mademoiselle Fifi.* Cain has only one novel to his name, a forgotten noir masterpiece called *Fast One,* published in 1932. Cain's novel actually evolved as Denis's would, starting in magazine form. It originally appeared as five separate stories in *Black Mask,* a Depression-era publication devoted to hard-boiled crime fiction, between March and September 1932. Denis latched on to a particular characteristic in Cain's writing: because he had been a screenwriter, Cain had eliminated all internalization. For Denis, this was yet another appealing idea to attempt; much of his prior writing existed predominantly in the interior.

What emerged from the parameters Denis had set for himself was a novel that felt like a backward reflection in the mirror of his earlier attempt at noir, *Already Dead.* Where that book had been four-hundred-plus pages of internal monologues, poetic ramblings, and psychobabble, *Nobody Move* was a sleek 196-page take on the classics of the genre, all action with no time for reflection, that could have worked in *Black Mask* just as easily as *Playboy.* The book's protagonist was a barbershop quartet singer named Jimmy Luntz who, about three pages into the story, leaves the barbershop singing world behind thanks to a gambling debt that sends him on the run from gangsters and fuels the plot. Luntz must avoid a large-headed enforcer named Gambol who, along with his mob boss, Juarez, claims to have dined on the testicles of a previous victim who didn't pay up. Subtlety was not, Denis surmised, what *Playboy* readers were looking for. Jimmy meets the obligatory femme fatale, a vodka-swilling divorcée named Anita Desilvera, and the story twists and turns on its way to its violent conclusion.

Under *Playboy's* monthly deadline, Denis eschewed the poetic flourishes found in most of his work and instead wrote bare-bone sentences and punchy, tough-guy dialogue. Though he had started working on the book months before the first issue appeared, he still viewed the tight schedule as an excuse to cast off the chains of literary pretension, an opportunity he seemed to relish. He gave a reading in Greenwich Village for the National Book Foundation where he read an excerpt from the first installment. He introduced it by saying, "This is from my work in progress. It's a short novel. It's pretty literary stuff, but you're sophisticated New Yorkers. You can handle it." He began reading from a scene that could have been right out of *Black Mask*. After a few pages, he stopped, put down the papers, and looked at the audience in mock surprise. "What the—? Where's the literary?" he asked. "I thought I put something literary in my suitcase, but this is just cheap pulp fiction," he said with a grin.

Nobody Move appeared in the July through October issues of *Playboy* with stylized cartoon illustrations and typewriter font. "An Exclusive Noir Novel Written in Four Parts on Deadline! Publishing History Begins Now!" screamed the headline in the July edition. The book version was published the following spring, to both acclaim and an acknowledgment that this time, Denis had aimed for pure entertainment and had achieved his goal. The story included enough sex, gore, gunplay, and vodka consumption to draw *Playboy* readers away, at least momentarily, from Miss July, and, in book form, it offered the page-turning experience of a pulp novel written by a sure hand.

Denis, as one reviewer would later note, had become the hermit crab of American novelists, crawling inside the shell of a particular genre, only to crawl out from under it once it had outlived its usefulness, ready to search for the next shell to occupy. By the time the dialogue from *Nobody Move* was spoken on the stage in San Francisco a few years later, he had long ago shed the shell of Raymond Chandler. For his part, he saw more in his creation than a rehash of an old form. "In a way, it's the most literary thing I've ever done," he told an audience at the University of Arizona. "Because I was conscious of the form, but when you get to the end, it's not quite what it should be."

*

The Club Bar in Troy, Montana, was a narrow building with wooden floors that sat next to the train tracks on Yaak Avenue, named for the nearby Yaak River. Along with assorted Americana such as pictures of Marilyn Monroe and John Wayne, a six-foot marlin hung on the wall below a fishing rod, spoils the owner, Tony Brown, had won in a poker game. Occasionally stray dogs from the street would wander in and plop down by the fire. In a back room, there was a coffin that Denis told Brown he hoped to be buried in, if Brown hadn't sold it to someone else before the time came.

Denis spent many evenings in the Club Bar and slept many nights in Brown's home a few blocks away. Shortly after he became acquainted with the place, he began to participate in an unlikely regular event that seemed to have been created just for him. The first-ever Club Bar Poetry Night took place on January 19, 1991, when a newspaper editor from nearby Libby, Montana, chose to honor the birthday of Edgar Allan Poe by reading some of his poems to a crowd at the bar. His audience grew impatient after a few stanzas, but a tradition was born in Troy.

Denis found the Club Bar a few years after Poetry Night had already been established. At first, the pool of participants was made up of amateur poets and performers from nearby towns, but soon Denis turned it into a regional gathering. He gave a reading in Spokane, Washington, about 140 miles from Troy. During the event, he challenged that town's "sissy, academic poets," who he said were probably the type of people "who played tennis with the net down," to come and experience a true western poetry venue. He sent faxes to universities with writing programs throughout the region offering similar challenges.

Poets from Eastern Washington University took him up on the offer, followed by more from the University of Idaho and the University of Montana. Soon poets were driving hundreds of miles from several directions for the chance to stand in front of Brown's blue marlin and read to an eclectic audience that one attendee described as a mix of "horse loggers, Vietnam vets, timber cruisers, back-to-the-landers and solar powered granola crunchers."

"Poets are like golfers," Brown said. "They'll drive a hundred miles, or ten hours to play a golf course, and these guys would do the same thing." Brown usually served as the MC. He played saxophone or trumpet between poems to enliven the crowd. He also liked to read Poe's poem "The Raven," cawing the words as if he were the titular bird. His version of performing the poem involved putting on a bird mask and cawing in various patterns for five minutes: "Caw! Ca-caw-caw! Ca-caw!"

Among the grad students and city poets were the more self-taught variety, who might incorporate chainsaws into their reading or begin to shed clothing as they performed. Much of the poetry read at the event was extremely fresh and raw, because it had been written during the evening between trips to the bar. Once in a while there would be a "hillbilly jerk" who would object to the entire premise, but they were easily overcome.

On occasion the event could edge in the direction of a celebrity literary affair. One such evening, Denis was chatting with writers Larry Brown, Kevin Canty, and Debra Magpie Earling, along with a young writing professor from Eastern Washington University whom he had befriended named Jonathan Johnson. Denis's attention was on the conversation when, out of nowhere, a young, bearded, football-lineman-size attendee who had been drinking at a nearby table stood up, ran over, and knocked Denis to the floor. The lineman stood up, turned in the direction of his table, and shouted, "Twenty bucks, motherfuckers, I just tackled Denis Johnson!" The room was momentarily stunned. Then Denis got up and jumped on the lineman's back, defusing the situation and leaving his misguided admirer with an even better story.

Poetry Night at the Club Bar delighted Denis. The lack of pretension appealed to him, as did the general unpredictability and the blurring of literary class distinction. A doctoral candidate might be followed on stage by someone reciting a bawdy limerick or just emitting a series of belches. Weirdness ruled the day. Denis's own contributions combined showmanship and diversion. He chose crowd-pleasers. A favorite was "Stewball Was a Racehorse," about the legendary Scottish thoroughbred.

Once he gave a reading wearing a turban and an eye patch. On another poetry night, he brought along an asbestos glove he had acquired from a movie stuntman in town for a shoot. When it was time for him to read that night, he put the glove on and picked up a copy of *The Throne of the Third Heaven of the Nations Millennium General Assembly.* He reached under the podium, came up with a can of lighter fluid, poured some on the book, took out a lighter, and set the book on fire. Then he raised the burning book, and, with his arm now a human torch and flames rising from the pages, he gave the patrons of the Club Bar a poetry recital they would never forget.

*

There was still the issue of the book of novellas to deal with. By 2010, the three novellas that were originally slated for that book, conceived a decade before, were in print. The only one that had not been published in book form in America was *Train Dreams*. It had appeared in the *Paris Review;* in the *PEN/O. Henry Prize Stories,* 2003 edition; and in book form in Europe, but not in the United States. An editor at FSG approached Jonathan Galassi with the idea of releasing it as a solo book. It was fewer than thirty thousand words and had been available to the public for ten years. But the very fact that it was difficult to obtain meant it had achieved cult notoriety. Galassi signed off on it, and in summer 2011, the thin volume of 114 pages hit the shelves.

It turned out to be a very good decision. The book was a critical success as well as a commercial one. Critics noted its cult status. The *Philadelphia Inquirer* called it a "long out-of-print B side treasured by those in the know." Others noted the language Denis had used to tell the tale, a pseudo-historic/mythic tone that brought to mind a particular type of ballad of the Wild West. In fact, a scene in the book aped the narrative of the American folk song "The Dying Cowboy," in which a fatally wounded ranger tells the story of his demise to another cowboy and implicates his murderer. In *Train Dreams,* the young protagonist, Robert Grainier, comes across an itinerant bum "holed up among some birches in a sloppy camp":

> "I been cut behind the knee by this one feller they call Big-Ear Al. And I have to say, he's killed me. That's the first thing. Take that news to your sheriff, son. William Coswell Haley, from St. Louis, Missouri, has been robbed, cut in the leg, and murdered by the boomer they call Big-Ear Al. He snatched my roll of fourteen dollars off me whilst I slept, and he cut the strings back of my knee so's I wouldn't chase after him. My leg's stinking," he said, "because I've laid up here so long the rot's set in. You know how that'll do. That rot will travel till I'm dead right up to my eyes. Till I'm a corpse able to see things. Able to think its thoughts. Then about the fourth day I'll be all the way dead. I don't know what happens to us then—if we can think our thoughts in the grave, or we fly to Heaven, or get taken to the Devil."

When award season rolled around, Denis was once again on the minds of the judges. *Train Dreams* was one of three finalists selected by the committee chosen to sift through the books submitted for the 2012 Pulitzer Prize for fiction. The others were *The Pale King,* a posthumous novel by David Foster Wallace, which had been left unfinished when he committed suicide in 2008 and later assembled by an editor, and writer Karen Russell's debut novel, *Swamplandia!* The selection committee, which included Denis's classmate from the Fine Arts Work Center, Michael Cunningham, put forward the three selections to the Pulitzer Prize board, which chooses the winner from the jurors' selections.

On April 16, 2012, the day of the announcement of the 2011 Pulitzer winners, the board revealed that the winner of the prize for fiction was, in fact, no winner at all. "The three books were considered, but in the end, none mustered the majority for granting a prize, so no prize was awarded," reported Sig Gissler, the administrator of Pulitzer Prizes. No further details were offered, even to the jurors (at least, none they would discuss publicly). The Pulitzers had not snubbed the fiction writers of America in thirty-five years. The previous time it occurred was in 1977. The Pulitzer spokesman of that era had been more forthcoming, rebuking all eligible novelists by announcing that it had been a "very thin year." Whether 2011 was a thin year or not was left to the reading public to interpret.

Despite the offense from the Pulitzers, there was no arguing that *Train Dreams* had been another one in the win column for Denis. "It was one of his best books," said Galassi, "and it turned out to be one of his greatest triumphs."

*

His quest to inhabit all of his literary heroes continued. He joked to Galassi that it wasn't that he was just trying to be Graham Greene this time; he felt that he truly had become Greene. With his new identity as the English champion of religious-themed international espionage thrillers, he traveled back to West Africa for the first time since the early '90s to gather some color and detail for what he said would be a literary spy novel set in the post-9/11 world of intrigue. In 2013, he flew from JFK Airport to Entebbe, Uganda, and then to Arua, a smaller city in the northeast corner of the country. He booked a room at the White Castle Hotel and spent a month there, exploring, taking notes, speaking into his recorder, and writing.

The protagonist that developed was one who would be recognizable to both Greene and Johnson devotees. Roland Nair was a spy with vague and shifting allegiances and a taste for booze and prostitutes who seemed to be after, more than any particular specific outcome, the stimulation and chaos he'd found in Africa years earlier. In the book, Nair is in Africa on a mission from his employer to find an old friend, Michael Andriko, with whom he'd shared escapades in the region a decade before. The story examines the state of international relations and politics to some degree, but for the most part, it is a buddy story about two men who travel deep into the African outback, facing increasingly bizarre circumstances. When one character asks Nair if he's just a "cheap adventurer," Denis's protagonist responds with a defense of thrill seeking for its own sake. "Why do you call it cheap? Adventure is glorious. I don't understand why people put it down."

The Laughing Monsters (the title refers to a local nickname for a Congolese mountain range) came out in the fall of 2014. Denis consented to an email interview with the *Los Angeles Times* and was typically opaque. "Since I select what appeals to me, to my soul or my ear or whatever part does the selecting, I'm not surprised if different settings seem facets all reflecting one image. I don't know what the image is. Something that's always changing and always staying the same," he wrote to David Ulin of the *Times.* "I suppose if I were in school today, I'd be diagnosed as attention deficient and dosed with speed. I get bored quickly and try another style, another genre, another form. To me the writing is all one thing, or maybe I should say it's all nothing. The truth is, I just write sentences."

The Laughing Monsters would be the last attempt at genre hopping that Denis would undertake. Privately, he had more pedestrian reasons for writing the book than the glories of trying out another new form and walking in the shoes of the legends. He told Morgan early in the writing process for *Monsters* that forty acres of property had been put on the market adjacent his land in Meadow Creek. To buy the land, he said, he would have to write another book.

Thc course of his life was about to take a turn that would lead Denis back to much more personal subject matter, and much more inward-looking sentences. In 2014, his friend Bill Winkelholz was diagnosed with liver cancer. Denis had recently relocated again to Arizona, but on hearing the news, he decided to take on the role of caretaker for his longtime friend. The two had bonded over their personal battles with addiction, and the relationship had endured. Now Denis returned to California and moved into Winkelholz's house on Fish Rock Road near Gualala. As Winkelholz's condition deteriorated over the course of the illness, Denis remained in the house, a witness to the devastations of the disease as it progressed. Winkelholz had been the model for a character in *Already Dead,* and now, as Denis tended to his dying friend, he knew that after this experience, he would write about him once again.

Winkelholz died on April 15, 2015. Denis contributed to the obituary in the local newspaper in Gualala. He told the newspaper the story of his friend's life and his battles with drugs. "Kindness and generosity seemed at the core of Wink's nature, and anyone who knew him… would agree that those qualities were miraculously undisturbed by the addictions that ravaged him."

DEATH IS THE MOTHER OF BEAUTY

27

At the last moment, my whole life will last a moment.

—**Antonio Porchia**

Throughout a life of writing, Denis had cultivated his past, allowing his experiences to ferment until he was ready to recreate them on the page. Sometimes, though, it was his past that chose when to reappear. In the late '90s, he had reconnected with some of his high school friends. One of them, Joe Cohen, happened to tell Denis that another friend of theirs, Carter Batchellor, had been diagnosed with hepatitis C. Denis likely had it as well, Cohen told him. They had all shared the same needles, so chances were they had also shared the same disease. "I feel all right. I don't feel sick. But it's funny," Denis wrote about receiving the unwelcome news. "Thirty years go by, and the moves we made just keep bringing this old stuff rolling over us."

Denis had indeed been living with the disease for much of his life. Hepatitis C was another of the treats of his generation. The Centers for Disease Control and Prevention estimated that 3.5 million Americans were living with the disease in 2016. Of those 3.5 million, 75 percent were baby boomers, having been unknowingly infected before it was discovered in 1989. During the 2000s, boomers were learning that they had the disease. Hepatitis C, once in the blood, goes to work destroying the liver. The process can take years or decades, but for a percentage of those with hep C, what's waiting down the road is cancer of the liver, one of the more deadly forms of cancer on the menu. By 2016, the CDC was recommending screening for hepatitis C and treatment was available, but to the thousands who had contracted it years before, much of the damage was already done.

In the fall of 2015, Denis took a position teaching in the creative writing program at Boise State University in Idaho. Two of his former students, Brady Udall and Martin Corless-Smith, were on the faculty at BSU and shepherded the invitation. Denis was to become the university's first distinguished writer and help launch an expansion of the program. He came to Boise and began working with the graduate students, offering versions of the literary counseling he'd now given to several generations of young writers. One grad student, Erin Rose Belair, came to him for guidance on a story she was writing for his workshop. She was struggling with a way to conclude. Don't worry, he told her, time is on your side. You might not know the ending of the story for five years, and that's okay. One day, you will open the window, and something will blow into the room, and there it will be, the ending you're looking for.

The final days of his friend Bill Winkelholz's life remained on his mind. He began a story, written in first person, in which the narrator is a caretaker for a dying cancer patient named Wink. The story would grow to include a number of deaths of people in the life of the narrator. It would evolve into a meditation on mortality.

The narrator visits a hospital emergency room, where he sees doors opening "onto a new phase of my own life, one I can expect to continue until all expectations cease, the phase in which these visits to emergency rooms and clinics increased in frequency and by now have become commonplace: trips with my mother, my father, later my friend Joe, then of course with my friend Link—and eventually me too—the tests, forms, interviews, exams, the journeys into the machines."

His own personal journey commenced in November, when doctors diagnosed him with stage 4 liver cancer. Though he had been undergoing treatment for hepatitis C (and had health insurance thanks to his employment at Boise State), tumors had developed in his liver. In

December, he underwent surgery to remove a large portion of the organ. The surgery was deemed a success. Doctors were hopeful that the cancer had been removed and recovery was possible. "It was a miracle," Udall said later. "He thought—we all thought—he dodged it."

*

It had been twenty-six years since he lived on the California coast, but now Denis told Cindy that it was his dream to return to Gualala. They bought a house in Sea Ranch, a community six miles south of Gualala that had been designed by University of California, Berkeley, architecture professors in the '60s to be in tune with nature and had earned a reputation for its unique design and breathtaking views. It was listed on the National Register of Historic Places. In March 2016, they relocated to their new home, a two-bedroom luxury cabin with wooden shingles, a hot tub, and a deck that overlooked the seventh hole of the Sea Ranch golf course.

Slowly, he recovered from the surgery and began to regain his health. He had lost significant weight in the fall, but now he started to put it back on. To some of his friends, he looked healthy and robust. He thought deeply about the journey to heal, physically and spiritually. He wrote about a middle-of-the-night epiphany in an email to his friend Elizabeth Cuthrell. "I had an insight, that I wish I could have held onto, that everything is renewed, replenished, perpetually," he wrote to Cuthrell. "And that's what we are, that replenishing. I'm not the one that is renewed, I'm the renewing itself. I'm not the one being healed, I'm the process of healing. That's the true me. I felt it was true, vividly."

As much as was possible, life returned to normal. He resumed attending Alcoholics Anonymous meetings and writing his sentences. He pondered the course of his life and how it hinged on a few chance meetings and occurrences. He began, once again, to think about November 1967, when he spent a week in jail and met John Dundon, the boy who became a link to a dangerous world—one that would first lead him to catastrophe and then, much later, to his greatest triumphs. He hadn't written about him in three decades and hadn't seen him in five, but now he brought him back, this time as a character called Donald Dundun. "Donald Dundun," he wrote, "showed me how to roll a cigarette. Dundun came from the trailer courts, and I was middle-class gone crazy, but we passed the time together freely because we both had long hair and chased after any kind of intoxicating substance. Dundun, only nineteen, already displayed up and down both his arms the tattooed veins of a hope-to-die heroin addict."

The story took place inside the walls of the Johnson County Jail, where an older prisoner, in jail for killing his wife, tells Dundun, the narrator, and another prisoner that they will all become murderers too. The prophecy comes true for all, including the narrator: "I'd shared dirty needles with low companions, my blood was diseased. I can't estimate how many people had died from it."

*

Time was precious, and he knew there might not be much of it left. The percentage of liver cancer survivors who were alive five years after it was diagnosed was frighteningly small. Affairs needed to be settled; books needed to be closed. He had already sold his papers to the Harry Ransom Center at the University of Texas nearly six years earlier. At the time, he joked that he hadn't been saving much of anything, but then he heard that his old friend and mentor Donald Justice had sold the drafts of one of his books for $17,000, so he immediately retrieved everything from his wastepaper basket and filed it for future sale. In reality, he had been saving letters, drafts, notebooks, and even paper plates and bits of paper with scribbles written on them, for most of his life and had accumulated reams of material. He had spoken earlier in his career of throwing away drafts as if they "were like skins [he] was shedding and leaving behind." But nearly everything he'd written since the late '80s had been meticulously collected, and his mother had saved correspondence and clippings from his younger days. The initial delivery to the Ransom Center was fifty boxes' worth, with more promised for the future.

He went back to Iowa City for a production of a play he'd written years before entitled *Des Moines*. The play features a character that was based on his college friend Bob Stall. Denis asked a mutual friend to look up Stall in the alumni directory and invite him to campus for the production. The two old friends hadn't seen each other in decades. Just as they had when they were freshmen in Hillcrest Hall, they talked about books and literature. Stall told Denis which of his books he liked the best. They laughed about people they'd known in those days, like Hardy, the young drifter who'd lived with them for a few months in the 1972, and who later appeared as a character in *Jesus' Son*. Denis, Stall remembered, was in a somber mood. "He knew he was under a death sentence," he said. Still, it was a satisfying reunion, and Stall told Denis he approved of his fictional version in the play.

His high school friend Joe Cohen was on a similar trajectory to Denis. He'd been living with hepatitis C and had been diagnosed with liver cancer as well. Now he was in the final stages of the disease. Denis went to see him in Massachusetts. Cohen was close to the end. They reminisced about their experiences in high school and the people they knew. Of their inner circle, only Denis and Joe remained alive. The others had all died of complications related to hepatitis C.

In April 2016, Denis went to Cornell University, where he had served as a visiting professor eight years earlier, for a reading. He appeared to be in good health, if a little thick around the waist, hair still brown and thinning only slightly in front, looking significantly younger than his actual age. He read a section from the story about Winkelholz's final days. He told the audience that he had entitled the story "Triumph Over the Grave," mostly because he liked how it sounded. The pages he read featured Winkelholz's real name, which Denis helpfully spelled for the audience.

"Triumph Over the Grave" was the second story he read to the audience that night. The first one, he told the crowd, was fiction, but this story was more memoir, leaning toward total truth. "It's about 62 percent me," he said. During the question-and-answer portion of the event, a woman asked him why he'd decided to switch from fiction to memoir for his new story. "I'm afraid I don't know," he said. Then he paused, took a breath as if he was about to elaborate, and concluded, "Yeah, I think that's the answer right there."

He continued to look backward, to go through the roster in his mind of the people who had played large roles in his life. At some point, his thoughts turned to Sue. He had made her a character on the page and on-screen, but he had not seen her in person since the '80s. In the '90s, when Sue was in graduate school in Montana, Denis spoke with her on the phone and made plans to go see her. The visit never happened. Now, he sat down at the keyboard to write her a letter and an offer an apology for some of the things he had done a half century before. "I felt better that he apologized," Sue said later, "that he realized he had hurt me."

He told friends he was feeling better and better every day, and that he was enjoying life. He wrote to Cuthrell that he had thought old age would be boring, but he was finding it to be exhilarating, like a trip over Niagara Falls. But privately, the stress of living under the threat of disease was weighing on him, bringing back the old demons. He spoke with Lucinda on the phone and said he wasn't doing well. He told his ex-wife that he had fallen off the wagon and had started drinking and had used hard drugs. He told Lucinda he was back on the program, but the admission shocked and saddened her. Those close to Denis, however, said no such slip-up occurred. Denis told his friend Sam Messer that he smoked "half a joint" to ease back pain, but nothing else.

He signed a contract to publish his first short-story collection since *Jesus' Son*. It was to be called *The Largesse of the Sea Maiden,* the title of a story he'd written and published in the *New Yorker* a few years before. The book would include two other stories that had been published previously, along with his story built around the death of Winkelholz, "Triumph Over the Grave," and the jail story about his time with John Dundon. It was October 2016, and Denis was looking forward to many more years of writing. The contract called for him to produce two books: the short-story collection and a novel about a deposed Middle Eastern dictator retelling the story of his life as he's being interrogated. Work continued on the new stories. The final manuscript was turned in to Random House soon after the contract was signed. Publication of *Largesse* was set for January 2018.

In spring 2017, he went to Austin to attend the retirement dinner of his friend James Magnuson, the director of the Center for Writers at the University of Texas. Denis agreed to give a short speech at the dinner. He and Cindy went to Arizona to visit Randy on the way to Texas. Denis started feeling nauseous while they were in Tucson. When they got to Austin, he still wasn't feeling well. It might be the flu, they thought. By the next evening, when he was scheduled to speak at the retirement event, it had gotten worse. Cindy spoke in his place at the dinner. An appointment at the doctor was scheduled. Initially, doctors diagnosed him with a case of vertigo, but soon Denis was vomiting blood. The morning after the dinner, a second set of tests confirmed that the cancer had returned. This time, doctors told him, it was terminal. It would be a good idea, they said, to get his affairs in order.

*

Denis and Cindy returned to their home in Gualala in April. The disease progressed rapidly. Denis was clear-eyed about what was going to occur. He'd had a front-row seat to the progression of the disease two years earlier, during the final days of Bill Winkelholz. He knew, step by step, exactly what was about to happen to him. As best he could, he maintained a positive attitude for his friends. He corresponded by email and talked on the phone with his friend Sam Messer, never letting on that the cancer had returned. He corresponded via email with his friend Lynne Tillman. He didn't mention the disease, but the sentiments he expressed revealed the truth. "Another day this side of the grass—I'll take it," he wrote. "And it's the only day there ever was—today. Every breath is sweet."

Magnuson was aware of the situation and continued to inquire about his friend's condition over email. Denis tried to reassure Magnuson that he was getting along fine. "I'm having a great day.... I'm set up to see some specialists and make new friends in lab coats," he wrote in one. A few weeks later, he sounded less convincing. "I'm weak as a wet sock, but in no discomfort."

Denis wanted to spend the remaining days and hours with his closest family members. His children came to visit him at Sea Ranch for several days. His brother, Randy, flew in from Tucson as well. His health was rapidly deteriorating. Every day, new signs of the disease were appearing. His visitors tried to comfort him when he was well enough and occupy themselves around the property when he needed his space. He told Randy he was worried that his family would be unhappy after he was gone.

Incredibly, there was still work to be done. His entire adult life had been spent with writing projects in various stages of completion, deadlines scattered on the horizon, puzzles to be solved, sentences to be sculpted, and edits to be made. As the end approached, all of it still hovered over him. The final galleys for *The Largesse of the Sea Maiden* arrived, his last chance to review the pages and offer any changes. When he was well enough, he went over them, line by line, massaging the last sentences that would be published in his name.

The effort required to keep going, to continue to perform the act that had been the very center of his existence on earth, finally became too much for him. One day near the end, he called Cindy over. Is it okay if I stop writing now? he asked.

Morgan came to Sea Ranch to spend time with his father in early May. Father and son spent time together talking about the past. They expressed their regrets and offered one another superficial apologies for past misdeeds. Denis, Morgan recalled, wasn't prepared for a deeper examination of their relationship. Instead, he asked Morgan to read him passages from *Leaves of Grass*.

He was tired all the time. Cindy told guests when to approach him and when not to disturb him. The family watched movies together, a long-standing tradition. Denis and Cindy watched videos about dying. Sometimes Denis would spend time sitting in the living room with his eyes closed, meditating. More often he would go out to the deck, where he could feel the mist come off the Pacific and gaze up at the herons and egrets migrating north for summer. He would look out over the golf course and pass the time in silence, deep in thought. One day, when he was in his room, Morgan knocked on the door and asked if Denis wanted to talk. Sure, Denis responded. We can talk about anything you want, with one exception: no speculation.

Of course, he didn't really need to spend his final days speculating about death, about what it would be like to go through those final moments. He had already done it, many years before. He had sat at his desk, and he had imagined those last few breaths. As had been his practice for all of his adult life, he had imagined it, and then, as best he could, he'd written it down. He had written of a dying man who, in that last moment, "felt he could hold his breath forever—no problem." He wrote about the man listening to the final beats of his own heart. "You can get right in between each beat, and let the next one wash over you like the best and biggest warm ocean there ever was." He had even written about the very last second, the moment life is extinguished. "He was in the middle of taking the last breath of his life before he realized he was taking it. He got right in the dark between heartbeats, and rested there. And then he saw that another one wasn't going to come. That's it. That's the last. He looked at the dark. I would like to take this opportunity, he said, to pray for another human being."

POSTSCRIPT

News of the death of Denis Johnson filtered into the world in the last days of May in 2017. Obituaries began to appear on May 26, two days after he had finally succumbed to the effects of liver cancer in Sea Ranch, California. It had been less than two months since the disease had reappeared. Journalists writing about his life focused on the beauty of his language; his flawed, desperate characters; the spiritual transcendence found in his most famous works. The *New York Times* described him as a chronicler of "the fallen—junkies, down-and-out travelers, drifters and violent men in the United States and abroad" who "emerged in ecstatic, hallucinatory and sometimes minimalist prose." In the *Los Angeles Times,* his writing was described as "a slab of brilliance, incinerated diamonds," "metaphysical and at the same time rooted in the real world."

The most hallowed names in American literature were invoked in the many articles that appeared across the spectrum of English-language publications: Whitman, Melville, Hemingway. Most acknowledged *Jesus' Son* to be the magnum opus in a lifetime of creation, but lines from many other entries in the pantheon were quoted as well. As the weeks went by, remembrances from current writers, contemporaries, students, and admirers continued to appear in print and online. Writers of all levels of literary success wrote of their moment with Denis. Those who never met him wrote of the story or line of his that changed their lives.

Over the next several months, ceremonies were held across the

United States to remember his life and celebrate his work. In New York, friends and family gathered to hear some of his greatest hits read out loud again and to listen to stories about Denis told one more time. Billy Crudup read from *Jesus' Son*. Michael Shannon, who played Dundun in the movie version, sang a song. Sam Messer, Jonathan Galassi, Arliss Howard, and many others took a turn at the microphone. Friends and admirers from many generations of the Writers' Workshop got together at Macbride Auditorium on the campus of the University of Iowa in September. Stories from his years in Iowa City were revisited, poems were read, and Morgan offered a tribute to his father. Similar ceremonies were held at the University of Texas in Austin, and in San Francisco by Campo Santo and the theater community.

Almost a year after his death, the events were still going on. In 2016, Philip Roth had nominated Denis for the Prize for American Fiction, a designation awarded annually by the Library of Congress. Denis had learned of the award just a few weeks before he died. In the summer of 2017, Cindy accepted the award at the National Book Festival in Washington, D.C. A while later, an event called "Stories from a Fallen World" was held at the Library of Congress to tie a ribbon on the award. It was a black-tie affair, with tribute videos and important remarks delivered by dignitaries from behind a podium on stage. It was the polar opposite of Poetry Night at the Club Bar, and it was the kind of event Denis usually skipped. More praise was offered, some of it from those who hadn't had their turn to pay tribute yet, and some who already had. All expressed their heartfelt admiration and shared a few more stories. The words of his contemporaries and friends, Don DeLillo, Marilynne Robinson, Joy Williams, and many others, were put on plaques to commemorate the occasion. "I have never known a writer who was so identical with his work," wrote Robinson, "whose thoughts and passions and energies were so entirely of one substance with the world he re-made as fiction."

*

The analysis and acclaim of the Denis Johnson canon barely had a chance to die down before some fresh wood was tossed onto the fire and the flames grew once again. Just as it had been written in the contract the year before, *The Largesse of the Sea Maiden* was published in January 2018. The fact that publication came less than a year after his death and that the book contained ominous subject matter combined to generate the feeling from many readers that the stories had been composed in the last few hours of Denis's life. Most of the contents of the book had actually been written before Denis got sick, and the manuscript had been submitted at a time when he was in relatively good health. But it was difficult to read the stories without being overwhelmed by their posthumous nature, which Denis helpfully spelled out for his readers. Many a review quoted the final, prophetic lines of the story "Triumph Over the Grave": "The world keeps turning. It's plain to you that at the time I write this, I'm not dead. But maybe by the time you read it."

Another popular reading of *Largesse* was that it was a sequel of sorts to *Jesus' Son*. "A tempting answer to the question of what happened to Fuckhead is that he became his author," wrote Christian Lorentzen in *New York Magazine*. "None of these narrators is Fuckhead, but all of them, we suspect, could be. After all, we never learn his real name." Because Denis had become sewn into the fabric of contemporary American literary fiction to such a degree, his life story acted as liner notes to the stories in the new collection. "There's a new, metafictional undertone to much of the book, too: novelists and poets pop up again and again," wrote Anthony Domestico for the *Boston Globe*. "Johnson's own life, transformed into art, haunts the margins."

His life was, of course, not only in the margins of *Largesse* but also in the center of the page, as it was in most of his best work throughout his life. He had even diagnosed it himself, on stage a few years earlier: it was 62 percent Denis Johnson. He offered, right there in the text, a helpful guide, the Johnson instruction manual to life:

> Writing. It's easy work. The equipment isn't expensive, and you can pursue this occupation anywhere. You make your own hours, mess

> around the house in your pajamas, listening to jazz recordings and sipping coffee while another day makes its escape. You don't have to be high functioning at all. If I could drink liquor without being drunk all the time, I'd certainly drink enough to be drunk half the time, and production wouldn't suffer. Bouts of poverty come along, anxiety, shocking debt, but nothing lasts forever. I've gone from rags to riches and back again, and more than once. Whatever happens to you, you put it on a page, work it into shape, cast it in a light. It's not much different, really, from filming a parade of clouds across the sky and calling it a movie—although it has to be admitted that the clouds can descend, take you up, carry you to all kinds of places, some of them terrible, and you don't get back where you came from for years and years.

When it came time to produce the audio version of *Largesse,* several actors who had known or worked with Denis were brought in to read the stories, including Will Patton, Nick Offerman, and Michael Shannon. The reading of "The Starlight on Idaho" fell to Shannon. "Starlight" is narrated by an addict in a rehab center formerly known as the Starlight Motel. Shannon began recording and quickly realized that the narrator was Mark Cassandra, the same character he had portrayed on the stage years before. As he began to read, the memories of playing Cass, and of Denis himself, washed over him. Being the voice of his friend from the grave was "one of the trippiest things I've ever done," Shannon said.

Like clockwork, *Largesse* found its way onto many year-end best-book lists and was a finalist for the National Book Critics Circle Award for fiction. More importantly, it had given his legions of fans a way, one last time, to spend a few more moments in the mind of an author who had provided them with so much wonder throughout the years. It offered some closure, tied up some of those loose ends, and now, with Denis's final, Johnsonian sign-off—"Elvisy yours"—the book could be closed.

*

But what, you ask, ever happened to Dundun, the kid Denis met in county jail in November 1967, doing time for "theft of merchandise from the home of an elderly woman"? The "hope-to-die heroin addict" who Denis had named a story after in *Jesus' Son,* who had been portrayed by Shannon in the movie version, and who had reappeared, fifty years later, in *Largesse* to once again ply a Denis Johnson narrator with heroin? What about Dundun?

The last Denis ever heard of the real John Dundon was that he was in jail in Colorado. The few people I found who remembered Dundon assured me that, like most of those who hung around the farmhouse on the outskirts of Iowa City in the late '60s, he was long dead, living on only in the pages of his friend's imagination. But in fact they were all wrong.

When Denis died in 2017, Dundon was very much alive, drawing breath just a few hours from the old farmhouse, in the little town of Jacksonville, Illinois. His life had taken a vastly different path in the fifty years since he'd met that Vietnam War protester in Johnson County Jail. Some of those years were indeed spent in a Colorado prison. After his release, he managed to get off drugs and find work assembling grain elevators in Illinois. He got married, moved his family to North Carolina, and had three children. (This was his second marriage; he had been married with two kids when he knew Denis.) By the time his last child was born, he was back in prison in North Carolina on drug-related burglary charges. This is the point at which his life, which had already literally been in a Denis Johnson story, became like a Denis Johnson story.

He found God and was saved in the North Carolina prison. He worked nights at a slaughterhouse. His conversion to Christianity wore off. He became, according to his wife, Mary, "a worse drunk than he ever was a drug addict." Mary took the kids back to Illinois. Dundon followed them back, drank day and night, slept in the street, went from one Salvation Army to another, and fell into a series of alcoholic comas. Eventually Mary started telling the hospital not to call unless he was dying. That call eventually came. She went to the hospital and spoke to the doctor. This time, he said, John had a 10 percent chance of regaining normal brain activity, and if he somehow woke up, he would live out his years in a nursing home. He was thirty-seven years old.

He woke up. The doctor made him sign a form that said if he came back, they didn't have to treat him. The doctor told him if he drank alcohol, he'd be dead in three days. He left the hospital, got drunk, and passed out on a park bench. When he woke up, he looked at his watch, and three days had passed. He was, apparently, still alive. He called Mary and pleaded for help. She sent someone to pick him up. On the way home, they had to stop for booze to keep him from succumbing to the DTs. Mary arranged for him to go to a rehab center, where, once again, he found God.

Around the time that Denis was beginning to publish novels, John Dundon began to find his own place in society. He moved back in with his family. He was unfit to hold a job, so he took care of the kids while Mary worked at the local car dealership. He made them lunch, had dinner ready when Mary got home. He cleaned the house, did the laundry. Mary bought him a $25 set of golf clubs at a garage sale. John applied the same addictive personality that he'd trained on heroin and booze to his golf game. He played regularly with men he met through church. "He was around guys that drank, but he was known as the only guy out there that didn't swear when he hit a bad ball," Mary told me.

When their youngest son went to high school, John went back to work and became the No. 2 salesman in the state of Illinois for a lumber company. Though he suffered through bouts of depression, as he had when he was younger, he worked for years and maintained a good relationship with his children, until, like his old friend from Johnson County Jail, his past caught up with him, in the form of hepatitis C and then liver cancer. John Dundon died on July 4, 2021, just about a week after a certain biographer had discovered his whereabouts.

Dundon went to his grave unaware that he'd been featured in books and that his life had been portrayed on-screen. "I wish John had known that. He would have been thrilled," Mary told me when we finally connected. I sent her a copy of the story "Dundun," in which his character famously shoots another character, McInnis, who dies while Fuckhead drives the two of them to the hospital. Mary sent the story to John's sister, Sandy Wray, who was more than ten years younger than John and remembered him mostly as an abusive older brother who used to leave syringes around the house. She read the story and recognized her brother in it instantly. "There's no doubt in my mind that he killed that guy," she told me.

*

Northwood, Iowa, is a quiet little town about twenty minutes off Interstate 35, an hour's drive from Minneapolis. A few blocks of tired-looking brick buildings, several boarded up, make up a tiny downtown that surrounds a single stoplight. It's the kind of place where, if you ask at the library for a place to eat lunch, you'll be directed to the R80 gas station and convenience store. I went to Northwood in the summer of 2022 to visit the Eckharts, the family that picked Denis up on the highway that night fifty years before. They live two streets over from the R80 in a two-story house with white vinyl siding on a well-manicured lawn. It's where they've lived since a few months after the crash, where they raised the two girls, and where they host their grandchildren. (Lori lives in Park Rapids, Minnesota; Cindy lives right down the street.)

After some understandable confusion due to the unexpected arrival of a stranger with intimate knowledge of their personal history, the Eckharts were welcoming and invited me in. The living room was homey, decorated with family photos, including one of their recently departed schnoodle, Gibbs, and framed words of wisdom—"Family Always & Forever," "There's No Place Like Grandma and Grandpa's Place." Craig is a jovial fellow, quick with a joke and a gift for understatement. "It's a surprise to see you," he told me. Janice laughs easily and finishes her husband's sentences.

A note from somewhere in the middle of "Gypsys, Tramps & Thieves" was the last sound Janice heard for a week after the accident, she told me. She woke up in the hospital in Mason City with brain trauma and several other injuries. Lori, the older daughter, broke a bone near her hip and was in traction, then in a cast from her waist down for months. Craig fared better, but still has a bum shoulder from that night. Though he teases his wife that her brain still isn't quite right, Craig's shoulder is the only lingering physical effect of the crash.

That night on Big Creek Bridge is never far from their thoughts. Several years ago, they traveled back to Bethany, Missouri, and saw memorials to those who'd been killed on that deadly twenty-two-mile stretch. The hitchhiker is always the phantom in the story. "We didn't really get to know him," Craig said. "We didn't have time!" Janice broke in.

Craig painted Denis's actions on April 20, 1972, in a heroic light. He still remembers hearing the slam of the back door minutes after the crash and realizing that Cindy was no longer in the car. "[He] took her back and put her in a nice warm car with a couple, thank goodness, and kept her there until everything started getting sorted out." In the fictional version that he published twenty-five years later, Denis described those actions differently. Fuckhead takes the baby to a trucker, who declines to keep her: "By his manner, he seemed to endorse the idea of not doing anything about this. I was relieved and tearful. I had thought something was required of me, but I hadn't wanted to find out what it was." Craig and Janice took me through the events of the night, ending up at the hospital, where Craig recalled a moment when all the tension built up from the horrors of the crash was temporarily relieved. He had been worried about getting the hitchhiker's bag back to him. He searched the hospital and finally found Denis standing with John Jones, a highway patrol officer who had responded to the accident call. Craig gave Denis his bag back. Then Craig asked Denis what he planned to do next.

"I'm gonna take a bus," Denis replied.

"I don't know who laughed loudest, the trooper or me. We just couldn't help it," Craig recalled.

We'd been chatting for about an hour when I got out a copy of *Jesus' Son* and flipped to "Car Crash While Hitchhiking." The cult of Denis Johnson didn't make it to Northwood in the '90s or any of the subsequent decades, so when I began to read from the story—a story that had been read by millions and been viewed on the big screen by millions more, a story that was about the most traumatic hours of their lives—Craig and Janice Eckhart were hearing it for the first time.

Denis had started the story with a few foggy memories of the chemically aided road trip that brought him to Kansas City. Then his narrator is on the highway, feeling eerily prophetic: "My jaw ached. I knew every raindrop by its name. I sensed everything before it happened. I knew a certain Oldsmobile would stop for me even before it slowed, and by the sweet voices of the family inside it I knew we'd have an accident in the storm." The car Denis had climbed into in 1972 was actually a Buick. As I read, the Eckharts noted that the make of their vehicle was one of the few details that was off the mark. They were impressed with how closely the words Denis wrote lined up with their memories. The few deviations from their recollections of the night, such as the fact that he believed the baby to be a boy, were bits of knowledge Denis could not have known. Finally, we reached the moment of the crash: "I was thrown against the back of the seat so hard that it broke. I commenced bouncing back and forth. A liquid I knew right away was human blood flew around the car and rained down on my head." It didn't feel as if Denis had meant it as a punch line, but after hearing that paragraph, Janice was laughing. The red liquid, she said, was actually taco sauce that she'd made to bring to her in-laws. It had been in a Tupperware container by the back windshield. Later, when Craig's father, a state police officer, went to see the remains of the Buick, he mentioned all the blood in the back seat and asked whether it was from the baby or the hitchhiker.

When the story was over, Craig went upstairs to search for some long-buried photos and news clippings related to the night of the crash. Janice called up directions so he could find the correct boxes. He brought them down and put them on the living-room floor, and Janice began flipping pages and removing faded photos from the early '70s, mementos of that period in their lives when they were young parents. She told a few stories from those years. "Back then, we were the young people on the block," she said. She went through box after box, but the crash photos were elusive. "What we need to have you do is go drive down the street, like you're going away someplace, because that's when we find it," Craig told me. Finally, Janice found the photos. There were six or eight old glossies of the wrecked cars that her father-in-law had taken a few days after the crash. One showed the remains of the Buick. The front end was completely caved in; from the image, it didn't appear to be a vehicle from which somebody could have come out unscathed.

The knowledge that they had been featured in a movie and a famous book seemed to have far less meaning to the Eckharts than the fact that they now had the answer to a mystery that had vexed them for fifty years. They had been present for a single hour of the life of Denis Johnson, a life that produced poetry and prose that would be read by millions while he was alive and take a place in American literary history. They had, in those few short moments, become part of the experience of a writer who was able to take such moments and, through language, use them to find the beauty and agony of human existence. They had crossed paths with him at a time when he was only beginning to understand his calling. But to the Eckharts, he had always been a phantom, one who vanished after that night on Big Creek Bridge and left them with unanswerable questions.

Who was that hitchhiker? What ever became of him?

"God, it's nice to know," Craig told me. "There's been many times when we wondered what happened to him," Janice added. "Every once and a while, we'd say, 'I wonder what happened to that kid we picked up on the highway.'"

—SEPTEMBER 2024, GAINESVILLE, FLORIDA

AUTHOR'S NOTE

Early on in the course of writing this book, I began to realize that it had a unique characteristic, one that it doesn't share with any other biography that I can think of. It turns out that this is a book about a person who is only the second most famous person of this name. (This only includes regular people, not all the various kings and queens with the same name, of course.) In the past few years, I've had the following conversation too many times to count:

SOMEBODY: Who's your book about?

ME: Denis Johnson.

SOMEBODY: D.J.? The basketball player? He's a great subject for a biography. One of the best defensive guards of all time. I can't wait to read this book. Remember when Bird stole the ball and passed it to D.J. cutting to the hoop for the layup to beat the Pistons in the '87 Eastern Conference Finals?...

ME: Uh, no, not him.

So I think it's only appropriate to acknowledge the most celebrated of the Den(n)is Johnsons, which would be Dennis Johnson, a six-foot-four guard out of Pepperdine who played for fifteen years in the NBA, including on championship teams with the Seattle SuperSonics and the Boston Celtics, and was elected to the Basketball Hall of Fame in 2010. I will also admit here to spending far too much time considering the possibility of these two famous Johnsons crossing paths. Denis Johnson was living in the Seattle metropolitan area in 1976, the same year that Dennis Johnson was drafted by the Sonics. Maybe Denis

Johnson went to a game at the Seattle Center Coliseum during Dennis Johnson's rookie season. Coincidentally, Dennis Johnson was traded to the Phoenix Suns right around the time that Denis Johnson moved to that same city to go to rehab and revive his writing career. Then in yet another incredible coincidence, Denis Johnson moved to New England for a writing fellowship around the same time Phoenix traded Dennis Johnson to Boston for Rick Robey and some draft picks. It's hard for me to believe that none of these overlapping coincidences produced a chain of events that placed the two D.J.s in the same place at the same time. Surely Denis Johnson found himself at an NBA game at least once during those years and cheered for his namesake. Or perhaps this would be a less likely scenario, but maybe Dennis Johnson found himself with nothing to do on a night he didn't have a game, and he decided he'd use his free time to attend a poetry reading and listened pensively to his namesake deliver the stanzas. Who knows? I'll add one final twist of fate to this list: I'm writing another book, and in that book, Dennis Johnson (the basketball player) appears. If that book is ever published, there's no question in my mind that I'll tell somebody that I wrote a book about Dennis Johnson and they'll say, "You mean the author of *Jesus' Son*?"

NBA legends aside, it took a lot of help from a lot of people to bring this project to completion. Without the people who were willing to take my phone calls and spend time digging back into the recesses of their minds to share their stories (and believe me, there were many who politely or less politely declined to do so), this would have been an exercise in futility. Thanks to all who helped out. Special acknowledgment goes to some participants who went above and beyond, sitting through several rounds of interviews, and even on some occasions finding old letters in between the pages of books and sending them to me, like Maury Barr, Randy Johnson, Will Blythe, Sam Messer and Chuck Hadd. Much gratitude to the Eckharts of Northwood, Iowa, for inviting an unexpected, unannounced guest into their home. And special thanks to Tess Gallagher, to whom I somehow accidentally mailed my car registration form. She took time away from preparing to host a party to call me and warn me that I may be driving illegally.

Thanks to all of the librarians, researchers, and records officials who took the time to field my requests and provide guidance I didn't know I needed, including Amy Snyder at the Mount Airy Museum of Regional History, Nan Cinnater at the Provincetown Library, Katherine Hertelendy at George Washington University, Julia Derzay and Kayce Harris at University of Wisconsin–Madison, David McCartney at the University of Iowa, Kathy Shoemaker at Emory University, Kathryn Millan, Amy Wagner, and several guys named Steve at the Ransom Center at the University of Texas in Austin, Tara Boes at the Missouri Highway Patrol, the staff of the Santa Fe College Library, and many others whose names I've misplaced or never caught. Thanks to Wink Weinberg for his vast medical knowledge.

I also could not have made it to the finish line without the tremendous support and encouragement from the Valdosta State University community, especially James LaPlant, Adam Wood, and the troops in the English department, as well as Greg Brown and all the hardworking journalists who hang out in the newsroom at the *Spectator,* Georgia's top student news organization. Thanks to Jim McCoy, Susan Hill Newton, and all the talented folks at the University of Iowa Press.

Everything I write goes through my No. 1 reader, Stuart Taylor, who always offers excellent critiques and needed reassurance. This time around, I also had the privilege of working with Gainesville, Florida's, premiere arbiter of all things literary, Huntley Johnson, former attorney and consigliere to Harry Crews. Huntley even brought in Harry's doctor to carve up the first half of an earlier draft in a very Crews-like fashion before he sailed to Panama. Also from the Crews universe, my friend and literary psychotherapist Jay Atkinson spent many enjoyable hours on the phone with me breaking down our writing projects and imagining what Harry would do if he had lived to see Instagram or Gen Z.

So many people listened or pretended to listen (some more convincingly than others) to me talk about the only somewhat interesting travails of book writing or unknowingly helped me clear my head when it got stuck in a loop of some minute detail related to this project. For anyone on this list, I'll buy you a drink (if you happen to see this): Richard and Annette Anguiano, Dave Schlenker, Mike and Lisa Miller, Paul Myer, Becky Gaskins, Scott Dudley, the entire Goede family, Dillon and Sarah Banerjee, Linda, Bill, and everybody associated with the Jim Murray Memorial Foundation, all the men, women, children, and dogs of South-Central Lexington Farms, McShane, Park, Devin, Chuck, Sherman (Slim, I would have mentioned you here if you had come with us to Nashville), Spiker, Tim, Spiker's neighbor Wayne, everyone at the Saturday morning workout, Spiro, Joe the dentist, and the rest of the Thursday night ballers, Kevin "Squeeze" Givens, Grigsby, Two-Beer Todd, the great Burt Gundleson—and finally Mom and Dad, Cassie, Ella, Bethany, Mollie, Luke, Lainey, and nearly last but definitely not least, my partner in everything, Jill, and, finally, finally, really last this time, thanks to everyone, present and future, who reads this far, and even thanks to those who checked out many, many pages ago.

NOTES

Prologue

2 *The scene on Big Creek Bridge:* Phillip Conger, interview with author, June 15, 2022.

2 *Denis Johnson had hitched:* Craig and Janice Eckhart, interview with author, June 14, 2022.

3 *Toward midnight: Bethany Republican-Clipper,* April 26, 1972.

3 *In the Buick:* Eckhart and Eckhart interview; Traffic Accident Report No. 10220, Missouri Highway Patrol, April 21, 1972.

3 *The front end:* Denis Johnson, *Jesus' Son,* 6.

3 *On the other side:* Eckhart and Eckhart interview.

5 *"My jaw ached"*: Denis Johnson, *Jesus' Son,* 4.

Chapter I. International Matters

7 *One of the memories:* Robert Stall, interview with author, June 11, 2021; Robert Steven, Association for Diplomatic Studies & Training.

8 *Oshkosh, Wisconsin:* United States World War II draft card, Alfred Nair Johnson, October 16, 1940.

9 *It was the early 1930s: Green Bay Press-Gazette,* September 21, 1948. According to the University of Wisconsin archives, Alfred N. Johnson is listed as an electrical engineering sophomore through 1932. There is no record of his attending UW later than 1932 or obtaining a degree.

9 *By the time: Capitol Times,* September 7, 1948; Randall Johnson, email to author, November 30, 2021.

10 *Al went before:* Christopher Argyle, *Chronology of World War II,* 5, 8, 194; Lee Kennett, *G.I.,* 4–5.

10 *It was nearly:* U.S. Department of State, *Biographic Register,* 279; J. P. Benjamin and H. S. Covington, *March Order.*

11 *Before leaving Europe:* Randall Johnson, email to author, November 24 and 27, 2021; Department of Veterans Affairs Death Files, 1850–2010; *Wisconsin State Journal,* September 7, 1948.

11 *Just a few months:* "United States Army Hospital Munich History: 98th General Hospital, Munich, Germany"; Randall Johnson, email to author, January 26, 2022; birth certificate, July 15, 1949, Denis Johnson Papers, Harry Ransom Center, University of Texas, Austin (abbreviated DJP hereafter).

12 *The Johnsons:* List of inbound passengers, United States Citizens and Nationals, form I-416, United States Treasury Department, United States Customs Service, October 10, 1949; Neil A. Hamilton, *Atlas of the Baby Boom Generation,* 18.

13 *Al did his part:* Randall Johnson, email to author, December 24, 2021.

14 *In August:* U.S. Department of State, *Biographic Register,* 279; Robert W. Chandler, *War of Ideas,* 14; *The World Within,* 184; Denis Johnson, interview with Gary Kamiya, Santa Fe, New Mexico, April 11, 2007.

15 *Denis and Randy:* DJP; a conversation with Denis Johnson, *The World Within,* 186.

16 *Life in Tokyo:* Susan Yuzna, interview with author, August 11, 2021; DJP; U.S. Department of State, *Biographic Register,* 279; *Japan Times,* June 7, 1959; Nancy Lister-Settle, interview with author, October 22, 2021; DJP.

17 *The Promotion:* Donald Bishop, email interview with author, April 7, 2021; DJP; Denis Johnson, "Jungle Bells, Jungle Bells," in *Seek,* 173–74; Doris Hourihan to Vera Johnson, February 28, 1962, DJP; *New York Magazine,* June 17, 2002; *The World Within,* 185–86.

18 *In April 1965:* Yuzna interview; Randall Johnson, email to author, December 10, 2022.

19 *A few of his classmates:* Denis Johnson, "Hippies," in *Seek,* 33–34; Leah Kunkel, interview with author, July 2021; Denis Johnson, public reading, University of Iowa, 2001.

20 *The summer before:* Denis Johnson to Vera, Alfred, and Randall Johnson, July 26, 1966, DJP; Lister-Settle interview; A Celebration Honoring Denis Johnson, September 15, 2017, MacBride Auditorium, Iowa City, IA.

Chapter 2. Blood on the Steps

21 *Denis was just:* Alan Soldofsky, in *Word by Word,* 29; Denis Johnson to family, September 1967, DJP; Robert Stall, interview with author, June 11, 2021.

22 *During Alfred Johnson's:* Nicholas J. Cull, *The Cold War and the United States Information Agency,* 219; Nicolas J. Cull, email interview with author, March 31, 2021.

22 *Al's own feelings:* Randall Johnson, emails to author, November 15, 2021, and September 23, 2022.

23 *Denis did not:* Johnson interview with Kamiya.

24 *Early in his first:* Lister-Settle interview; Denis Johnson to Family, October 1967, DJP.

25 *Across the country:* Hamilton, *Atlas of the Baby Boom Generation,* 92–93, 98–99; Terry H. Anderson, *The Movement and the Sixties,* 139, 160–61.

27 *Along with Denis:* Philip Schultz, interview with author, February 8, 2021.

28 *The sky was gray: Daily Iowan,* November 2, 1967; Bill Wernz, interview with author, February 8, 2021; Schultz interview; *Iowa City Press-Citizen,* November 2, 1967.

30 *The protest: Daily Iowan,* November 4, 1967; *Des Moines Register,* November 4, 1967.

30 *The following week: Daily Iowan,* November 7, 1967; *Iowa City Press-Citizen,* November 17, 1967; Wernz interview.

32 *From Friday afternoon:* Thomas Hauser, *Muhammad Ali,* 166, 173; *Iowa City Press-Citizen,* November 20, 1967.

32 *Denis remained incarcerated:* Peggy Lamar to Denis Johnson, November 22, 1967, DJP; *Iowa Press-Citizen,* November 8, 1967; Denis Johnson, "Strangler Bob," in *The Largesse of the Sea Maiden,* 99.

Chapter 3. Adult Education

34 *When his week:* Denis Johnson to family, November 1967, DJP.

34 *The events:* Lister-Settle interview.

35 *Near the end:* Stall interview; Richard M. Trumpe to Denis Johnson, May 29, 1968, and H. E. Kelso to Denis Johnson, July 24, 1968, DJP.

36 *The second problem:* "Engagement Announced," July 26, 1968, publication unknown; Norma Jean Settle to Vera Johnson, August 23, 1968, DJP.

36 *The plan was:* Robert Stall, email to author, July 6, 2021; untitled, undated newspaper clipping, private collection.

37 *After the ceremony:* Lister-Settle interview.

38 *The newlyweds:* Alan Soldofsky, interview with author, November 6, 2021; Lister-Settle interview; Denis Johnson to family, January 1969, DJP.

38 *The story of the birth:* Lister-Settle interview. The movie discussed here was also known as *Morgan: A Suitable Case for Treatment.* It was released in 1966.

Chapter 4. From Nowhere in Particular

41 *Sometime during:* John Morgan, email to author, November 19, 2021.

43 *In the fall:* Tom Meschery, interview with author, May 18, 2021; *Los Angeles Review of Books,* October 3, 2020.

43 *Sometimes Bell's:* Tess Gallagher, interview with author, May 5, 2021; Meschery interview; Eric Olsen and Glenn Schaeffer, *We Wanted to Be Writers,* 94.

44 *Bell's poetry workshop:* Soldofsky in *Word by Word,* 29; Soldofsky interview.

45 *As the semester wore on:* Yuzna interview; Marvin Bell, interview with author, July 4, 2018; Soldofsky in *Word by Word,* 30.

46 *Though the other:* Maury Barr, interview with author, May 13, 2021.

48 *Denis's excitement:* Denis Johnson to family, undated, DJP.

48 *There was soon evidence:* "Denis Johnson Wins Hallmark Poetry Award," undated, DJP; Denis Johnson to family, undated, DJP.

49 *Quickly Aging Here:* Geof Hewitt, ed., *Quickly Aging Here,* xv, 367.

49 *The extended life: Quad City Times,* February 28, 1968; Denis Johnson, *The Man among the Seals,* 23.

50 *The raft of publications: New York Times,* May 27, 2013; Denis Johnson to family, undated, DJP.

51 *The jinx was avoided:* Stall interview; request list, June 1969, Vera Johnson, DJP.

52 *Merker printed:* Johnson, *The Man among the Seals.* Bell's dedication is included in the original version of the book published by Stonewall Press. It was omitted when Carnegie Mellon University Press republished the book in 2017.

52 *The following year:* "Notes on Current Books," *Virginia Quarterly,* Winter 1971, viii; Lister-Settle interview.

Chapter 5. Berkeley of the Midwest

54 *The Iowa City:* Phil Ajioka, interview with author, June 1, 2021; *Daily Iowan,* June 27, 1969; Joe Price, interview with author, May 27, 2021; Scott Walker, interview with author, May 12, 2021; Morty Sklar, Cinda Kornblum, and Dave Morice, *The Ultimate Actualist Convention,* 223–24.

56 *The idea was:* Lewis Dundon obituary, *Iowa City Press Citizen,* June 12, 1978; Sandy Wray, interview with author, November 6, 2022; Maryann Dundon, interview with author, March 9, 2022.

57 *Dundon and Griffith:* Lister-Settle interview; Stall interview.

57 *Dundon reluctantly: Iowa City Press-Citizen,* June 23, August 9, and August 11, 1969.

58 *Another friend of Denis:* Ajioka interview; *Iowa City Press-Citizen,* March 15, 1971.

59 *Because it was now:* Lister-Settle interview; Denis Johnson to family, June 1970, DJP.

60 *The need for money:* Denis Johnson to family, July 16, 1969, DJP; Bell interview.

60 *The illustrious institution:* John C. Gerber, "The Emergency of the Writers' Workshop," in Robert Dana, ed., *A Community of Writers,* 225–27; Olsen and Schaeffer, *We Wanted to Be Writers,* 76.

61 *Engle took: Life,* 1956; Bharati Mukherjee, "A Tale of Two Fathers," and Marvin Bell, "He Made It Possible," in Dana, *A Community of Writers,* 91, 73–76.

61 *Engle was in his 60s:* Denis Johnson to family, June 1969; Denis Johnson to family, May 1969, DJP.

62 *Denis was provided:* Denis Johnson to family, February 1, 1970; Denis Johnson to family, April 30, 1970, DJP; Lister-Settle interview.

63 *Being in the orbit:* Denis Johnson to family, June 1970 and July 19, 1970, DJP; *Des Moines Register,* July 17, 1970.

Chapter 6. Introducing the Town Moron

65 *It was in a review*: Denis Johnson, "On Fat City," in Elizabeth Benedict, ed., *Mentors, Muses and Monsters,* 205–7.

65 *Leonard Gardner, the author: New York Times,* May 30, 2017; *Sacramento Bee,* October 13, 2015.

66 *Gardner's other fans:* Schultz interview; Tracy Kidder, interview with author, May 11, 2021; Leonard Gardner, *Fat City,* 23.

67 *The phrasing and tone:* Johnson, "On Fat City," 207.

67 *Even as Denis:* University of Iowa, report card, Denis Hale Johnson, February 12, 1969, DJP; *New York Times,* July 23, 1999.

68 *In his typewriter:* Bell interview; Denis Johnson, "The Taking of Our Own Lives," *North American Review,* Winter 1970.

69 *The publication further:* Stephen Minot and Robley Wilson Jr., eds., *Three Stances of Modern Fiction,* 46–58.

69 *The initial success:* Denis Johnson to family, February 1, 1970; April 30, 1970; and Fall 1970, DJP; Stall interview.

70 *An incident on a bus: The World Within,* 188.

71 *From that moment:* Denis Johnson, "There Comes After Here," *Atlantic,* April 1972, 96.

72 *The business card:* Yuzna interview; John Skoyles, interview with author, May 7, 2021.

72 *A phone conversation:* Denis Johnson to family, July 14, 1972, and September 5, 1972, DJP.

Chapter 7. Marriage Story

74 *Money, or the lack of it:* Denis Johnson to family, July 16, 1969; Bell interview.

74 *They weathered:* Denis Johnson to family, undated, DJP.

75 *Not all of Nancy:* Denis Johnson to family, December 1969, DJP.

75 *During the summer:* Nancy Jo Johnson to Alfred and Vera Johnson, July 7, 1969, and August 1969, DJP.

76 *Denis resolved:* Denis Johnson to Alfred and Vera Johnson, June 1, 1971, and undated, DJP.

77 *Living day after day:* Lister-Settle interview; Stall interview.

79 *It was soon apparent:* Lister-Settle interview; Denis Johnson to Alfred and Vera Johnson, December 1971, DJP.

Chapter 8. Crash Landing

81 *The students:* Gary M. Pomerantz, *Wilt, 1962,* 87–88.

82 *The quixotic journey:* Gallagher interview; Stuart Dybek, interview with author, April 19, 2021; David Dowling, *A Delicate Aggression,* 252–53; Jane Smiley, interview with author, April 2, 2021.

82 *It was a time:* Dana, *A Community of Writers,* 74–75; Olsen and Schaeffer, *We Wanted to Be Writers,* 59.

83 *Denis had explored:* Bell interview; Michael Waters, interview with author, May 24, 2021.

84 *His reputation: Rolling Stone,* January 6, 2017, and August 16, 1973.

84 *Denis arrived back:* Stall interview; Eckhart and Eckhart interview.

85 *Denis also told:* Yuzna interview; Maury Barr, interview with author, May 13, 2021.

86 *When the fall:* Denis Johnson to Alfred and Vera Johnson, undated, DJP; Yuzna interview.

87 *Denis had recently:* Scott Walker, interview with author, May 12, 2021.

88 *Denis and Sue's:* Yuzna interview; Denis Johnson to Alfred and Vera Johnson, Fall 1972, DJP.

Chapter 9. Double Life

89 *Each of us: Iowa City Press-Citizen,* June 23, 1972.

89 *To many of the graduate:* Dybek interview; Kidder interview; Gallagher interview; Steve Mortensen, interview with author, April 6, 2021.

90 *He also:* Olsen and Schaeffer, *We Wanted to Be Writers,* 81; William Logan, interview with author, June 3, 2021; Bill Herz, interview with author, June 7, 2021.

90 *His offbeat sense:* Dybek interview; Denis Johnson to Alfred and Vera Johnson, July 14, 1972, DJP.

91 *The writing community:* Olsen and Schaeffer, *We Wanted to Be Writers,* 77, 232; Schultz interview.

92 *Engle's International: Iowa Press Citizen,* April 10, 1973; Dybek interview.

92 *The visiting writer:* Carol Sklenicka, *Raymond Carver,* 250–51, 176–78; Raymond Carver, "Neighbors," *Esquire,* June 1970, 137–39.

93 *His newfound:* Sklenicka, *Raymond Carver,* 247, 252–53; Olsen and Schaeffer, *We Wanted to Be Writers,* 93.

94 *Carver was an extremely:* Dan Guenther, interview with author, April 23, 2021; Sklenicka, *Raymond Carver,* 262–63, 526.

95 *Carver invited:* Walker interview; Maury Barr, interview, July 13, 2021. Lish said he had trouble remembering details from that era because of his advanced age and had no recollection of this particular incident. "I have no information to offer," he wrote. "Lucky I can still recall my middle name." Gordon Lish to author, May 25, 2021.

95 *Workshop parties:* Meschery interview; Waters interview.

96 *Sometime during:* Raymond Carver, *All of Us,* xxiii; Gallagher interview.

96 *The name "Raymond Carver":* Rick Bass, *The Traveling Feast,* 66.

97 *The students:* Soldofsky interview; Herz interview.

97 *There were several:* Skoyles interview; Mortensen interview; Dan Guenther interview.

98 *Though he spent: Iowa City Press-Citizen,* June 23, 1972; Dan Guenther interview; Soldofsky interview.

98 *The owners of the Vine:* Soldofsky in *Word by Word,* 30; Skoyles interview; Robert Stall, email to author, June 19, 2021.

99 *Denis and Sue:* Yuzna interview; Jane Ann Russell, obituary, *Iowa City Press-Citizen,* June 29, 1972.

100 *Yet another:* Robert Stall, interview with author, June 11, 2021; *Iowa City Press-Citizen,* January 10, July 9, and July 12, 1974; Denis Johnson, "Out on Bail," in *Jesus' Son,* 39.

100 *The denizens of the Vine:* Maury Barr, letter to author, December 2, 2022; Yuzna interview; Denis Johnson, "Dirty Wedding," *New Yorker,* November 5, 1990, 44–46.

101 *Denis continually:* Yuzna interview; Denis Johnson, notes, undated, DJP.

102 *Dealing drugs:* Elizabeth Evans, email to author, October 11, 2021; Denis Johnson to Alfred and Vera Johnson, undated, DJP; Ron Hansen, email to author, April 10, 2021; Mary Swander, interview with author, May 24, 2018.

102 *The job at the International:* Yuzna interview; Soldofsky interview.

102 *Denis was not always:* Chris Offutt, email to author, December 22, 2021.

103 *The withdrawal:* Denis Johnson, "Homeless and High," *New Yorker,* April 22, 2002.

103 *Despite such setbacks:* Evans interview; Denis Johnson to Alfred and Vera Johnson, November 1973, DJP.

104 *The job ended up:* Denis Johnson to Alfred and Vera Johnson, undated, DJP; Bell interview. The journals that had published poems found in *The White Fires of Venus* included *North American Review, Iowa State Liquor Store, Iowa Review, L, Cloud Marauder, Sou'Wester, Kansas City Times, Utunk* (Romania), and *American Poetry Review.*

105 *Graduation failed:* Denis Johnson to Alfred and Vera Johnson, DJP; "Drug Overdose Results in Death," *Cedar Rapids (IA) Gazette,* November 25, 1974. The fictionalized version of Hottel's death appears in the story "Out on Bail" in *Jesus' Son.* Maury Barr, interview with author, July 13, 2021; Yuzna interview.

Chapter 10. Adrift

107 *A year or so:* Maury Barr, interview with author, May 13, 2021.

107 *Inviting a group:* Yuzna interview; Swander interview.

108 *He settled:* Denis Johnson, "Secret Agent," in Will Blythe, ed., *Why I Write,* 98–99; Yuzna interview.

108 *Denis did not:* Swander interview; Barbara Guenther, email to author, May 28, 2018; Sue Fletcher to Vera Johnson, July 19, 1974, DJP.

109 *In Chicago:* Yuzna interview; Johnson, "Dirty Wedding," in *Jesus' Son,* 92; Swander interview.

111 *Denis turned twenty-seven: New York Times,* July 5, 1976; Denis Johnson to Al and Vera Johnson, June 15, 1976, DJP.

111 *The wedding:* Walker interview; Scott Walker to Denis Johnson, April 7, 1975, DJP.

112 *Denis and Sue:* Morgan Johnson, interview with author, December 7, 2021.

113 *A few buckets:* Barr interview, May 13, 2021; Walker interview; Denis Johnson to Al and Vera Johnson, 1973, DJP.

113 *In Washington:* Walker interview.

114 *There was a fledgling:* Copper Canyon Press, mission and history; *Port Townsend Leader,* October 30, 2012; Jim Heynen, email to author, December 28, 2021.

115 *In his homelife:* Morgan Johnson interview.

115 *Denis did not:* Yuzna interview; Bell interview; Heynen interview.

Chapter 11. Unpredictable Weather

117 *Scott Walker had:* Walker interview; *Minneapolis Star-Tribune,* April 6, 1994; *CityPages,* October 29, 2008.

118 *The next step:* Gallagher interview; Walker interview; Scott Walker to Denis Johnson, undated, DJP.

119 *For his next release:* Walker interview; Scott Walker to Denis Johnson, March 29, 1975, DJP.

120 *Graywolf Press almost: CityPages,* October 29, 2008; Elliston Book Award winner announcement, DJP. Gallagher and Walker split the $1,000 monetary prize.

120 *The prizes: Tacoma News Tribune,* August 4, 1985; *Minneapolis Star-Tribune,* April 6, 1994. "History," Graywolfpress.org.

121 *Denis and Sue:* Barr interview, May 13, 2021; Denis Johnson, "Happy Hour," in *Jesus' Son.*

121 *Denis soon:* Barr interview, May 13, 2021; Yuzna interview.

122 *The desperation: New York Magazine,* June 17, 2002; *Arizona Republic,* August 5, 1979; Soldofsky interview.

123 *Somehow, Denis:* Yuzna interview.

123 *There began to be:* Yuzna interview; Jon Jackson, interview with author, May 17, 2021.

Chapter 12. A Place for People Like Us

125 *The Maverick House: Arizona Republic,* March 6, 1980; *Arizona Republic,* July 7, 1982.

126 *When Denis started: Hi-Desert Star,* March 25, 1981; *Missoulian,* May 6, 1980; *New York Times,* June 16, 2002.

127 *Denis soon: San Francisco Weekly,* February 2003; Morgan Johnson interview; *Fresh Air with Terry Gross,* radio show, February 21, 1991.

127 *The search for spirituality:* Morgan Johnson interview; Bob Stall, email to author, June 24, 2021.

128 *Number nine:* Walker interview; Denis Johnson, *The Incognito Lounge,* xi.

129 *Though he was:* Jane Krause, interview with author, December 2, 2022.

129 *They shared:* Ed Montini, interview with author, April 26, 2021; Denis Johnson, poetry reading, University of Iowa, 1991.

130 *Denis and Jane:* Krause interview.

131 *He threw himself:* Denis Johnson to Paul Zimmer, September 8, 1979, DJP; David Chorlton, interview with author, May 29, 2018.

131 *Once again:* Barbara Pearlman, "He's a Winner: Six Books by 40 Is the Goal," clipping, DJP; Susan Fletcher to Denis Johnson, undated, DJP; Yuzna interview.

132 *Gradually, the circumstances: Poetry* 134, no. 2 (May 1979); *Arizona Republic,* August 5, 1979.

133 *An area school district:* Business office, Litchfield School District #79, to Denis Johnson, September 26, 1980; *Arizona Republic,* May 18, 1981.

134 *He took a job:* Contract, Scottsdale Center for the Arts, September 9, 1979, DJP; notes, undated, DJP.

134 *With the increased: Arizona Republic,* August 5, 1979; *The World Within,* 188; Consultant's contract, Arizona Commission for the Arts and Humanities, May 11, 1980, DJP.

Chapter 13. The South Unit

136 *The heat drifted up:* Montini interview.

136 *Once he arrived:* Richard Shelton, *Crossing the Yard,* 97, 22–23.

137 *The prison poetry:* Shelton, *Crossing the Yard,* 13–14, 20–25, 63–64, 93, 65–66, 77–79, 97–103. Jimmy Santiago Baca won the American Book Award in 1987 for *Martin and Meditations on the South Valley.*

140 *For his first class:* Chuck Hadd Jr., interview with author, June 8, 2021; Montini interview.

140 *One morning in July: Arizona Republic,* June 3, 2017; *Arizona Republic,* July 27, 1980.

141 *A student named:* Hadd interview, June 8, 2021.

142 *On November 12, 1966: Arizona Republic,* November 13, 1966; *Arizona Daily Star,* October 25, 1967; *Tucson Daily Citizen,* August 21, 1971, and July 29, 1972.

143 *Montini went back:* Montini interview; Ed Montini to Denis Johnson, undated, DJP.

144 *As the class progressed:* Hadd interview, June 8, 2021.

144 *Occasionally, class discussion:* Morgan Johnson interview; Hadd interview, June 8, 2021; Chuck Hadd Jr. to Denis Johnson, December 15, 1980, DJP.

145 *Robert Smith attended:* Robert B. Smith, email to author, November 2, 2021; Denis Johnson to Ellis McDougal, December 26, 1980, DJP.

146 *One day in January:* Jane Krause, interview with author, December 2, 2023. The details and effects of the murder of Jane's mother are covered by the *Mourning the Murdered* podcast, episodes 28–30, entitled "Glenna Krause."

147 *Denis returned:* Denis Johnson to Jake and Lois Krause, January 23, 1979, private collection; *Journal-Herald* (Dayton, OH), May 2, 1979; Krause interview.

147 *Denis continued: Arizona Republic,* May 18, 1981; contract for *The Incognito Lounge,* Random House, undated, DJP; Krause interview.

Chapter 14. Life on the Cape

149 *In the fall of 1980:* Sam Messer, interview with author, July 9, 2021; *Days Lumberyard Studios,* art exhibition program, Provincetown Art Association and Museum, Provincetown, MA, 1978; "History," Fine Arts Work Center, Provincetown, MA.

150 *Denis and Messer:* Messer interview; Catherine Gammon, interview with author, March 26, 2021.

151 *The fellows at the Work Center: Opening to Wonder: Sam Messer in Conversation with Will Blythe,* May 6, 2021, Fine Arts Work Center, Provincetown, MA; Messer interview; Bert Yarborough, interview with author, July 15, 2021.

152 *One of the attendees:* Lucinda Johnson, interview with author, November 21, 2021; Gammons interview.

153 *Earlier that year:* Gary Fisketjon, interview with author, April 30, 2021; *Arizona Republic*, May 9, 1982.

154 *Fisketjon's hopes: Publisher's Weekly,* March 12, 1982; radio script, KUSC, Los Angeles, June 2, 1982, DJP; Howard Moss to Denis Johnson, April 22, 1982, DJP; *People,* July 13, 1982.

155 *It was an extraordinary reaction:* Soldofsky interview; Denis Johnson, Q&A following reading, University of Arizona, Tucson, April 9, 2009.

156 *In the spring of 1982:* Messer interview; Robert Cornfield, email to author, March 23, 2022.

Chapter 15. Going up the Pipe

158 *When their fellowships: Arizona Republic,* September 30, 1985; Lucinda Johnson interview.

159 *"Burglary is insanity":* Denis Johnson, *Angels,* 100–101.

160 *Denis had kept:* Chuck Hadd Jr. to Denis Johnson, May 26, 1982, DJP.

160 *From Robert Smith:* Robert Smith to Denis Johnson, June 14, 1982, DJP.

161 *Denis thanked Smith:* Robert Smith to Denis Johnson, July 28, 1982, DJP; Johnson, *Angels,* 174–75, 205–7; *Bookworm,* radio program, KCRW, March 16, 1992.

162 *Denis deemed:* Inscription from Denis Johnson, private collection. Years later, Denis would still be wearing the jacket as a visiting professor at Texas State University in Austin. (Stacy Muszynski, interview with author, November 11, 2022.)

163 *In his acknowledgments:* Johnson, *Angels,* 210; Robert Smith to Denis Johnson, July 4, 1983, DJP; Chuck Hadd Jr. to Denis Johnson, July 6, 1983, DJP; Chuck Hadd Jr. to Denis Johnson, December 17, 1983, DJP.

164 *The widespread positive:* Johnson, *Angels,* 193; Lucinda Johnson interview; Skoyles interview.

164 *Lucinda's father:* Yarborough interview; Lucinda Johnson interview.

165 *His friend:* Gammons interview; Lucinda Johnson interview.

Chapter 16. A Trip to Twicetown

167 *The genesis of:* Sam Messer interview, July 9, 2021; Barr interview July 13, 2021.

168 *Another reason: Washington Post,* August 9, 1981; *Opening to Wonder,* May 6, 2021; Messer interview.

170 *Much of the work: Boston Globe,* June 12, 1983.

170 *Denis settled in: New York Times,* May 26, 1985; Denis Johnson, *Fiskadoro,* 45–46.

171 *Growing out the world: Boston Globe,* June 12, 1983; Denis Johnson, *The Throne of the Third Heaven,* 199.

172 *The small steps: Bookworm,* radio program, KCRW, March 16, 1992; *New York Times,* September 28, 1986; *Los Angeles Times,* October 14, 2022.

173 *Shortly after:* Skoyles interview.

173 Fiskadoro *began: New York Times,* May 1, 1985; *Philadelphia Inquirer,* July 14, 1985; *Austin American-Statesman,* July 30, 1985.

174 *He had avoided:* Denis Johnson to Maury Barr, October 15, 1985, private collection; *Esquire,* December 1985.

Chapter 17. Hiding Out

176 *The problem:* Denis Johnson to Maury Barr, October 16, 1985, private collection; Lucinda Johnson interview.

177 *The same sequence:* Sam Messer interview, July 9, 2021; Lucinda Johnson interview.

178 *In the summer:* Denis Johnson to Al and Vera Johnson, October 15, 1985, DJP; Lucinda Johnson interview.

178 *Shortly after:* Barr interview, May 13, 2021.

179 *At first, life:* Lucinda Johnson interview; Denis Johnson, *Already Dead: A California Gothic; North Country Blade-Citizen,* June 8, 1990.

180 *Another friend: Ventura County Star-Free Press,* December 27, 1962*; Los Angeles Times,* June 6, 2010; *Independent Coast Observer,* April 7, 2015.

180 *It wasn't long: New York Times,* September 28, 1986; Denis Johnson, *The Stars at Noon; Chicago Tribune,* October 12, 1986.

181 *Elliott Lewitt was:* Lucinda Johnson interview. According to Lewitt, Denis was paid for the rights to *Angels.* He did not receive a salary or compensation for writing the screenplay.

182 *Once* At Close Range*:* Elliott Lewitt, interview with author, February 6, 2023.

182 *Still, Lewitt's vision: Los Angeles Times,* April 11, 1988; Arliss Howard, interview with author, December 17, 2022; Lewitt interview.

184 *If his first foray: Daily Advertiser,* January 7, 1987; Richard Pearce, interview with author, November 18, 2021.

185 *The small country: Los Angeles Times,* May 10, 1989; Pearce interview. Hull was arrested in Costa Rica in connection with a bombing that killed four people and fled to the U.S. in 1989. He died in 2017.

186 *Denis decided:* Susan Meiselas, interview with author, November 18, 2021; Pearce interview.

Chapter 18. Looking for Zealots

188 *When Denis walked:* Blythe interview; *New York Times,* July 24, 2017.

189 *At Patsy's: New York Times,* May 10, 1988, and June 25, 2016.

190 *This was exactly:* Denis Johnson to Will Blythe, June 18, 1988, DJP; Denis Johnson, notes, untitled draft, DJP.

192 *In the end:* Lucinda Johnson interview; Morgan Johnson interview; Randall Johnson, email to author, January 12, 2022.

192 *Still, Denis chose:* Lucinda Johnson interview; Denis Johnson, untitled draft, February 1989, private collection; Blythe interview.

194 *In the end:* Blythe interview; *New York Times,* July 24, 2017.

195 *Unlike the Muslims: New York Times,* January 31, 1990, May 25, 1990, and August 14, 1990; Blythe interview.

196 *Between the time:* Patrick Robert, email to author, March 30, 2022; *Guardian,* October 2, 1990; *Sunday Independent,* July 15, 1990.

196 *Unlike what Denis: Esquire,* December 1990; *Guardian,* October 3, 1990.

197 *They stayed long enough*: *New York Times,* July 24, 2017; *Esquire,* December 1990; *Opening to Wonder,* May 6, 2021; Blythe interview.

Chapter 19. Out of the Drawer

200 *At a particularly: Washington Post,* February 3, 1993; Denis Johnson, "Lying Down in the Dirt."

201 *Denis's own:* Yuzna interview; Johnson, "Lying Down in the Dirt."

202 *Denis had come:* Offutt interview; Blythe interview; Denis Johnson, "Work," November 14, 1988, *New Yorker.*

203 *With his newfound outlook:* Robert Cornfield, email to author, February 14, 2022; *San Francisco Weekly,* February 2003.

204 *The stories made their way:* Chip McGrath, interview with author, March 31, 2022.

205 *The stories began:* Denis Johnson, "Two Men," September 19, 1988, "Work," November 14, 1988, *New Yorker;* Dan Guenther interview, April 23, 2021.

205 *The publication of "Work"*: *New Yorker,* June 1, 2011; McGrath interview; *Globe and Mail* (Canada), March 4, 2011.

206 *Another story:* Denis Johnson, reading, University of Arizona, Tucson, April 9, 2009; *Opening to Wonder,* May 6, 2021; Mike Judge, interview with author, August 3, 2021; Denis Johnson, "Car Crash While Hitchhiking," *Paris Review,* spring 1989.

206 *Over the next few years:* Denis Johnson, "The Bullet's Flight," *Esquire,* March 1989; *Iowa City Press-Citizen,* June 23, 1969; Maryann Dundon, interview with author, March 22, 2022.

207 *The remaining stories:* Denis Johnson, "Emergency," September 16, 1991; Johnson, "Dirty Wedding," *New Yorker,* November 5, 1990; *The World Within.*

Chapter 20. New Life

209 *Just a few weeks:* Denis Johnson to Maury Barr, November 19, 1983, private collection; Jonathan Galassi, interview with author, March 18, 2022; Publishing contract, Denis Johnson and Farrar, Straus and Giroux, October 28, 1988, Farrar, Straus and Giroux Papers, The Brooke Russell Astor Reading Room for Rare Books and Manuscripts, New York Public Library.

210 *Though the setting: Bookworm,* radio program, KCRW, March 16, 1992; *New York Times,* September 4, 1870; Lucinda Johnson interview; Denis Johnson, *Resuscitation of a Hanged Man.*

211 *He sent the final:* Jonathan Galassi to Denis Johnson, April 10, 1990, Farrar, Straus and Giroux Papers; *News and Observer* (Charlotte, NC), April 14, 1991; *Chicago Tribune,* February 1, 1991.

211 *The reading public:* Royalty statement, Farrar, Straus and Giroux, January 1, 1992, to June 30, 1992, DJP; *Washington Post,* February 3, 1993.

212 *The arc of the relationship:* Lucinda Johnson interview; *Ottawa Citizen,* April 13, 1987.

213 *When Denis and Lucinda:* Sam Messer interview, July 9, 2021; Walker interview; Denis Johnson to Carol and Maury Barr, July 5, 1989, private collection.

214 *He went back:* Messer interview; *Washington Post,* February 3, 1993.

Chapter 21. Reluctant Journalist

216 *On the night: Spin,* April 1998; *Esquire,* March 1991; Sam Messer interview, July 9, 2021; *Longview (TX) News-Journal,* January 17, 1991.

216 *Military officials: New York Times,* January 17, 1991; Johnson, *Seek;* Carol Polsgrove, *It Wasn't Pretty, Folks.*

217 *Unlike his previous: Esquire,* March and April 1991.

218 *Once the air war began: Esquire,* April 1991; *Opening to Wonder,* May 6, 2021; *Condè Nast Portfolio,* March 2008; Blythe, *Why I Write.*

219 *Back in New York: New York Times,* July 24, 2017; Blythe interview; *Esquire,* April 1991.

221 *In 1992: Harper's,* October 2002.

223 *Such a pronouncement:* Messer interview; *Spin,* April 1998; *Fresh Air with Terry Gross,* radio program, aired February 21, 1991.

223 *It was 100 percent: Esquire,* April 1997; *Spin,* April 1998; *Open City,* Volume 4, 1996.

224 *The thrill of it:* Reading and discussion, Denis Johnson, April 9, 2009, University of Arizona Poetry Center, Tucson.

224 *He began to take: Esquire,* July 1995; Blythe interview.

226 *"The Militia in Me": Rolling Stone,* August 17, 2000; Blythe, *Why I Write.*

Chapter 22. Just a Short Little Book

229 *The Fuckhead stories: The World Within;* Dave Zollo, interview with author, July 16, 2021.

229 *The publishing contract:* Morgan Johnson interview; Boris Kachka, *Hothouse;* Galassi interview; Robert Cornfield, email to author, March 30, 2022.

230 *But for now:* Anthony DeCurtis, *Lou Reed;* Phyllida Burlingame to Denis Johnson, June 5, 1992, DJP.

231 *When he was sent a copy:* Offutt interview; *Capitol Times* (Madison, WI), February 26, 1993.

231 *Regardless of the size: New York Times,* December 11, 1992; *San Francisco Examiner,* March 1, 1993; *Newsday* (Melville, NY), December 10, 1992.

232 *Praise for* Jesus' Son: Barry Hannah to Denis Johnson, March 22, 1993, DJP; *New York Times,* May 26, 2017; October 13, 1993; Jonathan Galassi to Denis Johnson, March 3, 1993, DJP.

235 *Sales of the books:* Chuck Klosterman, interview with author, May 20, 2022.

236 *The stories in* Jesus' Son: Denis Johnson, *Jesus' Son;* Klosterman interview.

237 *Nathan Englander was:* National Public Radio, May 26, 2017; *New York Times,* January 28, 2018; 25th Anniversary of *Jesus' Son,* panel discussion, March 29, 2017, Manhattan, New York.

238 *Whether it was:* Denis Johnson, reading and Q&A, April 11, 2007, Santa Fe, New Mexico.

Chapter 23. Knife in the Eye

239 *Denis's third wedding:* Tony Brown, interview with author, July 11, 2021; Maury Barr interview, July 13, 2021.

239 *The original idea: Esquire Sportsman,* Fall/Winter 1993.

240 *Denis was once again:* Morgan Johnson interview.

241 *That semester:* Mike Judge, interview with author, August 3, 2021; Blythe interview.

242 *In his own writing:* Blythe interview; Bill Knott to Jonathan Galassi, June 10, 1994, DJP.

243 *Bill Knott was: New Yorker,* March 17, 2014.

243 *Whether it was:* Bill Knott to Jonathan Galassi, June 10, 1994, March 17, 1996, March 18, 1996, DJP.

244 *It was a deflating: Town Talk* (Alexandria, LA), October 12, 1997; *Rutland (VT) Daily Herald,* August 10, 1997; *New York Times,* August 12, 1997; Denis Johnson, reading and Q&A, April 11, 2007, Santa Fe, New Mexico.

245 *In the 1990s:* "Stories from a Fallen World," Library of Congress Tribute, Washington, DC, March 28, 2018; *Opening to Wonder,* May 6, 2021.

245 *His association: Record* (Hackensack, NJ), October 2, 1998; *Yale Literary Magazine,* Fall 2013.

246 *It didn't always:* Denis Johnson, "Liberia Notes: Act One," DJP; Offutt interview.

246 *Denis understood:* "Stories from a Fallen World," March 28, 2018, Library of Congress, Washington, D.C.; Pearce interview.

247 *So when Denis: Los Angeles Times,* June 23, 2000; Denis Johnson, reading and discussion, April 9, 2009, University of Arizona Poetry Center, Tucson; *Independent* (London), July 7, 2000.

247 *When the producers: Boston Globe,* July 2, 2000; *Los Angeles Times,* January 22 and June 23, 1999.

248 *The film had:* Nicki Lederman, interview with author, August 25, 2022; *Los Angeles Times,* June 23, 1999; Michael Shannon, interview with author, December 17, 2022.

249 *For Denis's scene:* Denis Johnson, *Jesus' Son;* Lederman interview.

250 *The film was ready: Fresno Bee,* September 3, 1999; *National Post* (Canada), September 13, 1999; *National Post* (Canada), September 18, 1999; *Arizona Republic,* November 22, 1999; *Santa Fe New Mexican,* November 12, 1999.

Chapter 24. Plot Is Character, Character Is Plot

252 *Agreeing to take part:* Johnson, "Lying Down in the Dirt."

252 *Another factor:* Howard interview; *Los Angeles Times,* October 15, 1991; Denis Johnson, reading and discussion, April 11, 2007, Santa Fe, New Mexico.

253 *His new identity: San Francisco Examiner;* February 8, 1999; Sean San José, interview with author, September 27, 2022. *Dead Man Walking* was a 1995 movie starring Sean Penn and Susan Sarandon about a death-row inmate.

254 *The two eventually:* San José interview.

255 Hellhound on My Trail: *McSweeney's Internet Tendencies,* May 29, 2017; Denis Johnson, *Shoppers: Two Plays by Denis Johnson;* San José interview.

255 *Two more plays: San Francisco Examiner,* January 20, 2003; *San Francisco Weekly,* February 2003; *The World Within.*

256 *Though he was:* "Stories from a Fallen World," Library of Congress, Washington, DC, March 28, 2018.

257 *In all, Campo Santo: Los Angeles Review of Books,* September 6, 2022; *Chicago Tribune,* November 21, 2003, *New York Times,* July 2, 2002; San José interview.

257 *One of Denis's:* Sam Messer interview, December 16, 2022. Denis would tell people that he liked only the early version of Elvis, before he went into the army.

258 *Grainier eventually:* Blythe interview.

259 *Another of the works:* Robert Cornfield, email to author, October 14, 2022; Denis Johnson, *The Name of the World.*

Chapter 25. Another Apocalypse

262 *For a writer: The World Within;* Denis Johnson, reading and discussion, April 11, 2007, Lensic Theater, Santa Fe, New Mexico.

263 *The manuscript was:* Galassi interview; Denis Johnson, reading and discussion, April 11, 2007, Lensic Theater, Santa Fe, New Mexico.

264 *As it turned out: New York Times,* September 2, 2007.

265 *If reviewers buried: South Florida Sun-Sentinel* (Fort Lauderdale), October 14, 2007; *Boston Globe,* September 2, 2007; *Arizona Republic,* May 18, 1981; *New York Times,* September 23, 2007.

266 *On November 14, 2007: New York Times,* November 15, 2007; 2007 National Book Awards Ceremony, November 14, 2007, Marriot Marquis, New York City.

267 *Morgan Johnson worked:* Morgan Johnson interview.

269 *The fight to remain:* Sam Messer interview, December 17, 2022; Denis Johnson, reading, University of Iowa, Iowa City, 2001.

270 *In the late '90s: Paris Review,* Summer 2000.

270 *Relapses like:* Morgan Johnson interview, Alan Soldofsky interview.

Chapter 26. The Revelator in Repose

272 *Because Denis: San Francisco Weekly,* February 2003; David Byrne to Denis Johnson, April 17, 2003, DJP; San José interview.

273 *One entity: McSweeney's Internet Tendencies,* May 29, 2017; *Granta,* June 1, 2017.

274 *Visitors who made:* Chorlton interview; *McSweeney's Internet Tendencies,* May 29, 2017.

274 *Time spent with friends:* Bell interview; San José interview.

274 *He was more than willing:* Offutt interview; "Stories from a Fallen World" Library of Congress, Washington, DC, March 28, 2018; *Los Angeles Review of Books,* November 8, 2022; Bass, *The Traveling Feast.*

275 *When he heard:* Jim Galvin, interview with author, July 14, 2021; San José interview; Ron Hansen, email to author, April 20, 2021.

276 *In 2014, Denis:* Awards, American Academy for Arts and Letters, artsandletters.org; Allan Gurganus, interview with author, May 24, 2018.

276 *He continued:* Denis Johnson, Reading and Q&A, University of Arizona, Tucson, April 9, 2009; June 11, 2008, *New York Times.*

277 *To prepare:* Paul Cain, *Fast One;* Blackmaskmagazine.org.

278 Under *Playboy's: New York Times,* April 21, 2018.

278 Nobody Move *appeared: Playboy,* July 2008; *Desert Sun* (Palm Springs, CA), January 4, 2015; *San Francisco Examiner,* May 26, 2011; Denis Johnson, Reading and Q&A, University of Arizona, Tucson, April 9, 2009.

279 *The Club Bar:* Johnson, *Seek; Spokesman-Review* (Spokane, WA), November 16, 2005.

279 *Denis found:* Jonathan Johnson, interview with author, January 11, 2023.

280 *"Poets are like golfers":* Brown interview; Jonathan Johnson interview; Bass, *The Traveling Feast.*

281 *There was still:* Galassi interview. The material that was originally to be a novella called *Door in a Blank Wall* had appeared in altered form in *Tree of Smoke.*

281 *It turned out: Philadelphia Inquirer,* August 30, 2011; Denis Johnson, *Train Dreams.*

282 *When award season: Albuquerque Journal,* April 17, 2012; *Indianapolis Star,* April 19, 1977; Galassi interview.

283 *His quest: Yale Literary Magazine,* Fall 2013; Denis Johnson, *Laughing Monsters; Los Angeles Times,* November 2, 2014.

284 *The Laughing Monsters:* Morgan Johnson interview; *Independent Coast Observer* (Gualala, CA); April 17, 2015.

Chapter 27. Death Is the Mother of Beauty

286 *Throughout a life:* Johnson, *Seek.*

286 *Denis had indeed:* CDC.gov; *Idaho Statesman,* May 26, 2017; glimmertrain.com.

287 *The final days:* Johnson, *The Largesse of the Sea Maiden.*

287 *His own personal journey: Idaho Statesman,* May 26, 2017.

288 *It had been twenty-six years: Independent Coast Observer* (Gualala, CA), October 6, 2017; *New York Times,* June 11, 2019; *Los Angeles Review of Books,* September 6, 2022; "Stories from a Fallen World," Library of Congress Tribute, Washington, DC, March 28, 2018.

288 *As much as was possible:* Johnson, *The Largesse of the Sea Maiden.*

289 *Time was precious: Ransom Center Magazine,* July 7, 2010; Stall interview.

290 *His high school friend:* Leah Kunkel, interview with author, July 2021. Cohen died December 9, 2016.

290 *In April 2016:* Denis Johnson, public reading, Cornell University, Cornell, New York, April 21, 2016.

291 *He continued to look backward:* Yuzna interview; "Stories from a Fallen World," Library of Congress, Washington, DC, March 28, 2018; Lucinda Johnson interview; Sam Messer interview, December 17, 2022.

291 *He signed a contract: New Yorker,* March 3, 2014; Sam Messer interview, June 9, 2021.

291 *In the spring of 2017:* Messer interview; *Los Angeles Review of Books,* September 6, 2022.

292 *Denis and Cindy:* Messer interview; *Los Angeles Review of Books,* September 6, 2022; "The Tears of Denis Johnson," Longreads, June 16, 2017; Randy Johnson, email to author, September 28, 2022.

293 *Incredibly, there was:* Randy Johnson, email to author, September 28, 2022; Messer interview; Morgan Johnson interview; Denis Johnson, *Angels.*

Postscript

295 *News of the death: New York Times,* May 27, 2017; *Los Angeles Times,* May 30, 2017.

295 *Over the next:* Sam Messer, email to author, October 16, 2022; Galvin interview; San José interview.

296 *Almost a year: News from the Library of Congress,* June 11, 2017; "Stories from a Fallen World," Library of Congress, Washington, DC, March 28, 2018; DJP.

297 *The analysis and acclaim:* Johnson, *The Largesse of the Sea Maiden; New York Magazine,* January 8, 2018; *Boston Globe,* January 14, 2018.

299 *But what, you ask: Iowa City Press-Citizen,* November 8, 1967; Maryann Dundon interview; Wray interview.

301 *Northwood, Iowa:* Eckhart and Eckhart interview; Denis Johnson, *Jesus' Son.*

BIBLIOGRAPHY

Alcoholics Anonymous: The Story of How Many Thousands of Men and Women Have Recovered from Alcoholism. 4th ed. New York: Alcoholics Anonymous World Services, 2001.

"Alfred Johnson Is Food Official for Munich Government." *Green Bay Press-Gazette,* September 21, 1948.

Ambrose, Stephen E. *Citizen Soldiers: The U.S. Army from the Normandy Beaches to the Bulge to the Surrender of Germany*. New York: Simon & Shuster Paperbacks, 1997.

Amsden, David. "Denis Johnson's Second Stage." *New York Magazine,* June 17, 2002.

Anderson, Terry H. *The Movement and the Sixties: Protest in America from Greensboro to Wounded Knee*. New York: Oxford University Press, 1995.

Andrews, Robert M. "Arts in America: Feast or Famine?" *Arizona Republic* (Phoenix), September 30, 1985.

Argyle, Christopher. *Chronology of World War II*. New York: Exeter Books, 1980.

Asher, Colin. *Never a Lovely So Real: The Life and Work of Nelson Algren*. New York: Norton, 2019.

Baca, Jimmy Santiago. *Feeding the Roots of Self-Expression and Freedom*. New York: Teachers College Press, 2019.

Baca, Jimmy Santiago. *Working in the Dark: Reflections of a Poet of the Barrio*. Santa Fe, NM: Red Crane Books, 1992.

Bailey, Blake. *Cheever: A Life*. New York: Knopf, 2009.

Baird, Robert, P. "Remembering Bill Knott." *New Yorker,* March 17, 2014.

Bass, Rick. *The Traveling Feast: On the Road and at the Table with My Heroes*. New York: Little, Brown, 2018.

Benedict, Elizabeth, ed. *Mentors, Muses and Monsters: 30 Writers on the People Who Changed Their Lives*. New York: Free Press, 2009.

Benjamin, J. P., and H. S. Covington. *March Order: The 567th Anti-Aircraft Artillery Automatic Weapons Battalion (Mobile), A Short History*. Epernay, France: The Muzzleburst, 1945.

Bennett, Eric. *Workshops of Empire: Stegner, Engle, and American Creative Writing during the Cold War*. Iowa City: University of Iowa Press, 2015.

Benson, Bob, Sr., and Michael W. Benson. *Disciplines for the Inner Life*. Nashville, TN: Thomas Nelson, 1989.

Benson, Sheila. "Some Upcoming Major Readings." *Los Angeles Times,* October 15, 1991.

Best of Tin House. Portland, OR: Tin House Books, 2006.

Bigart, Homer. "Calley Guilty of Murder of 22 Civilians at My Lai; Sentence Expected Today." *New York Times,* March 31, 1971.

Bingham, Clara. *Witness to the Revolution: Radicals, Resisters, Vets, Hippies, and the Year America Lost Its Mind and Found Its Soul*. New York: Random House, 2016.

Biskind, Peter. *Down and Dirty Pictures: Miramax, Sundance, and the Rise of Independent Film*. New York: Simon & Schuster, 2004.

Blades, John. "Novelist Turns Nicaragua into a Tropical Inferno." *Chicago Tribune,* October 12, 1986.

Blythe, Will. "A Lot Like Prayer: Remembering Denis Johnson." *New York Times,* July 24, 2017.

Blythe, Will, ed. *Why I Write: Thoughts on the Craft of Fiction*. New York: Little, Brown, 1998.

Bogosian, Eric. *SubUrbia*. New York: Theatre Communications Group, 1996.

Bosnak, Cilla, "Man Gets 6 Months in Death." *Journal-Herald* (Dayton, OH), May 2, 1979.

Boudreaux, Richard. "Contra Backer Hull: An American 'Don' Falls in Costa Rica." *Los Angeles Times,* May 10, 1989.

Bouw, Brenda. "Bruce the Restauranteur Reels in Fellow Stars." *National Post* (Canada), September 18, 1999.

Brondoli, Michael. "A Mythic Tale of Survival after the Apocalypse." *Philadelphia Inquirer,* July 14, 1995.

Cain, Paul. *Fast One*. New York: Fawcett Popular Library, 1932.

Caldwell, Gail. "Nietzsche Noir." *Rutland (VT) Daily Herald,* August 10, 1997.

Caldwell, Gail. "The Things They Carried: Denis Johnson's novel of Vietnam Novel Weighs the Burdens of Delusion and Faith." *Boston Globe,* September 2, 2007.

Cano-Murillo, Kathy. "24 Hours." *Arizona Republic* (Phoenix), November 22, 1999.

Carver, Raymond. *All of Us: The Collected Poems*. New York: Alfred K. Knopf, 1998.

Carver, Raymond. "Neighbors." Esquire, June 1970.

Carver, Raymond. *No Heroics, Please: Uncollected Writings*. New York: Vintage, 1992.

Cassill, R. V., ed. *Intro #2: The Annual Collection of the Best College Writing in America*. New York: McCall, 1969.

Chandler, Robert W. *War of Ideas: The U.S. Propaganda Campaign in Vietnam*. Boulder, CO: Westview, 1981.

"Channeling Noir, Dickens-Style." *New York Times*, June 11, 2008.

Cheever, Susan. *My Name Is Bill: Bill Wilson—His Life and the Creation of Alcoholics Anonymous*. New York: Simon & Shuster, 2004.

Chinlund, Chris. "A Poet Turns to the Past for Inspiration." *Boston Globe*, June 12, 1983.

Clark, John. "Stars Find Their Independents." *Los Angeles Times*, January 22, 1999.

Conrad, Joseph. *Typhoon and Other Stories*. New York: Knopf, 1991.

Conroy, Frank, ed. *The Eleventh Draft: Craft and the Writing Life from the Iowa Writers' Workshop*. New York: HarperCollins, 1999.

Coolidge, Joy. "Big Writing Award Lets Office Worker Develop his Talent." *Arizona Republic* (Phoenix), August 5, 1979.

Covert, Colin. "Graywolf Split Felt in Pack of Small Presses." *Minneapolis Star-Tribune*, April 6, 1994.

Cull, Nicholas. *The Cold War and the United States Information Agency: American Propaganda and Public Diplomacy, 1945–1989*. Cambridge: Cambridge University Press, 2008.

Dana, Robert, ed. *A Community of Writers: Paul Engle and the Iowa Writers' Workshop*. Iowa City: University of Iowa Press, 1999.

Dean, Paul. "Youth Slays Five in Mesa to Make a Name for Himself." *Arizona Republic* (Phoenix), November 13, 1966.

DeCurtis, Anthony. *Lou Reed: A Life*. New York: Little, Brown, 2017.

DeLuca, Dan. "A Novella of Mighty Things Done by a Lonely Man." *Philadelphia Inquirer*, August 30, 2011.

"Demonstration at Union Ends as Police Move In." *Iowa City Press-Citizen*, November 2, 1967.

Domestico, Anthony. "A Dark World in Gem-Like Sentences." *Boston Globe*, January 14, 2018.

Doubler, Michael D. *Closing with the Enemy: How GIs Fought the War in Europe, 1944–1945*. Lawrence: University of Kansas Press, 1994.

Dower, John W. *Embracing Defeat: Japan in the Wake of World War II*. New York: Norton, 1999.

Dowling, David O. *A Delicate Aggression: Savagery and Survival in the Iowa Writers' Workshop*. New Haven, CT: Yale University Press, 2019.

"Drug Overdose Results in Death." *Cedar Rapids (IA) Gazette*, November 25, 1974.

Dunnigan, James F. *How to Make War: A Comprehensive Guide to Modern Warfare*. New York: William Morrow, 1982.

Ebert, Roger. "Movie Buffs Find Paradise." *Fresno (CA) Bee,* September 3, 1999.

Ebert, Roger. "Sorry, Sadness, Poignancy: *Jesus' Son* Has It All." *Calgary Herald,* July 28, 2000.

Elder, Robert. *The Information Machine: The United States Information Agency and American Foreign Policy*. Syracuse, NY: Syracuse University Press, 1968.

Engle, Paul. *American Song*. Garden City, NJ: Doubleday, Doran, 1934.

Engle, Paul. *Break the Heart's Anger*. New York: Doubleday, Doran, 1936.

Engle, Paul, ed. *Midland: Twenty-Five Years of Fiction and Poetry Selected from the Writing Workshops of the State of Iowa*. New York: Random House, 1961.

Estes, Jack. "Indeed, the City Has a Poet." *Port Angeles (WA) Daily News,* December 19, 1976.

Farley, Ellen. "The Toughest Act to Call." *Los Angeles Times,* April 11, 1988.

"Fourth Youth Faces Charges of Burglary." *Iowa City Press-Citizen,* November 8, 1967.

Fox, Margalit. "Owsley Stanley, Artisan of Acid, Is Dead at 76." *New York Times,* March 14, 2011.

Gallagher, Tess. *Soul Barnacles: Ten More Years with Ray*. Ann Arbor: University of Michigan Press, 2000.

"The Gallows: Execution of John H. Skaggs at Bloomfield, Mo.—A Remarkable Case of Partial Strangulation, Resuscitation of the Body, Horrible Scenes, etc." *New York Times,* September 1, 1870.

Gardner, Leonard. *Fat City*. Berkeley: University of California Press, 1969.

Gavin, Jennifer. "Prize for American Fiction to Be Awarded Posthumously to Denis Johnson." July 11, 2017, Library of Congress.

"Gina Berriault, 73, an Author of Deft Novels, Short Stories." *New York Times,* July 23, 1999.

Gioia, Dana, and William Logan, eds. *Certain Solitudes: On the Poetry of Donald Justice*. Fayetteville: University of Arkansas Press, 1997.

Green, Andy. "*Rolling Stone* at 50: Making the First Issue." *Rolling Stone,* January 6, 2017.

Green, Michael, and James D. Brown. *Patton's Third Army in World War II*. Minneapolis, MN: Zenith Press, 2010.

"Gunshot Injury Here." *Iowa City Press-Citizen,* June 23, 1969.

Hagengruber, James. "Salon Meets Saloon at Bar's Poetry Night." *Spokesman-Review* (Spokane, WA), November 16, 2005.

Halberstam, David. *The Best and the Brightest*. New York: Random House, 1969.

Hamilton, Neil A. *Atlas of the Baby Boom Generation*. New York: Macmillan, 2000.

Hauser, Thomas. *Muhammad Ali: His Life and Times*. New York: Simon & Shuster, 1991.

Henry, Ted, and Susan Hooven. "Demonstrators Spill Blood, Give Petition to Bowen." *Daily Iowan* (Iowa City), November 4, 1967.

Hewitt, Geof, ed. *Quickly Aging Here: Some Poets of the 1970s*. New York: Anchor Doubleday, 1969.

Hibbs, Robert. "Clay Talks of Draft Problem, Civil Rights, Ring Foes and Justice." *Iowa City Press-Citizen*, November 20, 1967.

Hodder, Jim. "Deaths: Jim Hodder." Obituary. *North County Blade-Citizen* (Oceanside), June 8, 1990.

Hohenadel, Kristen. "For Crudup, a Chance to Expand Horizons." *Los Angeles Times*, June 23, 2000.

"Hottel Found Innocent in Alleged Incident." *Iowa City Press-Citizen*, July 12, 1974.

Howard, Rachel. "Loner No More: Campo Santo Brings Johnson Out of Hiding." *San Francisco Examiner*, January 20, 2003.

Howe, E. W. *The Story of a Country Town*. Cambridge, MA: Harvard University Press, 1961.

Huband, Mark. "City Where No One Sleeps at Home." *Sunday Independent*, July 15, 1990.

Huband, Mark. *The Liberian Civil War*. London: Frank Cass, 1998.

Huband, Mark. "Liberian Rebels Replay the Last Hours of President Doe." *Guardian*, October 3, 1990.

Huband, Mark. "Monrovia Peace Force Moves In." *Guardian*, October 2, 1990.

Huband, Mark. "Nigerian Jets Bomb Rebels in Monrovia." *Guardian*, November 7, 1992.

Hurwitt, Robert. "Weirder Living through Chemistry: Jesus' Son Takes Short Trips through the Druggie Life." *San Francisco Examiner*, February 8, 1999.

Johnson, Denis. *Already Dead: A California Gothic*. New York: HarperCollins, 1997.

Johnson, Denis. *Angels*. New York: Knopf, 1983.

Johnson, Denis. *Fiskadoro*. New York: Harper Perennial, 1985.

Johnson, Denis. *The Incognito Lounge: And Other Poems*. New York: Random House, 1982.

Johnson, Denis. *Jesus' Son: Stories*. New York: Farrar, Straus & Giroux, 1992.

Johnson, Denis. *The Largesse of the Sea Maiden*. New York: Random House, 2018.

Johnson, Denis. *The Laughing Monsters*. New York: Farrar, Straus & Giroux, 2014.

Johnson, Denis. "Lying Down in the Dirt: An Interview with Denis Johnson." Conducted by Janet Steen. Longreads, February 2018.

Johnson, Denis. *The Man among the Seals and Inner Weather*. Pittsburgh, PA: Carnegie Mellon University Press, 2017.

Johnson, Denis. *The Name of the World*. New York: Perennial, 2000.

Johnson, Denis. *Nobody Move*. New York: Farrar, Straus & Giroux, 2009.

Johnson, Denis. *Resuscitation of a Hanged Man.* New York: Farrar, Straus & Giroux, 1991.

Johnson, Denis. *Seek: Reports from the Edges of America and Beyond.* New York: Perennial, 2001.

Johnson, Denis. *Shoppers: Two Plays.* New York: HarperCollins, 2002.

Johnson, Denis. *The Stars at Noon.* New York: Vintage, 1986.

Johnson, Denis. "The Taking of Our Own Lives." *North American Review* 55, no. 4 (Winter 1970): 32–37.

Johnson, Denis. *The Throne of the Third Heaven of the Nations Millennium General Assembly: Poems, Collected and New.* New York: Harper Perennial, 1995.

Johnson, Denis. *Train Dreams.* New York: Farrar, Straus & Giroux, 2011.

Johnson, Denis. *Tree of Smoke.* New York: Farrar, Straus & Giroux, 2007.

Johnson, Denis. *The White Fires of Venus.* Master's thesis, University of Iowa, 1974.

"Johnson Takes Bavarian Post." *Wisconsin State Journal,* September 7, 1948.

Jones, Chris. "'Soul,' a Haunting, Provocative Drama." *Chicago Tribune,* November 21, 2003.

"Judge Admonishes, Fines 77 Protesters." *Iowa City Press-Citizen,* November 17, 1967.

Kachka, Boris. *Hothouse: The Art of Survival and the Art of America's Most Celebrated Publishing House, Farrar, Straus & Giroux.* New York: Simon & Shuster, 2013.

Kakutani, Michiko. "Books of the Times." *New York Times,* May 1, 1985.

Kakutani, Michiko. "The Mystical and the Damned." *New York Times,* August 12, 1997.

Kakutani, Michiko. "Stories that Range from Bleak to Bleaker." *New York Times,* December 11, 1992.

Kallen, Stuart A. *Sixties Counterculture.* San Diego, CA: Greenhaven, 2001.

Karnow, Stanley. *Vietnam: A History.* New York: Penguin, 1997.

Kennett, Lee. *G.I.: The American Soldier in World War II.* Norman: University of Oklahoma Press, 1987.

Ketchum, Diana. "Sea Ranch, California's Modernist Utopia, Gets an Update." *New York Times,* June 11, 2019.

Kidder, Tracy, and Richard Todd. *Good Prose: The Art of Nonfiction, Stories and Advice from a Lifetime of Writing and Editing.* New York: Random House, 2013.

King, Loren. "Redeeming *Jesus' Son:* Alison Maclean Loved the Challenge of Converting the Cult Book." *Boston Globe,* July 2, 2000.

Klett, Mark. *Traces of Eden: Travels in the Desert Southwest.* Boston: David R. Godine, 1986.

Klosterman, Chuck. *The Nineties: A Book.* New York: Penguin, 2022.

Knott, Bill. "Bill Knott, 74, Widely Admired as a Poet, Emerson Professor." Obituary by Bryan Marquard. *Boston Globe,* March 31, 2014.

Knott, Bill. *Laugh at the End of the World: Collected Comic Poems, 1969–1999.* Rochester, NY: BOA Editions, 2000.

Kushner, Rachel. *The Hard Crowd: Essays, 2000–2020.* New York: Scribner, 2021.

Lavine, Harold, and James Wechsler. *War Propaganda and the United States.* New York: Arno Press, 1972.

Leahy, Colleen. "Remembering the Dow Protest and Riot 50 Years Later." *Wisconsin Public Radio,* October 18, 2017.

Levine, Jerry. "7 Protesters Convicted." *Daily Iowan* (Iowa City), November 7, 1967.

Lewis, Jim. "The Revelator." *New York Times,* September 2, 2007.

"Local Girl Free on Bond in Drug Case." *Iowa City Press-Citizen,* August 11, 1969.

Lorentzen, Christian. "Denis Johnson Left Us with One Final—And Terrific—Book." *New York Magazine,* January 8, 2018.

Lowry, Malcolm. *Under the Volcano.* New York: Harper Perennial Modern Classics, 1947.

Mansfield, Stephen. *Tokyo, a Biography: Disasters, Destruction and Renewal: The Story of an Indomitable City.* Tokyo: Tuttle, 2016.

Mare, Chauncey. "Apocalypse Again." *South Florida Sun-Sentinel* (Fort Lauderdale), October 14, 2007.

Margolis, Susan. "100 American Seducers on Their Art and Sullen Craft." *Rolling Stone,* August 16, 1973.

Margoshes, Dave. "Demonstration—The Way It Was." *Daily Iowan* (Iowa City), November 2, 1967.

Maslin, Janet. "A Future without a Past." *New York Times,* May 26, 1985.

"Mass Killer Smith Again Sentenced." *Tucson Daily Citizen,* July 29, 1972.

Matsuda, Takeshi. *Soft Power and Its Perils: U.S. Cultural Policy in Early Postwar Japan and Permanent Dependency.* Stanford, CA: Stanford University Press, 2007.

McClurg, Jocelyn. "Small Book Is Now Big Trend." *Capitol Times* (Madison, WI), February 26, 1993.

McDonald, Charles. *The Last Offensive: The European Theater of Operations.* Washington, DC: Office of the Chief of Military History, 1973.

McKeen, William. *Outlaw Journalist: The Life and Times of Hunter S. Thompson.* New York: Norton, 2008.

McManis, Sam. "'Fat City' Author Still a Contender." *Sacramento Bee,* October 13, 2015.

Meschery, Tom. *Over the Rim.* New York: McCall, 1970.

Messner, Sam. *Opening to Wonder: Sam Messer in Conversation with Will Blythe.* Provincetown, MA: Fine Arts Work Center, May 6, 2021.

Meyers, D. G. *The Elephants Teach: Creative Writing since 1880*. Englewood Cliffs, NJ: Prentice Hall, 1996.

Miller, John, and Tim Smith. *Cape Cod Stories: Tales from Cape Cod, Nantucket, and Martha's Vineyard*. San Francisco: Chronicle Books, 1996.

Minot, Stephen, and Robley Wilson Jr., eds. *Three Stances of Modern Fiction*. Cambridge, MA: Winthrop, 1972.

Mitchell, Susan. *Generation X: The Young Adult Market*. Ithaca, NY: New Strategic Publications, 1997.

Montini, Ed. "Escape: The Outside Is as Close as a Pen for Students in Prison Writing Class." *Arizona Republic* (Phoenix), July 27, 1980.

Montini, Ed. "Poet Touches Realm of Man in 'Incognito Lounge.'" *Arizona Republic* (Phoenix), May 9, 1982.

Montini, Ed. "Prize-Winning Poet Works in the Meter of Everyday Life." *Arizona Republic* (Phoenix), May 18, 1981.

Montini, Ed. "That Day I Went to Prison with Denis Johnson." *Arizona Republic* (Phoenix), June 3, 2017.

Moody, Rick. "The End: Denis Johnson's Long Preoccupation with Mortality Culminated in a Posthumous Story Collection." *New York Times*, January 28, 2018.

Moore, Michael Scott. "Denis Johnson, Poet of the Fallen World: How a San Francisco Theater Troupe Turned Johnson into a Playwright." *San Francisco Weekly*, February 2003.

Morgan, John. *Forms of Feeling: Poetry in Our Lives—Essays and Interviews*. Cliffs of Moher, County Clare, Ireland: Salmon Poetry, 2012.

Morrell, David. *First Blood*. London: Headline Book Publishing, 1972.

Morris, James, Jr. "Johnson's Novel about a Man on 'A Place Apart.'" *News and Observer* (Charlotte, NC), April 14, 1991.

Moses, Kate. "Tales of the Blessed and the Wretched." *San Francisco Examiner*, March 1, 1993.

Nance, Kevin. "Laughing Monsters Takes Espionage Caper for a Ride." *Desert Sun* (Palm Springs, CA), January 4, 2015.

"Narrow Bridge Claims Life." *Bethany (MO) Republican-Clipper*, April 26, 1972.

Nickel, Lynette. "Breaking the Bottle Habit." *Missoulian* (Missoula, MT), May 6, 1980.

Noble, Kenneth B. "Liberia Capitol Fearful as War Nears." *New York Times*, May 25, 1990.

Noble, Kenneth B. "Liberia Rebel Agrees to Cease-Fire Talks." *New York Times*, August 14, 1990.

Noble, Kenneth B. "Masses of Liberian Refugees Flee Rebellion and Reprisal Killing." *New York Times*, January 31, 1990.

"No Fiction Book Gets Pulitzer This Year." *Albuquerque Journal*, April 17, 2012.

"No Help in Sight for Alcohol Center." *Arizona Republic* (Phoenix), July 7, 1982.

Oland, Dana. "Denis Johnson, Author of *Jesus' Son* and the First Distinguished Writer at BSU." *Idaho Statesman* (Boise), May 26, 2017.

Olsen, Eric, and Glenn Schaeffer. *We Wanted to Be Writers: Life, Love, and Literature at the Iowa Writers' Workshop*. New York: Skyhorse, 2011.

"On This Wall, in This Town, in Their Own State: Paul Engle's Memorial Sonnets Salute the War Dead of Iowa." *Life*, May 28, 1956.

"One Day at a Time: Film Recounts AA History." *Hi-Desert Star* (Yucca Valley, CA), March 25, 1981.

"On OMG Staff." *Capitol Times* (Madison, WI), September 7, 1948.

Overby, Erin. "Bonfire of the Profanities." *New Yorker*, June 1, 2011.

Passaro, Vince. "The Chronicler of a Wounded World." *Newsday* (Melville, NY), December 10, 1992.

Pekar, Harvey. *Students for a Democratic Society: A Graphic History*. New York: Farrar, Straus & Giroux, 2008.

Perlez, Jane. "Writing in a Female Voice." *New York Times*, September 28, 1986.

Perren, Alisa. *Indie Inc.: Miramax and the Transformation of Hollywood in the 1990s*. Austin: University of Texas Press, 2012.

Phillips, Larry W. *Ernest Hemingway on Writing*. New York: Scribner, 1984.

Pierson, John. *Spike, Mike, Slackers and Dykes: A Guided Tour across a Decade of American Independent Cinema*. New York: Hyperion, 1995.

"'Pigs' vs. 'Freaks' in Softball Sunday." *Iowa City Press-Citizen*, June 23, 1972.

Pomerantz, Gary. *Wilt, 1962: The Night of 100 Points and the Dawn of a New Era*. New York: Crown, 2005.

Posgrave, Carol. *It Wasn't Pretty, Folks, but Didn't We Have Fun?* New York: Norton, 1995.

"Pour Blood on Steps of Union." *Des Moines (IA) Register*, November 4, 1967.

Powell, Padgett. *Indigo: Arm Wrestling, Snake Saving, and Some Things in Between*. New York: Catapult, 2021.

"A Prodigal Son Turns Novelist Turns Playwright." *New York Times*, June 16, 2002.

Resteker, Alan. "Mood Was Set for Leary." *Daily Iowan* (Iowa City), June 27, 1969.

Richburg, Keith. "Philippines' Moslem War Stalled: Long Rebel Insurgency Falters on Southern Island of Mindanao." *New York Times*, May 10, 1988.

"Robbery Suspect Arrested, Two Facing Drug Charges." *Iowa City Press-Citizen*, March 15, 1971.

"Robbery Suspect Bound Over." *Iowa City Press-Citizen*, January 10, 1974.

Rosenthal, Andrew. "U.S. and Allies Open Air War on Iraq; Bomb Baghdad and Kuwaiti Targets; No Choice but Force, Bush Declares." *New York Times*, January 17, 1991.

Ross, Robert. "Drugs Seized in Raid Here." *Iowa City Press-Citizen,* August 9, 1969.

Rushkoff, Douglas, ed. *The Gen X Reader.* New York: Ballantine, 1994.

Sacks, Peter. *Generation X Goes to College: An Eye-Opening Account of Teaching in Postmodern America.* Chicago: Open Court, 2000.

Sale, Kirkpatrick. *SDS.* New York: Random House, 1973.

Sandomir, Richard. "Denis Johnson, Who Wrote of the Failed and the Desperate, Dies at 67." *New York Times,* May 26, 2017.

Schiffman, Jean. "Characters on Course of Disaster in 'Nobody Move.'" *San Francisco Examiner,* May 26, 2011.

Schoemer, Karen. "In California, Finding 'Fat City' with the Man Who Wrote It." *New York Times,* May 30, 2017.

Schwartz, Richard A. *Cold War Culture: Media and the Arts, 1945–1990.* New York: Facts on File, 1998.

"Seals' Tipsy Pal Fined after Dip." *Quad City Times* (Davenport, IA), February 28, 1968.

Seibold, Douglas. "After Much Praise, a Puzzling Failure." *Chicago Tribune,* February 1, 1991.

Shanon, Philip. "Awesome Scene as Jets Go to Iraq." *Longview (TX) News-Journal,* January 17, 1991.

Shelton, Richard. *Crossing the Yard: Thirty Years as a Prison Volunteer.* Tucson: University of Arizona Press, 2007.

Shepherd, Richard F. "Panoply of Sails: Harbor Armanda Led by Tall Ships in Salute to Fourth." *New York Times,* July 5, 1976.

Shields, Charles J. *And So It Goes: Kurt Vonnegut: A Life.* New York: Henry Holt, 2011.

Simpson, Mona. "Resuscitation of a Hanged Man." *New York Times,* February 24, 1991.

Sklar, Morty, Cinda Kornblum, and Dave Morice. *The Ultimate Actualist Convention: A Detailed View of Iowa City Actualism in the 1970s and 1980s and Its Migration to the San Francisco Bay Area.* Jackson Heights, NY: Spirit that Moves Us Press.

Sklenicka, Carol. *Raymond Carver: A Writer's Life.* New York: Scribner, 2010.

Skoyles, John. *A Moveable Famine.* Sag Harbor, NY: Permanent Press, 2014.

"Small Newspaper Wins Pulitzer." *Indianapolis Star,* April 19, 1977.

Smith, Dave. "Benny Smith and the Drama No One Likes." *Tucson Daily Citizen,* August 21, 1971.

"Soviet Poet Brodsky to Give Reading Here." *Iowa City Press-Citizen,* April 10, 1973.

Strand, Mark. *Collected Poems.* New York: Knopf, 2014.

Streitfield, David. "The Ghost in the Addict: Denis Johnson's Books Explore the Grim World of the Junkie He Used to Be." *Washington Post,* February 3, 1993.

Tarkington, Booth. *Penrod.* New York: Grosset & Dunlap, 1914.

Taylor, Marilyn. "Halfway House Urged for Alcoholic Women." *Arizona Republic* (Phoenix), March 6, 1980.

"Tokyo Women's Club Holds Last Pre-summer Meeting." *Japan Times,* June 7, 1959.

"Tournament Semifinals Set for Tonight at Fillmore." *Ventura County Star-Free Press* (Camarillo, CA), December 27, 1962.

Thomas, Bob. "Richard Pearce Loves Saturday Night Films." *Daily Advertiser* (Lafayette, LA), January 7, 1987.

Thompson, Toby. "The Throne of the Third Heaven of the Nations' Millennium General Assembly." *Washington Post,* August 9, 1981.

Trillin, Calvin. "How I Got Dirty Words into the *New Yorker*." *Globe and Mail* (Canada), March 4, 2011.

Turner, Dan. "AIDS Driving Africa towards the Brink of Calamity." *Ottawa Citizen,* April 13, 1987.

"Two Face Weapons Counts." *Iowa City Press-Citizen,* July 9, 1974.

Ulin, David. "Chaos and Literature: Denis Johnson Deals in Carefully Arranged Derangement." *Los Angeles Times,* November 2, 2014.

Ulin, David. "A Vision at Once Mystical, Other Worldly." *Los Angeles Times,* May 30, 2017.

U.S. Department of State. *The Biographic Register.* Washington, DC: U.S. Government Printing Office, July 1967.

Van Zyl, Miezan, *The Vietnam War: The Definitive Illustrated History.* New York: Penguin Random House, 2017.

Verkamp, Jane. "Mesa Youth Found Guilty of First-Degree Murder." *Arizona Daily Star* (Tucson), October 25, 1967.

Vitello, Paul. "Kim Merker, Hand-press Printer of Poets, Is Dead at 81." *New York Times,* May 27, 2013.

Wakefield, Dan, ed. *Kurt Vonnegut: Letters.* New York: Delacorte Press, 2012.

Wallace, Frank R. *Poker: A Guaranteed Income for Life by Using the Advanced Concepts of Poker.* Wilmington, DE: I&O Publishing, 1968.

Waters, Chris. "Nuclear Plot Mushrooms into Riveting Tale." *Austin (TX) American-Statesman,* July 30, 1985.

Webber, Bruce. "Distressed by the Taming of the West." *New York Times,* July 2, 2002.

Webber, Bruce. "Michael Herr Is Dead at 76: Author of a Vietnam Classic." *New York Times,* June 25, 2016.

Weingarten, Marc. *The Gang that Wouldn't Write Straight.* New York: Crown, 2006.

Westad, Odd Arne. *The Cold War: A World History.* New York: Basic Books, 2017.

Westhoff, Ben. "Graywolf Press Is Lone Wolf in Book Publishing." *CityPages* (Minneapolis, MN), October 29, 2008.

Whitman, Walt. *Leaves of Grass.* New York: Simon & Schuster Paperbacks, 2010.

Winkelholz, William. "Obituary: William 'Wink' Winkelholz." *Independent Coast Observer* (Gualala), April 17, 2015.

Wolff, Alexander, ed. *Basketball: Great Writing about America's Game.* New York: Library of America, 2018.

The World Within: The Tin House Interviews. Portland, OR: Tin House Books, 2007.

Wright, James. *Enduring Vietnam: An American Generation and Its War.* New York: Thomas Dunne Books, St. Martin's Press, 2017.

Yagoda, Ben. *About Town: The New Yorker and the World It Made.* New York: Da Capo Press, 2001.

Yardley, Jonathan. *Misfit: The Strange Life of Frederick Exley.* New York: Random House, 1997.

INDEX